D0744006

The World Court in Action

The World Court in Action

Judging among the Nations

Howard N. Meyer

ROWMAN & LITTLEFIELD PUBLISHERS, INC.
Lanham • Boulder • New York • Oxford

ROWMAN & LITTLEFIELD PUBLISHERS, INC.

Published in the United States of America
by Rowman & Littlefield Publishers, Inc.
4720 Boston Way, Lanham, Maryland 20706
www.rowmanlittlefield.com

12 Hid's Copse Road, Cumnor Hill, Oxford OX2 9JJ, England

Copyright © 2002 by Howard N. Meyer

All rights reserved. No part of this publication may be reproduced, stored in a
retrieval system, or transmitted in any form or by any means, electronic,
mechanical, photocopying, recording, or otherwise, without the prior permission
of the publisher.

British Library Cataloguing in Publication Information Available

Library of Congress Cataloging-in-Publication Data

Meyer, Howard N.
  The World Court in action : judging among the nations / Howard N. Meyer.
    p. cm.
  Includes bibliographical references and index.
  ISBN 0-7425-0923-0 (cloth : alk. paper)—ISBN 0-7425-0924-9 (pbk. : alk. paper)
    1. International Court of Justice. 2. International law. 3. U.S. foreign relations.
  4. Peace studies. I. Title.
KZ6275 .M49 2002
341.5'52—dc21

                                              2001031795

Printed in the United States of America

♾ ™The paper used in this publication meets the minimum requirements of American National Standard for Information Sciences—Permanence of Paper for Printed
Library Materials, ANSI/NISO Z39.48-1992.

For our grandchildren

Daniel

Justin

Mary

David

Jonathan

Debra

Emma

and theirs

NATIONAL UNIVERSITY
LIBRARY   SAN DIEGO

And He shall judge among the nations
and rebuke many people
and they shall beat their swords into plowshares
and their spears into pruning hooks;
nation shall not lift up sword against nation,
neither shall they learn war any more.

—Isaiah 2:4

NATIONAL UNIVERSITY
LIBRARY - SAN DIEGO

Contents

Foreword

This book opens with a daunting question. A representative of President George Washington asks why nations do not settle otherwise intractable disputes with the aid of neutral third parties. Having just succeeded in such an effort in solving a disputed Canadian border question, he wants to know why nations compete in killing off each others' people until one side or the other gives up.

Of course, in Washington's time there was no standing procedure for peaceful third-party judging. Nations that were already at odds and hostile could not easily agree on who should decide between them, when and where, and under what rules. And there was no pressure, legal or moral, for them to accept a third-party settlement.

Now there is a standing instrument for peaceful solution, the International Court of Justice, with its own rules, a body of law, a home at The Hague, and international financial backing from the United Nations. There is also available an optional procedure for shared legal acceptance of an obligation among nations to submit to the Court's judgment. Until 1985, the United States subscribed to that elective compulsory jurisdiction (albeit with a controversial reservation), and Washington had been a persistent advocate of wider acceptance of that obligation.

In May 1985, Pope John Paul II, during a visit to the Court at The Hague, called on the nations for "wider acceptance of the so-called compulsory jurisdiction of the Court." At that very moment, the United States administration was pondering a different course, as it had publicly warned earlier in the year. In December, as threatened, it did indeed revoke President Harry Truman's pledged acceptance of the commitment to compulsory jurisdiction.

Howard N. Meyer, attorney, labor arbitrator, and civil rights historian, was troubled when he learned in 1985 that his country had thus "turned its back not only on the International Court of Justice but on forty years of leadership in the cause of world peace through law," as that action had been described by the editor in chief of the *American Journal of International Law.* This book is his personal response to that reversal of course, and to his concomitant realization of how little was known, or taught, about the history and scope of the U.S. contribution to the Court or to the functioning and achievement of the tribunal.

His work traces the role of prominent Americans—many of whom were members of the early peace movements, international lawyers, and leaders of industry and government—in making the Court possible. As he covers its accomplishments he makes a convincing case for its capacity to serve as sane resource for global conflict resolution.

I share his conviction that the end of the Cold War made it possible for the United States to lead the world in returning to wholehearted acceptance of the peace-serving principles of the Law of Nations. Our leadership in this is essential to enable the Court to play its full part in establishing peace under law, as its founders had contemplated and fondly hoped.

To this end it is critical to eliminate public ignorance about the Court and its history. To meet that need this book can make an important contribution.

Fr. Theodore M. Hesburgh, C.S.C.
President Emeritus of Notre Dame

Preface

"World Court" is the long-established, if unofficial, name that has identified a court that was formed more than half a century ago. Its official name is the International Court of Justice, and its mission is to judge and decide disputes that nations are unable to settle between or among themselves. This book's focus is the Court's origin (and the U.S. contribution to it), makeup, history, and functioning. It also offers an appraisal of the Court's role.

From its very beginning, it was agreed that only nations could sue or be sued at the International Court of Justice (ICJ). However, in recent years individual crimes, such as acts of terrorism or genocide, have aroused the international community. So, too, has the increase (and the increased visibility) of atrocities perpetrated by individuals in the course of civil wars. Special *criminal* courts of limited scope have been created to deal with such individuals in the former Yugoslavia and Rwanda.

In the summer of 1998, representatives from 160 nations met in Rome and agreed on a treaty that would create an international criminal court not so limited to specific places. The purpose of punishing people guilty of misdeeds of global importance is a worthy one. But it is quite different than the business of the tribunal known as *the* World Court. The distinction should be made clear and observed. It has not been. Even among media there has been careless use: "U.S. Pushes to Weaken World Court on Atrocities" (*New York Times,* June 9, 2000); "Yes, a World Court," in an op-ed piece decrying Washington's attitude to a universal criminal court (*Washington Post,* June 27, 2000). Confusion of the identity of the two tribunals can affect adversely the effort to enlist the United States in support of the two needed instruments of international law and order.

The active ICJ and the proposed criminal court, different as they are, do have a common problem: resistance in Washington to submitting national actions to judicial examination when challenged as to the legality at the ICJ. A similar position is being taken as to Americans being tried before international judges, who will have jurisdiction to try crimes of nationals of all other countries.

The U.S. initiatives early in the last century that led to the founding of the first World Court and its major role in formation of the ICJ after World War II, are worthy segments of our heritage of which we can be proud. It is in our interest that the origin and business of the World Court be better known. It is important that we recognize its potential—if and only if backed by U.S. leadership—to aid in the defense of peace and protection of human rights.

To say that, if properly supported by the United States, the Court provides an authoritative voice to administer the Law of Nations and an alternative to violence in conflict resolution, is not to say that it is a panacea. Hardy C. Dillard, one of the great U.S. jurists who served on the World Court, also a professor, dean, and colonel, said in addressing one of the audiences to whom he explained the Court: "International law and third-party judgment suffer from the two extremes of those who claim too much for both and those who claim too little for either."

He would have learned with regret that, since his death in 1982, those who claimed too much have all but disappeared, as those who glibly say the Court and international law are irrelevant have come to be treated as stating conventional wisdom. Their perception is distorted by utter ignorance or denial of knowledge of the record of the business of the World Court.

On another occasion, Dillard, as Virginia Law School dean before his election to the Court, addressed a congressional conference on justice, convened in 1970 after the troubled 1960s: "If we are going to talk about law and order nationally [as was then all the rage] we ought to be willing to commit ourselves to law and order internationally."

The American people's pride in and striving for a domestic government marked by respect for the Rule of Law should be matched by enthusiasm for achieving supremacy of the Rule of Law in global affairs.

Acknowledgments

Holdings of the uniquely well-furnished International Law Library at Columbia Law School were my principal source. They include, for example, seminal activity of the early twentieth century, when the idea of a Court was a U.S. cause—even the reports and proceedings of annual meetings at Lake Mohonk.

The initial impetus for this book was the content of a 1985 lecture by Felix Frankfurter Professor (and former deputy legal adviser) Abram Chayes, now deceased. This was delivered as one of a series supported by the Samuel Rubin Foundation at Columbia Law School (later published, *Columbia Law Review* 85: 1445). The fact that one who had been a lawyer for half a century did not know anything about much of the law discussed was a revelation. It was shocking to learn of the actions of the U.S. government in the Nicaragua case, especially to reject and disregard, after going to The Hague to submit argument on it, a Court decision on jurisdiction and to refuse to go before the Court to defend the legality of U.S. actions. That instigated the years of study and effort to publish this book.

While they have no responsibility for anything contained in the work, most of which they never saw, appreciation for occasional tips and guidance must be given to Columbia Law School Professors Oscar Schachter, Lori Damrosch, and Louis Henkin.

Professor Schachter told me of a lecture titled "Between a Rock and a Hard Place," which appeared later in the American Bar Association's *American Lawyer,* by Keith Highet, now deceased, then president of the American Society of International Law. I later met attorney and Professor Highet, whose encouragement and help were important.

The papers delivered at the annual meetings of the American Society of

International Law and its journal and other publications have been helpful, as have a kind word, now and then, from such members as Thomas M. Franck and Richard Bilder.

Interviews with judges of the World Court, including Stephen Schwebel, Manfred Lachs, Taslim Olewale Elias, and Ni Zhengyu, were stimulating, and supplemented by Judge Lachs's correspondence.

I am grateful for the loyal support of my agent, Luna Carne-Ross, and for the inspiration and intermittent editorial assistance of my dear friend Gertrude Lang.

There were many individuals whose words were supportive or encouraging, many of whom do not know of the fact. Outstanding among these was Michael Kinsley, then writing as "TRB" in the *New Republic,* October 1, 1990:

> [U]sefulness of international law depends on others believing that this time we really mean it.
>
> Really meaning it means giving up our own freedom of action on occasion, and allowing our own case-by-case moral assessments to be constrained by rules that will sometimes strike us as wrong. . . .
>
> Law that need not be obeyed if you disagree with it is not law. If we want meaningful international law to be available when we find it useful, we must respect it even when we don't.

Prologue

Before the Civil War the United States had fought two wars with England. Then, during that bitterly fought conflict, a grievance against England arose that threatened yet another.

In 1862, the Union was in danger; its only real victories were General Grant's in the west. There slid down the ways at Liverpool an armed frigate built in England and manned by British seamen. The ship flew the Confederate flag, yet it was never to enter a rebel-held port.

Ship No. 290, the British shipbuilder Laird called her; at sea she was christened the *Alabama*. She entered a career unlike any in the history of warfare: during a two-year period, resupplying only in English and French ports, she conducted a series of attacks on U.S. merchant ships that can be compared only with the Kaiser's unrestricted submarine attacks on allied and U.S. merchant vessels that drew the United States into World War I.

She attacked seventy ships, burning most of them down to the water's edge. Other roving ships, all from English shipyards, joined in the attacks, the total of which numbered 270.

"We shall have a day of reckoning for these wrongs," wrote Gideon Welles, Lincoln's Secretary of the Navy, in his diary, "and I sometimes think I care not how or in what manner that reckoning comes."

How severe the damage and how outraged the U.S. public were reflected in Welles's entry in July 1864, when the USS *Kearsage* engaged and sank the *Alabama:*

> Our *Alabama* news comes in opportunely to encourage and sustain the nation's heart. It does them as well as me good to dwell on the subject and the discomfiture

1

of the British and the Rebels. The perfidy of the former is as infamous as the treason of the latter.

Five years later, Britain's day of reckoning seemed to be on hand. One topic that was receiving serious debate was whether the United States should take over British North America—Canada as we know it now. In his final observation on the subject, Welles tells us, "the English are fully conscious of the great wrong they have done us. They are more apprehensive of war than they are willing to confess, and hostilities may be nearer than our people suppose."

That there was no war can be credited to the determination of President Grant and the skill of Secretary of State Hamilton Fish. In accordance with a treaty that they negotiated, the *Alabama* claims were submitted to a board of arbitrators with neutral members selected by the heads of state of Brazil, Italy, and Switzerland. They sat and heard evidence and rendered their decision in Geneva, inaugurating that city's modern role in international affairs.

The verdict was an award of $15.5 million, a sum quite commensurate with the dollar value of the destroyed ships. "The greater victory," as admiral and historian Samuel Eliot Morrison has written, "was for peace and arbitration."

The method used for arriving at the peaceful *Alabama* settlement was not unprecedented. It was but one instance of an ongoing contribution of the United States to the potential for peace in the world.

The initial demonstration of this came under President George Washington's leadership. After the American Revolution, when British forces had been withdrawn from the former colonies, there remained a number of exasperating differences concerning borders, fishing rights, and confiscation of property. In its early days, the U.S. Supreme Court was not very busy. Having confidence in Chief Justice John Jay as a negotiator, President Washington sent him to London to try to settle matters.

The issues seemed intractable. Jay and his English negotiating partners then agreed on a solution: each side would appoint commissioners who would go to the border areas in question; if they were unable to settle an issue, they would select someone believed by both to be neutral to make the decision. Included in a record of the proceedings was a most quotable remark by one of the commissioners: "Why shall not all the nations on earth determine their disputes in this mode, rather than choke the rivers with their carcasses and stain the soil of continents with their slain."

The agreement that provided for that became known as the Jay Treaty. It is regarded as having introduced international arbitration to the modern world. Arguably our Founders' generation made, in this, quite as important a contribution to the peoples of the world as they had by the Declaration of Independence and the Constitution.

Chief Justice Jay, doubling as special envoy, did not "invent" arbitration. Something very like it had a place in the relations of the Greek city-states three millennia ago. Reference has been made to use of impartial persons for the settlement of controversies in medieval times by the Catholic Church. But with the rise of nationalism and the predatory interrelation of European states, the process seems to have been ignored for centuries. The success of Jay's Treaty brought about a revival. During the nineteenth century, there was increasing use of arbitration to settle minor difficulties.

There was an important domestic consequence. Already existing U.S. peace societies, which with the Quakers and others, constituted a "peace movement," were stimulated into activism in behalf of arbitration. These groups— historian Merle Curti has referred to them as the "American Peace Crusade"— interrelated with the abolitionists and the reformers of the first half of the nineteenth century.

Taking a cue from the Jay Treaty's success, the American Peace Society called on the government to urge other nations to resort to arbitration instead of war to settle differences. Their efforts won from the Massachusetts state legislature in 1835 a resolution calling for the "establishment of some mode of just arbitration for all international disputes." Soon afterward their leader, William Ladd, personally published a plan—perhaps the first of its kind here—for a permanent court of the nations as an auxiliary body to a "Congress of Nations." The Ladd Plan was advocated in Boston 1845 at what had become a significant annual event, the Fourth of July Address.

The speaker was Charles Sumner, a relatively unknown young Boston attorney who was later to be a national figure as a senator and leading abolitionist. During the Fourth of July speech, which was titled "The True Grandeur of Nations" and was published and reprinted in Europe, he identified war as essentially a "mode of litigation between nations," which he denounced as constituting "international lynch law." If international law at the time permitted war as a legal instrument, he argued, it could be changed.

An alternate plan, more attainable than the full international organization, was conceived by William Jay, who succeeded Ladd as leader of the American Peace Society. He suggested that all treaties on any subject should contain in their very text an arbitration clause, an agreement that any disputes arising with regard to the subject of the treaty go to arbitration. Although commonplace now, Jay's idea was then a radical advance. It won practical realization in a clause placed in the treaty concluding the Crimean War.

The foregoing only outlines the rising sentiment for arbitration as a tool of peacekeeping before the Civil War. That sentiment must be recognized as background to the successful peaceful settlement of the grievous *Alabama* claims. The arbitration cause was also fed and notably enhanced by the outcome at Geneva. Credit can be given to persistent and growing activism from below, and government advocacy and occasional action above.

Members and supporters of the peace societies saw the vindication of their stance and a growth in the societies' membership. There were tangible consequences, beginning, on June 17, 1874, with the U.S. House of Representatives unanimously urging "an international system" to facilitate arbitration.

The 1880s saw a stepping up of activity for a broad, general British–American arbitration treaty, visualized as a precursor to a network of such pacts. A British Labor leader arrived in the United States with a petition signed by 234 members of Parliament, and secured an introduction to President Cleveland through the intervention of multi-millionaire Andrew Carnegie. A group of distinguished citizens appointed by New York Mayor William R. Grace drafted and submitted a statement in support of such a treaty.

At the 1889 centennial celebration of Washington's inaugural, Edward Everett Hale, New England writer, reformer, and sometime radical, predicted a permanent court of arbitration would come in the twentieth century, brought into being by U.S. initiative. However, at an early Pan-American Conference of 1889, Secretary of State James Blaine's plan for an inter-American comprehensive arbitration treaty drew cheers, but no ratifications.

The 1890s had a similar pattern. In early 1895, 300 notables at a major conference on arbitration backed the idea of the treaty with Britain. Another unofficial meeting, the first of twenty-two such annual gatherings for gaining influential support for the international arbitration idea, was held at a Catskill resort at Lake Mohonk, New York. These sessions played such a significant role that the place, still functioning as a vacation spot, is a national historic landmark. These were by no means the only efforts made on the subject during that decade.

A treaty of general arbitration with Britain was signed in January 1897, at the end of Cleveland's presidential administration. His successor, President McKinley, supported the treaty with real bipartisan enthusiasm. The church groups, women's clubs, and chambers of commerce, alerted by peace and arbitration advocates, made their views known to the U.S. Senate.

But the senators were not enthusiastic. They looked jealously at a measure that might have an impact on their power to participate in making foreign policy. They flexed their muscles with a series of amendments, stripping the pact of any real meaning. They went on to defeat the treaty by withholding the two-thirds majority vote needed for "advice and consent."

Arbitration proponents were dismayed but not discouraged. Rolling up their sleeves, they resumed their campaign, mutually pledging greater efforts. Welcoming valued new supporters, the participants at the Second Mohonk Conference of International Arbitration were happy to join in endorsing publicly an elaborate plan for a permanent international court, drawn up by the Bar Association of the State of New York.

The "Platform"—as the Mohonk convenors called the resolution adopted at the end of the first meeting—for 1895 began, "the feasibility of arbitration as a substitute for war is now demonstrated."

The second resolution, in 1896, went further:

In the settlement of personal controversies civilization has substituted the appeal to law for the appeal to force. . . . Such a substitution of law for war requires a permanent tribunal to which all nations may appeal. Its personnel may change but its judicial life should be continuous.

European peace advocates had responded in a manner similar to their U.S. counterparts to the peaceful settlement of the *Alabama* claims, and an arbitration movement developed among them. After news of the agreement of Americans on a permanent court reached them, they began to call the idea of a permanent tribunal the "American plan."

A FEW WORDS ABOUT
INTERNATIONAL LAW

It was understood by the advocates of a court that by "Law" they meant international law, the "Law of the Nations," as it was referred to in our own 1787 Constitution. That international law existed and should be recognized in guiding national conduct was no secret in 1897, any more than it had been in 1787. Indeed in 1900, in the case called *The Paquete Habana*, the U.S. Supreme Court said:

International law is part of our law and must be ascertained and administered by the courts of justice as often as questions of right depending on it are duly presented for their determination.

It may be noted at this point that in 1987, the Midwest philosopher Haskell Fain wrote, "Once most educated people knew quite a lot about international law, but it says something significant about our international problems that today international law is a subject for specialists; it is not even part of the standard curriculum in law schools." Since it is not expected that the readers of this work will be among the "specialists" referred to by Fain, a few words about international law may be in order.

Like the English Common Law, the 800-year-old source of most of our domestic law, international law did not spring into being all at once, or by the act of any legislature or supreme ruler. Just as common law developed slowly over the centuries, the Law of Nations has developed slowly since about 1648, the time of the Peace of Westphalia, which ended the Thirty Years' War in Europe.

The rules of behavior and principles governing the states in their relationships came from no sovereign's decree. It was called "Customary Law." It was to the Customary Law that Supreme Court Justice Horace Gray referred when he wrote in the 1900 *Paquete Habana* case, "resort must be had to the customs and usages of civilized nations, and as evidence of these, to the words of jurists and commentators."

The American Founders' familiarity with the Law of Nations is evidenced by their inclusion, at the 1787 Convention, of the power to punish "offenses against the Law of Nations" among the powers of the Congress. In another clause, that original Constitution pays its respects to international law, with the clear implication that the executive and legislative branches of our government are duty-bound to respect and abide by it. Along with the Constitution itself, "Treaties . . . shall be the supreme Law of the Land."

Treaties, of course, are agreements between or among nations. They are specifically identified by Justice Gray's opinion in the *Habana* case in differentiating the status of treaties from the normal sources of Customary Law: that customs and usages may be resorted to only "where there is no treaty."

In the early period during which international law was recognized, Customary Law constituted the major portion of the body of the Law. Treaties, where appropriate, constituted "Conventional" law. Two types of treaty, by the mid-twentieth century, came to overshadow "customs and usages," as representing what the law was.

Multilateral treaties restating the law represented the agreement of many state parties, on the subject of what Customary Law had come to be. That is, just as domestically we have codified large portions of the Common Law, groups of states—more frequently the United Nations itself—delegate to experts the task of drafting codifications of the Customary Law; these are finalized in the diplomacy of interstate relations.

Treaties among many nations were and are useful with regard to "new" law. This refers to the agreement of states to adjust their relations as necessitated by changes and advances in technology and its targets. The problems of aerial hijacking, exploitation of the Arctic region, and undersea oil drilling justify and are best treated at multilateral meetings and by collectively made treaties.

At the turn of the twentieth century, when our story begins, international law was less developed than it has come to be in our time. Nevertheless, Customary Law had come into being to deal with such subjects as recognition of states, rights and duties of diplomatic missions, the making and interpretation of treaties, and a cluster of the problems relating to the seas and rivers.

Useful as it might be in the solution of international difficulties that might otherwise lead to armed hostilities, the Law of Nations did not—in 1900—treat war itself as illegal. War was considered to be a legitimate arm of national policy; a favored cliché was that it was an extension of diplomacy by other means. While there was some rudimentary regulation of the manner of conduct of armed combat, war itself was as legitimate as dueling had been in earlier societies.

There was a central feature of international law that when observed helped to preserve peace and, when ignored, could lead to conflict: this was "*pacta sunt servanda*," a Latin maxim well known to scholars and students of foreign affairs, as well as to diplomats and foreign affairs officers: "Treaties *must* be obeyed." *Pacta sunt servanda* was important in view of the delicacy of interstate relations. It was chief of the rules that were obeyed mutually by the nations because it was in their own interest so to behave.

It was assumed and legally recognized that each state was "sovereign"— meaning that it was the sole source of power to rule over territory within a delineated geographical subdivision of the globe. This meant it was the exclusive representative and guardian of its people and institutions.

HOW INTERNATIONAL LAW IS "MADE": ONE CASE STUDY

In the nineteenth century, examples of "law" making by treaty set up some useful and durable multinational instrumentalities. These included the Universal Postal Union, commissions to regulate traffic on rivers that bordered on or were used by more than one state, and so on. But the great modern period of codification of multiple rules began later.

Customary Law was evidenced by behavior: conduct of states in circumstances or in ways that reflected a sense of legal obligation. That a practice was accepted as law could be ascertained best by examining instances of such acceptance. Perhaps the most celebrated of the nineteenth century was the episode referred to in the books as the case of the *Caroline*.

The affair began with a domestic rebellion, like many international controversies that resulted in the use of force by one nation against another. British North America (not yet the "Dominion of Canada") was suffering Tory misrule in the 1830s, a condition not unlike that which had provoked the American Revolution sixty years earlier. Insurrections began in the provinces of Quebec and Ontario, led by William Mackenzie in the English-speaking area and Louis J. Papineau in the French region.

Defeated, Mackenzie's forces retreated to sanctuaries along the New York border. Some of them were resupplied with the aid of U.S. sympathizers using a riverboat, the U.S. paddle wheeler *Caroline,* plying the Niagara River. One night a picked squad of British volunteers boarded and seized the boat, killing one American and wounding others. They set fire to the *Caroline* and sent her to the bottom near Niagara Falls.

Not long after the rebellions ended, a supposed former Canadian commando raider was reported to have boasted in a New York barroom of killing the American crewman. When he was arrested and indicted for murder, Lord Palmerston, the British prime minister, protested and demanded the man's release. He claimed the destruction of the *Caroline* was a government act, justified by the British territory's right of "self-defense."

The diplomatic exchanges between U.S. Secretary of State Daniel Webster and the London Foreign Office are still quoted today and accepted as a statement of a principle of customary international law. Responding to the British claim that such a soldier was immune to local criminal laws, Webster's message conceded that one "forming part of a public force, and acting under the authority of his Government is not be held answerable as a private trespasser or malefactor."

But, Webster argued, the action of the British force that sank the *Caroline* in U.S. waters was a wrongful intrusion and a violation of our rights as sovereign. The first answer from London was that the past and possible future use of the *Caroline* to supply scattered rebels who might cross the border justified the raid as "self-defense."

Webster's response drew a distinction between force legally acceptable as a protective measure, and action that, after a passage of time, sought revenge or redress. Only where the "necessity of that self-defense is instant, overwhelming, and leaving no choice of means, and no moment of deliberation is the use of force legitimate."

The British acquiesced and apologized. The case of the boastfully confessing commando was closed when a jury acquitted him.

The *Caroline* standard is of importance for the still-quoted statement of the principle defined by Webster: A state that claims (to justify an action that would ordinarily be clearly illegal) to have acted in self-defense, must show: (a) instant, overwhelming necessity; (b) no alternative choice of means; and (c) an obvious need to ignore deliberate processes.

Caroline is a striking example of how customary law comes into being; it is moreover an excellent case of two-party settlement of an international disagreement.

HOW INTERNATIONAL DISPUTES ARE DECIDED

As we have just seen, individual states through diplomats can achieve peaceful settlement of clashes by the kind of rational discussion that Daniel Webster and his London counterparts had in the *Caroline* case, "talking out" their differences as to what the law provided. Then, as now, most differences between states were settled through diplomatic negotiation.

When such exchanges fail to bring about a meeting of minds, a third party can often help. That can be done, as we often see in labor disputes, by a method that will still leave the ultimate decision to the contenders. "Good offices" is a technical term in transnational affairs for a friendly act of a concerned outsider, encouraging two stubborn opponents to talk. A more active, but still not decisive, role is played by the outsider in "mediation"—a technique very familiar when the contenders are a stubborn company and an aggressive union. The neutral outsider will take part in the talks, sometimes in caucus separately with each side, exploring their positions, making suggestions for a formula that may bring them together. However, the final decision is still left to the opponents.

Arbitration that came to be more popular in the years after Jay's Treaty meant submission to an outsider for final decision after hearing both sides. It began to play a significant role in international affairs, and to win appreciative "fans" among antiwar activists who sought to push governments into greater use of this peace process. But unlike the use of arbitration in domestic commercial or industrial cases, international decision making by outsiders did not emerge as an alternative to a mandatory, established judicial system. There was nothing in the Law of Nations that made submission to and acceptance of neutral decisions mandatory. On the contrary, nations had been free to settle arguments via "trial by battle." Arbitration arose as the civilized alternative.

Though voluntary, and created on an episode-by-episode basis, arbitration as a way of deciding between nations has played a worthy role, but only when two states—already at odds and glowering—take the trouble and effort to:

1. Select a person acceptable to two foes to serve as neutral.
2. Agree, at least, on the wording of the issue to be decided—no easy task itself.
3. Work out all the ground rules: where and when and how the hearing/ decision process was to be conducted.

And so, as the nineteenth century was coming to a close, peace activists, lawyers and businessmen, increasingly involved in foreign affairs, talked more often about the virtues of a permanent court, composed of professional judges, with its own rules. That would make all that preliminary maneuvering unnecessary. A court in existence before a dispute breaks out has an enormous advantage. Afterward, without a court, cooperation on a solution is so much harder.

The existence of a court could bring growth and development and clarification of the law: the English common law could not have achieved its acceptance without the role played by judges. Customary international law had no such advantage.

Since the people of the United States had seen their several sovereign states (with one glaring exception of the Civil War) peacefully adjust their border, water rights, citizens' travel, and business disputes by a single, permanent federal Supreme Court, they could more easily imagine and more ardently strive for an equivalent for the separate states of the globe.

Such a mode of decision among nations—indeed the hope for expansion of arbitration itself—seemed remote indeed, as the nineteenth century drew to a close. The defeat of the bipartisan effort of 1897 (Cleveland's Treaty endorsed by his successor McKinley) was discouraging. If two English-speaking nations that had been drawing closer could not agree to replace war with a mechanism for peaceful settlement to which they'd be bound, what hope was there for the already feverishly arms-racing rest of the globe?

The struggle to establish an answer took most of the century that followed.

1

A Century Ends, an Effort Begins

A SIGNAL FROM SAINT PETERSBURG: 1898

Those in the United States who had hoped to promote law as an alternative to war were discouraged as the turn of the century approached. After the defeat of the British Treaty, they had received a short-lived lift in morale when President McKinley responded favorably to a call from the third Lake Mohonk conference, asking that he try again. The good news was that he agreed and sent a message to Congress, declaring, "The best sentiment of the civilized world is moving toward the settlement of differences between nations without resorting to the horrors of war."

Then came the bad news. It was a time of rising popular indignation with Spain's behavior toward its subjects in its colony of Cuba. There was widespread sympathy with the insurrectionists there, and revulsion at reports of brutal repression. All fine words and sentiments about arbitration and third-party settlement were forgotten when the U.S. battleship *Maine* sank as the result of an explosion in Havana Harbor.

Instead of seeking a peaceful settlement the administration turned to war. The efforts of the Spanish king's ministers to keep the peace were rejected, even though he agreed to most U.S. demands and offered to arbitrate the rest. Other European nations urged Washington to seek a peaceful solution. Instead, President McKinley yielded to the advice of expansionists and big navy advocates ("navalists") and to what he perceived as popular clamor for war to free Cuba and revenge the *Maine*. When he asked for and secured a declaration of war against Spain in April 1898, the arbitration movement seemed thoroughly stalled. This was not altered by the sudden and easy victory in the war that might have been avoided.

At this point an unexpected lift for America's battered peace advocates came from a most surprising quarter. There arrived in Washington, and in the rest of the world's major capitals, a message from St. Petersburg, the capital of Imperial Russia.

11

One of the world's last absolute monarchs, Czar Nicholas II, leader of a nation that was a principal actor in the ever-more frightening arms race, proposed an international conference to consider ways for ending competition in armaments. The message, called an imperial rescript because it was signed by the czar himself, hoped such a conference would prove to be "a happy presage for the century which is about to open" and focus the efforts "to make the great idea of universal peace triumph over the elements of trouble and discord."

The czar's foreign minister handed out copies of the rescript on August 24, 1898. A dozen days earlier the United States and Spain had initialed an armistice; European capitals had been discussing the humiliation of Spain, which was once one of the globe's great empires, and whether the United States would take over the Philippines and thus enter the World Power club.

That question receded in importance as the czar's seemingly bizarre initiative became the topic of the day in foreign ministries and embassies, and even some throne rooms. Although there were kind words for the czar's rescript in public, all were at best skeptical in private. The German kaiser told his foreign minister it was a "bit of deviltry"; France, Russia's ally, was miffed at not being given advance notice, and concerned that its own long-range plan to retake Alsace and Lorraine might be endangered. The mood was one of suspicion, confusion, or both.

U.S. supporters of international arbitration and other peace advocates were neither suspicious nor confused. The day after the news became public, the *New York Times* reported that peace leaders were "jubilant." The American Peace Society sent a congratulatory message to the czar through his embassy in Washington. They called on President McKinley to accept the invitation and instruct delegates to push for a general arbitration treaty. The Episcopal Church convention, meeting at the time, went one step further and called for a system of "judicial arbitration."

In 1879, at the Washington Inaugural Centennial, Edward Everett Hale had predicted that "the United States . . . will propose to the other great powers to . . . form a permanent tribunal of the highest dignity" by the turn of the century. Addressing the delegates at the 1899 Lake Mohonk Fifth National Arbitration Conference, Hale said of the czar's initiative, "It was indeed like a sudden flash of lightning in a clear sky."

> [I]f I had stood up here and said that . . . the head of the largest army in the world, the emperor of the largest empire in Europe, would have gone farther than the rest of us had gone in proposing universal peace . . . you would have certainly said that here was such a crank as never got even to Mohonk before.

The peace activists felt no need to speculate about the Russian autocrat's possible motives. What he did and what he said had come to erase recent setbacks and renew energy and effort for the future struggle. This applied not only to those in the United States, but to many peace societies in Britain and other parts of Europe that were avid supporters of what had come to be known among them as the "American idea" or "plan" of substituting law for war.

After the Imperial Archives were opened to scholars and historians by the Bolshevik Revolution of 1917, they found that a cynical view of the czar's motives might have been warranted. There is evidence that the idea of sending out the invitations to a meeting supposedly aimed at reducing the pace of the arms race was prompted by fear that the Russian economy could no longer stand the strain of matching every German or Austro-Hungarian advance in heavy artillery. One verdict, cited by Calvin Davis, was that the rescript had been "conceived in fear, brought forth in deceit, and swaddled in humanitarian ideals."

But that interpretive judgment may not fairly appreciate the whole story. A contemporary report stated that the czar was moved by more than his minister's parsimony. He had been impressed by talks with Ivan Bloch, a Polish scholar and pacifist, who had recently published a six-volume warning to the world, titled *The Future of War*. Its central message was that modern war was "futile and would result simply in bankruptcy if fought to a finish, with victory for neither side." Even more persuasive—and prophetic—was Bloch's warning that the ultimate result would be "social revolution."

By the autumn of 1898, the czar and his ministers were aware that they had scored what could be called a public relations coup. The most eloquent symptom was the spontaneous cry from Ernest H. Crosby, who had resigned as judge of the Alexandria "capitulations" court (forced on Egypt by colonial powers to safeguard subjects from local justice) after coming under the influence of Count Leo Tolstoy's writings and personality. By now an anarchist sympathizer and a leader of a New York Committee for Russian Freedom, Crosby said on hearing of the first rescript: "God bless the czar."

ON TO THE HAGUE

As if responding to the warm reception of the pacifists and others usually hostile to autocracy, the Russians issued a supplemental rescript in January 1899. It repeated the czar's invitation and proposed a specific list of subjects to be discussed at the contemplated conference. Added to talks on limiting arms were three ideas for prohibition or restriction of new instruments of warfare, changes in the wartime law of the sea to benefit neutrals, and improvement in an earlier declaration of purpose to impose "humane" conditions and limitations on the conduct of hostilities. The eighth point expressed in plain language what the United States and world peace forces had read between the lines of the first rescript: "improvement and extension of arbitration and mediation."

At this news, U.S. peace groups went into high gear. The American Peace

Society, the sometimes more militant rival Universal Peace Union, and church-sponsored and religiously oriented organizations—including the Women's Christian Temperance Union, powerful enough, later, to lead in putting over the Prohibition [Eighteenth] Amendment—all joined in agitating for U.S. participation in favor of an effective plan for peace through arbitration.

Hale was elated that his prophecy was being fulfilled. Once active in pre-Civil War abolitionism and its allied reforms, he was a preacher and prolific author. His book *The Man without a Country,* a lesson in patriotism, by which he is still remembered, was aimed at those who opposed the Union in the Civil War. A perennial and leading figure in the Lake Mohonk conferences, he led the New England effort. Hale was no minor or fringe figure in public life, and was soon to lead a vast throng on Boston Common to pay the city's respects to the coming of the twentieth century, and shortly thereafter, he was named chaplain of the U.S. Senate.

Hale launched a Boston Peace Crusade, a group active in the months prior to the conference that was to assemble in response to the czar's call. His partner in the effort and editor of a similarly named paper published during the period was Edwin D. Mead, no minor figure himself in reform activities that Van Wyck Brooks has called "New England: Indian Summer." During these few months, Hale addressed more than fifty meetings in thirteen states, and organized committees in other cities to help promote the coming conference. Repeatedly, he stressed the theme that he had successfully stressed at the Mohonk meetings, his intuitive notion, even as a nonprofessional in transnational legal affairs, that an established court was superior to one-shot arbitration settlements: "We will have a permanent tribunal for the twentieth century."

In his advocacy he frequently argued, "The United States of America is the oldest, as it is the largest and most successful peace society which the world has ever known." By this he meant that the original thirteen independent states and those that were set up to join them had had dozens of differences, all of which (save for the slavery/Union question) had been settled by a single, permanent tribunal, the U.S. Supreme Court, "so peacefully that nothing gets into the histories. That is the general rule for a history, to leave out what is important and to put in what is unimportant if only it be noisy."

Meanwhile, back in Europe, the Russian government wisely chose to seek neutral territory for the conference's location, so that the invitations could be formalized and the meeting could begin. The Netherlands was the first to be asked, and offered its capital, The Hague. The Dutch took over the responsibility of sending out the invitations and thus began a century of use of The Hague, not only for the conference to come but also as a place where the institution that emerged, and a variety of future international meetings, official and unofficial, would be located. Invitations were limited to states with diplomatic representation at St. Petersburg, thereby excluding most of Latin America, an omission that would be remedied on a similar occasion at a later date.

It cannot be said for certain that the intensive campaign led by Hale and his colleagues influenced the choice of the U.S. delegation or the instructions they received. But there was a "strong" delegation chosen, headed by Andrew D. White, former president of Cornell University and at the time U.S. ambassador to Germany. Another member of the mission was Frederick Holls, an international lawyer who was notably active in German-American political circles. His presence was to be helpful at a crucial moment. When the time came for the U.S. State Department to instruct the group, the result was quite in accord with what Hale and the activist arbitration advocates would have wanted.

John Hay, the new Secretary of State (and one of Abraham Lincoln's former secretaries) had just returned from an ambassadorship to Britain and was arbitration-minded. The administration, under the influence of the navalists and their allies in Congress, was not going to have its people talk disarmament, the czar's supposed top priority. The army's standard arsenal, in the old U.S. peacetime tradition, was so meager that there was nothing to spare. The powerful navalist lobby would not hear of any reduction in the still-growing fleet that had humbled Spain across the waters. They saw to it that Captain Alfred Mahan, one of the most celebrated of their group, was placed on the delegation to The Hague, as if to see that the peace thing did not get out of hand.

So the State Department focused the delegates' attention on international arbitration, with the admonition that the second rescript's addition on this point was "likely to open the most fruitful field for discussion and future action." There was even annexed to the written instructions an exhibit, consisting of a plan for a permanent arbitration tribunal, modeled on the recent proposal of the New York State Bar Association. This the delegates were authorized to propose if the opportunity presented itself.

This was a principal U.S. negotiating position in a multination, multisubject conference. Both in the United States and abroad, it was sensed by the leaders of the peace movement that this was a rare opportunity. They knew that it required effort to yield the result that they had envisioned when they praised the czar's original initiative. Their response sparked the first stage, one that had brought delegates to The Hague, of whom a majority was surprisingly ready to advance the subject of a substitute for war. This could be credited in no small part to the work of arbitration peace advocates everywhere.

Now came the second stage, something unprecedented in world history, a sort of peoples' lobby at an international conference of diplomats and other officials representing their separate national states. Their purpose, not only among Americans but also voiced by a rising chorus in every nation represented and some others, was to influence the conference by intense pressure on the individual conferees, to advance the cause of arbitration and/or a court for international disputes.

Despite the time and expense of travel, all branches of the U.S. peace movement had members and leaders who traveled to The Hague to observe the conference at one time or another. There came also many personalities not traditionally identified with peace advocacy, such as Archbishop John Ireland of St.

Paul, Minnesota, and Thomas B. Reed, Speaker of the House of Representatives. Dr. Benjamin Trueblood, secretary of the American Peace Society (also the official representative of the rival Universal Peace Union) came on May 19, 1899, the day after the conference opened, and stayed for many weeks.

Aside from the stream of visitors, scholars, and peace delegations, every mail brought many letters and every day saw dozens of telegrams from overseas and petitions signed by many thousands. Naturally, the English and the European peace groups outnumbered those from across the Atlantic. They made an impressive showing.

As the cosmopolitan group of peace and arbitration advocates continued to buttonhole and attempt to convert or neutralize the delegates at The Hague, a crisis developed. It became evident that the German delegation would block any movement toward an agreement on third-party intervention for legal solution of international problems. Their delegates had been instructed to do so presumably because their high command's military theory was based on the value of, and their skill at, surprise attack.

Holls, a member of the U.S. delegation, had been (as a second-generation German-American) politically active among his compatriots and an advocate of Teutonic language and culture. On hearing of the possible impasse, he was chosen by the U.S. delegation to make a quiet, unofficial side trip to Berlin. He visited Chancellor Hohnelohe and Foreign Minister von Bulow to induce them to have their delegates' instructions modified.

The Germans, asserting that they saw no great enthusiasm among their own people, questioned whether Americans really cared. Holls gave them evidence that moved them. As Lucia Ames Mead, an activist and historian of the U.S. peace movement, described in her report:

> They [the German cabinet members] were amazed to see that multitude of letters and cablegrams from all over the country which [Holls] showed as evidence of our concern. Among them was a telegram from [thirty-one] Baptist clergymen, each of whom had paid a dollar to send it. Another was a prayer written by a bishop of Texas, to be prayed every Sunday in every church in his diocese. These simple documents had weight.

The earlier preconference enthusiasm of the people of the United States seemed to be paying off.

SOMETHING UNPRECEDENTED DONE: MUCH MORE TO DO

The conference opened on May 18, 1899. It was the kind of spring day that was ideal for those who were looking for good auguries. At The Hague's little seaside suburb of Schveningen, balmy salt breezes blew about a Russian Orthodox chapel, where European delegates joined their Slavic colleagues at a mass celebrated to honor Czar Nicholas II's birthday. The delegates then proceeded to the meeting at a Royal Dutch summer residence not half an hour from the heart of The Hague, named the House in the Woods. As thousands lined the route of the procession, flags of all twenty-six nations in attendance waved.

The conference opened with a congratulatory telegram to be sent to the czar, and the election of Baron de Staal, the Russian ambassador to London, as president of the gathering. Getting on with its business, the body voted to set up three commissions, among which to divide the eight points of the ambitious and diversified program that had been projected by the second rescript. One was to deal with the supposed leading question presented by the ongoing arms race; one on the points dealing with the rules of warfare; and a third to consider proposals and plans to avoid war by alternative methods of dispute resolution.

Holls, Chairman White, and Seth Low were the three members of the U.S. delegation assigned to the arbitration commission, as the third came to be known. (Low was then president of Columbia University, and was the last mayor of Brooklyn before it merged with its neighbors.)

No action of any consequence was taken by the meeting on the prime topic of disarmament. Thus was fulfilled Andrew White's forecast, confided to his diary, "never has so large a body come together in a spirit of more hopeless skepticism as to any good result." The conferees went no further on the armaments buildup than to "resolve"—an expression of pious wish but no more—that an end to the constant *increase* in spending for warfare would be "extremely desirable." To avoid the label of "do-nothings," the first commission added to this nonaction three "declarations," statements of policy that nevertheless did not amount to agreed-upon prohibitions bearing the weight of treaty commitments. These denounced the use of poison gas and so-called dum-dum bullets that expand after entry, imposing added torture to the injured. On the insistence of Captain Mahan, the United States joined Great Britain in voting against the poison gas and dum-dum bans.

A third declaration, unanimously adopted, expressed the opposition of the assembled representatives of the civilized world to "the launching of projectiles from balloons *or other similar new methods*" (emphasis added). The "similar new method" that the Wright brothers would reveal in their first flight at Kitty Hawk, North Carolina, was yet to come.

The second commission, on laws and customs of war, did provide for the participating states something more substantial: a multination treaty, called a "convention," designed to regulate and limit specified conduct that, by consensus of the period, made war too barbaric. This task was facilitated by preliminary work on the subject that had taken place independently from, and in some instances long prior to, the conference at The Hague.

Professor Charles de Visscher, a Belgian international legal scholar who was to become a World Court judge, has given us a fine epigrammatic critique of the effort in his book *Theory and Practice in Public International Law* (Princeton University Press, 1957):

> They embarked on the vain enterprise of regulating what is the anarchic phenomenon *par excellence* by prescribing laws for the use of forces which, once loosed, know no law but success.

It was in the work of the third commission—assigned to evaluate plans for "good offices, mediation, arbitration"—that the Hague Conference of 1899 accomplished something of enduring value. In 2001, with an international Court more than fifty years old, successor to one that lasted almost twenty years, what they did may not seem sensational. Yet in that turn-of-the-century world, the delegates at The Hague took what was then a giant step forward: they created what was called a "Permanent Court of Arbitration."

An interesting feature expressly provided that signatory states should consider themselves duty-bound to remind any others that seemed on the verge of imperiling the peace of the very existence and the utility of the "Court." Members of the third commission also broke new ground by supplying a technique for creating "Commissions of Inquiry" to work where fact-disputes had the effect of hampering diplomacy.

The Court of Arbitration was a partial victory for the U.S. plan, but not nearly so complete as Secretary Hay thought when he cabled his congratulations to the delegates. Believing that the "Convention for the Pacific Settlement of International Disputes" included "the essential features of the American plan," he saluted them for what he declared they could always think of as the crowning achievement of their lives. The delegates had, in fact, backed off in midsession (with his approval) from pushing for a true Court, with permanent career judges, which lay advocates such as Hale and professionals in the New York State Bar had drafted.

The U.S. delegation had joined in producing an institution that was a "court" in name only. What had been brought into being (subject to ratification) was an international body that consisted of two interdependent features: First, a "panel" or list of distinguished jurists, with stipulated qualifications, was to be nominated by the participating states—but no more than four from any one nation. Second, the panel was to be coordinated in function by a standing administrative council, consisting of the members' regular diplomatic representatives at The Hague. The council would appoint and oversee a group of international civil servants to act as the Secretariat of the Court. Their function would be clerical rather than judicial, but their existence would make possible elimination of many of the time-costly delays that impaired the effectiveness of the customary voluntary arbitration of the past. They provided standing rules, and an available place—in neutral territory— and were in a position to facilitate selection from the list of qualified judges.

The process of arbitral decision would lose none of its voluntary character:

it would gain in efficiency and availability—the quality of "being there." The very existence of this new entity seemed to introduce a significant new factor in global affairs. That perceived penumbra was deemed more important than the very tangible and obvious creation of new machinery to facilitate going to arbitration.

"For the scholar interested in world organization," historian Warren F. Kuehl has written, "The Hague Conference of 1899 contributed substantially to the movement . . . a genuine international gathering had taken place. . . . It proved that nations could unite on a broad scale to discuss their problems."

That modern evaluation was anticipated by Hale, when the final structure (and limitations) of the so-called Permanent Court was still on the drafting table. He summed up the achievement as he addressed the conferees at the May 1899 Mohonk conference:

> This conference at The Hague marks an epoch in the history of the world. It is the first step toward the federated peace of the world. The czar is entitled to gratitude and respectful admiration for his noble initiative.

The conference at The Hague closed on July 29, 1899. The convention that created the Court contained no commitment to arbitrate; the Senate would be free to veto U.S. participation in individual cases. The U.S. Senate, under the influence of the administration and sensing the enthusiasm of the peace movement, ratified the agreement in twenty-five minutes.

A bright and shining light had opened the century. But it did not reach far. Something unprecedented had been done. But the beginning of wars within a year in distant China—where European nations intervened to repress the Boxer rebellion—and in South Africa—where British troops began a costly war to terminate the existence of the Boer regions that had declared their independence—and in the Philippines, where the U.S. Army was warring on the indigenous peoples who sought their independence, showed that a great deal more had to be done. Still another bloody conflict, in Russian Asia, between Russia and Japan, brought the final demonstration that a great deal more had to be done if the peace program established at The Hague was to fulfill its purpose.

2

Onward Movement until a Tragic Halt

BUILDING ON THE NEW FOUNDATION

When the peace pact of The Hague opened the twentieth century, the reception was widely enthusiastic. This did not abate even when it became apparent that the Permanent Court of Arbitration was less than had been hoped for. The fact that it existed, the manner in which it was created, inspired renewed effort to craft a tribunal that would deserve the name "Court." All they really had secured, however, was a better arbitration agency. The limited practical success nevertheless helped to spread the message. With new recruits the early advocates addressed two types of action that would move their efforts onward. These were compatible and interacted for one another's benefit.

One option was a supplementary network of treaties. Any two nations, by separate treaty between them, could commit each other to go to The Hague for the selection of arbitrators from the permanent panel, should there be a deadlocked dispute. Thus could be created a fragmentary islet of obligatory arbitration. A sufficient number could create an impressive archipelago, though it could not convert the noncourt into an entity with all the advantages of a true panel of permanently sitting judges. The nations' response to the 1899 agreement was the negotiation of dozens of such treaties beginning in 1901, more than 150 within a few years. (More than 1,600 would have been required at the time to bind all the existing nations with each other).

Another option was a second Hague conference, at which, it was hoped, the movement to a real World Court could be advanced by another giant step. Considering what had been created from a zero base in 1899, the prospect was not at all dim. Partisans of the peace movement saw the opportunity and began to arouse public opinion in that direction. A decade of progress ensued during which the U.S. peace movement grew dramatically. A further spur came with the response of the public sector.

21

At first, the president and secretary of state were reluctant to join the treaty networking by reviving the British pact that had been rejected by the Senate in 1897. But they did address one deficiency in the initial Hague structure. The omission of all Latin American states, save for Mexico, was a reflection of the isolation of Imperial Russia from South and Central America: invitations to The Hague meeting had been sent only to states with diplomatic ties to the czar's regime, thus excluding South and Central America.

What made the omission especially ironic was that during the nineteenth century, theory and practice of international arbitration had developed and flourished independently among the Latin states. Though not always effective in preventing local conflict, arbitration was, at the turn of the century, on the verge of one spectacular success, which was to leave a lasting tangible symbol of the potential for peace between states via third-party settlement. That reminder was the noted sculpture towering over the Argentina–Chile border known as "The Christ of the Andes." It celebrates the peaceful end of the decades-old conflict between the neighbors over the territory of Patagonia to the south of them: Edward VII of Britain had acted as arbitrator.

President McKinley and Secretary of State Hay were being urged to call a second Pan-American conference; especially interested were those in the business community concerned with foreign trade. Assistant Secretary of State David J. Hill, in charge of preparation, included in the agenda a vaguely worded hemispheric arbitration proposal. The president went on a nationwide tour devoted primarily to promoting the conference. In his last scheduled stop at a Pan-American exposition at Buffalo, New York, his overview of the century just ending was summarized: "No nation can any longer be indifferent to any other." He urged the people of the world to recognize the need "when we have differences, to adjust them in the court of arbitration, which is the noblest forum for the settlement of international disputes."

He may have been expressing regret for allowing himself to be stampeded by the media, the Congress, and many in his cabinet, into war with Spain despite that nation's avowed willingness to settle the Cuban issue by arbitration. His last words were forgotten as the nation and historians were preoccupied by the tragic event of the following day, September 6, 1901. President McKinley was assassinated and Theodore Roosevelt was catapulted into the White House.

The conference opened in Mexico City a few weeks later without any change in plan offered by President Roosevelt. The idea of a separate Western Hemisphere arbitration scheme ran into trouble with the Latin delegates, as well as with many of the U.S. peace movement, who had been following the meeting closely. Edward Everett Hale, reliable activist of the Mohonk conferences and other centers of arbitration advocacy—himself among the pioneers of the increasingly popular Court idea—wrote to President Roosevelt: "[T]hose of us who count the Hague as a real step upward and forward, hate to see a fifth wheel put on the coach . . ." The majority of the delegates agreed with that view and rejected the idea of setting up a new arbitration center. It was agreed to extend The Hague system to the Americas.

This significant victory for a one-world system of peace-by-adjudication was followed by another that increased the enthusiasm and activism of the U.S. peace people. The Mexico City meeting unanimously adopted a resolution proposing a third Pan-American conference within five years. The idea of having regular international conferences that had been discussed among the activists both in the United States and in Europe was brought to a higher level. A second Hague conference now seemed closer to realization.

Other developments helped advance the "Hague II" idea. One was the advocacy from newcomers, not primarily interested in arbitration or a court so much as they were in a broad-ranging internationalism, a "League of Nations," as some U.S. groups called their project. Meanwhile, there had been increasing restiveness about the failure of the many governments of the world to put the "Court"—the arbitration machinery established at The Hague—to work as a system of dispute resolution.

Some counseled patience, arguing that there was no pressing need. But Hale saw a need—the British began a conflict with the Boers, the would-be independent Afrikaans states of South Africa. He called upon Secretary of State Hay to intervene under The Hague convention's provision that recommended calling on the disputants to use the arbitration machinery. Hay ruefully responded that The Hague convention did not apply to a conflict between the British and the areas dominated by descendants of Dutch settlers over which Britain claimed sovereignty.

THE FIRST CASE AND THE COURTHOUSE

A more appropriate and successful initiative came from Baron d'Estournelles, a French Parliament member who had been a delegate to The Hague in 1899, and was impatient about the blank score sheet at the tribunal. D'Estournelles had given his name to the clause in the convention whereby the signers agreed that it was their duty to remind others who were quarreling that the "Permanent Court is open to them," and that such advice "can only be regarded as friendly." Now he was going about—hardly two years later—denouncing the great powers for ignoring the Court. Hale and his colleague in the American Peace Society, Benjamin Trueblood, were less concerned; the latter told European delegates at a Glasgow peace meeting about the first years of the U.S. Supreme Court, when it seemed to languish for lack of business.

D'Estournelles was not to be put off. During a visit to the United States, he sought to give his message to the highest level. The French ambassador prevailed on Hay to set up a White House meeting in February 1902. D'Estournelles challenged Roosevelt, who had been known for his advocacy of the idea that "only through strife, through hard and dangerous endeavor, that we shall ultimately win the goal of true national greatness," to show that he was not a danger to the world. The president asked how he could prove himself a man of peace. The baron replied, by "giving life to the Hague Court." Roosevelt promised to try; he did so, and succeeded.

Lower echelons of the State Department had been having futile negotiations with Mexican diplomats about the "Pious Fund," fruit of a 200-year-old Jesuit investment that had supported priestly work in California when it was only a remote province of Mexico. The fund was banked in Mexico City. After the United States invaded Mexico in 1846 and seized California, the bishops of San Francisco and Monterey were denied access to the fund. The United States took up their claim through diplomacy in the 1870s, and a mixed claims commission ruled that the bishops' rights survived the separation of California from Mexico. Despite that ruling, Mexico had stopped payments again some years later. It was probably only a delaying action by the Mexican authorities, was not a serious dispute, and would not have led to war in any event.

Nevertheless, a full and formal hearing was held at The Hague. Five arbitrators ("judges" of the Court) sat for the case; there was much paperwork and ten days of hearings. The award that directed payment to the bishops was promptly made and promptly obeyed. The event was exciting and provided another impetus in building sentiment for a second Hague meeting. Its effect was exceeded shortly thereafter by an even more stirring event.

Andrew Carnegie, the multi-millionaire industrialist, had already participated in several nineteenth-century peace-and-arbitration initiatives. He had let it be known that he was about to retire, to sell his properties, and enter a broad-ranging career as philanthropist. An immense number of libraries, as well as music halls, trusts for educational purposes, and the like were on his agenda.

It occurred to Frederic Martens, a noted Russian international lawyer who was now a counselor to the czar and a Hague Court arbitrator, that this was a likely source for funding an edifice of which he had dreamed: a suitable home for The Hague tribunal and its library, instead of the makeshift rented quarters that had been provided for its use.

At Martens's suggestion, Ambassador Andrew White, whom he had met at the 1899 founding meeting, approached Carnegie in 1900. Carnegie postponed a decision. He was at that time fully committed to the "anti-imperialist" group supporting Philippine independence. He was trying to buy freedom for the Philippines, making a vain offer to pay Washington the $20 million that had been paid to Spain for the Philippines, Cuba, Puerto Rico, and Guam.

When Carnegie ultimately agreed in January 1903 to make the gift of $1.5 million to build the courthouse that came to be known as the Peace Palace, the news (as with previous movement gains) had a significant "ripple" effect. The sensational publicity it received added to the momentum of prior events to increase the pressure for a second Hague conference.

The Lake Mohonk annual conferences had become semi-institutionalized, with a small staff conducting a year-round effort to reach and enlist business interests. After 1902, chambers of commerce and the like responded favorably. "Peace" was then an unmixed blessing, conducive to expansion of trade without interruption.

The old-line American Peace Society successfully petitioned the Massachusetts legislature in 1903 to endorse regular international peace meetings. A European-based Interparliamentary Union, composed of a handful of legislators from Britain and some continental nations, which had long supported the "American Plan" for a Court, met in the United States for the first time in 1904 and called on President Theodore Roosevelt to support the idea. He agreed.

The 1904 election was coming and Roosevelt wanted badly to be reelected on his own, having entered office on McKinley's assassination as accidental president. He knew of his earned reputation as a navalist and was conscious of the controversial impact of his intervention against Colombia that helped create the Republic of Panama to secure a zone for building a canal. He wanted to win the support of as many as possible in what he correctly perceived to be a growing and increasingly influential peace movement.

"HAGUE II" AND ITS STEPCHILD IN CENTRAL AMERICA

Immediate action by Roosevelt to fulfill this promise was delayed. War had begun in February 1904 between Japan and Russia, although each had signed the 1899 Covenant of The Hague. The conflict was the first of a century showing that the Permanent Court of Arbitration (or, later, each of the World Courts) could have no more importance than the signatory powers would voluntarily assign to it. Correction of that flaw remains a prime peace problem of today and tomorrow.

The war brought Japan stunning victories. It brought prestige for Roosevelt by casting him in a role as peacemaker. Russian defeats and Japanese exhaustion brought the foes (after covert signals from Tokyo to Washington) to the mediation table in the United States. For this serendipitous feat, Roosevelt, the advocate of the strenuous life and strife, won the 1908 Nobel Peace Prize.

Peace cleared the way for the diplomatic activity needed to set up Hague II. Worth noting, before reviewing that, were two demonstrations of the Hague I machinery at work. One was an arbitration proceeding. The issues were more serious than the Pious Fund case: German, British, and Italian warships in the Caribbean were menacing the coast of Venezuela. That South American state was swamped in debts incurred by its military ruler. The European fleet was a collection agency, moving to take over the local ports and seize customs revenues. The U.S. Navy had responded with warning maneuvers. Rising tension was quelled when debtor and creditors agreed, with President Roosevelt's help, to arbitration at The Hague.

That was the good news. The bad news was withheld until after the 1904 election: Roosevelt announced a "corollary" to the Monroe Doctrine, to keep European fleets away in the future: the U.S. Navy would see to it that Latinos were more responsible debtors; the U.S. Marines would land if they were not. This was to happen some dozen times in the next generation—even after an agreement was reached at Hague II that cured the problem of having European navies serve as debt collectors.

The other case was a Commission of Inquiry, a by-product of the Russo-Japanese War. The Hague conferees had anticipated that, sometimes, potential adversaries might be unaware of the whole truth about an episode. They might benefit from impartial assistance in finding out just what had happened. That sort of fact-finding could lead to a settlement without the embarrassment of a third-party judgment against one side or another. The inquiry commission clause was successfully invoked when a trigger-happy Russian admiral, on his way from the Baltic to Japan, ordered a big gun broadside on a suspected foe. The target proved to be a covey of fishing craft, off the Dogger Bank of Britain. When the facts were ascertained by the Hague-initiated Commission of Inquiry, the "case" was quickly resolved; meanwhile, the admiral and flotilla reached the Pacific, to be sunk in their first encounter with the Japanese.

One striking feature of the events since 1899 was the response in educational circles. In 1905, soon after the Massachusetts Legislature's unanimous call for a second Hague meeting, the state's school superintendent, James van Sickle, issued an order for all schools in the state to celebrate May 18, the anniversary of the first Hague meeting. Within a few months, Ohio's school chief followed suit, and a campaign was begun to spread the idea to other states. Then, the U.S. Commissioner of Education began preparing and distributing to school superintendents across the nation special material to be used when such observance was conducted in the schools.

One of the proponents and a leading force in implementing such educational activity was Lucia Ames Mead, who wrote a book published in 1906 "to aid the teachers to prepare for the commemoration of this epoch-making event [Hague I] and to remind them of the principles involved in patriotism *and* internationalism . . ." (emphasis added). No reader could miss Mead's point that her emphasis was on the linkage. With a wealth of literary allusion, aphorism, and lesson plans, she proposed that:

> The teacher of history who knows where to place the emphasis . . . will not hesitate to say with General Grant that "the Mexican War [of 1846] was an iniquitous war," and teach that the English statesmen who "rejoiced that the colonies had resisted" were loyal in a fashion higher than loyalty to king or party, and that while emphasizing our country's noble inheritance . . . and dwelling especially

upon the glorious principles and achievements of the founders of the Republic, the patriotic teacher will indicate the points wherein we have failed and fallen short of our ideals, as well as those in which we have excelled.

This distinctive teacher's manual was called *Patriotism and the New Internationalism*. It was published by an affiliate of wealthy textbook publisher Edward Ginn, created for the purpose of distributing peace education material.

There had been a touch of romance in the entry of Lucia Ames into the arbitration movement. Lucia Ames had been president of the Massachusetts Women's Suffrage Society and active in other reform causes, where she met Edwin Mead, Hale's lieutenant and successor as editor of the progressive *New England Magazine*. Mead took her, as a friend, to one of the early Lake Mohonk meetings. The seemingly practical path to peace via the rule of law caught her imagination; during their joint attendance there arose a relationship that transformed their lives—and led to their marriage.

As Edwin Mead became a pamphleteer on peace for Ginn & Company, she worked on every front, in lectures, at conventions, and writing incessant letters to the editor. She helped create the conditions that made possible a major event of the decade, the 1907 peace demonstration, held over a three-day period at New York's Carnegie Hall in April 1907. This was planned as prelude to the now-imminent Hague II conference.

Modern activists may ponder the attendance recorded in its published proceedings:

> [T]here were enrolled among its membership and supporters two men who had been candidates for the presidency of the United States, eight Cabinet officers, ten United States senators, nineteen members of the House of Representatives, four justices of the Supreme Court, twelve state chief justices, nine state governors, sixty New York editors, thirty labor leaders, ten mayors, eighteen college and university presidents, twenty state superintendents of public instruction and forty bishops.

Andrew Carnegie himself served as president, and while Ms. Mead spoke on the movement's history, star billing went to U.S. Secretary of State Elihu Root. His presence as keynote speaker at such a mass meeting was a symptom, similar to the attendance roll presented above, of the snowballing growth of the U.S. movement to substitute the path of the law for the warpath when disagreeing nations were at an impasse.

Unlike Lucia Ames Mead or Hale, who came to the movement as passionate multisided reformers, Elihu Root had not been a man for causes. Born of a modest family in upstate New York, he had been single-mindedly successful in his chosen career as an attorney, just as Carnegie had as a businessman. Root was founding partner of one of the great Wall Street law firms that produced wealth for its members by its skilled services to men of wealth and the corporations that they controlled. A keen and sagacious adviser, a prudent analyst of problems his clients faced, a hard worker and skilled negotiator, he had become by the end of the nineteenth century a leader of the bar. His "call" to become a constructive worker for peace had come to him after he entered government service, and because he took very seriously and in earnest the role of U.S. Secretary of State as chief peace advocate of the administration.

Carnegie, on the other hand, even while adding to his fortune by the sale of armor plate to the new U.S. fleet, had become a peace activist in general, and an arbitration advocate in particular. Despite some contemporary cynicism, his peace activity was spontaneous and sincere; he put his own body and soul into the movement. As his wealth and power made him a celebrity with easy access to people of prestige and influence, he willingly aided various groups in making contacts. He was as ardent an opponent of the Philippine policy of McKinley and Roosevelt as the organizers of the Anti-Imperialist League and financed much of the public advocacy that they had conducted.

Root did not agree with any of that. His introduction to government service was as secretary of the War Department, a post for which he was chosen because of skills shown as civilian problem solver. He reorganized the U.S. Army and eliminated organizational flaws exposed in the island campaigns. He had no qualms about the Philippines policy.

When recalled to service as secretary of the State Department, he strove to improve relations with and among the nations of the Americas. He was to learn from their diplomats about the utility of international dispute resolution by impartial third parties. The lesson of the settlement between Chile and Argentina and the meaning of the construction of the monument of the Christ of the Andes were much appreciated by the new secretary of state.

Root's acceptance of Carnegie's invitation to attend and speak at the 1907 National Peace and Arbitration Congress was natural, and as to differences over Philippines policy, bygones were bygones. The split in the business and establishment world that the anti-imperialist movement had produced was now healed. Both factions saw world peace as a desirable objective in the then early stages of the United States' development as a world trader. Carnegie warmly introduced Root to the audience as the secretary of state who had traveled farthest "carrying the olive branch of peace"; it was the beginning of a relationship that would grow ever closer until Carnegie's death in 1919.

While telling his audience, "The thoughts of all men who hope for the peace of the world are now turned toward the second peace conference so soon to meet at The Hague," Root uttered a prescient prediction: "Let me add a few words of warning concerning your anticipations of what the conference is to do. Do not expect much."

Though not optimistic, Root set his sights high. As an able and experienced attorney, his professional judgment agreed with the conclusion Hale had come to by intuitive preference: that for a tribunal to be useful in replacing force in settling quarrels among the nations, a permanent court of independent judges was far superior to "ad hoc" (occasional, chosen for the moment) boards of arbitration.

He promised his audience that he would seek at The Hague the "establishment of a court of permanent judges who will have no other occupation or interest but the exercise of the judicial faculty." In keeping this promise, he echoed—in his formal instructions to the U.S. delegates what Hale had told the Mohonkers repeatedly since 1900—he wanted a "tribunal which would pass upon questions between nations with the same impartial and impersonal judgment that the Supreme Court of the United States gives."

What was actually achieved at Hague II was less. Those who then and since belittled its work have overlooked the second "giant step" taken there, under U.S. initiative and leadership: drafting a plan of organization on which the first World Court was modeled in the 1920s. This was not merely agreement in principle on precisely the institution that Root had told the U.S. delegates to aim for; it was sweetened by the expression of a wish by the majority of the delegates that submission of disputes to the Court be "obligatory."

Unhappily, the forty-six nations present (Root had seen to it that all of Latin America had been invited) could not come to agreement on a method of selecting judges that would keep the number on the bench manageable, so that they could work together judicially. The entire working plan for an operational court compatible with the U.S. plan was perfected—and then shelved. A few years—and millions of lives—afterward, it was dusted off, refurbished, and put to work.

The conference, thus, did not achieve Root's major aim—but he had not seriously expected that it would. Those attending amended and expanded provisions of the first Convention for Pacific Settlement of 1899. Although doing nothing, again, on disarmament, they made further paper provisions to "humanize" warfare. The guidelines for the functioning of the Commissions of Inquiry were amplified. Ground rules for the conduct of Permanent Court of Arbitration's proceedings were supplemented.

Of special interest to the Americas was the article severely limiting the use of force or threats of force in the collection of debts owed by nations; in effect this did away with the international law sanction that had previously permitted such events as the blockade of Venezuela by European warships. This dispensed with the excuse that had been given for the Roosevelt "corollary" to the Monroe Doctrine, but the interventions conducted under it continued. The conferees formally called for a third Hague conference, seven or eight years later. War prevented that.

A moving interlude occurred on July 30, 1907: time was taken out to lay the cornerstone of what was to be the "world's courthouse," the building for which funds were given by Andrew Carnegie, that came to be known as the Peace Palace. Carved on the side of the great granite block were the words:

PACI
JUSTITIA FIRMANDAE
HANC AEDEM
ANDREADE CARNEGIE
MUNIFICENTA
DEDICAVIT

As the ceremony began, two flags were flying, the American and the Dutch. In words that were echoed two wars and forty years later, the president of the second conference, Russian Ambassador Count Nelidow, described the tower that had been included in the plans of the building-in-progress as a "lighthouse, showing to the nations the way of right and justice, the immutable pillars of peace."

TRIAL AND ERROR IN CENTRAL AMERICA

James Brown Scott was a Columbia Law School professor who had become U.S. State Department solicitor in 1906 and editor of the newly founded *American Journal of International Law* in 1907. He became a close and trusted aide of Elihu Root for many years. He saluted the acceptance in principle of the idea of the Court by the nations at Hague II:

> It is of little moment whether the court is constituted now or later, for the recognition of the idea makes the ultimate realization a certainty. The American delegation forced the idea on the Conference, and, notwithstanding bitter opposition, the idea stands.

An unexpected mini-vindication of the confident forecast emerged just two months after the closing of the sessions at Holland. It came from the Central American Republics at Washington, D.C. (While the phrase "Central America" sometimes includes other nearby states, it then included only Costa Rica, El Salvador, Guatemala, Honduras, and Nicaragua.) Intermittent internecine combat had been chronic among these small states, ever since the breakup of their early federal union that followed independence from Spain seventy years before. Responding to a new flare-up of 1906, Secretary of State Root and Mexican President Díaz called for a conference with the five at Washington that began November 14, 1907.

Knowing their history as a united federal nation for a brief time, Root asked a rhetorical question with a relevant answering comment:

> Why should you not live in peace and harmony? You are one people in fact; . . . It can be nothing but the ambition of individuals who care more for their selfish purposes that for the good of their country, that can prevent the people of the Central American states from living together in peace and amity.

The delegates responded to Root's leadership and the "Hague spirit," as the sentiment of the period has been called. They crafted an agreement to solve future differences by, as described by their chair, Luis Anderson of Costa Rica, a body that would be "no mere commission of arbitration, but a genuine judicial tribunal . . . the practical realization of the ingenious plans formulated and recommended by the [United States] delegates at the Second Conference at The Hague."

To spare the impoverished little nations the expense, Andrew Carnegie contributed funds to build a courthouse. And so was launched what was not merely the *first* international court of continuous and compulsory jurisdiction; it has been so far the only one available for suit without consent.

Root's aide William I. Buchanan, who helped the group with their negotiations, warned in his report that it couldn't solve Central America's "most basic problem . . . how to avoid internal outbreaks" that would attract outside intervention. That seemed prescient, yet in its first big case (revolution in Honduras in December 1908, and alleged intervention by Guatemala and El Salvador) the court's orders to stop fighting, pending judgment, were indeed obeyed.

Interference from the outside brought about the court's end. The treaty creating the court limited its life to ten years: it was to expire in 1917 unless unanimously renewed. Seven years of quiet unspectacular success had followed the court's first successful peacekeeping venture. The fateful difficulty came when the United States (having intervened in Nicaragua with 2,000 marines to install a friendly government in 1913) "negotiated" a canal rights treaty. The purpose was to forestall possible competition with the Panama route that had just been completed. Most of the $3 million paid to Nicaragua went to repay earlier loans made by Wall Street bankers.

Costa Rica challenged the making of the treaty by Nicaragua's Chamorro regime as a violation of Nicaragua's obligations to its neighbor. The charge was based on a pact about the two country's common border, the San Juan River. In September 1916, the court sustained the complaint against Nicaragua, but declined to nullify the treaty outright since the United States, the other party, was not subject to the court's authority. Nicaragua ignored the ruling.

A similar scenario was enacted between Nicaragua and El Salvador, with a similar result in March 1917: the court sustained a complaint that Chamorro's concession of a naval base to the United States in the bordering Gulf of Fonseca violated Salvador's coastal rights.

U.S. encouragement to Nicaragua to ignore the court ruling and to refuse to extend the court's existence proved fatal. Elihu Root, now a senator from New York, but in a minority party, protested without avail at the strangling of the court that the United States under his leadership had brought into being.

Summarizing a single episode, the brief life (1907–1917) of the Central American Court of Justice, took us a bit out of chronological order. But it seemed best to tell it as a unit: That court's career did not intersect significantly with the progression toward a multicontinental World Court. Nor did the fate of the Central American court seem to matter much to its contemporaries. Yet its history and the events leading to its demise have relevance to us today.

ADVANCES, DISTRACTIONS, AND (TEMPORARY?) DEFEAT

Interest in the peace movement continued to swell up to and beyond Hague II in 1907 and continued until 1914, when it fell victim to the Guns of August. But in 1908, more people began to accept first, the idea that, peace could be secured if a process of impartial judgment between nations could be established, and, second, that this process could best be accomplished by establishing a single, continuously sitting world court, rather than by sitting arbitrators, chosen from a pool of qualified individuals, on a sporadic basis.

Both of the major party candidates for the presidency in 1908 concurred: the winner, Roosevelt's selected successor, William Howard Taft, who had been governor general of the Philippines during the imperialist controversy; and the loser—for the third time—the still popular, William Jennings Bryan. Outgoing President Theodore Roosevelt, still distrusting and distrusted by the peace people, endorsed the concept in his speech accepting the 1908 Nobel Peace Prize, awarded for mediating the settlement between Japan and Russia.

The fine Rule of Law language used by those three—Roosevelt, Taft, and Bryan—conflicted sharply with the role played by each in disrupting Central American harmony and the undermining of the Central American court. The treaty with Chamorro for an alternate canal route disregarded treaty rights of Costa Rica and El Salvador; it was made with Nicaragua under a protectorate produced by the "Roosevelt corollary," negotiated by Taft's administration and implemented by Bryan as Woodrow Wilson's secretary of State. (Bryan was no longer at State when the court was torpedoed.)

The post-1907 (after Hague II) consensus of politicians was a response to public enthusiasm for arbitration and a court. Support had grown to an extent that its sponsors of hardly a decade earlier could hardly believe. The organized peace movement in the United States consisted in the mid-1890s of a small handful of impoverished societies with little claim to power or influence, as stated in *The Eagle and the Dove*, a 1976 book by John Whiteclay Chambers II. They generated little enthusiasm. In 1900, even the oldest and largest group, the American Peace Society, remained a small, Boston-based organization with an annual budget of less than $6,000. Now they had become so influential that they were imagining that the world was close to victory over war.

The extraordinary expansion of the support base for the idea of "The Supplanting of the System of War by the System of Law" (the subtitle of Lucia

Ames Mead's 1912 book, *Swords and Ploughshares*) was not primarily in the empowerment by megagrowth of the formerly impoverished societies. Their membership and branches had grown significantly, but not overwhelmingly. But from being based mainly on the East Coast, they now reached to the Midwest, to Texas, Utah, and California. Even more significant and impressive was the growth of new societies—one count tells of forty-five in all having begun in the 1901–1914 interval.

The newer peace-and-arbitration groups reflected a major change in composition. The enlistment of business leaders begun with a "call" from Mohonk in 1902, expanded enormously after the Great New York Carnegie Hall Meeting of 1907 and the Hague conference thereafter. "Business leaders," Charles DeBenedetti wrote, "who were directing the country's corporate consolidation, turned to the peace reform out of an interest in the extension of order at home and abroad." That their motives were less idealistic than Andrew Carnegie's did not lessen the value of their interest and support.

Lawyers and judges had shown an early interest in application of the Rule of Law to international affairs. In 1896 the New York Bar Association developed the first modern plan for a court of nations. Now, as international trade and commercial arbitration expanded, a community of international lawyers began to develop. Two mutually complementary organizations were formed. The first, the American Society of International Law, was created to promote the study and teaching of international law (from an idea born in a caucus at a 1906 Mohonk meeting). That group's still widely respected journal began publication in 1907. The second, formed in 1910, was the perhaps clumsily—but lucidly—named American Society for the Judicial Settlement of International Disputes. The two groups agreed on an objective. There was overlap in their membership: the latter, less confined to a scholarly orientation, was willing to propagandize and lobby actively for the cause.

Educators, too, were active. At the college level, work was carried on through an organization of internationally minded Cosmopolitan Clubs. At the secondary- and grade-school levels, organization and dissemination of the ideas was conducted through the American School Peace League, founded in 1908. Its work had the blessing of the U.S. commissioner of education and it was for all practical purposes an affiliate of the National Education Association (NEA), the major teachers' membership association. The league's support of the arbitration court cause was a feature of the NEA's annual meetings until 1915.

Religious leaders had always been prominent in the membership and some had been and were still active in the direction of the older, pre-Hague organizations. Now there was activity on several fronts to develop their own societies. The most notable was the formation in 1911 by the Federal Council of Churches of Christ in America of a separate Commission on Peace and Arbitration.

Activity of the various groups was seen, for example, in the official school celebrations of the anniversary of the opening of Hague I in activity programs.

Another was a frank willingness, as urged by Lucia Ames Mead, to face the facts of the country's history and imperfections in past performance. Former Secretary of State John Foster spoke in this vein at a 1910 meeting of the Judicial Settlement Society, of which President Taft was honorary chair. Professor James Brown Scott, long Elihu Root's right-hand man, introduced Foster— grandfather of John Foster Dulles, and father-in-law of Robert Lansing, secretary of state under Wilson—with the observation that "it is necessary that we set our own house in order, that we examine our own conduct in the past."

Foster's thesis was that every nineteenth-century foreign war the United States had been involved in "could have been submitted to arbitration and decided without recourse to war." He argued that an international commission of inquiry should have looked into the blowing up of the battleship *Maine* in Havana Harbor, that diplomacy, or arbitration, would have succeeded, that "had not the president [McKinley] yielded to the war clamor and the demands of Congress, the [Spanish] war might have been averted."

Andrew Carnegie chose the conclusion of this speech as the moment to announce publicly the $10 million grant that began the Carnegie Endowment for International Peace (CEIP). In his brief talk, Carnegie argued for resisting those who "arouse the passions of the people" to get votes for war expenditures, adding:

> Our country, right or wrong, is still a potent cry . . . and well do demagogues understand this. That is the kind of patriotism which [British writer Samuel] Johnson said was the refuge of scoundrels and so it is today the refuge of scurvy politicians.

He had been wise when, resisting some of the many voices seeking handouts, Carnegie said, "There is nothing that robs a righteous cause of its strength more than a millionaire's money." Unfortunately, the instant aphorism was proven true in the CEIP's early years. The choice of trustees and administrative personnel, particularly Nicholas Murray Butler, president of Columbia University, served to sap the activism of the movement, branches of which came to depend financially on its grants. Michael A. Lutzker wrote in his account of the CEIP's beginnings that Carnegie himself "was disappointed with the work of the endowment in its early years."

Scanning the list of trustees who had been selected to administer the grant, O. G. Villard of the New York *Post* complained, "Not a single radical opponent of war is on the list, but many who . . . express an intellectual interest in peace, but are hot for battleships too." And it was not long before the London *Times,* on January 11, 1911, analyzed CEIP's activity as avoidance of "promiscuous preaching against war and armaments."

Carnegie himself seemed oblivious to these developments that proved his aphorism to have been an accurate forecast. But in 1913, at the formal opening of the Peace Palace that his funds had built, he made a prediction that has not yet been justified, and which many, within a year, were to think back upon as a manifestation of senility:

> Looking back a hundred years . . . the future historian is to pronounce the opening of a World Court . . . the greatest one step forward ever taken by man, in his long and checkered march upward from barbarism. Nothing he has yet accomplished equals the substitution for war, of judicial decisions founded upon International Law.

One year later came the catastrophic conflict that had been brewing since well before the turn of the century. Fear of its coming had accentuated the efforts to implement the U.S. plan for worldwide agreement for judicial settlement of all disputes among nations. Not enough had been done.

3

Not a *Whole* World's Court

Preparing a feature article for their November 1914 issue, the editors of the *Ladies' Home Journal* sought from the "two most prominent advocates of universal peace" the answer to the question, "Is the Peace Movement a failure?" One answered on his letterhead as secretary of state. "No," wrote William Jennings Bryan. He added:

> The European war may better be interpreted as the final object lesson needed to convince mankind of the folly of war. This war will teach a truth that will not be soon forgotten, namely that "preparedness" directly encourages the very carnage which it is supposed to prevent.

The other answer, datelined at Hull House, Chicago, was signed by Jane Addams and read in part:

> [T]his great war cannot stamp International Arbitration as a failure.... When the thirteen original states united and each agreed . . . to submit all differences to a Supreme Court . . . [the founders] had every right to look forward to centuries of unbroken peace, although in less than seventy-five years these States were engaged in a prolonged civil war. Yet no one would call our Federal Government a failure nor the establishment of the Supreme Court a mistake.

THE COURT IDEA LIVES AS EUROPE'S WAR BECOMES OURS

The two overlapping, early twentieth-century attempts to move the world toward "universal peace" reached their zenith in 1914. One was the drive to promote arbitration as the rational and moral alternative to the use of force when settling international differences. The other was the effort to create an international court, a permanent body of independent, qualified jurists, to offer a mode of impartial judgments on international disputes that would be more effective than arbitration in peacekeeping.

Neither Addams nor Bryan was a leader in, or even prominently active among, any of the diverse social, business, educational, lawyer, or clergy groups that were collectively called the "peace movement." They *were* "prominent," but not primarily as advocates of universal peace. Bryan had become a celebrity as three-time candidate for the presidency, during which he won more popularity as a loser than had many winning candidates. Addams had won worldwide fame as a social worker, a pioneer in Chicago's Hull House, a "settlement house" effort to ameliorate the suffering of the poor and the exploited victims of predatory, unregulated business.

Although not prominent as such, each actively supported the idea of replacing war with law as the ultimate resort in conflict among nations. They had in common with some Americans of that period an interest in the radical ideas of Count Leo Tolstoy. This had brought each to take a pilgrimage to his Russian estate to meet with him. That chance coincidence could hardly have been the reason they were chosen by the editors of the *Ladies' Home Journal* to comment on the onset of the European war, rather than Carnegie or Root, or any of the functioning leaders of the peace organizations.

Addams had, as her statement to the *Journal* showed, accepted the ideals and principles of the arbitration movement. Bryan illustrated the movement's nonpartisan character when he endorsed arbitration treaties proposed by Taft, who had defeated him for the presidency in 1908.

Bryan's Plan Pushed Aside by War

Bryan had seen Taft's proposed arbitration treaties go down in a third round of Senate intransigence, in spite of overwhelming public support. As Wilson's secretary of state, he devised a new approach. The modest plan, inspired a bit by The Hague "Commission of Inquiry" provisions, had won Senate approval because it did not commit the nation to agreeing to outside judgment. The parties to the Bryan treaties agreed to set up fact-finding commissions, ready to act when incidents threatened to provoke hostilities; while inquiry into a controversial incident was pursued, a cooling-off period of one year was mandated.

But the war came. The Hague system was purely voluntary, hardly fifteen years old, with a technique new to a war-accustomed world. It was not able to pass a test involving many nations and many long-smoldering issues that began with the murder of an Austrian prince in Serbian territory, and Serbia's offer to arbitrate was spurned.

Bryan's version had hardly circulated; the ink was still wet on the signatures in August 1914. The U.S. ambassador to Belgium, Brand Whitlock wryly recalled a message from the State Department urging him to follow up with the Belgians to sign the Bryan treaty when the Germans had already crossed the border. British Ambassador Sir Cecil Spring-Rice wrote that a student of the events could not "speak lightly of Bryan's idea . . . even one week's delay would have saved the peace of the world."

Bryan's statement to the *Journal* about the "preparedness" movement could serve not only as analysis of the causes of the war in Europe, but also as a warning or forecast of U.S. involvement. He saw in Wilson a pro-allied tendency that he tried to curb, believing neutrality to be the United States' best safeguard. Wilson's tilt worsened when a U-boat's torpedo slammed into the *Lusitania*. Bryan protested without avail his chief's hard line that followed the sinking of the *Lusitania;* when Wilson declined to propose an impartial inquiry Bryan resigned in protest. In response to a fellow cabinet member who warned that he'd be committing political suicide by such an action, Bryan, the Tolstoian, agreed:

> I think this will destroy me; but whether it does or not, I must do my duty according to my conscience and if I am destroyed, it is, after all, merely the sacrifice that one must make to serve his God and his country.

Bryan was never to hold public office again. But he was not, in a larger sense, "destroyed." His popularity and reputation were to flourish later when he took a major part in opposition to entering the war. At a meeting in Carnegie Hall, Meyer London, a Socialist member of the House of Representatives, compared Bryan to Tolstoy. But when war was declared on Germany, Bryan felt it his duty to be silent: as a member of a democracy, he yielded to the majority that had spoken.

Addams Looks at the Big Picture

Addams, on the other hand, never gave in. Her vision of peace and her feeling for the possibility of achieving it came from the years she had spent in a sustained, self-sacrificing effort to create a sense of community among people of diverse ethnic origins. She accepted and agreed with the goal of the arbitration advocates, but reserved her activism for such social justice causes as remedial labor laws, that would aid the clients of the Hull House community, and especially feminism, which at that time focused on women's suffrage.

She differed with many of the leaders of the old-line organizations, who believed, as such historians as Charles Chatfield and Charles DeBenedetti had shown, that their peace movement was not simply an antiwar movement but a prolaw movement. Being not merely for peace but decidedly against war, Addams responded actively to the crisis in U.S. life precipitated by onset of war in Europe in 1914. She led an emergency social workers' revolt against the war, which was soon expanded into a women's revolt.

Her efforts led to formation of two new organizations—Union Against Militarism and a Woman's Peace Party, which later became the Women's

International League for Peace and Freedom—that filled a gap created by the dismaying drift of the new groups that had appeared and the old groups that had grown so much from 1899 to 1914. In addition to these, Addams presided over meetings in Chicago of an Emergency Federation of Peace Forces, and at The Hague in April 1915 at an International Congress of Women. The groups' common effort was to secure an organization of neutral countries that would bring about effective mediation between the warring nations. For the postwar world, they sought, above all, "an international court for the settlement of all disputes between nations."

Other Groups Push Own Ideas

The Carnegie-related and other peace groups ultimately espoused the view that for the sake of ultimate peace it was necessary that the United States cast aside its neutrality and join the British and French forces, but they and the so-called preparedness people continued to support the idea of an international court.

The non-antiwar peace organizations further divided into two factions. One was the fast-growing League to Enforce Peace, which, as its title reflected, stressed advocacy of economic and ultimately military sanctions—primarily to force recalcitrant nations to a world court. This contributed greatly to President Wilson's developing idea of bringing about a League of Nations. The other faction, those who objected to the "force" element in the League to enforce peace, united to work for a new World's Court League.

President Wilson was a reluctant and belated supporter of the Court idea. He agreed, only late in the Versailles negotiations, that it be created as an affiliate of the League of Nations. Peace historian David Patterson has written "that the [Court] was established in the face of Wilson's resistance suggests the pervasive influence of the movement for a world court before 1914 and its survival during the war years." That movement was bipartisan in a rare sense: both prowar preparedness activists and antiwar peace advocates supported the idea of a court to prevent future wars.

The Covenant of the League of Nations, drawn up by the Versailles conferees, reflected the extent to which U.S. impetus for world organization was given credit for the formation of the association of nations. It contained an express provision that initial meetings of assembly and council "be summoned by the President of the United States of America." The treaty and covenant having been rejected by the U.S. Senate, the United States never joined the League. A by-product of that rejection was that the United States was not automatically eligible to be affiliated with the Court that the Covenant of the League pledged to create.

The League's covenant directed its council to create what was named the Permanent Court of International Justice. It was felt that the structure and details of organizing a court of the nations, unprecedented in global history, presented challenges too complex to be handled by peacemakers who were facing a host of other problems. At their first meeting, the council agreed that the League should invite a commission of distinguished jurists to draw up the plans for the peace court.

AFTER THE WAR:
THE COURT WE WANTED

Woodrow Wilson has been criticized as having been headstrong and partisan—so much so that many believe he shares blame with the Senate for the Versailles Treaty's defeat. But when he was asked to supply an outstandingly qualified attorney from the United States for the League's commission to draw the detailed Court plan, he promptly proposed Elihu Root, who by now was seventy-five years old. Root, who for fifteen years had contributed so much to the victory of the Court idea, accepted with pleasure. He relished the formal invitation's declaration that the Court could "contribute more than any other single institution to maintain the peace of the world and the supremacy of right among the nations."

Jurists came from twelve nations. Typically for that time, nine were from European states, two from South America, and one from the United States. When they met at The Hague in June 1920, Root took the leadership. In his opening remarks he urged that they get a head start by using as a basis for their work the plan developed under his instructions and agreed to in principle at Hague II in 1907. As a result of his leadership, a complete plan for a court was ready for the League of Nations Council's action in six weeks.

The main problem again was size: how to have a manageable number (not more than twelve or fifteen) when the judges are to be selected from forty-six (as it was then—more than 180 now) nation states. Moreover, the large powers were unwilling to be subject to a court dominated by small states, and vice versa. To introduce the solution he had devised, Root reminded the jurists of the impasse of 1907, adding: "It seems to me that both views are, in a broad sense, right."

How could the nations cope with this? Root, a former secretary of state and U.S. senator, answered: "Allow me to refer to an example which naturally arises in the mind of an American." He recalled the analogous problem that had arisen in 1787, when there were delegates from thirteen independent and sovereign states: the tiny ones wanted equal power and the larger sought power at the center, proportional to population. Root told them of the compromise that had resulted in the creation of the two-chamber U.S. Congress, with equal representation in the Senate and proportional representation in the House. While the analogy was not exact, the idea was fruitful, made possible by the structure of the League of Nations, with Great Powers dominant in the Council, and all equally represented in the assembly. And so the compromise emerged that broke the deadlock: the Court's judges were to be subject to a vote—separately but concurrently—in each house, and had to muster a majority in each.

In any electoral process, the method of nomination is at least as important as the final vote. Root objected to nomination made by government heads: to act and be respected for acting judicially, the Court should be depoliticized, he said. Others agreed. The scheme chosen to insulate the procedure was to delegate nominating authority to the national groups of eminent jurists previously designated to serve as Hague Tribunal arbitrators. It was stipulated not only that the candidates be required to have stated judicial qualifications, but also that they represented "the main forms of civilization and the principal legal systems of the world."

Some debatable problems remained but none were insurmountable. The initial agreement provided that there be eleven judges and four deputies, all with nine-year terms of office. The Court was to elect its own president, or chief justice; in case of a tie vote, the president would be given a "casting" vote that would serve as a tiebreaker. A variety of provisions were included to treat Court members as international civil servants, rather than as national representatives. Before sitting, each was to make a "solemn declaration" in open court to exercise his powers impartially and conscientiously. This was backed up by several ways to keep outside influence at bay. The judges were exempt from all taxes at home or in the Netherlands; precluded from holding any other office or engaging in any professional occupation; and forbidden to act as counsel or serve in any case in which the judge had previously played a role. All were give diplomatic immunity; none could be removed from office unless by unanimous vote of the rest of the Court.

Debate—but no fundamental disagreement—ensued when the jurists were reminded of the unanimous resolution of the 1907 Hague II conference, "That they accept the principle of obligatory jurisdiction." As International Law then stood, no state could be required, without its consent, to submit a dispute to either mediation or arbitration. Now the most important issue to face the jurists was whether this should be altered for the sake of the Court's peacekeeping mission.

Root argued "strenuously and successfully," as his biographer Philip Jessup put it, for elimination of that fragment of old-fashioned sovereignty, the right to withhold consent to be sued; it was obsolete in the epoch of total war. He was backed by Dutch Judge Bernard C. J. Loder, one of several commission members who later became judges of the Court. If the League Covenant were not construed, as Elihu Root had argued, "to open the doors of the court to any party without previous consent between it and the defendant party, it would not take the world further on the road to peace than had the purely voluntary arbitration tribunal first created at The Hague in 1899." The British and French jurists agreed, and so a plan for obligatory (sometimes called "compulsory") jurisdiction was included in the package sent to the League Council for final approval, needed before the Court statute was to become a multination treaty by the necessary ratifications.

At this point, before summarizing the balance of the Court's structural outline as contained in its statute, we must look forward a few months. The right of a victim state to get a ruling that another member state was in the wrong, even when the adversary refused to litigate, is a crucial and perhaps indispensable element of judicial peacekeeping and peacemaking. This was removed by the League Council.

The jurists' commission was but the League's agent, and Britain and France were dominant in the Council, the body (predecessor to the present-day UN Security Council) that had a veto power over the final draft. Despite the agreement among expert legal scholars, neither the French nor the British foreign offices were willing to give up the freedom to use force to settle a dispute.

The League's other body, the Assembly, where the smaller states outnumbered the greater and all were equal, did not acquiesce quietly to the council's decision. They recognized and wanted the protection of an automatically available resort to the Rule of Law. Debate was acrimonious and seemingly futile, but not without result. A limited step was taken when a Brazilian delegate put forward a compromise proposal. His idea was that states that wanted the compulsory plan could have it in greatly limited form—confined to litigation with states that were willing to join them in a voluntary commitment to submit themselves to hearings in future cases. Thus, ten or twenty— it could start with two; any number could play—of the League's members, forty-six at the time, could agree to accept obligatory jurisdiction among themselves. Those who so chose would, in effect, be creating a little club of real law-and-order observers who feared not to be sued and obtained the unconditional privileges of suing others in the "club."

The plan was adopted without difficulty; it soon became known unofficially as the "optional" plan of jurisdiction, since each nation had the option of subscribing to it. Nonmembers of this insiders' club would appear before the Court only by mutual agreement, which was like the traditional mode of arbitration that the Court plan was supposed to be improving on.

Selection of judges, voluntary versus involuntary jurisdiction, and all other details that had been left to the Council's commission of jurists were settled within six weeks. Among the subjects covered with ease were: official language, which was to be both French and English; the locale, which was The Hague; provision for interim protection (equivalent to a "temporary injunction" in U.S. courts); and intervention, that is, participation by an interested third state in a case in which two others contended. There was an additional feature to deal with: *advisory jurisdiction.*

While everything else was open, the treaty makers' covenant mandated that the Court should have an unusual power: to "give an advisory opinion upon any dispute or question referred to it by the Council or Assembly." This proviso had unforeseen potential—it later came to account for a substantial part of the body of the Court's work, and is still producing some historic rulings. To a very limited extent, it makes up for the absence of obligatory jurisdiction. From an Anglo-American point of view, it was indeed something new. With a few exceptions in a handful of states (and Canada), the United States has been accustomed to the idea that the adversary process develops law the best, and that truth (and/or justice) can be most clearly discerned by the process of evaluating conflicting presentations. For a court to give "advice" in the abstract was not favored.

The treaty-making group that was working on Woodrow Wilson's proposed covenant was not bound by Anglo-American notions. Members were drafting for the community of states a compact that had no precedent. Suppose there should be a clash of ideas as to the meaning of a sentence of the new covenant. How would it be settled? A French delegate came up with the idea of having the very Court that was in the planning stage save time and trouble later by deciding the issue. Now there would be no wait for an issue to be framed in a lawsuit or the consent of the state nominally sued to get the ruling. Thus the Court, itself a novelty, was given the relatively novel authority to "advise" international agencies.

Those trained in and familiar with the adversary system, as were Root and his British colleague Lord Phillimore, sought to set safeguards so that the power to render advisory opinions would have procedural protection for states with a special interest in the subject matter of the question under review. A scheme was agreed upon by the planning commission, but rejected by the League Assembly. The matter was left to the Court's own Rules of Procedure, not yet drafted. These, when developed by the judges themselves, were quite adequate: there was to be no secret advice; any state was entitled to be heard if it believed it had an interest in the outcome.

The question of housing was deferred. The Carnegie Foundation, "landlord" of the Peace Palace built with Andrew Carnegie's grant and host to the Hague arbitration tribunal, was expected to help. In fact, the Great War of 1914-1918 broke out so soon after the Peace Palace had been dedicated and opened for use that arbitration had not begun there. There was as yet only a clerical staff and a rudimentary law library. In August 1914, as the clash of arms that would change the map of Europe began, some wit hung a sign on the iron gates: TO LET.

The conferences and hearing of cases began after the war, in August and September of 1920. The first arose from damage to or destruction of church property in Portugal, resulting from the Portuguese revolution of 1910. The claimants were from Britain, France, and Spain, and their respective countries had joined in initiating the cases for arbitration. The agreement submitting the cases for hearing (called a "compromis": defining the question to be decided) was signed in July 1913, but the hearing had been deferred. The arbitration board consisted of Swiss and Dutch nationals and was chaired by Elihu Root. At the closing session of September 4, 1920, Root declared:

> It remains for me to state that for the first time since the completion of the Peace Palace, an international judgment has been delivered within these walls. Our judgment is, therefore, an inauguration; it is an important day in the history of this building and we hope that this award will be followed by many another in the interest of peace, and of accord among the nations.

REJECTING WHAT WE WANTED:
A WISHBONE INSTEAD

The bruising, bitter battle over the ratification of the 1919 Versailles Treaty and the 1920 presidential election were behind the United States. A minority of the Senate had succeeded in keeping the United States out of the League of Nations. But what of the Court that was getting ready to go to work? What of applying the Rule of Law for the peaceful disposition of dispute between nations? We had almost the Court we wanted. Still lacking was obligatory jurisdiction; a device approaching that was in the so-called optional clause. What was the United States going to do about that?

Nonmembership in the League was no obstacle. Provision had been made in the protocol, a treaty to subscribe to the Court's statute, enabling outsiders, such as the United States, to participate in the Court's work. However, even though it was clearly evident that a majority of Americans wanted the Court, it was opposed by the "irreconcilable" Senate minority, men of seniority in that body, who had defeated the League.

It was evident that the new tribunal could not be a "whole" world's court, as the new rulers of Russia, the Soviets, made it clear that they would not participate. But that was not considered a problem; and indeed, for the first years the former allies—British, French, and the United States—were waiting and hoping for the Soviet Union's overthrow by former czarist generals and admirals, in whose favor the United States had intervened by sending troops to Siberia.

The Court's opponents put forward two arguments that conflicted each other: on the one hand they argued that entry into the Court was simply the back door for entry into the League, a way of getting around what the Senate had voted down; on the other, they claimed that being outsiders, the United States would be at the mercy of the League members dominating the Court.

Neither of these objections should have been enough to resist the public opinion that had built up since the concept of a world court was first proposed. But there were delays and distractions. As time passed, the sentiment that had seemed so strong began to ebb. There was single-minded, stubborn, and skilled leadership among the senators opposed to the Court, while those in favor were divided; not all were as determined, and their leadership was hesitant.

The opposing leaders in the contest were, at first, two Americans of great stature, whose careers were parallel, beginning with birth in families that were not very well off and that lived in small towns. Charles Evans Hughes, President Harding's secretary of state, and William Edgar Borah, senior senator from Idaho, were self-made and successful lawyers who became active in the Republican Party and then held office.

Each was a genuine liberal: Hughes was a leader for reform and liberal causes until his first (1910–1916) term on the Supreme Court, which was followed by an unsuccessful run for the presidency of the United States in 1916 against Woodrow Wilson. Borah opposed the World Court but not as a conventional isolationist. In many other foreign affairs issues, he advocated a liberal position. For example, he opposed the nonrecognition policy that Republicans applied to relations with the USSR, and in the 1920s he opposed the intervention into the affairs of Nicaragua when the U.S. Marines were sent there to fight the rebels led by Augusto Sandino. He was a notable dissenter for much of his career and became known as the "conscience" of the Republican Party.

Their careers ended almost simultaneously in the late 1930s, when Borah was still a Senate notable and old-fashioned debater, and Hughes was chief justice of the United States. The struggle drifted without effective leadership after Hughes's retirement on the death of President Harding. But in his initial efforts, Hughes was undermined by his own chief.

The formal transmission to Washington of the Court Protocol (the instrument whereby the United States, by special annex to the League Covenant, could participate equally with League members in the work and administration of the Court) was completed on August 15, 1921. Action was deferred for almost two years—an error on the administration's part for which Hughes must share responsibility—because of preference and concentration given to a naval arms limitation conference. (This, coincidentally, had been initiated by Senator Borah, but no evidence suggests that his motive then, as in a later initiative, was to derail the Court.) After making several persuasive, but low-key statements in support of the protocol, Hughes induced Harding to commend it to the Senate for ratification.

However, less than four months later President Harding reversed himself. Despite agreements entered into by the many nations via the League Covenant, he demanded that the Court be completely divorced from the League, to become "beyond shadow of doubt, a World Court, and not a League Court." Thus he gave seeming validity and high-level currency to the meaningless slogan that the minority had been harping on: "back door to the League." In the same speech Harding gave the pro-Court majority an even more serious setback: he demanded the abolition of the provision that the rest of the world had agreed upon, giving the Court advisory opinion authority. Harding died in 1923, but the damage he had done proved to be irreversible.

While the Senate committee headed by Borah stalled on the resolution to accept the Protocol, outside of Congress there was continued pressure for action from supporters, still very much of a majority. On March 3, 1925, the House of Representatives (though having no authority in the matter) expressed the consensus of their constituents in support of affiliation by a vote of 301 to 28. In this, the House was responding to such views as that expressed by former Attorney General Wickersham in an address later circulated as a pamphlet in support of affiliation with the Court:

> We cannot decently urge the creation of such a Court as this upon the rest of the world through a long series of years and then repudiate the Court when they consent to it, unless we offer some adequate reason.

The cue for the "reason" that developed in Borah's Foreign Relations Committee had been given by Harding in his reversal: the advisory authority of the Court became the focus of the objectors. Doubts were created by the invented threat that by advisory opinions the Court would be used to undermine the Monroe Doctrine, that it might interfere with the then-prevalent high tariff policies; above all that the Court might stand in the way of the United States' anti-alien policies and laws, which embodied, particularly, anti-Oriental exclusions.

That there was little or no objective basis for the fears expressed was made evident by early experience with the Court's "advisories," showing them to be a promising and useful innovation in international law. The senators were not persuaded. An interim committee reported that the power to render advisories was "believed by the committee to be a highly dangerous and undesirable jurisdiction." When the objectors could no longer hope to prevent a favorable Senate vote, that committee's quite unsupported condemnation of the Court's advisory opinion power was exploited successfully to defeat it.

The defeat of the Court was accomplished by the "reservation" device that had been used in the resistance to and final rejection of the Versailles Treaty. A majority of senators were persuaded to make ratification of the Court subject to a condition that had to be met by all members of the League. The United States would participate only if it were granted unique veto power; the Court was not to be allowed "without the consent of the United States [to] entertain any request for an advisory opinion touching any dispute or question in which the United States has *or claims* an interest."

That further delayed a vote. In 1935, Franklin D. Roosevelt was president and saw Hitler building the Nazi war machine. Wanting to ally the United States with supporters of international law and order, he urged the Senate to accept the Court without conditions. Demagogic opposition was now led by radical right priest, Father Charles Coughlan, the Hearst press, and Senator Huey P. Long. A majority of the Senate voted "aye," but the Court was defeated by the two-thirds rule.

The long delay had been fatal. Part of the story worth mentioning briefly is how efforts that led to the 1928 Pact of Paris, the so-called Kellogg–Briand Pact "outlawing" war, contributed to the delay. This treaty originated with an idea that came to Salmon O. Levinson of Chicago, who stubbornly pursued it to realization. He had made a fortune as a lawyer, rehabilitating shaky or failed business ventures, but had never been concerned with international law until his generation was shaken by World War I. When he learned that war was permitted by the Law of Nations as it then stood, he decided to change it.

Levinson succeeded in a way by launching and carrying to success a movement that required the agreement of all the world's great powers. The treaty that capped his effort, less than ten years after he began, became a "scrap of paper" for most of its life—but was not ignored during the Nuremberg trials that followed World War II. The judges there respected it and made the historic ruling: a plea of self-defense as justification for armed attack necessarily had to be subjected to the judgment of a court and, if challenged, could not be sustained by the one-sided claim of the accused nation. Thus they rejected the Nazi plea that Poland had attacked Germany in 1939.

Our concern is with the impact of Levinson's endeavor as an inadvertent impediment to the peace movement's effort to campaign for the affiliation of the United States with the Permanent Court of International Justice. The Outlawry Movement, as it was called, was not merely a distraction; it was seized on astutely by Senator Borah, interested in any device to obstruct completion of the Senate action on the Court resolution.

Levinson's original plan, as espoused by Borah, had called for creating an international court to pass on violations of the bar against levying war; Borah insisted that he was for "a" court, but could not accept the idea of a League Court. Something funny happened to Borah on the way to the treaty table: when the prospect of success was offered, it dropped out of sight and out of mind. French statesman Aristide Briand's acceptance of the idea of renouncing war omitted any new or additional court: France was quite satisfied with the existing Court, as founded in 1921.

U.S. citizens who supported the idea of affiliating with the existing Court were not dismayed in 1928 when Borah's alternate Court idea vanished. Many of them joined the campaign to win ratification of the Briand version of Levinson's idea, to which the name of Frank Kellogg, then secretary of state, was added in the popular media references. One group, the Committee on the Cause and Cure of War, founded and led by pioneer feminist orator Carie Chapman Catt, was said to have sponsored thousands of public meetings to support action by the Senate for the outlawry pact. At one major session, a pioneer woman appellate judge, Florence Allen of Ohio, told the delegates it was "up to women to teach the world that there was no situation 'in which the law of justice can not and does not function if applied' between nations and individuals."

When Levinson's dream appeared near realization—without a court to give it force—two contemporary leaders of public opinion bluntly noted the new pact's major flaw. Walter Lippmann, superpundit of his era, wrote in the *New Republic* about the courtless agreement, "until a man is willing to say that he is ready to submit any and every dispute affecting the peace of the world to adjudication, he has not made up his mind to outlaw war." And limiting himself to two cheers, Rabbi Stephen S. Wise, respected by many outside his own faith, was quoted in the *New York Times* as having declared:

> The Kellogg-Briand Pact is a forward step but not a forward march. . . . It is just a kindly, pious wish. In other words, the treaty is a sort of wishbone of peace lovers, and what we need is backbone.

He meant an effective Court, of course.

4

The Part-World Court Functions

The Court effort began shortly after the 1919 ratification of the U.S. Constitution's Eighteenth Amendment, outlawing intoxicating liquor. When the Court's protocol was ultimately defeated in 1935, national prohibition had already been dead for more than a year, killed after fifteen years of turmoil and controversy. The mass movements that led to each of these attempts to rid humanity of an evil had shared beginnings in America's Age of Reform (1830–1860); their defeat in 1933 and 1935 was due to entirely different factors. But in defeat they were linked by some wags overseas, who stated that the United States had given the world two great ideas and had turned their backs on both: the International Court and the mixed drink.

The hope of the rest of the world for U.S. participation in the Court for which it had done so much dimmed over the years. Without it the new tribunal would be less of an all-world court. But the nations that had agreed with the United States at Versailles to create the Court that had been outlined at The Hague in 1907 did not wait for the United States to make its decision before getting to work. Having drawn up the statute that defined the authority, outlined the structure, and established a mode of choosing the judges, they proceeded to finish the job. The "protocol" by which countries could accept and agree to the statute was quickly ratified by the necessary minimum. All was in readiness for the election of judges, as the Second Assembly of the League of Nations met in Geneva in September 1921.

USING THE BLUEPRINT:
ELECTING THE JUDGES

Eleven judges and four alternates were to be chosen; eighty-nine nominations had been received from the thirty-four national groups of arbitrator members of the Hague Tribunal. The president of the assembly explained the procedure: Voting was to be by secret ballot, with the council meeting in private, the assembly in public. They were to act simultaneously, so that neither would know the results of the other before the tallies were compared—to ascertain who and how many had received simultaneous majorities.

"Some nervousness was felt in the Second Assembly," wrote Manley O. Hudson, who was then a Harvard professor of international law and who, fifteen years later, would be elected a judge of the Court. Such tension was appropriate to a historic task, the first effort of its kind: to vest in a standing judicial body the authority to make decisions that would replace the barbarism of war as a mode of settlement of differences between the nations.

Representatives of five nations nominated Elihu Root to serve on the Court, intending thus to honor him for his service. By then he was seventy-six years old, and he declined. But he was eager to see an American jurist on the Court. This was possible despite U.S. nonmembership, since the judges, as defined in the statute, were international public servants, not chosen to represent their states or the governments in power. Root hoped that the presence of an American on the bench at The Hague would help to induce the United States to reconsider and participate in the Court, despite the stubbornness of the U.S. Senate.

John Bassett Moore, Root's first choice, was nominated and easily elected. For thirty-five years, Moore had been known and respected as scholar, writer, and State Department aide. He had been a frequent Mohonk conference participant and lecturer, and an outstanding international law professor at Columbia University and its law school. As a historian, he had written, before the turn of the century, a six-volume encyclopedic history of international litigation. In it, he unearthed and made available to his contemporaries the records of the 1796 arbitration under Jay's Treaty. Intriguing details about border conditions were brought to light. It was there he salvaged the observation of one of the U.S. delegates, asking why all nations should not settle disputes by arbitration, rather than choking the rivers with carcasses and staining the continents with blood.

At the twenty-first Mohonk meeting in 1915, Moore prophetically asserted that it would be "unreasonable to expect that international wars will cease before civil wars end," pinpointing the chronic *casus belli* of conflicting interventions. He went on to stress the "essential" principle that "no nation is so high . . . as to be above the law." During another Mohonk session, Moore gently rebuked his own country's ambivalence in its foreign policy. His target was the infamous sabotage by the Senate when arbitration treaties had been submitted after diplomatic agreement:

> As we are somewhat prone to boast of leading the van in the cause of peace, it may be worthwhile to consider whether we should not gain a position far in advance of that which we now hold if we were to recur to the practice we followed a hundred and twenty years ago.

Equally qualified were the others elected to the initial bench of the Permanent Court of International Justice. Nine of the eighty-nine candidates were elected on the first ballot; Moore was elected on the second; and three more ballots were required before a final choice was made for the last regular judgeship. All of those elected were men. It was not until 1990 that a woman was elected to serve on the World Court.

From the Netherlands came Bernard Cornelis Johannes Loder, who was elected by his fellows as the Court's first president. He had been Root's staunch ally and articulate colleague on the Commission of Jurists that prepared the first draft of the Court's statute. Loder was the founder and active participant in the work of several international professional associations, notably the International Maritime Association, and had represented his nation at international diplomatic conferences on maritime law; he helped in the drafting of the Covenant of the League of Nations.

The oldest member of the First Court, elected at the age of eighty, was Robert Viscount Finlay of England. Finlay, who was born in 1842, had begun his professional career as a medical doctor. After going into politics, he had entered the House of Commons, where he represented several constituencies, and by 1900 was appointed attorney general. He represented Great Britain—and had been Elihu Root's opponent—in the first major twentieth-century arbitration, between Britain and the United States over their respective rights in the North Atlantic fisheries. In the midst of World War I he was made lord chancellor. Finlay was not at all limited by his age: after serving with him on the Court, Judge Moore told a gathering of Columbia Law School alumni that Finlay had to be regarded "as still in the prime of life if judged by the vigor and alertness of his faculties."

Another judge from the Western Hemisphere was Antonio Sanchez de Bustamente, who had been born in Havana when Cuba was a Spanish colony. As a lad, Antonio had lived in Madrid, where his father, former dean of medicine at Havana University, had served as a member of the Senate from the then Cuban province. When he was but twenty-six years old, Bustamente won the chair of international law at the University of Havana.

Like Judge de Bustamente, Dr. Max Huber of Switzerland had been a delegate to the Hague Conference of 1907. He was widely recognized in the international law community during twenty years of service at the University of Zurich as professor of international law. He had been one of a small group assigned to do preparatory work for the third Hague Conference of 1915, which never took place. He was to succeed Judge Loder as president of the Court. Judge Huber, during his incumbency on the Court, was chosen to serve as sole arbitrator of a dispute between the United States and the Netherlands over title to the tiny islet of Palmas, midway between the then Dutch East Indies and the Philippines. The Coolidge administration thus accepted a World Court judge as an individual, to arbitrate its rights, while scorning the Court in which he sat.

Another of the judges was André Weiss of France, a longtime academic who had won appointment in 1907 as legal advisor to the French Foreign

Affairs Ministry, and represented France in several international arbitrations. Weiss was initial vice president of the Court. Others in the initial group of judges were D. G. Nyholm of Denmark, Yorozu Oda of Japan, and Dionisio Anzilotti of Italy. Each of these, like several of their colleagues on the initial bench, had previously been a member of The Hague's Permanent Court of Arbitration. There were also four deputy judges—selected to fill in when a member of the regular bench was unable to serve.

Throughout the Court's history (and that of its successor) there have been few judges found lacking the requirements of the office. Reflecting the consensus was a remark made to Elihu Root by a colleague representing Italy at Geneva, as they were trying to find the key to overcoming the U.S. Senate's objections, specified in its reservations to joining the Court. The colleague complained to Root about the Court's handling of requests for advice: members of the League of Nations Council "found that the Court was too judicial and independent; they [the League members] could not get the kind of advice that they wanted." Similar comments are made about the judges in the successor Court.

FINDING A COURTHOUSE

The Netherlands capital city of The Hague had, by 1921, been identified with a number of efforts to promote peace among the nations. When the advisory commission that was drawing up the Court's statute addressed the subject, they chose The Hague, rather than Geneva, home of the League itself, to be the Court's seat. This vote was unanimous. In the course of the brief discussion of the point, Japan's jurist on the committee said that in the island empire, "when The Hague is mentioned, it means Peace and Justice." The French delegate gave an additional and persuasive reason: it was desirable, he declared, "to separate the political functions of the League of Nations from its judicial functions by assigning different seats to the two groups of institutions." (When the time came to reestablish the Court in 1945, the statute was updated with a vision of things to come by a provision that allowed the Court to sit wherever it chose.)

The newly elected bench and its staff needed a courthouse. The advisory committee itself had met in Andrew Carnegie's Peace Palace. This was by courtesy of the Dutch Carnegie Foundation, a nonprofit corporation organized to receive the U.S. steel magnate's bounty, and to build and maintain the edifice. But to install, on a nontransient basis, an entity comprising eleven judges, four deputies, a registrar, and his retinue presented quite a different question.

The advisory committee's Netherlands delegate, Dr. Loder (the Court's first president), had declared, as his colleagues completed their work, that he expected that the new Court would sit in the building where they had themselves worked. But this could not be taken for granted, as there was a satisfied tenant already installed: The Permanent Court of Arbitration created by the Hague Conference of 1899.

Carnegie, sharing the belief of some of his contemporaries that his beneficiary was *the* "world court" that the U.S. delegation had been instructed to support, had in his gift stipulated that the funds provided were for "building, establishing and maintaining in perpetuity at The Hague a Court House and Library for the Permanent Court of Arbitration." The bureaucracy that ran the arbitration agency that went by the name of "Court" had the advantage of being a tenant in possession at the Peace Palace; it could also have claimed that it was the sole intended beneficiary of Carnegie's generosity. The secretary-general of the League of Nations had the problem of setting up the new Court for housekeeping. He disregarded the technical obstacle that loomed. Immediately on the assembly's approval of the Court's statute, he approached the Carnegie Foundation in behalf of the Permanent Court of International Justice for a lease for "premises in the Peace Palace for its meeting and offices."

The foundation's board agreed, heedless of its tenant. The latter, being composed of substantially the same nations as those in the League (save that the United States was on the board but not in the League) could not very well stand on its full legal rights as it was about to be displaced and forced into smaller quarters. But it did not want to be the new Court's landlord. "Thus, on its coming to the Peace Palace," historian Arnoldos Lysen wrote, "this new Court was faced by two hosts who disputed each other's honor to grant hospitality." The Permanent Court of International Justice nevertheless moved in; the squabble was settled within a year.

There was thus fulfilled the 1907 prediction of Dutch Foreign Minister van Karnebeek, president of the Carnegie Foundation, that both the arbitration body and a court of "international judicature" would be housed at the edifice.

AN OPERATIONAL JUDICIAL BODY

On January 30, 1922, the new group of judges convened for the first time. The initial order of business was to settle details of administration that would transform an unorganized group of jurists into a functioning Court. They prepared to elect standing officers—this Court would always elect its own president, to serve three-year terms—and set up their clerical administration. Then it was necessary to adopt the body of rules, characteristic of any court of record, that would govern (a) their internal operations and (b) the procedure whereby cases would be begun, and the interaction among parties and court that would follow the inception of a proceeding.

Looking back, eighty years after the event, in a global society accustomed to—if not accepting wholeheartedly all the implications of—a standing international judiciary, the assignment undertaken by the newly elected judges may seem humdrum and routine. It was far from that in 1922. Not only was the Court itself a revolutionary advance in international organization; it was also totally unprecedented as a judicial body for which no model was known that could be looked to as a guide.

To begin with, the judges had been trained in and were familiar with the traditions of disparate systems of law: Anglo-American, Napoleonic-European, Latin American, Muslim, and Sino-Japanese. In writing the rules of procedure they had to select acceptable features of each and compromise among them. They were aware that the parties to come before the Court in an adversary proceeding were each sovereign states, more accustomed to making and enforcing laws than obeying them. They displayed special sensitivity to the concerns of states whose legal systems had no advisory opinion procedure. No advisory opinion request could be considered without a hearing for any state that might conceive its interests to be affected. Whenever a petition for an advisory was filed, all members of the League were to be notified.

The rest of the rules, regarding initiation of cases, form and content of papers filed, time limits, objections to jurisdiction, intervention, and so on are of interest only to practitioners. One feature worthy of note was avant-garde in 1922 and anticipated a reform that in some courts only came years later. This was the requirement, usually called "discovery," that litigation not be affected by maneuvering and surprise tactics. The Court rule required that in sufficient time before the opening of oral proceedings, each party must inform the Court and the other parties of all evidence it intends to produce, together with the names, description, and residence of witnesses whom it desires to be heard, with an outline of the kind of evidence, that is, the content, each is expected to offer. Playing the game of lawyers outwitting other lawyers was intolerable when the interests of whole peoples, represented by their governments, were at stake.

OPEN FOR BUSINESS:
ADVISING THE NATIONS

> An international court will be organized without reference to any special case under discussion. Its members will prepare themselves as they choose for its great duty. Timidly at first, and with a certain curiosity, two nations will refer to it some international question, not of large importance, which has perplexed their negotiations. The tribunal will hear counsel and will decide. . . . That first decision will be accepted. The next question may be of more importance, the next of even more; and thus gradually the habit will be formed of consulting this august tribunal on all questions before states . . . the decisions, though no musket enforce them, will one day be received of course.

So prophesied Rev. Edward Everett Hale, when called to the nation's capital to preach on the occasion of the centenary of Washington's inauguration. It did not turn out altogether that way, but over the years, just as Hale had forecast in 1889, the questions increased in importance. And over eighty years, after scores of decisions, nearly 200 in all by two successive international courts, only two decisions were ignored as if they hadn't been made.

One of Hale's Mohonk colleagues had once mused that when the Court they had been wishing for was formed, it might be necessary for it to advertise, to hang out a shingle proclaiming JUSTICE BETWEEN NATIONS ADMINISTERED HERE and then to wait a year or two for customers. But the new Court did not have to sit listening for a knock on the door. There was a question ready and waiting when the Court's regular sessions opened on June 15, 1922.

The first case presented a request for exercise of the controversial new power: to render an advisory opinion on the request of the Council of the League of Nations. It was a good way to break the ice. This first case, and the next two (also advisories), dealt with problems passed on to the council by the new International Labor Organization (ILO). (In fact, eight of the first nine cases were exercises of the advisory power.)

The ILO showed that the realization of the American dream of a World Court was by no means the only constructive job of the oft-deprecated Versailles Peace Conference. In those days, protective labor legislation was in a rudimentary state; the treaty conferees responded to an international movement of labor that wanted a peace settlement that would advance social and economic justice. They created a new kind of international body to research and promote the raising of labor standards. Even the isolation-minded United States joined by 1934, and the ILO exists and works today as a specialized agency of the United Nations.

Unique among such organizations, the ILO was set up with a tripartite form of representation from member states. Not only were governments themselves represented, but each member nation also had in its delegation separate representatives of capital and labor. The ILO's constitution provided that each nation's labor delegation should be selected by the organizations "most representative" of the working people in that country. The problem arose when the Netherlands delegation was selected by consultation with three smaller labor groups, whose aggregate membership was greater than the Netherlands Federation of Trade Unions, which had a membership much larger than any of the three.

While the question presented to the Court had to do only with events within a single state, it became one of international law as needing interpretation of the multination Treaty of Versailles. The rejected group, the NGCTU, had been allowed to choose the delegates to the first two ILO conferences and protested to the credentials committee of the third. The ILO decided to seek legal advice, and the League Council formulated the question for the Court.

At the Court's opening, President Loder announced for the bench that on this (and any future) question, it would hear views of any interested party.

This included not only ILO member states but also several international labor organizations. The latter appeared and were even allowed to make oral presentations, as did the British and, naturally, the Dutch governments. The Court ruled unanimously that, in deciding who was "most representative," there might be selected the collected voice of several groups combining to outnumber the single largest; there was immediate compliance.

Another ILO case with broader implications came on the opening day. Did the Versailles Treaty empower it to look into and make recommendations about working conditions on farms? The ILO officials and delegates had been acting on the assumption they could; at an early point the French government objected, and the problem was processed through the League Council to an advisory. The issue: should "industrial" include agricultural workers?

Again several governments were heard, as well as a number of international labor organizations. The Court took an expansive view, asserting that farming was "the most ancient and greatest industry in the world"; any ambiguity in the word "industrial" had to be addressed with deference to the overriding purpose of the framers of the treaty, which they had declared was to improve the "conditions of labor . . . of large numbers of persons," whose hardship and privation could "produce unrest so great that the peace and harmony of the world were imperiled."

In a pamphlet published with the cooperation of the American Federation of Labor, with an introduction by AFL President William Green, written a few years later, George W. Wickersham, a former U.S. attorney general, used the ILO cases to explain and defend the role of the Court to U.S. workers. The writer, later head of a presidential commission that looked into and denounced widespread domestic "lawless enforcement of the law," praised the opinions as a "perfect example of the Court's procedure and a clear instance of the worldwide nature of the tribunal."

The Permanent Court of International Justice was, in time, to take on four more advisories with regard to ILO powers, and its activities resolved them; its rulings were accepted as guides. The Court's first dissents came in the agricultural labor case, one by the Court's vice president, André Weiss, who was from France. But there was no thought of French nonacquiescence or further resistance within the ILO. And Judge Weiss was soon to demonstrate (as others did repeatedly during the years) that he did not serve as representative or agent of his government or nation; that his role, as defined in the "solemn declaration" required when he took office, was to "exercise his powers impartially and conscientiously." In the first advisory that came up after the ILO cases, Judge Weiss, as noted with some pleasure by the *Harvard Law Review,* contemporaneously "joined in repudiating the position solemnly taken by the French Government."

This occurred in a case that followed a bitter dispute between France and Great Britain. France, as colonial power then in possession of Tunisia, sought to impose French nationality on all Europeans who lived there. Since this subjected these "involuntary" Frenchmen to military service as draftees, Britain acted vigorously in behalf of its nationals. When France refused to arbitrate or let the Court adjudge the matter, Britain took the dispute to the League Council as a threat to peace. (Neither had yet accepted the optional clause, so there was no French consent to be sued for the English to utilize.) The French then claimed that the League Council could not act, because the covenant excluded matters "solely within the domestic jurisdiction of a party."

The impasse was made susceptible of resolution because the French member of the League Council was Leon Bourgeois, who had distinguished himself at both of the Hague conferences in his advocacy of the American plan for a Court. He and the British council member, Lord Balfour, agreed to an ingenious solution: the two sparring nations would suggest that the council ask the Court *not* whether France's forced-nationality decree was wrongful, an issue that government was too proud to submit; instead the Court was to be asked only whether it was correct, as France had been saying in its diplomatic exchanges, that its new law's legitimacy was purely a question of "domestic jurisdiction," excluded from the council's consideration by the very words of the covenant.

Bourgeois was well known as a longtime supporter of the Rule of Law as vested in the Hague courts and had been awarded the Nobel Peace Prize in 1920. He was now able to persuade his chiefs that a question, put as an advisory, avoided the awkwardness of France being a defendant. In Court it was presented solely by counsel representing France and Britain—just as if it were a case brought by one against the other. The Court agreed with the French that in the current state of international law, nationality questions were ordinarily within domestic jurisdiction only, but agreed with the English that, Britain being party to treaties relevant to French occupation of Tunis (and Morocco as well), the possible effect of those treaties made the case one of international and not merely domestic law.

The Court's limited and complex ruling has been admiringly described by one lay observer as having the "charm of half-understood poetry." It was, in any case, a victory for legality in that it opened the door for a solution. France gracefully accepted the limited ruling, and announced that it would put its case on the merits, the right and wrong of its decrees, to the Court for solution. This proved unnecessary when further talks led to an out-of-court settlement, whereby Britons then alive would not be forced to become French citizens, if they wished—a kind of "grandfather" clause.

5

Judging "Between the Nations" Begins

The usefulness of the advisory opinion for dispute resolution as well as organizational guidance had been a pleasant surprise. The result of the expected sight of nation opposing nation before the judges remained to be been. That historic beginning was to wait almost a year after the initial nonconfrontational "advice" cases were presented.

THE SEAS AROUND US FOR A STARTER

The seas and oceans comprise 70 percent of the earth's surface. They have been used since the beginning of civilization for travel and transport among the globe's nations, and as a source of food for their peoples. The so-called high seas belong to no one, which means that they belong to everyone in common. Disputes about an asset commonly owned or commonly used cannot be sent for decision to judges sitting in the courts of one side or the other: an international court is needed for fair resolution. So it was fitting that after the world's courthouse opened for business, its first contested case should deal with a ship's right of passage from one international body of water to another.

The beginning of nation-versus-nation litigation at the Court followed an unwanted interruption of a voyage of the SS *Wimbledon*. Brought back to life by the 1919 Versailles settlement, Poland was engaged in 1921 in a brand new war—one of intervention. It was being waged under instigation of the Allies, who were seeking to overthrow the young Soviet state. The *Wimbledon* was a British ship that had been chartered by a French syndicate formed to supply munitions to the Poles. The object of the voyage was to get a load of munitions that had been assembled in the Mediterranean to the port of Danzig in the Baltic Sea, since there was no feasible route for overland shipment. Danzig is now called Gdansk, and still the major harbor serving Poland.

The last leg of the *Wimbledon*'s voyage, from the North Sea to the Baltic, would ordinarily have been through the German-situated Kiel Canal, built to save ships from having to sail around the Jutland Peninsula, via the straits of Skagerrak and the treacherous Kattegat. For the benefit of the new states carved out of Russia and Germany at Versailles—Poland, Finland, Esthonia, Latvia, and Lithuania—the treaty provided that the Germans should keep the canal "free and open" to "nations at peace with Germany." The canal manager had received orders via telegram from the new Weimar Republic in Berlin to bar the *Wimbledon*'s transit because of the munitions she bore. The ship was stopped.

The Germans said they were entitled to disregard the treaty rule because of a legitimate national interest that should justify an implied exception. Britain, the ship's owner, and France, main sponsor of the shipment to aid the anti-Soviet Polish rebels, joined with Italy and Japan as principal treaty sponsors to initiate a suit for damages at the new Permanent Court of International Justice (PCIJ), the World Court that the treaty had provided. The resulting case was a multiple "first," as it was also the first case of a kind of "compulsory," that is, involuntary, jurisdiction. Germany's consent was deemed to have been given in advance by her signature to the treaty. It was also the first use of a privilege given a state that had no jurist on the bench: the option to name one, ad hoc, for this case only.

When the case came on for hearing, there was no dispute about the facts. The central issue was whether the obligation, imposed by the Versailles Treaty, to keep the canal open to all was affected by the war of Germany's neighbors. The language of the treaty provided only one express exception: when Germany herself might be at war. The Court declined to create an implied exception, as the defense had proposed.

Counsel for the Weimar Republic put up a good fight. Their arguments were persuasive enough to win three dissents. Noteworthy, since Italy had joined the plaintiffs suing Germany, was the vote of Dionisio Anzilotti, one of the three against Italy and her partners. He had been professor at several Italian universities before joining his nation's Foreign Affairs Ministry; while there he had been Italy's advocate in several international arbitrations. Neither Anzilotti's dissenting vote nor later independence prevented his renomination and reelection; during part of one term his colleagues elected him Court president. With his French colleague André Weiss, in the Tunis/Morocco advisory, he was among the first to demonstrate that the judges were truly international civil servants, that the phrase "Italian judge" (or "Polish" or "British" judge) is misleading when applied to jurists of the caliber elected to serve at The Hague.

The Court's majority opinion in SS *Wimbledon* included points that became part of the developing body of international law. The ruling's components vindicated the professional forecast of Elihu Root and the common-sense judgment of Yankee layman Edward Everett Hale: that a permanent body of career judges would help to create a collection of precedential rulings that, in turn, would guide the nations' legal advisers and result in the predictability so essential to respect for the law and the Court.

One example was the Court's handling of the argument that to prevent Germany from enforcing her neutrality would impair a sovereign right. The answer was that the very act "of entering into international agreements is an attribute of state sovereignty," and thus its independence and dignity are respected when its agreement is enforced. The U.S. Supreme Court referred to that ruling during the early Roosevelt New Deal. The U.S. attorney general argued that "sovereignty" prevented challenge to the nation's repeal of its pledge of gold bond repayment. Not so, said the Supreme Court, echoing The Hague: "The power to make binding obligations is a competence attaching to sovereignty," which is respected by giving force to the obligation as written.

Likewise still relevant is rejection of the argument that the Kiel Canal Commission, in barring the *Wimbledon,* was obeying a valid German law. The Court ruled that international law must necessarily be superior to the laws and decrees of any single state. The penalty for violating an international obligation cannot be evaded by referring to what a local law has provided.

Several years later, another interruption of another voyage—with more tragic consequences—brought another maritime case to The Hague. The fate of the SS *Lotus* and its legal implications were to prove to be of importance to more nations and to more individuals than those immediately involved. It has reverberations to this day, as when the United States tries in its own court a defendant who has never been in the United States and whose alleged terrorist acts were committed outside this country.

The case of the SS *Lotus* began around midnight, August 2, 1926, in the waters of the Aegean Sea, when the ship, a French mail vessel headed for Constantinople (now Istanbul), rammed and sank a Turkish collier. Lieutenant Demons, the French officer on watch at the moment of the collision, rescued a few seamen from the waters that had closed over eight of their shipmates, and proceeded to his destination—their homeland. Expecting at worst a disciplinary hearing on his return to the *Lotus*'s homeport of Marseilles, Demons was in for an unpleasant surprise when he reached Turkey. He was arrested and charged with manslaughter, and convicted at the Istanbul criminal court. A protest by the French consul was brushed aside.

An attempt at a higher diplomatic level to work out the incident was unsuccessful because of an impasse as to the central issue: under international law, may Turkey try a French citizen for mishandling a French ship in international waters? The lieutenant's advocates contended that what happened was subject only to French law and the judgment of French courts; the Turkish diplomats answered with a claim of right based on the effect on Turkish seamen and a Turkish ship. The adversaries agreed to a hearing at the Hague Court. Turkey, following its defeat as an ally of Germany in World War I, was not yet a member of the League of Nations, nor a party to the PCIJ's protocol. Her diplomats nevertheless agreed to accept the Court's ruling on what was a seemingly insoluble difference.

When the case came on for hearing, the proceedings were marked—just as they had been in the hearing of the Allies versus Germany in the *Wimbledon* case—by mutual and judicial respect for recent war foes. One observer noted that states began accepting former enemies as normal litigants under the law. The Court, in turn, paid states a compliment by treating them with equal formality, courtesy, and consideration.

The division between the parties on the legal issue was to divide the judges as well. It was accepted, in customary international law, that a ship on the high seas had to be treated as the territory of the state whose flag it flew. The French argument was that Demons's handling of the wheel took place on their territory and could be judged only by their courts. The Turkish claim was that the effect of what had been done must be taken into account: the Turkish ship represented Turkish territory, impacted by the bow of the SS *Lotus,* and therefore they had concurrent jurisdiction.

Though the judges were (with one exception) from nations that had been allied with France, or neutral in the Great War, the decision went to Turkey. It was a close one: the judges had divided six to six. The statute had anticipated such an event and provided for a tiebreaker, a "casting" vote assigned to the Court's president, who thus voted twice. (In domestic appeals courts this is not needed, as a tie favors the decision appealed from.) The Court's president at the time was Max Huber of Switzerland, so well reputed that the United States had accepted him as single arbitrator in the *Isle of Palms* case. Judge John Bassett Moore dissented, but not on the ground of the other five. He agreed with the ruling that Turkey could exercise authority, but he viewed the Turkish law as overbroad.

The *Lotus* ruling turns out to have great importance as nations are affected and aroused by acts of hijacking and other lawlessness outside their territory. Initially, however, the idea of concurrent jurisdiction, two nations having authority to try for one offense, was unpopular among maritime states and it was overruled by later treaties. But as the nations became preoccupied with terrorism, new rounds of treaties were negotiated under UN auspices that restored a limited *Lotus* rule: that nations whose citizens or property are affected by intentional acts of violence may seek to try and to punish the perpetrators. The United States has taken advantage of this by passing laws that make it possible to put people on trial for actions that occur overseas but that affect U.S. citizens. But in cases of accidental injury, the French losing position in the case of Demons is the law today.

EXTRA DIVIDEND: HUMAN RIGHTS

Neither Poland nor Czechoslovakia, Finland nor Lithuania—nor others that are now familiar—existed as nation states prior to World War I. The peace treaties of that postwar period created an unfamiliar map of Europe. The treaty makers were aware that the peace of the new Europe they were fashioning would be endangered by new minority problems: Germans and Russians under Polish rule; Germans and Hungarians under the new Czech Republic; and Greeks in Albania, a tiny state created just before the Great War (the result of the Balkan conflicts that led to it.)

First fruit of the discussions of the problem came with a condition imposed on the recognition of Polish independence. New Poland agreed that all its nationals "shall be equal before the law and shall enjoy the same civil and political rights without distinction as to race, language or religion" and also that "racial, religious or linguistic minorities shall enjoy the same treatment and security in law and in fact as the other. . . ." Similar pledges were soon made by a dozen other European states, old and new—raising to a global level the substance of the U.S. Fourteenth Amendment and much of the U.S. Bill of Rights.

It was one thing to write such pledges; it was another to have them become meaningful in real life. One necessary condition was to have a Court that would be there to adjudge differences between or among nations as to the meaning and the application of the so-called minorities treaties. Another was access to the Court: while that was not provided for individuals, as such, they had a route via the League council, which was given power to ask for advisory opinions on the subject. State-versus-state questions, when raised, had the benefit of a kind of "compulsory" jurisdiction, as the treaties themselves constituted consent in advance to having the PCIJ pass on such disputes. And so, from the first 1923 case, involving what were called German settlers in Poland, until 1935, when the Court, in its twilight years, heard from Greek parents in Albania who complained of denial of educational opportunity, there was established a firm foundation for *international* judicial protection of what we now refer to as "human rights."

It was not merely that the paper protection provided in the minorities treaties was backed by a Court. It had a sympathetic Court. The diversity of national origin among the members of the bench, it may be suggested, helped to account for this. Judges from eleven countries (fifteen now) were not as a body or as individuals accountable to any single national power center or bloc of powers. Their independence from the political and diplomatic forces in the League council and assembly was written into the Court's statute.

In one of the first minorities treaty cases that came before it, the Court rejected application of narrow or "strict" construction to the clauses on minority protection. The controversy involved the German-speaking minority that was settled in territory that had been taken from Poland when it had been partitioned among Russia, Prussia, and Austria more than a century before. In declaring that it had the authority to decide who could assert the right to claim Polish citizenship, the Court would not heed the Polish government claim that only persons that *it* recognized as Polish citizens could complain under the pact. The contention that treaty language limiting its benefit to "Polish nationals" was rejected. The usually local question of who had or had not attained citizenship was for the Court to decide since the purpose of the treaty had to be given effect. When the ruling came down, the Polish authorities respected it.

In the last of the World Court human rights cases of the minorities treaty type (there have been none since the revival of the Court in 1945, because the nations united at San Francisco declined to give it authority to act), the ruling—in 1935—set an example worth recalling. At stake was an Albanian "declaration" (with the force of a treaty) that racial and religious minorities should "enjoy the same treatment and security in law and in fact as other Albanian nationals." When the regime abolished parochial schools, Greece protested to the League in behalf of the Greek Catholic minority who were hard hit.

The Albanian lawyers at The Hague defended their nation's action with an argument that may sound familiar in the United States today. They reasoned that there was "equality," since the Albanian majority population had no greater right to attend private church schools than the Greek Catholics. The Court responded with a formulation not cited as often as it might well be, a classic in this area of the law:

> Equality in law precludes discrimination of any kind; whereas equality in fact may involve the necessity of different treatment in order to attain a result which establishes an equilibrium between different situations. . . . The equality between members of the majority and the minority must be an effective genuine equality.

The Court's realistic and compassionate treatment was approved by Manley O. Hudson, a professor of international law at Harvard, because the parochial schools, important to the Greeks only, "are essential to the needs of the minority group and their abolition would destroy equality of treatment." The Albanian government promptly complied with the ruling.

John Humphrey's review of the entire period summarized the PCIJ's achievement, saying that:

> [It] took a strong stand against any interpretation of the treaties which would diminish protection for minorities. It rejected the view that treaty protection applied to citizens alone and maintained that the provisions of the treaties provided only the minimal obligations. It tried to maintain for minorities not only legal equality but factual equality, interpreting the treaties always in a broad sense and with due regard for their spirit and intention.

While the minorities protection system ceased to function when the European crisis of 1939 and war supervened, it offers a model that can be consulted. That the system did not revive has been attributed by a UNESCO-supported study to an improper action of the UN Secretariat in 1950 in deciding and announcing that the treaties were no longer in force.

MAKING HISTORY BY MAKING LAW

Few of the cases that come to the Supreme Court of the United States have historic dimensions. A major segment of its service has been to develop, incrementally, the rules that govern relations between the states and the federal government—and with each other. Included in this has been treatment of the people and businesses of one state, working or investing in another. Guidelines have been worked out by decision of cases, quite important to the participants, but rarely seen as significant at the time and only dimly recalled later on, except by professionals.

So it was with the first World Court. A variety of cases (and requests for advisory opinions) came its way, of which few were of much enduring significance. As the Court decided these, one by one, it fulfilled the hopes of the early peace and Rule of Law advocates and activists that it would give authoritative expression to a code of behavior governing relations among the globe's nation states. It was expected that while doing this, the Court, just as Anglo–American courts in developing the common law, would build useful principles of international law. Ingredients that were intended to make possible fulfillment of that expectation were spelled out in its statute. These were (and still are: the statute of the present International Court of Justice adopted in 1945 did not change them):

- First, the kinds of treaties that participating states intended should serve as rules of legal significance between or (as more and more frequently till the present day) among them, in so-called multilateral pacts.
- Second, the international customs accepted among the nations, such as diplomatic immunities, and matters like the definition of "self-defense" formulated by Daniel Webster as U.S. Secretary of State in the case of the British commando-style raid that sank the U.S. paddle wheeler *Caroline*.
- Third, "the general principles of law recognized by civilized nations," which was meant to be, and taken as, a grant of authority to incorporate into the Law of Nations some basic notions of fair play and decency—not linked to or dependent on any one of the principal legal systems of the world: precepts based on such ideas as, one who has caused another's wrongful act cannot ordinarily complain of it, or expressed in the almost universal maxim, "No one can be judge in his own case."
- Fourth, earlier judicial decisions, "and the teachings of the most highly qualified publicists [scholars] of the various nations." The quoted clause

reflected a state of affairs that had already developed by 1920, and continues today: the existence of a wide scholarly interest in researching and writing about the customs and practices that have made up the body of principles recognized as the "Law of Nations," and the tendency of many— even discounting such nationalist bias as they may be likely to entertain— to seek common ground with mutual respect.

Development of Judicial Collegiality

The first group of World Court judges, some of whom had a bit of experience in international arbitration, others in diplomacy, nevertheless had no difficulty in understanding and using these guidelines. They became a unified body, relatively quickly, with a common sense of responsibility to the Court as an institution and to its purposes—a characteristic of the membership that has followed ever since. They accepted their responsibility, and went on to accomplish the initial breakthrough of winning acceptance of the fact of international adjudication in action.

The body of law that is the legacy of the PCIJ touches on many types of problems. They did not each make a new contribution to international law; but all the cases that came to the Court participated in an ongoing demonstration that it was readily possible, with assurance of a result based on "neutral principles," and without the expense, delay, and, sometimes, stalling that marked the arbitration process, to secure the dispensing of international justice.

Some instances are worthy of mention, not for their importance but as a sketch of what went on in the Peace Palace, in addition to the shipping and International Labor Organization cases that were discussed in chapter 4. One early case questioned whether Britain, as holder of a mandate for Palestine, had to respect and give effect to a concession that had been granted by Turkey, whose possession it had been, to a Greek to operate utility concessions in the Holy Land. (The "mandate" was a Versailles Treaty device for transfer of control, supposedly temporary until "fit" for self-government, of property of a former enemy to a victor.) The principle was established that, even though the Court was confined to state-versus-state cases, a government could come there on behalf of one of its nationals to complain of an allegedly illegal act causing loss or injury. (Incidentally, this was again a case of a judge of nationality of one party, voting for the result that he thought right and fair: in this case, the judge from Britain voted against "his" nation.)

Boundary disputes were repeatedly settled between such adversaries as Czechoslovakia and Poland; Albania versus Greece; and Britain (again as mandatory, this time of Iraq) versus Turkey. Two of the cases dealt with the binding effect of a decision by the post-Versailles Conference of the Ambassadors of the Great Power victors. The third presented for judgment a League of Nations Council decision that wasn't unanimous (the covenant required that League decisions be without dissent, that is, any member could, in effect, cast a "veto," predecessor to the crippling feature of the UN Security Council). The Court ruling was that unanimity "does not involve the concurrence of the representatives of the parties to the dispute." Neither adversary, in other words, could block the effectiveness of an otherwise unanimous council decision, because, as the Court said, "The well-known rule that no one can be judge in his own suit holds good."

In a variety of other cases the Court dealt with issues presented by treaties regulating traffic on the Danube and the Oder, two important European rivers that were used by several nations; other treaty interpretation questions, laying down rules for future guidance of both treaty negotiators and future Courts; enforcement of a "gold clause" in foreign loan agreements; and enforceability of foreign concessions, such as the operation of lighthouses. There were further calls on the Court for advice concerning spheres of activity in which the International Labor Office could function.

THE GERMAN–POLISH POWDER KEG

Close to a third of the Court's business arose as a result of the revival of the Polish state, which had been removed from the map by the aggression of her neighbors, at the same time as the United States was beginning its independent existence in the late eighteenth century. The adversary was Germany, which (unlike Russia and Austria, the other partners in the partitions) encouraged settlement on the West Bank of the Vistula, in occupied territory.

Had Germany not fallen into the hands of the lawless National Socialists, the decisions in the cases of Poland and Germany would be better remembered. Their litigation resulted in the kind of exemplary transborder justice that proves the capacity of a cosmopolitan court to contribute to peaceful settlement of inter-nation irritations. Almost every decision was in favor of the German Republic's representatives, as were the advisory opinions delivered on complaint of German settlers, whose cases were presented to and taken up by the League council. And any one who was doubtful of Nazi intentions could have discerned what they were from actions of October 1933: two cases that had previously been filed on behalf of German settlers were withdrawn; not long after, Germany would withdraw from the Court and the League altogether.

Prior to that withdrawal, it seemed as if there should have been commutation tickets available for travel from Berlin and Warsaw to The Hague. One case, in fact, required seven trips to Carnegie's Peace Palace, and along the way resulted in a number of still useful principles of international law. Its origins are in the checkered history of Upper Silesia, a province of the ancient Polish Kingdom, that for 1,000 years had been a football of Eastern Europe. Over the centuries, it was taken from the Poles by Bohemia, which then lost it to the Austrians, from which it was snatched in the eighteenth century by Frederick the Great of Prussia. It gave Prussia a strategic base for offense or defense against Russia or Austria that was also mineral rich—including Europe's second-largest coal deposit. The possession of this territory was the key to Prussia's rise to dominate the rest of Germany and the latter's rise as a military power. About 100,000 German settlers moved into Poland, joining those who had moved in during Austrian occupation.

Following a Versailles decision to give it all back to Poland, there was guerrilla warfare, and a dispute plebiscite. Finally, a formula for dividing the province between Germany and Poland was agreed upon by the Allies, and the two contesting nations made a 1922 treaty accepting the settlement. But the Germans had foreseen the possible result and made preparations for it. They sold, before the treaty was made, an immense nitrate factory at Chorzow, owned by the Reich, to a private concern, the Oberschlesischer Stickstoffwerke, A. G. Disregarding this, the Polish authorities took over the plant as if it had still remained property of the Reich when they were granted ownership of the province. Germany instituted suit in the PCIJ, on behalf of its company's stockholders.

The tangled series of seven decisions in one contest is not of interest to many. But in the course of the decision on questions of jurisdiction, the merits, and damages—all leading up to a final decision favoring the German claimants—the Court enriched the body of the Law of Nations. Its decisions included, as British scholar Sir Hersch Lauterpacht (himself later a judge of the International Court of Justice) ticked them off, such points as:

- The conditions of jurisdiction of international tribunals.
- The question of litispendency [effect of another case pending in a different court].
- State succession.
- Expropriation of alien property.
- The position of ceded territory in the period between the signature of a treaty and its ratification.
- The plea of nondiscrimination in the treatments of aliens.
- The competence of the Court to issue declaratory judgments.
- Its right to decide on claims for compensation in the absence of express treaty provisions for this effect.
- The implication of state control over private claims.
- Measure of damages, counterclaim, and set-off.

It is not necessary for the lay reader to learn the "law" on these points, or to understand the complexities of each, in order to have a picture of the Court as accepted arbiter of international law principles. Each was debated vigorously (and, in some instances, ingeniously) by Polish and German advocates at The Hague. To show how they worked out, let us look at the right to decide on claims of compensation, called "damages" in domestic lawsuits and "reparations" in international law.

The German-Polish treaty agreeing to the division of Upper Silesia had given to the Court at The Hague the power to decide differences as to its construction or application. On Germany's suit, after the initial set of rulings, the judges decreed that Poland was not justified under the pact in taking over the Chorzow factory. The parties accepted the verdict—every one that the old PCIJ handed down was agreed to—but were not able to come to terms on the nature and amount of restitution.

When another application on this subject was made to the Court by the Germans, the agents for Poland argued that the only power given to the Court by the treaty was to settle disagreements as to "interpretation or application" of its words. Nothing was said in writing about money. But the Court ruled that it *had* to be a principle of international law "that the breach of a Treaty involves a duty of reparation." In the words of the Court:

> An interpretation which could confine the Court simply to recording that the Convention had been incorrectly applied . . . without being able to lay down the conditions for the reestablishment of the treaty rights affected, would be contrary to what would, *prima facie* be the natural object of the clause; for a jurisdiction of this kind, instead of settling a dispute once and for all, would leave open the possibility of further disputes.

After the Court named experts to determine the amount due, the parties to the case saved The Hague further trouble. They settled it between themselves. This was international adjudication at its best: bringing the parties to a point where they could turn to their respective constituencies, unembarrassed by having to make an agreement that would seem to be giving in or yielding points—after all, the Court had settled the principle—and have a free hand to avoid the ultimate discomfiture of an adverse decision.

PROMOTING PEACE: DISPENSING JUSTICE

The Court did well in fulfilling its mission to build the structure of international law. However, its existence did not prevent the outbreak of World War II. That did not prove it to have been a "failure." It lacked compulsory jurisdiction and was only a part-World's Court. And worst of all, there was absent the kind of public determination that the Court's proponents had agreed was needed, that insoluble international differences be settled by impartial strangers. Also needed was the existence of responsive governments, the kind that would permit popular will to influence a nation's leaders.

With all its handicaps, the Court in the interwar period gave evidence that such a tribunal could be a global asset for the preservation of peace and promotion of justice.

Greenland

However unlikely it may seem, in view of their joint membership in the community of states we call Scandinavia, a serious dispute broke out between Denmark and Norway in 1931. Troops were sent overseas, strategic points fortified, and bristling notes exchanged. The quarrel had erupted over conflicting claims of ownership in Greenland—that great, mostly icy, island off the northeastern Canadian archipelago.

Most of Greenland is above the Arctic Circle. Fishing and hunting were its only significant economic activities. The only settlements on the island worth referring to as such were on its southwest coast. These were Danish in 1931 when the trouble broke out. Their history, briefly, was: Greenland's early settlers of nearly a millennium ago, mainly Norsemen, had disappeared. Colonization was resumed by a Danish missionary in the eighteenth century, while Norway and Denmark were united; when their union was dissolved in the nineteenth century, Denmark was given ownership—which in actual fact related only to the new southwest settlements.

The east coast was practically vacant. Norwegian armed hunters moved in during early 1931, and their coup was followed by a declaration of ownership by the Norwegian state. Denmark replied, not with guns—although it did reinforce its western settlements—but with briefs and oral pleadings.

Each Scandinavian state had been an early signer of the "optional clause," agreeing in advance to submit to Court decision any dispute of a legal nature with a state that was also a signatory. There was thus, for this dispute at least, compulsory jurisdiction. Nevertheless, feelings were running high, newspapers in each nation were provocative, and while the briefs in the case were being written, there was a new Norwegian occupation and declaration of sovereignty, this time on the island's southeast quadrant.

When a Danish expeditionary force was being readied and threatened to go to the new occupation area, Norway responded by filing a new case, to which Denmark filed a cross-claim. Norway, as the new plaintiff, asked for "interim measures of protection," the phrase Root and his founding colleagues gave to what we'd call an application for temporary injunction. In the presence of the judges at this first hearing, the parties backed off from their truculence, gave assurance that they would abstain from further forceful action pending decision, and the Court stayed its hand.

The earlier Eastern Greenland case went on shortly thereafter, with forty-eight hearings devoted to a full history that began with Eric the Red, the Norse discoverer, who, in 982 landed and settled on the west coast. After a review of the history, the Court, with four dissents, decided in favor of Denmark. Its decision was controversial; scholars denounced certain aspects, especially that the judges seemed to disregard that it was only paper possession that Denmark had had on the east. Questionable, too, was the emphasis given to an oral acknowledgment of Danish rights given by a Norwegian foreign officer, unratified by Norway's king.

Controversial or not, the decision disposed of the case and ended the threat of conflict. As implied in a pledge in its submission of briefs to the Court and as expressly provided in the Covenant of the League of Nations, each contestant had agreed to obey the Court's ruling. Following the announcement of the judgment in the first case, the Norwegian proclamation of July 1931 that it was ruler of eastern Greenland was promptly withdrawn. Just as quickly Norway withdrew the later provocative declaration of ownership of southeastern Greenland and eleven days later both nations asked the Court to drop the second case without further action.

Germanic Unification?

In 1931, two years after the start of the worldwide economic disaster of the 1930s, and two years before Adolf Hitler's rise to power in Germany, much of Europe awoke to a nightmare. Austria, the severed German-speaking portion of the former Austro–Hungarian empire, had agreed with Germany, its defeated ally, to establish a customs union—elimination of trade barriers between them—that would also involve the full integration of their economies.

Against the better judgment of some statesmen, Germany had been left united in 1919, save for the restoration of Alsace-Lorraine to France, and the subtraction of former Polish lands to contribute to the re-creation of Poland. But Germany was still potentially the strongest power on the continent and was beginning to regain that status. With the addition of Austria and the geo-strategic as well as population gain, she would soon become a threat to peace. U.S. President Herbert Hoover compared the announcement to the 1914 assassination in Sarajevo of the Austrian crown prince, and the barrage of ultimata that followed, which seemed inevitably to have led to the "Guns of August" that began the Great War of 1914-1918.

It was natural that a storm of protest erupted when the preliminary commitment for "Zollverein"—customs union—was disclosed. There was ample nineteenth-century precedent to indicate that such a union preceded and led to "Anschluss"—unification—in the first creation of the unified German Reich. But there was some controversy as well. Sympathy was evoked by the seemingly helpless and isolated situation of "little" Austria (as she strikingly did appear on maps, in contrast with its prewar Kaiser Franz Joseph's empire). Sympathy was particularly evident among those who weren't vulnerable neighbors; Britain was ambivalent and the United States appeared to have a majority that did not object.

There was a potential legal problem. The postwar treaties provided—precisely because of fear of the politico-military effect of unification—that Austria's independence "is inalienable otherwise than with the consent of the Council of the League of Nations." Also, Austria had agreed not to take steps that would "compromise" that independence without such consent. As France, Czechoslovakia, and others who felt the heat were putting political and especially economic pressure on Austria to break off, Britain took the case to the League council. But council members, rather than take the responsibility of acting—as it would have had to if Austria had asked for its consent—preferred to pass the buck to the Court in the form of a request for an advisory opinion.

The Court took the case, but divided closely in its ruling, 8 to 7, with four different opinions. While the case was pending and being argued, the French economic steps bankrupted the Creditanstalt Bank, Austria's greatest, a failure that had a domino effect culminating in U.S. bank closings at the end of the Hoover presidency. Sympathy for Austria grew. The Court's tangle of opinions and the economic effects of the pressure on Austria combined to bring some discredit to the judges. Some now argue that they should not have taken the case, as there was discretion to decline requests for advisories, and that the question presented was a "political" question, not a "legal" one.

That may be the wisdom of hindsight. The case did bring before the Court the interpretation of a treaty. That the judges had to decide what the effect of the customs union might be did have its political elements, but there is a degree of politics in every judicial decision by an international court. The judges were faced with the problem of making a factual judgment; that is an element of most cases. The decision that was made did have the potential to preserve peace. There is always the possibility that a judgment may be controversial, that it may create criticism of a court. To allow that to influence an abstention from decision is itself a choice that lacks impartiality: it is a ruling that disregards the merits, the rights and wrongs of a case, which it is the sworn obligation of judges to confront and grapple with.

There was an anticlimactic element: two days before the advisory opinion was released, Austria and Germany chose to yield to the political-economic pressure that was brought on them from the day the news of their agreement had been disclosed. The final tragedy came when, seven years later, Nazi troops moved across the border, proceeded unopposed to Vienna, and were led by Hitler through cheering streets on the road to war and all of its holocausts. That was the war makers' way of overruling a judicial decision.

Decency in Danzig

Now known as Gdansk, Poland's principal port, where a shipyard strike made Lech Walesa world-famous in the 1980s, Danzig—the independent "free city" created by the League of Nations in 1920—is hardly remembered these days. It had a checkered history, somewhat like that of Upper Silesia. Teutonic knights took it from the old Polish kingdom in the middle ages; repolonized, but with the quasi-independent spirit of a cosmopolitan seafaring town, it was taken for Prussia by Frederick the Great in the eighteenth-century partition; it was thereafter thoroughly Germanized by a new wave of settlers.

As part of the re-creation of Poland after World War I, it was necessary to give her a Baltic Sea port. The early League of Nations shrank from placing the Teutonic city under Polish rule. Using a medieval concept, they made it a Free City, under a high commissioner appointed by and responsible to the League. The port was to be within the Polish customs frontier, and the revived nation would have control of all railways, waterways, and docks, with the right to conduct such foreign relations as the independent city might have. The people would have their own legislature and elect their own local government.

That government was German-dominated from the start. It adopted the Weimar Republic's policy of incessant nonviolent conflict, aimed at ultimately undoing the Versailles settlement. In all, six Danzig-spawned cases plagued the PCIJ during its twenty years. The last of these cases—and the final advisory opinion rendered by the PCIJ—came when Nazi politicians took over the Danzig government. The last German free election held before World War II revealed the state of mind of the majority of Germans, who had come, after two years of Hitler's rule, to support him and what he stood for.

The Nazi rulers of Danzig issued a decree in September 1935, aping the totalitarian law of the Reich that was designed to eliminate personal freedom and due process of law. It provided that people could be prosecuted not only for violations of the provisions of existing written laws, but "also in accord with sound popular feeling . . . left to the individual judge or public prosecutor to determine." Danzig's Social Democrats and other minority parties petitioned the League council, as ultimate authority over Danzig, for help. The council, typically, evaded responsibility, and voted to pass the question on to the Court at The Hague.

The outcome was another historic expression of support for human rights, in advance of our era when the concept became widely popular. This time, the result was even more striking, as creative jurisprudence was required. The Court found a basis for international jurisdiction in the League's "guarantee of the Danzig Constitution" that its council had drafted. That constitution provided for what the Court called "essential individual rights." These the Court identified as liberty of the person, and freedom of movement, of speech, and of assembly and association. These were all threatened by the wide discretion that was given to the local judges and prosecutors by the Danzig decrees, said the Court. Since the Danzig Constitution established a "state governed by the rule of law," all could be subjected to arbitrariness that varies from judge to judge, from prosecutor to prosecutor, uncontrolled by standards laid down in advance. Hence the Court was constrained to hold that the decrees that attempted to put Nazi justice into effect in Danzig (the judges did not put it quite that way) were not consistent with the guarantees of the Danzig Constitution.

No fireworks followed. Talk of "nullification" of the Court's ruling or disregard of it was not heard. The Danzig legislature repealed the decrees in compliance with the judgment of the Court. Thus ended what Professor (later Judge) Sir Hersch Lauterpacht called a case "of great significance, as it constituted the first instance of international judicial review of a national enactment in the sphere of fundamental human rights."

At the end of the decade—as some were repeating the slogan "Why die for Danzig?"—the dictator who demanded that the League turn Danzig over to him overruled the Court with his Panzer battalions within hours of the start of World War II. And now there is Gdansk, not Danzig, cradle of the Polish revolution.

6

A Palace as a Courthouse

Inspired by his fellow peace activists, Andrew Carnegie, a naturalized American, had financed the building of the world's courthouse. The Hague, where it was built, had since the seventeenth century played an important role in the emergence and development of modern international law. Carnegie hoped it would serve as a "Temple of Peace" and be called by that name. It did come to be officially named the Peace Palace.

The architect was influenced by the extravagant affectations of the immediate post-Victorian era. The exterior was a baroque reflection of Renaissance Gothic. The interior was to be a lovely representation of the optimistic sentiment that prompted the sending of gifts from across the globe. Fitting out the building as an international project was the idea of Baron d'Estournelles. It was d'Estournelles's idea and it was his hope that such donations would give all nations a symbolic stake in the Peace Palace and the tribunal that was to function there. He had been an occasional speaker at the Lake Mohonk assemblies and a delegate to the second Hague conference. It was he who had persuaded President Theodore Roosevelt to identify a pending dispute that would furnish a first case for the arbitration court.

The main entrance door, of iron and bronze, as well as the bronze vestibule doors came from Belgium; the exterior gates of exquisite wrought iron were supplied by Germany—the gates on which, after Germany had invaded Belgium in 1914, someone had hung a sign reading "To let." For the approaches and columns, Sweden and Norway furnished granite from the best quarries; the marble columns in the vestibule were sent by Italy, which also supplied marble for flooring. Bronze and crystal candelabra came from Austria, and a variety of objects of art—precious vases, paintings, and tapestries—were obtained from Russia, Hungary, China, Holland, France, and Japan.

Turkish and Romanian rugs covered the floors, and stained glass windows for the great hall came from British craftsmen as their nation's offering. The United States supplied sculptured figures for the grand staircase, itself a gift of The Hague; there stands as well a miniature replica of the Christ of the Andes, given by Argentina, which had helped erect the original to commemorate the arbitration that brought peace between that country and Chile. A cutting of ivy for the exterior (taken from Washington's Mount Vernon) was the gift of the Daughters of the American Revolution.

While the creation of the Court was the result of a surge of strong public interest, inspired by the hope and belief that it would help ensure world peace, there was and still is public ignorance as to what went on inside the palace. Foreign service officials and diplomats and the fraternity of international lawyers who helped realize the idea knew what it was all about. But from its earliest days, the Court lacked the appeal, the charisma, that the ideal of judicial conflict resolution had won: the idea that had become so popular that statesmen bowed to it in creating a court. The media soon shared the lack of interest that marked the public attitude.

Diplomat and historian Sir Alfred Zimmern observed this with regret and analyzed it in his League of Nations history, *The American Road to World Peace*. Arguing, back in the 1920s, that although U.S. and British statesmen associated world peace with the Rule of Law "because they hope[d] to transfer to the international realm the deep respect which their peoples feel for *their own law,* with the ethical values that have become bound up with it over the years," Lord Zimmern ruefully concluded, "the relationship between the new Court set up at The Hague and the peoples whose law, or laws, it interprets is still extremely tenuous." Still relevant is Zimmern's observation:

> An English lawyer, a great devotee of the Court, once remarked to the writer that he hoped to live to see the day when the *London Times* would give as much space to the proceedings at The Hague as it was in the habit of allotting to the British Law Reports. That day still seems distant.

Charles Evans Hughes was introduced in chapter 3 as leader during the first part of the long and unsuccessful effort to bring the United States to support the old Court. His life of public service ended as chief justice of the U.S. Supreme Court, during the controversial years of the New Deal, 1933–1938. But even among lawyers, there are few who are aware that, after service as U.S. secretary of state and before being named chief justice, he had been elected to and served on the Permanent Court of International Justice (PCIJ). This was to fill a vacancy created in 1928 when John Bassett Moore, the first U.S. national to serve as a World Court judge, resigned.

Hughes relinquished his post at The Hague because President Herbert Hoover appointed him chief justice of the United States. He was sensitive, during his tenure at The Hague, to the pervasive problem of lack of knowledge of and accompanying indifference to the Court. In an address on its work at the New York Bar Association, he said:

There is profound ignorance on the subject in the most unexpected quarters. From the sort of questions put to me in this country, even by lawyers, I am persuaded that . . . there is but little knowledge on the part of most people of the facts relating to its constitution and actual working.

A strikingly similar view came sixty years later from Sir Robert Jennings, who served on the Court from 1982 until 1995 and was president from 1991 to 1994. He remarked how distant the Court must seem to lay people, "if it appears in their vision at all." The Court, he continued, is "not supposed to be newsworthy by the media," and the person "in the street seems to be invincibly ignorant of its existence."

What happens in the Peace Palace, when cases are brought to the Court (either the former PCIJ or the present International Court of Justice [ICJ]) is not at all secret. The date and time cases will be heard is published in advance, and the court is open to all who wish to attend. All the briefs and evidence submitted are released and published by the Court. (One sorry note: The UN financial crisis of recent years has had a disproportionately heavy impact on the Court, and so it has fallen behind somewhat in this.) Finally, decisions are announced, and often read from the bench in summary form, exactly as is done by the justices of the U.S. Supreme Court.

How the Court—eleven judges at first; fifteen since 1930—functions in deciding cases, the judicial process, is not confidential. Several of the judges at The Hague have spoken about and/or published papers on the subject, beginning with Judge Hughes; more recently three successive Court presidents during the last decade have written on the subject: Sir Robert Jennings, Mohammed Bedjaoui, and Stephen Schwebel of the United States.

In comparing the description of their working methods given by Judge Hughes and the three contemporary Court presidents, one is struck by one overriding fact: the original group of judges from widely diverse legal systems and national cultures worked together so well from the very start in 1922, that by 1928 they had developed a satisfactory working method. More than half a century later we see the routine described by Hughes and that which the three most recent presidents have written about resembled more than they differed from each other.

The judges of U.S. and British nationality, in their writings, took pains to stress that the "collegiality" of their bench was unaffected by the so-called Cold War, which did not end until 1989. By collegiality, they did not mean just good manners and ordinary courtesies. There was an esprit de corps; the Court, wrote Judge Hardy Cross Dillard (in pre-Court life a University of Virginia professor and an asset of the Army's judge advocate corps), is "not merely a handful of judges, but an institution, most of whose members are animated and sustained by common aims and a sense of pride and tradition."

Turning now to the Court's internal procedures, we may begin with Judge Dillard's description of the open sessions of the Court: The hearings "are held in an atmosphere of imposing solemnity accentuated by the almost cathedral-like setting of the Peace Palace, with its marble corridors, vaulted roofs, stained glass windows and majestic chandeliers. . . ." Adding to the solemnity is a practice that developed early in the Court's history. Counsel who appear for a country traditionally appear in whatever formal dress is customarily worn for appearance in the highest Court of the respective nation. Amid what is sometimes a riot of color, the English barristers come with their usual wigs.

Preceding the appearance of counsel in court is a variety of paperwork. Timing, content, and volume depend on certain variables. The first is *advisories.* The preliminaries to the making of an advisory opinion are less complex. The entity authorized to request advice will draft it carefully and either send it direct to the Court or via the secretary-general of the United Nations. Accompanying the request will be such documentation as the presenter's legal adviser or team decides may be necessary to inform the Court of background and context. All members of the League (now the United Nations) are notified that a request for advice is pending, lest any have an interest that may be affected. Each is free to file such submission as it chooses. Oral presentation is not automatic: the Court will decide whether it desires to hear from counsel.

Contentious (adversarial) cases can begin on application of a state choosing to bring another state to Court to resolve a question between them, or by mutual agreement jointly signed and presented. In these cases, there may be as many as three separate procedural steps. Two preliminary phases of a case are possible; one might be for emergency relief, where delay presents a risk of irreparable damage or loss. Possible, in cases not brought by mutual agreement, is a separate and early contest about jurisdiction, with such questions as whether the Court is empowered to hear the case, and whether consent of the defendant has been effectively given, by treaty or acceptance of the optional clause.

After the principal part of the paperwork phase of the case is concluded, a date will be set for oral presentation. A nation will not show up with only one attorney; there may be as many as six or even a dozen. The points to be argued are supposed to be divided up, but not always with success. Argument is a strictly formal affair. One attorney may not interrupt another. The judges themselves do not suddenly interrupt to ask a question. The Court president may; he also acts to transmit in writing questions suggested by his colleagues. The side questioned can, if they wish, take their time to respond, even overnight.

American lawyers would take pleasure in avoiding the peppering of questions that is most often faced in the U.S. Supreme Court, spoiling plans for an oral argument carefully worked out, and often causing premature termination—time limit expiring before a statement is complete. Moreover, they might welcome a chance to try a presentation utterly unlimited as to time. For that is the rule in the World Court. Judge Hughes, who would later as chief justice control the flashing of a red light on the lectern that can stop a speaker in midsentence, wrote that the absence of time limits at The Hague is "a paradise for advocates. . . . How I have envied them." Stephen Schwebel of the more modern Court, on the other hand, wrote, "the cases are overargued . . . often they are somewhat repetitious."

When the lawyers have finished, the process of fashioning a judgment begins. The method by which the Court arrives at a decision and issues a judgment is quite structured, so much so that a formal instruction as to how to proceed is prescribed in a resolution that was adopted under the Rules of Court. To begin with, the president outlines his view of the issues in the case. These are presented to the whole Court in a meeting; any judge may comment or suggest an addition. At this point the resolution calls for a "deliberation," a session during which any judge may speak.

"It does not follow," wrote Judge Sir Robert Jennings, "that there is no discussion." There ensue informal talks in smaller groups, sometimes as few as two. Then, after what the rule itself calls a "suitable interval," each judge is called upon to prepare a written note, to be distributed to the other judges. As in all Court proceedings, translations in English and French are required: these are provided by the hardworking registry ("Clerk's office" for the U.S. equivalent). The registrar's office is required to arrange for this distribution in anonymous form. This supposedly avoids any undue influence by any particular judge. Preparation of the note is a serious business: each judge is expected to give a well-considered outline of what he thinks the decision should be. This necessitates a careful study of the evidence, arguments, and briefs. For each case the oral presentation is promptly translated and distributed in both languages.

At this point it should be observed that the individual judges at the International Court of Justice do not, like the justices of the U.S. Supreme Court, have four law clerks each to help them with their labors. They do not have even one. Each judge must do his or her own work; the only help is what a single, very competent librarian can furnish on request.

The individual notes tend to be of very high quality. "No judge cares to appear at a disadvantage," wrote Hughes. "He does not care to disclose a failure to study the case or to apprehend its points or to appreciate the weight of the respective arguments."

The judges are given time to study, compare, and reflect on what may be as many as fourteen other notes—fifteen or even sixteen if they are ad hoc judges serving on the case. After the judges have had an opportunity to study and to consider the written notes of their colleagues, there is a further and formal deliberation. During that rather structured meeting, each judge is called upon to express a viewpoint. This (as in the U.S. Supreme Court) is scheduled in reverse order of seniority: the most recently elected judge first, the president last. This may be followed by a modest debate. Any judge is free to comment or to request from any other judge an explanation of the views given in that oral statement. At this point, it has been observed, the earlier anonymity of the written notes is lost, since recognition can come during the oral statements. But the purpose of the anonymity by then has been served in the initial decisional process.

Judge Bedjaoui tells us, "it is always stimulating" to listen to and to question brethren originating in different cultures and trained in different traditions and bodies of law. Counterposed to the value of explaining oneself and answering questions is that the process "sometimes manage[s] to shake conclusions for which one had thought one possessed cast iron justification."

These discussions may last for three or four days. When a majority trend emerges the Court proceeds to elect a drafting committee: two colleagues who will serve with the president in preparing a preliminary draft of an opinion for consideration and detailed review by every member of the Court. If the president be in the minority, the senior judge on the majority side will preside over the committee. Once completed and translated, the preliminary draft is circulated. Written amendments are invited and considered by the drafting committee. Upon review of the proposed amendments and any comments received, the committee will then prepare a working draft of opinion for a mandatory "first reading," a meeting at which all the members of the Court are to attend.

At the first reading, the working draft is read aloud in both French and English. It is then discussed with care, paragraph by paragraph. There is often as much commentary contributed by judges contemplating dissent as from members of the prospective majority. The judges who have written on the internal procedure have stressed that this session is where the content of every word and phrase is weighed. "The discussion proceeds quite slowly and meticulously," Judge Schwebel has written.

By the end of this meeting, any judge who decides to write a separate, perhaps dissenting, opinion must announce his or her intention. There is a time limit fixed for this and the opinion must be submitted to the Court before the decision is made final. The draft is circulated to all judges and read with special care by the drafting committee. The Court majority may be impressed by points made to reedit their own work accordingly. The author may then make an adjustment to the extent the separate opinion's merit has won approval.

After all this, a second reading is conducted, which proceeds more rapidly—page by page rather than paragraph by paragraph—and is concerned primarily with points of style—but not necessarily. After this reading, the final vote is held. Every judge must vote "yes" or "no"; abstention is not permitted. After the vote, the writers of separate opinions are allowed to make a final decision as to whether the opinion is to be labeled "dissent" or "separate."

The last point to be settled is whether the "official" text will be in French or English. This is intended to but does not always preclude later disagreement when there is a point made in one language that may seem ambiguous when read in the other. This settled, the judgment day is announced; the parties, press, and public—including usually the diplomatic community accredited to

The Hague—are invited to attend. In open Court the president will read the operative parts of the judgment and advance copies will be distributed.

Although admitting that the procedure overall is ponderous and slow-moving, former Judge Schwebel has written:

> [T]he parties, generally speaking at least, can be confident that they have had a full opportunity to present their positions, that the Court has considered their arguments fully, that every judge in the Court has had the opportunity to say what he thinks and to influence his colleagues and if he has not influenced them in the way he thinks they should be influenced to express his views in a concurring or dissenting opinion.

Intimately related to the need of the community of nations for confidence in fairness is the institution of ad hoc (for this case only) judges. Fashioned at the start for the PCIJ (the old Court), it proved to be a sound practice and was continued for the ICJ. It was created to meet the problem resulting when a Court limited to fifteen members has a constituency of fifty members (almost 190 now).

Since the Court's judges were international civil servants, it was considered inappropriate to assume that any judge would have bias requiring disqualification in any case wherein one of the states parties was of the judge's nationality. Indeed the record of both courts has been good (even if not perfect) in this respect. Nevertheless, when a judge of the nationality of only one of two contending parties is on the bench there is an evident "perception of fairness" problem. The press, the public, and the responsible foreign office of the contestant lacking a judge of its nationality would reasonably be expected to be uncomfortable, at the very least.

The Court's founders provided for this. When such a case arises, the "unrepresented" state is empowered to name a judge ad hoc. Such an appointee will sit with no less status or authority than any of his or her brethren on the bench. The idea is taken further when neither party to the case has given a judge to the Court: each may appoint one and there will be two ad hoc judges.

No one who is not an international jurist of standing is likely to be appointed or ever has been appointed; it is preferred, and the custom has been when possible, that a retired judge or a previous unelected nominee to the Court is chosen. In any case, such a person is required to have the minimum qualifications for election to the Court, to be free of the usual disqualification of having been connected in any way with the controversy. She or he (well before 1990, when the first elected female judge ascended the bench, there were women ad hoc judges) is obliged to take the solemn oath of impartiality that every judge avows on initial appearance. The ad hoc appointee takes a place as a member of the Court for the particular case, of equal authority with the rest. Such a judge hears arguments, may give opinion in the deliberations, and participates in review of a draft opinion and votes with the rest of the judges.

Although such judges have had a tendency to be somewhat less independent of the appointing authority than full members have been, the institution has a great advantage. It can help to forestall the feeling that a case has not been fairly considered or failed of decision on the merits. The ad hoc judge reads all the tentative opinions of the rest and sees how the case has impressed each. He or she meets in the consultations and hears every position discussed, with participation in every phase of the judicial process. If the court rules against the appointing state, the judge has had the chance to understand fairly well why it did; he or she is likely to go back with the message that whatever may be thought of the outcome, there was no question of the fairness and thoroughness of the consideration of the case. Were such an appointee not present and there was a judge of the nationality of the winning state on the bench, the likelihood of suspicion of partisan bias arising in the losing state would be far greater.

It was rare that a so-called major power, one of the five with veto power, had to appoint an ad hoc judge: from the start in 1921 and continuing today, it was an accepted custom that one of the permanent members of the League Council or UN Security Council would furnish a judge to the Court.

There is one exception to the rule that permits a state lacking a national on the bench to select an ad hoc judge. If such a nation should decline to appear, be unwilling to present its case, then it cannot appoint an ad hoc judge. But such nonappearance does not prevent the case from going forward.

That a nation might have consented to jurisdiction, either by acceptance of the "optional clause," or under a treaty, yet refuse to appear, had been contemplated at the very outset by the drafters of the Court's statute. They laid down the law very plainly: "Whenever one of the parties shall not appear before the Court, or shall fail to defend his case, the other party may call upon the Court to decide in favor of his claim." Like almost all the rest of the statute, that provision remains unchanged, illuminating the identity of the ICJ as a continuation of the PCIJ, rather than a "new" institution replacing a previous one.

The Court's responsibility in such a case is weighty; failure to appear to defend does not result in a mere perfunctory granting of a default judgment, such as some may be familiar with in domestic courts. The court is entrusted with a dual responsibility that it has discharged with care: it is directed to satisfy itself (1) "that it has jurisdiction," that is, the party not present had in one way or another agreed to have the Court pass on such a case, and (2) "that the claim is well founded in fact and law." In both endeavors, of course, it will expect, and receive, from the state that filed the case such assistance as it is capable of providing.

The World Courts have a unique character that must always be remembered as one examines the working methods. The Court is always the first to hear a case; at the same time it is the last. Therefore it does not have the benefit of sorting out the issues and the preliminary analysis of the facts that are available to an appeals court in each case. The World Court must start from scratch in identifying the issues and in distilling the essential and operative facts. This should help to explain the enormous documentation that accompanies almost every case. It also makes understandable the great length and detailed content of the oral presentations that were made before the PCIJ and that are still seen and heard at the ICJ.

In the opinion of all qualified and disinterested observers, the PCIJ functioned ably during its lifetime. Its judgments and advice were uniformly obeyed and accepted. While it did not prevent World War II, it must be emphasized that it was never given a chance to try. According to former Court Judge Stephen Schwebel, looking back at his Court's forerunner, "it was regarded as a marked success not only by international lawyers but also by diplomats and politicians."

During the Court's lifetime there occurred a promising shift in attitude on the "optional clause," the feature that had been devised to make up, to the extent that it was accepted, for the Great Powers' initial rejection of involuntary jurisdiction. In the very first years of the Court's existence, small or vulnerable nations, such as Bulgaria, Brazil, Costa Rica, Finland, Haiti, the Netherlands, and Panama, accepted the idea of advance committal to subject the legality of their conduct to scrutiny at the instance of any possible complainant that had also so agreed. No Great Power did so, until, ironically, the democratic Weimar Republic of Germany was admitted to the League—and promptly showed up its conquerors by signing. France, Britain, Italy, Spain, and the British Dominions rapidly followed suit.

This promising growth in acceptance of universal jurisdiction did not make up for two abstentions. One was the persistence of the Soviet Union—which did, for a part of the period, join the League of Nations—in declining to submit to outside judgment in international actions. The other, more dismaying after the long suspense, was the U.S. Senate's 1935 action, taken as the final refusal by the United States to join the international community.

Denna Fleming, a principal student of the U.S. policy toward international organization during the interwar period, has suggested that there was a direct relation between the U.S. Senate vote that ended any possibility of the United States joining the PCIJ and Hitler Germany's march in the spring of 1936 into the demilitarized Rhineland, the first of the major aggressions that led to the start of World War II in 1939.

During the period of the Permanent Court, there were several demonstrations of the proposition long espoused by its advocates and founders of the earlier years of the century: that the moral strength of Court rulings was such that neither the threat nor use of force was needed to secure compliance. Two were especially vivid. After the advisory opinion of 1922 upholding the power of the International Labor Office (ILO) to superintend farm labor standards, to the dismay of France whose farm employer-community had objected and prompted the request for a ruling, the Gallic delegate to the next ILO conference rose and said:

We have accepted the decision of the Permanent Court on this point with the loyalty and deference which is due to that great judicial body, and the best proof of the spirit in which we have accepted that decision is my presence here today.

More tense was the story of the reception of the ruling in the Free Zones case, which pitted France against Switzerland. The victorious power in World War I had sought to use some doubtful language in the Versailles Treaty to do away with a customs exemption that Swiss farmers around Geneva had enjoyed for a century, under an old pact. The Court gave judgment that the old treaty was still in force and directed the French to remove newly added customs stations.

Reminiscing, Harvard Professor Manley O. Hudson commented: "That was a very bold thing for an international court to do," France a recent victor in World War I and Switzerland being a weak small state. He and others then waited for word, "much concerned about what would happen we literally sat on the edges of our chairs. On the 31st of December 1933, before ten o'clock in the evening, the last of the French customs stations was taken away."

In 1940, the Nazis invaded Holland. The Court had shut down in September as the Germans entered Poland and the war spread. Foreign judges and clerks packed and left. The Dutch judge van Eysinga and a skeleton staff of registry people stayed. The day after the Netherlands surrendered, a German motor convoy swept up to the great iron gates that the German Kaiser had given the Court two decades earlier. Van Eysinga came to meet the colonel in command at the gate, looked him in the eye, and said the Court was an international institution and should not be molested. The colonel backed off.

During the occupation, members of the Wehrmacht entered individually as tourists or to use the library. In December, the local Nazi commander came and asked for a list of Jewish staff members. The Carnegie Foundation, which had assumed housekeeping functions for the duration, refused to comply. Again, the Germans backed off.

7

The Court's Second Coming

THE NEW COURT: ITS STATUTE
REVISED BUT NOT MUCH

The Japanese attack on Pearl Harbor in December 1941, followed by Nazi Germany's declaration of war, completed the discrediting of U.S. isolationism. It had begun to crumble as the Nazis swept across Europe and seemed poised to invade England. Fresh in memory was the defeat of Franklin D. Roosevelt's 1935 initiative for the Court. As plans began to develop for a new organization of nations, the need for international law and order entered the consciousness of many. With that came renewed recognition that international "law and order" needed a Court.

Within months after the Pearl Harbor disaster, U.S. Secretary of State Cordell Hull publicly called for a Court that involved the United States. Others agreed. Questions were raised not long after that. Was it to be a new Court or a revival of the old one, the so-called Permanent Court of International Justice (PCIJ)? In either case, were changes in its basic structure needed? The former Court had functioned under a charter called its "statute," which had been adopted in 1920 and was based on a model prepared at Hague II in 1907. Was the old statute still serviceable in the 1940s?

Then as now, most laypeople paid little or no attention to the Court. Those who needed to stay informed appreciated the year-by-year performance of the judges who had been at work in the Peace Palace. This was in sharp contrast with the prevailing view about the League.

There were several conferences of diplomats and international lawyers in the years between 1943 and 1945—while war was raging. The consensus of all, in the words of one participant, was that the old Court "had functioned for twenty years to the satisfaction of litigants." Since it *was a court*, what better test of its merit, or of any court, was whether the litigants were satisfied. A conference of representatives of the "governments in exile," who met with their counterparts in London in 1943–1944, agreed. In fact, a legal committee formed by the South and Central American states declared that the Court that had functioned should simply be brought back to life and allowed to resume work.

The question of changes, if any, and of "old" Court or "new," were ultimately to be settled by the founding conference of the United Nations, held in San Francisco in 1945. In preparation for that conference a Committee of Jurists was created, representatives of the nations that were preparing to attend the meeting at San Francisco, persons well versed in international law and familiar with the Court's functioning. Their proposals were considered and their work continued to conclusion by a special technical committee of the San Francisco conference.

That conference decided on an important change in the Court's relation to international organization. The principal drafters of what was to become the UN Charter, led by the United States, agreed that the Court should not be merely a parallel organization, as the PCIJ had been with the League. This led to the decision to create a nominally "new" Court, which was to be a "principal organ" of the United Nations, of equal standing with the new Security Council and General Assembly. Its statute was to be annexed to and be adopted simultaneously with the UN Charter. Original signatories to the Charter and later additional members of the United Nations were to be ipso facto (that is automatically) parties to the Court's statute, entitled to its privileges and subject to its obligations.

The San Francisco conference committee on judicial organization debated the view that there need not be a "new" court, that the PCIJ should merely be continued. A factor favoring simple continuance of the same Court was the body of hundreds of international agreements, entered into during a quarter-century, which named the Court as the place to go if disputes under the particular pact required litigation. There was reluctance to let slip this modest system of agreed-on jurisdiction.

All this was outweighed by the problem of countries that, though parties to the statute of the PCIJ, were not slated to be "charter" members of the United Nations: the Axis and its allies, and some neutrals. Their treaty rights were respected by creation of a nominally "new" Court. As designed, it will be seen—in doctrine, procedures, acceptance and application of precedent, facilities, and most staff personnel, even a few judges-to-be, under the new name of International Court of Justice (ICJ)—as a re-created or revived Permanent Court of International Justice.

Another improvement sought for the UN Charter with regard to the Court dealt with compliance with Court rulings. The League covenant had provided no enforcement machinery: there was a declaration of the agreement of members to carry out "in good faith any award or decision that may be rendered." No back up was provided save that "the Council shall propose what steps shall be taken in case of refusal to accept a Court decision." Although compliance had been superb during the League era, the committee recommended to the

San Francisco conferees, "for the reign of law and the maintenance of peace," that there be a guarantee of "exact execution of the decision of the Court."

There was proposed at San Francisco an Article 94 for the Charter, in which the first section provided an obligation that was much more explicit than the old covenant:

> 1. Each Member of the United Nations undertakes to comply with the decision of the International Court of Justice in any case to which it is a party.

The smaller powers, led by Norway, sought to impose on the newly created Security Council a specific obligation of enforcement by use of the variety of peacekeeping tools that were envisioned for the new organization. The blocking team of the United States, the United Kingdom, and the USSR insisted on diluting that proposed new clause. All that was done was to allow "recourse" to the Security Council, but without any obligation imposed on that body to act: it "may, if it deems necessary, make recommendations or decide upon measures to be taken to give effect to the judgment."

As to the Statute of the Court itself, there was but one major change (dealing with election of judges), a few minor changes, and some of a purely technical character. The one really significant change corrected a flaw in the Court's original statute that was perceived when the second election cycle arrived: in a Court whose efficiency and repute required stability and continuity, to end the terms all at once was unwise. Students of the Court agreed on this and the unofficial committees that met as World War II was winding down sought a solution.

A cue was taken from another U.S. constitutional innovation of 1787: the staggering of election of senators. The San Francisco conference committee recommended and the conference adopted without controversy a plan to have a third of the membership of fifteen on the Court stand for election every three years: all would have terms, as before, of nine years each, but no more than five, at most, would leave the Court at any one time, should election results so dictate.

A minor, but potentially significant, change modified the clause that established the seat of the Court at The Hague: "This, however, shall not prevent the Court from sitting and exercising its functions elsewhere whenever the Court considers it desirable." This seemed to preview, at long range, the coming of a truly world court.

Another change was an ironic comment on the history of U.S. attitude to the Court as well as evidence of the value of one function of the judges. Back in the 1920s the novel power given the Court to give advice on request to the League's council and assembly had been a principal pretext for resistance of some senators who were blocking U.S. participation. After the first two decades it was universally recognized that the giving of advisory opinions was a useful function that gave needed guidance. Now, in 1945, with the U.S. diplomats concurring, the advisory function was readopted *and* its availability was broadened. More than a dozen UN-related groups were empowered by the General Assembly to petition the Court directly, including the World Health Organization, the International Monetary Fund, and the International Atomic Energy Authority.

The jurists on the conference's own committee were rebuffed on a more important change that they proposed. As in 1920, when the Charter was initially adopted, the experts favored universal jurisdiction for the Court, this is, presuming consent when a state entered the United Nations. If a state did not wish to consent, it could stay out of the United Nations; by joining it consented. This is what is inaccurately but most frequently referred to as "compulsory" jurisdiction. The proposal was met with a replay of a clash of a quarter-century before. The "villains" of the piece changed: what Britain and France had done in overruling the experts was now done by the United States and the Soviet Union.

At first, prospects looked good. President Truman had but recently succeeded Franklin Roosevelt. New and not yet aware of the interests of the Pentagon and State Department, he had said: "If we are going to have a court it ought to be a court that would work, with compulsory jurisdiction." But it was not long before he modified his stand, the departmental prejudice having been shared by congressional leaders with whom he was comfortable. He must have been persuaded by their belief and the view of the State Department, that the Senate was so far behind public opinion, which apparently endorsed universal jurisdiction, that it would not ratify a UN Charter so providing.

When a Soviet representative said that his nation would be unalterably opposed to accepting a Court with universal jurisdiction, this enhanced the resistance of U.S. diplomats. They said that they feared the Soviet Union would decline to join the United Nations if the Court were empowered to give any other nation its day in court regardless of the expression of consent for the particular case.

There may have been a pervasive, underlying sentiment that survived, whether or not isolationism had, that it was too risky to submit the legality of U.S. foreign policy decisions, especially with regard to the use of force, to a tribunal that the U.S. government could not control. President Truman retreated from his expression of a need for a "court that would work." In what one delegate optimistically called "a spirit of reconciliation," the majority, that is, the smaller, weaker nations, yielded to the great power combination. As they yielded, they were consoled in the same way that they had been in 1920 (see chapter 3), by the hope that with the optional clause winning more adherents, an effective Court with something close to universal reach, would eventually be formed.

Unfortunately that was not to be. As we shall see later in this chapter, when the Truman administration acted on U.S. acceptance of the optional clause, inept leadership or worse undermined the U.S. Senate subcommittee's effective support. The full body was brought to reverse it; as explained in chapter 16, the result was to undermine the effectiveness of the Court's defense of the Rule of Law.

When completed, the UN Charter and the ICJ statute were adopted by the delegates in San Francisco. On the very same day, without apparent ironic intention, a separate conference began to work on another charter: vesting power in an international military tribunal to sit in judgment at Nuremberg, on major war criminals of the immediate preceding period. Supreme Court Justice Robert Jackson, on leave to lead the prosecution, said, "The record on which we judge these defendants today is the record on which history will judge us tomorrow."

By a vote of 89 to 2, the U.S. Senate ratified the UN Charter and Statute.

RECONSTRUCTING THE COURT: WITH JUDGES OLD AND NEW

When the twenty-ninth state—the number needed to constitute a majority then—ratified the UN Charter and the Court's statute, President Truman himself made the announcement and added, "The charter of the United Nations came into force as a fundamental law for the peoples of the world."

Now the time had come to select the judges who would have the responsibility and authority to interpret and apply that "fundamental law." The rules guiding conduct that made up the "Law of the Charter" were, collectively, a significant addition to the entire body of international law. The whole of it was identified in the statute in four categories:

- "international conventions [treaties], whether general or particular," among which the Charter itself, by its own terms, became supreme
- "international custom," the "common law" of nations
- "general principles of law recognized by civilized nations"
- as "subsidiary" to the foregoing, the lessons learned from earlier court rulings and the "teachings" (scholarly writings) of qualified jural scholars

The Court's 1939 election had been canceled by the outbreak of Hitler's war. The judges became holdovers with no judicial duties. In late October 1945, the surviving members were called together for a closing session at the Peace Palace. Their final action was to continue their registrar in office, with instructions to serve until he could turn over to the coming International Court of Justice the archives, case records, and library of the PCIJ. They also recommended most of their staff to the coming Court.

In January 1946, the first session of the UN General Assembly met in London, and deliberated on a new round of nominations, following the procedure of the PCIJ. On February 6, the Security Council and the General Assembly elected the first group of judges to serve on the International Court of Justice. Symbolic of the continuity of the "old" and "new" Courts was the election of several judges formerly with the PCIJ. José Gustavo Guerrero was one of that first group of World Court judges. He had been elected to the PCIJ in 1930, after a career as a diplomat and participant in international juridical assemblies. In 1936 he was elected president of the old Court, and as it turned out, was the last to hold that title. Judge Guerrero was promptly elected president of the new Court for an initial term. This was followed by a term as a vice president, and he continued to serve with the ICJ until 1958.

Writing in the *American Journal of International Law,* Judge Hudson briefly summarized the functions of the office that Judge Guerrero had just left: "The President is far more than the director of the public proceedings devoted to hearing Agents and Counsel appearing in cases before the Court. He is the guardian of the strictly judicial tradition of the Court. Upon him falls the delicate task of threading the deliberations of judges to conclusions which will command the world's assent."

Another ICJ holdover from the PCIJ was the Belgian scholar-jurist Charles de Visscher, first elected in 1937, after a career combining an academic role with a variety of learned publications, as well as advocacy before the Permanent Court of International Justice, where he represented a number of nations other than his own. He went underground during World War II to serve with the Belgian Resistance, heading the political branch of the movement that served as liaison with the government-in-exile in Great Britain. Immediately before his election in 1946, he was a member of the Committee of Jurists that prepared the amendments to the Court's statute, as well as serving at the San Francisco conference itself.

Sergei Borisovitch Krylov was the first Soviet citizen to be elected to serve on the Court. Judge Krylov had studied law under the old czarist regime, and had written a thesis on international conferences. He had not only fought in the czar's army in World War I and been wounded, but also took part in the defense of Leningrad in 1941–1942. He had lectured in international law, as well as comparative constitutional law, for more than thirty years—bridging the revolution of 1917 that deposed first the czar, and then his successor, Aleksandr Fyodorovich Kerensky. Krylov served as dean of Leningrad's Institute of International Law from 1920, the year of the first Court's birth, until 1939. As legal adviser to the Commissariat of Foreign Affairs of the Soviet Union, Judge Krylov had been both at Dumbarton Oaks and San Francisco, and been a participating member of the pre-UN Conference of the Commission of Jurists.

Green H. Hackworth, the U.S. citizen who had chaired that Commission of Jurists while still legal adviser of the U.S. Department of State, was one of the first fifteen judges to be elected to sit at The Hague's present Court. (The title, "legal adviser," customary in foreign offices, is that of the highest law officer, comparable somewhat to "general counsel" in other U.S. agencies). It should be noted here that it came to be customary—even though the judges are clearly not serving as representatives of their nations—that a citizen of each of the five permanent members of the UN Security Council would win election to the Court.

In an address to an American Bar Association group in December 1945, on the eve of the first UN General Assembly, Hackworth said:

> Now we know that the mere existence of a court does not of itself solve any problems; it must be used. If the International Court of Justice is to be of maximum usefulness, the member States must come forward in good will and submit to it all international disputes of a justiciable nature which cannot be resolved by the parties; and they should do this with promptness.

Also elected in 1946 was Professor Jules Basdevant, who, under Hackworth, had served as rapporteur of the jurists' commission preceding the San Francisco conference. Basdevant was elected vice president of that first Court, and president for the three years following that first term. He had been a member of the "invisible college of international lawyers" (a concept invented by Professor Oscar Schachter, to which we shall return) since almost the turn of the century, served as French delegate to many international meetings during his professional career, and participated in a variety of arbitrations. He resigned as legal adviser during the Vichy regime in 1941, and was immediately, on order of the Germans, removed from the Paris University law faculty.

Others on the Court's first bench included jurists such as:

- Bodhan Winiarski of Poland, who had served the prewar Polish Republic after the nation was created in 1919. During the war he was seized by German troops, escaped, and joined the Polish government-in-exile. He was twice reelected to the Court and remained until 1967.
- Milovan Zoricic of Yugoslavia, who had been with the League of Nations in the interwar years and was appointed on occasion to function as an ad hoc judge with the PCIJ.
- Briton Sir Arnold McNair, a longtime professor of international law and respected writer-scholar in the field.

Most individualistic and colorful of that first bench was Alejandro Alvarez of Chile, whose writings before joining the Court and his role as its "great dissenter" at The Hague were notable. Although the oldest member of the Court by almost a decade, Alvarez, born in 1868, had the most modern ideas. He served but a single term on the Court, yet some of his iconoclastic views still reverberate. One of his major dissents became the "law" that led to the freedom of Southwest Africa as Namibia, de jure in 1970 and de facto in 1990 (see chapter 11).

From the start of his career, Judge Alvarez had been identified with the major established institutions devoted to the study and publicizing of the Law of Nations. Since the second Hague conference of 1907, he had been a member-arbitrator of the Permanent Court of Arbitration of The Hague. His writings were voluminous and covered many areas of the branch of the law to which he was devoted. He stressed the Latin American contribution to international law—exposing the parochialism of the European powers that had limited the first Hague conference by excluding most of the American nations. He had won the notice of many and the regard of the usually tight-lipped President Calvin Coolidge.

Alvarez's viewpoint, as stated in his 1916 book, *The International Law of the Future,* was drastically affected by the impact of the Second World War of 1939–1945. His verdict now was, "After the social cataclysm which we have just passed through, a *new order* has arisen and, with it, a *new international law*. We must therefore apply and interpret both old and new institutions in conformity with this new order and this new law."

Humanity's trauma of World War II had, according to the study of Alvarez in *Dissenting and Separate Opinions at the World Court* by I. Hussain, "opened a new era in world history, more important than any previous one, including the Renaissance, the French Revolution of 1789 and the First World War." Summarizing and evaluating the impact of the body of Alvarez's work as a judge, Hussain wrote:

> In his view, the result was that in almost every field of international activity, the psychology of peoples underwent great transformation. A new international/universal conscience was born which produced a regime of social interdependence [which] rendered the old community of nations into a veritable international society encompassing all States of the world, irrespective of their consent. These States had not only rights but also duties to one another and this society. Consequently, they were no longer absolute sovereigns, but interdependents . . . ruled by a law that was absolutely different from that of the classical law.

Upon the election of the new Court, the members of the PCIJ resigned en masse. The furniture, books, and supplies of the old Court, as well as its law library and case files, were turned over to the custody of the acting registrar of the new bench. Formal arrangements were made with the Carnegie Foundation, "landlord" of the Peace Palace, to lease the now vacant premises to the new Court.

On April 18, 1946, the Court held its formal inaugural sitting at the Peace Palace. Royalty, the diplomatic corps, and high officials of the new United Nations organization were present. The usual formal addresses were delivered. UN General Assembly President Spaak declared that no UN organ was more important than the Court and expressed the hope that the Court's "jurisdiction may become compulsory for all countries and for all disputes without exception." This because, "I am deeply convinced that peace will not be finally established until all countries have recognized the truth that there can be no civilized world nor any lasting peace, if there be not complete and absolute respect for international jurisdiction and its judgments."

UNDERMINING OUR OWN CREATION
WITH AN ILLUSORY COMMITMENT

The United States had ratified the Charter and was ipso facto into the Court. But what about the acceptance of the optional clause and, with it, leadership in winning global acceptance of the Rule of Law? On the day that the Charter was ratified in 1945, Senator Wayne Morse of Oregon acted, as he often did, in accordance with his own conscience. He introduced a resolution that called on President Truman to accept the option, offered by the Court statute, of agreeing to submit to suit without special agreement, by any nation that would have made a similar agreement. This was the "optional clause" for spreading acceptance of jurisdiction that a Brazilian delegate had conceived in 1920, to mitigate the Franco-British defeat of the majority sentiment for universal jurisdiction for the Court. Senator Tom Connally of Texas, chair of the Foreign Relations Committee, did not respond; he waited for "the word" from the White House.

It could be argued that no Senate or other congressional action was needed; within the scope of his broadly construed foreign affairs powers, the president could have made the commitment on his own. The treaty that the Senate already had ratified dispensed with further consent; agreement would not have been a "new" treaty that required further Senate action. Even if a commitment to submit to universal jurisdiction did require Senate ratification, the procedure followed was peculiarly inverted.

The president did *not* (as he ordinarily would have, if he thought "advice and consent" were required) submit a proposed agreement for Senate action. The White House, moreover, did not respond on the record to the Morse initiative. It seems to have been shelved at the administration's request. Nothing further happened for four months. Late in that period, Senator Morse quietly rounded up fifteen other senators, reportedly with State Department aid and approval, for another resolution proposing acceptance of judicial settlement of legal disputes with other nations. This time, modest limitations were included in the recommendation: one, barring submission when we and our adversary had agreed to some other means of decision; second, reserving disputes "essentially within the domestic jurisdiction of the United States." As written, that last seemed unexceptionable; it paraphrased a subparagraph of the UN Charter (Article 2.7). The Court's own statute limits it to disputes involving treaties and other aspects of international law, Article 36.1, and the very optional clause itself, Article 36.2, plainly restricts obligatory jurisdiction to international law matters.

Now, inexplicably, the revised Morse resolution was stalled for an additional eight months. Nor did there come from President Truman, who had once said no Court could be useful without compulsory jurisdiction, a bid for advice and consent. Finally, as if by secret signal, the Senate committee's hold on its own members' proposal was unlocked for hearings on U.S. acceptance of the optional clause.

During three full days, despite months of advance notice, no opposition at all was offered by witness or written statement to U.S. submission to the Rule of Law. A variety of organizations expressed support for acceptance of the optional clause, led by the American Bar Association and the American Society of International Law. The subcommittee's conclusion was that there was "relative unanimity of American public opinion" backing the action they recommended. Epitomizing what the witnesses wanted the Senate and the White House to know, was a statement made by Undersecretary of State Dean Acheson, who proclaimed: "The record of the United States in its international dealings is such that it should not dread to have its acts reviewed by a court of law."

The committee report resolved the troublesome "domestic jurisdiction" reservation with unanimity. They settled among themselves the question as to who was to decide the limits of the category "domestic jurisdiction." Here is how they saw it:

> The question of what is properly a matter of international law is, in case of dispute, appropriate for decision by the Court itself, since, if it were left to the decision of each individual state, it would be possible to withhold any case from adjudication on the plea that it is a matter of domestic adjudication.
>
> A reservation of the right of decision as to what are matters essentially within domestic jurisdiction would tend to defeat the purposes which it is hoped to achieve by means of the proposed declaration.

In sum, they accepted the view that Dean Acheson had expressed in his testimony, that the Rule of Law could not become effective if states reserve the right to decide when and how it is to be applied.

At this point, there came the unexpected posthearing intervention of John Foster Dulles, who had been an adviser on foreign affairs to two-time presidential nominee Thomas E. Dewey, and was taken into the State Department during the war to give a bipartisan tone to the peacemaking process.

Dulles gave lip service to the concept of compulsory jurisdiction. He then suggested a number of restrictive reservations, "in language characterized by deep suspicion of international law and the Court," as later described by distinguished Cornell Professor Herbert W. Briggs, lead committee witness at the hearings. The view that Dulles expressed, that international law had not yet "developed the scope and definiteness necessary to permit international disputes generally to be resolved by judicial rather than political tests," revived in Senator Connally, chair of the Senate Committee on Foreign Relations, all the old fears concerning the Court. As Denna F. Fleming put it, "In spite of the fact that Connally's full Committee had sent the resolution to the Senate unanimously, Connally offered in the Senate an amendment which once more drew the protective robes of the Senate around the mighty and unique United States."

What had he done? In effect, Connally double-crossed his own committee and canceled out their vote. To the reservations that limited the granting of U.S. consent to compulsory jurisdiction (to "disputes with regard to matters which are essentially within the domestic jurisdiction of the United States"), he added the fateful words, "as determined by the United States." The meaning of what he proposed was to reserve an unlimited unilateral veto power to the United States when a policy was questioned at the Court: whether relating to tariffs, immigration, or testing nuclear weapons—regardless of treaty commitments, we could immunize ourselves from Court review by refusing to submit to suit by declaring that we "determined" the dispute was within domestic jurisdiction.

"These six words ['as determined by the United States'] took us back to the year one," wrote Fleming. "They withheld from the Court perhaps its most fundamental function: the duty to decide . . . whether a particular case is wholly within domestic jurisdiction or whether it has international aspects that are justiciable."

The very statute of the Court provided, as he pointed out, that "in the event of a dispute as to whether the Court has jurisdiction, *the matter shall be settled by the decision of the Court*" (Section 36.6, emphasis added). The United States had already committed itself, by ratifying the statute of the Court, to the treaty obligation contained in those words. "The United States was not blithely free to act," added Fleming, "a reservation which negated [the Court's] jurisdiction was clearly illegal."

Connally's reversal ignored the potentially self-defeating nature of the added reservation. The optional clause, in its own words, is effective only "in relation to any other state accepting the same obligation." This principle of "reciprocity" limited the scope of the area within which any state could be involuntarily sued, to that on which the suing state could be taken to Court. The effect of Connally's clause was that any nation we sued, no matter how broad its consent, could claim its words were automatically limited so that it was no wider than ours.

A handful of senators, led by Claude Pepper of Florida, resisted the reversion to primitive isolationism called for by Connally ("We do not propose to have . . . alien judges . . . decide what question is international") but without avail. The Senate voted, 51 to 12 (thirty-three senators abstained out of fear or shame), to violate a treaty they had ratified only a year earlier. Pepper's point, that it was "fundamental in law that no one can judge his own case," was ignored.

Adoption of the Connally "self-judging" amendment, vitiating acceptance of the optional clause, was itself judged by the State Department's Ernest A. Gross, who was U.S. ambassador to the United Nations in the early 1950s: "Insistence upon keeping the key to the courthouse in our pocket is strangely out of keeping with the traditional American respect for the judicial process as prime guarantor of the rule of law." A more acerbic comment was made in 1928 by Manley O. Hudson, commenting, "the expression of the sentiment [U.S. loyalty to arbitration] has become so conventional that a popular impression prevails that it accords with the actual policy of the United States."

NEW WORLD OF THE "OLD" COURT

The Court was new in name, but as we have seen, save for a few changes in its statute and its designation as "principal judicial organ" of the United Nations carrying ipso facto membership of all UN members, it was a continuation of the Court that opened for business in 1922. While the old Court had been the dream of peace advocates for many years, it had actually been a novelty when it began to function. Diplomats and practical-minded statesmen had been understandably hesitant and doubtful. The group that ascended the bench in 1946 had a great advantage over its predecessor of 1922.

The new institution was familiar in world capitals and enjoyed approval for past performance. As it resumed, there was every reason for international adjudication to play an increasingly significant role in smoothing relations among the world's states, and to fulfill the promise that its early ardent advocates had hoped to see: substitution of the Rule of Law for threat or use of force to settle international problems.

The Court that began functioning in 1946 was faced at the outset with a daunting disadvantage, however: two great, unprecedented global conflicts that had been incubating during the final part of World War II emerged to dominate the postwar scene. The world came to be divided, increasingly, between what people came to call "East" and "West" and between "North" and "South."

The leading adversaries in the East/West clash were the two major allies who had together collaborated in winning the war and in shaping the new international postwar world organization: the United States and the Soviet Union. The suspicious and the traditionally hostile officials in each of these nations doubted that their alliance would last. Their pessimism became something of a self-fulfilling prediction. Each nation was led to foster and even create its own allies and satellites. Their conflict has gone down in history as the not very accurately named Cold War. It had a disheartening, disruptive effect on the functioning of the institutional arrangements they had put in place to preserve the peace—including disregard or attempted manipulated use of the Court by those who had concluded it was necessary to judge their law compliance for themselves.

The North/South division was one of a different sort. It began as the uprising of the colonized against the colonizers. As the victory of each former colony was won, in gaining statehood and an often nominal independence, another source of discord came to be called "haves" versus "have nots," or the "developed" versus the underdeveloped."

With all its differences and rivalries, the constituency of the earlier Court was a comparatively coherent, mainly European, community of nations. The growing number of states that were former colonies, the increasingly widespread instability of governments, and the jockeying for power or other advantage between the major combatants, created a different milieu for the Court that followed World War II. Despite all this and despite intermittent periods of involuntary inactivity, the Court compiled a creditable record. An impressive array of international law questions (controversies settled, treaties interpreted) were answered in the contentious (adversarial) and advisory (furnishing guidance) rulings of the Court. Much of the remainder of this book assembles and presents a picture of a good deal of this work. The cases are collected and classified by subject matter rather than simple chronology.

8

Advice about the UN Charter and Others

In its early years, the new International Court of Justice (ICJ) proved once again that the function of giving advisory opinions, when requested, was useful and a genuine asset. At times, the advisory device may have been used to gain a fancied advantage during the continual fencing of the Cold War. Apart from these instances there were helpful developments in international law. Problems that arose because of gaps or ambiguities in the UN Charter were solved. Other questions of importance in international relations were answered. Over the years, the cumulative effect was the transformation of the UN Charter, a paper produced at a conference table, into a living, international constitution.

NEW MEMBERS

The "charter" members of the United Nations were those nations that were represented at San Francisco and that accepted the Charter as drawn there. Provision was made for adding new members, especially those states that were absent from the founding sessions for a variety of reasons, principally because they were neutral or enemy states during the Second World War. Applications from new members were considered by the Security Council; if recommended there, the applications then went before the General Assembly for a vote. Conditions of membership were that the applicant state be "peace-loving," accept the provisions of the UN Charter, and be able and willing to carry the provisions out.

In the early years of the United Nations, admission of new members came to a halt because of the political conflict developing in the early years of the Cold War. The West declined to approve the applications of some Soviet client states, on the claim they were unqualified; a greater number, sponsored or approved by the West, were held up by exercise of the Soviet veto—a negative vote on an issue on which unanimity of the permanent members of the Council was required.

It was evident that unless the Soviet candidates were approved, the Western hopefuls would be barred. In an attempt to secure a solution for the political problem, it was decided to look to the Court for advice on the question: Was it legal for a vote on admission to be based not on the applicant's qualifications, but as leverage for approval of another candidate? A delegate from Argentina suggested that the question was being asked not to clarify the meaning of the UN Charter, but to "clarify" (meaning to spotlight) the conduct of some members. No one needed any clarification as to what was going on.

The Court answered that a state "is not juridically entitled to make its consent dependent on" anything other than the Charter conditions. The Court's answer was as futile as the question was pointless: the Security Council veto was not subject to limitation.

An interesting feature of the decision was the line-up of dissents on whether the "advice" should be given: the Court did have authority in its discretion to decline to answer any question it deemed inappropriate. Identification of the nationality of the dissenting judges showed the Court's and the judges' own independence of international political currents. Retired Judge Philip Caryl Jessup wrote of this case:

> It was one of the many instances in which those who would denigrate the Court . . . are baffled to explain how the dissenters included such a mixed group as judges from England, Canada, France, Poland, Yugoslavia, and the Union of Socialist Soviet Republics.

The UN Charter does not provide with respect to advisory opinions the same obligation of obedience imposed as to contentious, that is, adversarial cases. In this instance the reasoning of the dissents prevailed: the view that the basic character of a decision on admission of new states was political and not meant for judicial determination.

Ultimately the dissenting viewpoint can be said to have prevailed: the solution came after the General Assembly took note in a resolution of "the growing general feeling in favor of the universality of the United Nations."

THE CHARTER "IS A CONSTITUTION THAT WE ARE EXPOUNDING"

The second advisory the Court was called on to render was handled in the spirit of the words quoted above, used by U.S. Chief Justice John Marshall to explain liberal interpretation of the basic document, freedom to apply it in conformity with its purpose to achieve ends not precisely provided for in words. Called officially *Reparations for Injuries Suffered in the Service of the United Nations,* the case followed the death of a UN representative who was killed in the line of duty in Palestine in 1948.

The president of the Swedish Red Cross, Count Folke Bernadotte, was sent by the Security Council to mediate a conflict that began when the British Mandate terminated. Bernadotte was able to bring about a truce between Jews and Palestinian Arabs; he then tried to advance the idea of a united federal state with Arab and Jewish autonomous regions. Bernadotte's plan was rejected by both sides, and was said to have been particularly unacceptable to the would-be founders of the Israeli state. Three months later, while he was still engaged in his peace efforts, Count Bernadotte was murdered while traveling in a part of Jerusalem under Jewish control.

Bernadotte's successor, Ralph Bunche, an international civil servant from the United States, was aware that Israeli extremists who had been using terrorist tactics to drive out the British had been intensely hostile to Bernadotte's proposed federal solution. He reported that the assassination had been perpetrated by "Jewish assailants."

UN Secretary-General Trygvie Lie put to the third meeting of the General Assembly "the question of the right of the United Nations to demand reparations for injuries to its agents." Lie believed that the United Nations did have such a right but a legal basis for it was not at all clear. The character of the Bernadotte case offered an especially sympathetic basis for creative jurisprudence.

Customarily, an international claim—whether presented through diplomatic channels or by the use of an arbitration tribunal—could be pressed only against one nation state by another of its peers. The very word "reparations" meant, by the traditional use, an agreed-upon or adjudicated sum that represented damages for injury inflicted by one nation on another. In cases of loss inflicted on an individual he would be represented by his nation state, acting on his behalf.

Equally, if not more, serious was the question of legal authority. The capacity and powers of states to act in relation to each other were determined by the rules of customary international law, as developed over the centuries, or as amended by treaties that had gained general acceptance. But the United Nations was created by its Charter. This was, on paper, no more than a treaty among the founding nations, accepted as a condition of acquiring membership by all others. What did the Charter say, if anything, on action as a body, to assert claims on behalf of itself or its employees?

The purposes of the United Nations appear in Article 1. They were expressed in formulations that were clear and specific. Even where there were "open-end" concluding phrases—for example, "to take other appropriate measures to strengthen universal peace"—that purpose was still limited by the particular objective stated as the aim. Nor was anything to be gleaned from the statement of "Principles" in Article 2. That seemed designed only to guide the states-members in their conduct—with a cautionary "don't": The

United Nations was forbidden "to intervene in matters which are essentially within the domestic jurisdiction of any state."

In short, looking at the matter as a strict constructionist, one would be obliged to say that no power to seek redress seemed available. The state of which the agent was a national would have to be the one to act. If it chose not to do so for political or other reasons—say, disapproval of the UN mission on which the victim's life was lost—that would end the matter. And of course, what if the perpetrator was even instigated by the terminated agent's own state?

The General Assembly debated the report of the secretary-general on the murder of Bernadotte, in the same way that a legislative body of a democratic state would react to the killing of a diplomatic representative abroad. Some thought the issue required the making of new law by the Assembly itself; others felt that an affirmative answer to a request for advice, by the ICJ, could solve the problem. The majority thought the Court would help. The Court did so— and did not confine itself to a mere "Yes, the United Nations can assert a claim." Once more the functioning of a UN organ was aided by use of a modus vivendi borrowed from, or resembling, a key aspect of U.S. constitutional development.

This time, in a single major opinion (later to be supplemented) the Court applied the same expansive technique that had characterized early U.S. Chief Justice John Marshall's creative application of the U.S. Constitution. Granting generous respect to the breadth of purpose of the Framers and regard to the logical implications of their intention was the phrase Marshall used in one major opinion: "We must never forget that it is a *Constitution* we are expounding."

In a lecture given in 1982 to the students of Syracuse College of Law, the Court's then senior judge, Manfred Lachs, used two quotations from subsequent opinions by Justice Holmes to describe the judicial process that gave the *Reparations* case an "international context." In one Holmes said—and we substitute "Charter" for "Constitution"—"its provisions . . . are organic living institutions . . . [whose] significance is to be gathered not simply by taking the words and a dictionary, but by considering their origin and the line of their growth."

After reviewing the tragic events and General Assembly proceedings that gave rise to the request for advice, the Court said, "To answer this question, which is not settled by the actual terms of the Charter, we must consider what characteristics it was intended to give to the organization." Essential to the affirmative answer was the Court's finding—central not only to the opinion but to the future course of development of the law of the United Nations— that the organization possessed an "international personality"; that is, it was not merely an association of nations but was also an independent being, an entity apart from them, as a corporation has a personality apart from its individual stockholders. The Court explained that it had come to that conclusion on the basis of what had happened at San Francisco where the Charter was produced: "Fifty states, representing [in 1945] the vast majority of the members of the international community, had the power, in conformity with international law, to bring into being an entity possessing objective international personality, and not merely personality recognized by them alone."

The words "necessary implication"—hallmark of U.S. constitutional development by liberal construction, beginning in the days of Chief Justice Marshall—were used in a similar way: under international law, the organization must be deemed to have those powers that, though not expressly provided in the Charter, are conferred upon it by necessary implication as being essential to the performance of its duties. And so, added the Court (which had been unanimous in holding the United Nations could recover for damage to itself), the organization could claim in behalf of its agent's next of kin, "in claiming reparation based on the injury suffered by its agent, the Organization does not represent the agent, but is asserting its own right, the right to secure respect for undertakings entered into towards the Organization."

Judge Lachs maintained that the *Reparations* opinion ranks as a "landmark in the development of international law." He told his 1982 audience at Syracuse, "For the first time in history, an institution other than a State was recognized as a subject of international law. A whole series of political and legal consequences followed from these statements of the Court. . . . In 1949, during the formative years of the United Nations, states were still unsure what standing the United Nations would have and what relationships would exist between the organizations and its members."

There was the usual absence of media coverage that continues to cramp public understanding and knowledge about the role of the Court. The *Reparations* decision made little impression on the general public—this despite the global sensation attendant upon the assassins' attack on the UN peacemaking envoy.

The potential impact of the *Reparations* case as establishing the unitary and independent character of the United Nations as an entity independent of its states members has not yet been fully realized. Its converse has presented itself in at least one case in the former Belgian Congo, where members of the UN force, who had been sent to keep order amid the postindependence chaos, had looted property. After a claim was filed and investigated, the United Nations conceded its liability as a legal "person."

As to the claim against Israel, which had been the occasion for the advisory on *Reparations,* there was no problem. Ordinarily states interested in or possibly affected by the rendering of advisory opinions are notified formally of their submission to the Court and given an opportunity to be heard; the state of Israel was quite silent during the proceedings. When the claim for the damages the United Nations had sustained was presented, it was promptly paid in full by the government at Tel Aviv. Bernadotte's widow declined to make a money claim to be presented by the United Nations on her behalf.

THE ASSEMBLY'S RIGHT TO INQUIRE:
HUMAN RIGHTS-LINKED CASES

The UN Charter declares its founders' concern for human rights in its preamble and several of its articles. That interest was taken into account in several major advisory opinions. In addressing them the Court modified a rule laid down by the Permanent Court of International Justice (PCIJ) in which a request for advice could not be used to settle a dispute between states and thereby circumvent a nation's refusal to consent to exercise of the Court's jurisdiction.

Obligation to Arbitrate Human Rights Claims

When the Allies made peace in 1945 with states that had been dominated by Nazi Germany (Bulgaria, Hungary, and Romania), the treaties included human rights provisions. Guarantees for the inhabitants against discrimination because of race, sex, language, or religion were accompanied with assurance of the "fundamental human freedoms, including freedom of expression, etc. and public opinion and of public meeting." Bulgaria and the others, when liberated from German control, came under Soviet influence, with the continued presence of the Red Army units that had driven the Germans out. But then the laws supposedly intended to eliminate or control remnants of Nazism were used, as alleged by the United States, to repress others. The case of Cardinal Mindzenty in Hungary is an example.

The treaties each contained an arbitration clause, which the United States and the United Kingdom attempted to activate by notes proposing the appointment of an arbitrator by each side. Provision had been made for the UN secretary-general to appoint a third, neutral arbitrator, if the two designees could not agree. The UN General Assembly was also notified of the attempt to settle the dispute by the treaty method. The accused regimes rejected the request to appoint arbitrators and, in the UN debate, rejected diplomatic intervention as interference with matters solely of domestic concern.

Not willing to allow the cases to be closed by the refusal to arbitrate, the United States and the United Kingdom prevailed upon the General Assembly to submit a four-pronged request for advice to the Court. The four questions were:

1. Were there disputes between the parties to the treaties?
2. Were the respondent states required to appoint the respective arbitrators?
3. If the answers to questions 1 and 2 were "yes," could the secretary-general appoint the neutral arbitrator, if the state accused refused still to participate?
4. Could the resulting two-person board have the competence to decide the dispute?

The hearing on a request for advice can become two-sided, even though it is not formally an adversarial or contentious case. Since all states are notified when a request is filed, and each has a right to be heard and to give its view on the issue, there was opposition in the *Peace Treaties* case. One argument was that it was really, on the one hand, a controversy between the United States and its allies, and on the other, the states allegedly violating human rights. That this was superficially true and that Bulgaria and other nations had not consented to be sued did not trouble the majority of the Court. U.S. State Department Attorney Benjamin V. Cohen argued that the Charter, unlike the League covenant, was more than a mere treaty; it was the "constitution of the international community" (a claim made with a bow to the *Reparations* case language on that subject). Therefore, he said, the UN Charter authorizing advisory opinions "on any legal question" justified adjudication regardless of lack of consent.

In accepting this position the Court said, "no State . . . can prevent the giving of an advisory opinion which the United Nations considers to be desirable in order to obtain enlightenment as to the course of action it should take." Decision in the four questions was divided: on questions 1 (Was there a dispute?) and 2 (Were states required to appoint an arbitrator?), the answers were "Yes." But on questions 3 (Could the secretary-general appoint a neutral mediator if the state party refuses?) and 4 (Will the resulting two-arbitrator board have power to act?), the answers were "No."

Advisory rulings do not give rise to an enforceable duty. The affected states chose not to be guided. The negative answer to the third and fourth questions made any real benefit impossible at the time. But the lesson it gave was applied in future treaty drafting: it became customary to make provision for default appointments.

Effect of Reservations in the Genocide Treaty

We have met the concept of a "reservation" to a treaty: a condition of acceptance imposed by a person or entity that has power to ratify. In the case of the Versailles Treaty of 1919, the U.S. Senate used reservations as part of tactics to defeat the treaty. Not all reservations have a sinister purpose.

If only two states are involved, they will have to renegotiate, unless the reservation is accepted. International law had previously been unclear as to the effect when one of a multiparty treaty refuses ratification with a reservation. Prior law had been marked by different practices and frequent disputes. One school of thought insisted on a "unanimity" rule: no completed deal unless all other parties to the treaty acquiesce in the reservation. There were variations.

The problem was important to the functioning of the United Nations because the Charter made the secretary-general responsible for publishing treaties deemed effective. Another modern concern came from the number of multiparty pacts that require a percentage of ratifiers before going into force. After discussion of the issue at the General Assembly proved to be inconclusive, it was decided to submit the issue to the Court for advice. The Treaty for the Prevention and Punishment of Genocide had acquired a flock of reservations: it was selected as a good vehicle to carry the question.

The jurisdictional question—whether to entertain and consider the question—was not difficult for the Court. The General Assembly had been directly involved in the drafting and circulation of the genocide agreement. The Court stated, "In these circumstances, there can be no doubt that the precise determination of the conditions for participation in the Convention [Treaty] constitutes a permanent interest of direct concern to the United Nations."

The result of the submission of the *Reservations* question, unlike the *Peace Treaties* issue, was a complete success. The Court set out an improved and useful formula under which reservations were to be deemed valid if (and only if) compatible with the object and purposes of the Treaty. The Court's formula (as in other great multinational issues) became conventional law as well as common (customary) law for the nations: it was accepted by the drafters of a new multinational agreement on the interpretation and application of treaties.

UPHOLDING THE UN'S JUDICIAL
PROTECTION OF STAFF RIGHTS

It was inevitable, after the UN Secretariat settled at its new New York headquarters building, that the new organization would be scarred by the forces collectively called "McCarthyism," which peaked in about 1952. There were serious, even tragic in some instances, consequences in the impact on U.S. nationals who were working on the UN staff.

Articles 100 and 101 of the Charter were designed to guard the international civil service character of the secretariat: for example, Article 100.2, "Each member [nation] . . . undertakes to respect the exclusively international character of the responsibilities of the Secretary General and staff and not to seek to influence them in the discharge of their responsibilities." Domestic U.S. political forces that disregarded their own constitution and its human rights safeguards could not have been expected to respect that feature of the Charter—and did not.

Despite the plain language of the Charter, congressional committees pushing the McCarthyite agenda, with Secretary Dean Acheson's assistance, moved to attack the United Nations. They pressed Secretary-General Trygvie Lie to dismiss employees who exercised their constitutional rights at congressional hearings. Obviously, their UN staff performance had nothing to do with their actions at the hearings. Lie caved in and fired them. (He later wrote, "Being human, I of course made mistakes.")

The General Assembly had previously created an Administrative Tribunal, conferring on it independent judicial authority to hear appeals of staff members who alleged violation of their employment rights. The tribunal heard the appeal of twenty-one workers fired by Lie. It held in favor of eleven, and directed reinstatement of four. When Lie refused to reinstate any (permitted under the tribunal's ground rules) a total of $180,000 in damages was awarded.

Predictably, the U.S. Congress passed a joint resolution forbidding payment out of U.S. dues of the legally granted sum. It was the time in the United States that historian David Caute called "The Great Fear." The U.S. mission to the United Nations fought to have the General Assembly ignore the verdict of the very judicial body it had empowered to investigate and decide.

At this time—before the wave of decolonization and the addition of many new members to the United Nations—the United States usually could count on a mechanical majority in the Assembly. Not this time, though. Nations who were usually "allies" voted their conscience. They felt the Assembly was morally bound to honor the tribunal's decision. Instead of simply refusing U.S. demands, it decided to go to the Court for advice on the question of whether, under the law governing international organizations, the Assembly had the power to overturn the tribunal's findings. As a monograph on advisories of the ICJ concluded, it did so "less, perhaps, for clarification than for support."

The Assembly voted, 41 to 6, to ask the Court if it "had the right on any grounds to refuse to give effect to an award of compensation made by the Tribunal in favor of a staff member of the United Nations whose contract of services has been terminated without his assent." U.S. State Department attorneys submitted vigorous written and oral statements arguing that the Assembly had power to void the awards.

On July 13, 1954, with three judges dissenting, the Court held that the General Assembly had no right on any ground to refuse to give effect to the tribunal's award. It rejected the theory advanced by the United States that the General Assembly is all-supreme in budget matters, and is uncontrolled in use of the budget power. The Court further stated that, under the Charter, the Assembly has "a power to make regulations, but not a power to adjudicate upon, or otherwise deal with, particular instances . . . and in view of its composition and functions [the Assembly] could hardly act as a judicial organ."

The verbal response of the United States came from Senator William Fulbright, then a member of the U.S. delegation: "While the United States delegation did not share the Court's opinion as to the relationship between the Administrative Tribunal and the principal organs of the United Nations, it would maintain its consistent policy and continue to respect the Court's authority and competence." But the resolution barring payment from U.S. dues remained, and the secretary-general had to pay out of a special fund.

A comparable episode took place at the UN Educational, Scientific, and Cultural Organization (UNESCO), when four employees were denied contract renewal for refusing to appear before a body called the U.S. International Organizations Employees Loyalty Board. After a deliberate rejection of the UNESCO director's views, the tribunal overruled the negative personnel action. The U.S. UNESCO board member insisted on taking the issue to the Court, which rendered another prorights decision, and the U.S. board member declared that "since the U.S. government has a long tradition of respect for international law, it would not contest [the Court's] ruling."

"EXPOUNDING" THE CHARTER FURTHER: PEACEKEEPING AND CERTAIN EXPENSES

The word "peacekeeping" does not appear in the UN Charter. That instrument's primary declared purpose—"to maintain international peace and security"—as drafted by representatives of the recently united and victorious Allies, was supposed to have been achieved by "suppression of acts of aggression" through "collective measures" to "remove" threats to peace.

Authority and responsibility to accomplish this had been vested (seemingly exclusively) in an executive body, the Security Council, which could not effectively function without unanimous agreement; absence of that came to be called the "veto" of the five permanent members, the dominant powers of 1945 who had joined to win World War II. Their division by 1947 into two seemingly irreconcilable hostile blocs had vitiated, to a point of paralysis, the effectiveness of the security system so designed. They failed to create at once—or ever since—the essential arm of that system, the permanent united force mandated in Articles 43 to 47 of the Charter.

Even if that collective force had been created as designed by the founders at San Francisco it would not have been useful in another kind of conflict. A principal cause of many wars has been internal instability, or civil conflict. Outside meddling by other states sympathetic to one of the sides—without armed attack—can intensify and prolong such conflict. The Charter-designed force to suppress blatant aggression would be of doubtful utility in dealing with such crises.

The Court was soon to face the Charter-constitutional issue that emerged when the U.S. delegation took the lead in devising a remedy. It was to fill the gap that resulted from the Security Council's nonfunctioning peace-protecting powers. The major case that developed was a sequel to the passage by the Assembly, in late 1950, of the resolution that became known as "Uniting for Peace." Noting the lack of "restraint" in use of the veto by the Council, and its failure to provide the forces provided for by Charter Article 43, the Assembly announced its intent to "recommend" collective action when deemed necessary. In his argument in support of the resolution, which was to pass by a vote of 40 to 5, with 12 abstentions, U.S. Ambassador Benjamin V. Cohen dealt with the position taken by the East bloc: that strict construction of the UN Charter would not permit the assumption of such responsibility by the Assembly.

Cohen's argument was a preview of and set the tone for the later presentation of the U.S. side of the issue at the ICJ. Its success marked still another contribution of U.S. constitutional history to the development to the Court. Ambassador Cohen employed what international law professor and writer/editor Thomas Franck called "the uniquely American argument that the UN should follow our Supreme Court's practice of construing the Constitution flexibly." The historic path that had been followed since the days of Chief Justice John Marshall in the early nineteenth century allowed the system to create new methods of meeting difficulties unanticipated by the Founders—as long as they were not clearly forbidden by the language of the document. That view was based on the 1819 U.S. Supreme Court case of *McCulloch v. Maryland,* rejecting the notion of "strict construction," when a constitution was involved. Led by Marshall, the Supreme Court sustained the power of the U.S. Congress to charter a bank, despite the failure to include such authority among the carefully enumerated powers of the Congress.

The U.S. position was to be vindicated by the ICJ. Twice in the decade after passage of "Uniting for Peace," the Assembly used the powers claimed in the resolution. The first of these Assembly initiatives was launched in 1956. In the turmoil that followed Egyptian nationalization of the Suez Canal (owned mostly by French and British interests), Israel began an invasion aimed at a major canal port, from which her shipping had been excluded. France and Britain vetoed Security Council action to demand a cease-fire and withdrawal. The vetoes were followed in a day by Anglo-French invasions, which were checked and terminated by joint U.S.-Soviet demands.

At an emergency Assembly session, a resolution calling for a cease-fire and withdrawal to 1948 truce lines, to be supervised and policed by a UN joint force, was adopted. The Assembly called on the secretary-general to recruit the force. It was to be financed out of the UN budget—contrary to the practice envisaged in the Charter, which contemplated the contribution of troop units by powers that could afford to pay them. The force thus created (UNEF, for UN Emergency Force) was rather small, never exceeding 6,000 troops. Its purpose was to separate and observe the combatants, rather than to enforce collective action against either. This was the role to become known as "peace-keeping," a word and concept unknown to the Charter.

A similar force was created four years later when, after the turbulent transition of the former Belgian Congo to independence, the new state was endangered by a complex of internal and external forces. Called ONUC (for the French acronym), the new force, although launched "legitimately" by the Security Council, had to be adopted and taken over by the Assembly under Uniting for Peace, because changing winds of political influence altered the attitude of permanent members of the Security Council.

The refusal of France and the Soviet Union to pay their respective shares of the costs of UNEF and ONUC, motivated by policy differences but based on plausible claims of constitutional legality, brought the United Nations to the verge of a financial crisis. The argument that each defaulting member made—that because of the legal doubts, the assessments levied were not legitimate expenses of the organization—gave U.S. lawyers the opening for presenting a case to the Court that would vindicate the Assembly's powers as they had been exercised in the peacekeeping operations.

While the Charter limited the Assembly in almost every respect to discussions and recommendations, there was one supreme authority that the Assembly had: the power of the purse. The United States had tried to use this power in the case of the McCarthyite dismissals but the Court did not allow that to be done. But in the controversy over peacekeeping expenditures, it was felt, that problem did not exist. The Assembly had the exclusive power to "consider and approve the budget of the organization" (Article 17.1 of the Charter). And further, Article 17 stated, "The expenses of the Organization shall be borne by the Members as appointed by the General Assembly."

Under the leadership and the prompting of the U.S. delegation, the Assembly focused on the issue of whether the actions taken—under the Charter normally thought to be the responsibility of the Security Council—were legal, despite the variety of contentions made by the Soviets and the French. The Assembly used its power to request an advisory opinion to inquire, because of its need of legal guidance "as to the obligations of Members . . . in the matter of financing the United Nations operations in the Congo and the Middle East," as to whether "the expenditures authorized . . . constitute 'expenses' of the Organization within the meaning of Article 2, paragraph 2, of the Charter."

The French legal advisers saw danger for their case in that submission's wording. The ingenuity of the U.S. lawyers might enable to Court to duck, or bypass, what they saw as the real issue: flagrant violation of the Charter's intent to confine use of force to the Security Council subject to the veto. They sought to amend the formal request for the advisory, so as to force the Court to confront directly the bypassing of the Council's veto by the UNEF and ONUC actions. But the French amendment was defeated.

Even in the tricky formulation in which the case was now presented, there remained a risk in taking it to Court. There was no doubt that "a literal [strict] reading of the Charter left the Western powers with a . . . difficult case," as one sympathetic onlooker said. Britain's Professor Akehurst declared that the "legal basis for the creation of the force is obscure and controversial." The Court began its majority opinion with a deft parry: "expenses," it said, were the cost of carrying on the organization's work: if the money spent had been used for a purpose identified in the Charter, that should be all there was to it. But the opinion drafters did not confine themselves to that. They noted that the Security Council had "primary" responsibility for enforcement—but then observed that "primary" does not mean sole or "exclusive." Moreover, it stressed, there was no "aggressor" being chastened by UNEF or ONUC: in each case they functioned where they had been sent by permission of the host state—Egypt in one case and the Congo in the other. (Israel would not permit UNEF forces on its land.)

In these, and every other step in the Court's analysis, the judges of the majority mostly followed the U.S. presentation. With the hindsight of the decades that followed, one does not find it easy to quarrel with the majority decision, and its acceptance of the then—and long-prevailing—tendency of U.S. constitutional law to avoid strict construction. Even if the paralysis of the Security Council in straight "curbing-the-aggressor" cases had ended with the end of the Cold War, the deficiency of the original Charter (as previously noted) in regard to policing combatants in civil conflict cease-fire justifies the use of the Assembly's budget powers as upheld in the case called *Certain Expenses*.

The immediate aftermath of the ruling was not as satisfactory as one might have hoped. There is no international law requiring states to submit to advisory opinions, comparable to the Charter's agreed-on command for contentious cases that parties "comply" with the Court's judgment. The technical legal status of an advisory is just what the name implies: an expression of judicial opinion for the information and guidance of the international organization that requested it—in this instance, the General Assembly. Still, respect for the Court would ordinarily, and does usually, bring agreement by individual states to go along. In this case, the nature of the political background was such that France and the Soviet Union did not change position. Quite a few other states, which had held off, did respect the Court's opinion and paid up their respective shares.

There followed a near crisis in the life of the United Nations, because of Article 19 of the Charter, which deals not with the Court, but with general dues delinquency. The provisions of Article 19 deprive a defaulting state of its vote in the General Assembly "if the amount of its arrears equals or exceeds the amount of the contributions due from its arrears equals or exceeds the amount of the contribution due from it for the preceding two full years."

The United States and sympathetic states made preparations to move to deprive the USSR of its vote. The Soviet Union replied by threatening to leave altogether. A truce was called during one session of the Assembly, when no formal votes were taken, and decisions were arrived at by a "consensus" process. Eventually in 1965, the United States backed down, and the USSR agreed to make contributions that it called "voluntary" for peacekeeping.

The late Professor Wolfgang Friedmann, a highly regarded international legal scholar, declared in his *Certain Expenses* that the matter had been one of the most important of the Court's advisories, saying that its greatness "lay in the recognition of the shifts that had occurred in the United Nations as a living organism. . . . Any constitutional document is in large measure the formulation of expectations and purposes, rather than of specific commands." Thirty years later, his view was confirmed in his *British Yearbook* essay on the Court by retired Judge Jimenez de Arechaga, who saw in the Court's action the safeguarding of "an indispensable instrument in the hands of the UN . . . and the best contribution the organization may make today to the realization of its essential purpose: the maintenance of peace and security.

9

Transnational Force and Global Law

COLD WAR VIOLENCE EXPLODES:
MINES OFF ALBANIA

The Corfu Channel is a saltwater strait connecting the Mediterranean with the Adriatic Sea. It runs along the island of Corfu, while the mainland opposite is shared by Albania and Greece. Cross-border violence struck there less than six months after the Court's 1946 inaugural session. Two British navy destroyers were hit by mines off the Albanian coast as they were passing through the channel. One sank and forty-four seamen were lost.

In a time of peace, even warships have a right of "innocent passage" through a strait that is an international waterway. This is so even when it is so narrow that a navigable part lies in a state's territorial waters. Showing no hostility, the ships had that right. Soon after the disaster, Britain sent armed minesweepers through the channel. They were not on a voyage of innocent passage through Albania's waters. It was announced that their purpose was to invade the sea off the coast of Albania to clear the Corfu Channel and to seize any mines that were found, to be used as evidence.

These events, the first violence in the Cold War, were incidental to hostilities in Greece, marked by British intervention in civil conflict before the end of World War II. The United Kingdom sought after the Germans left to prevent the anti-Nazi resistance from replacing the Greek regime that had coexisted with Nazi occupation. The conflict was adequately described by playwright and White House speechwriter Robert E. Sherwood, in his book *Roosevelt and Hopkins:* "All that was apparent on the surface was that British troops, engaged in the task of 'Liberation,' were killing Greek patriots who had been fighting the Germans." The Greek resistance fighters were being aided by Albania, then under Soviet influence. English naval forces had been using the waterway to carry aid to the Greek royalist regime. Albania's coastal guns had failed to stop this. After futile diplomatic exchanges, the fatal mine explosions occurred.

Both Britain and Albania carried the dispute to the UN Security Council, the former complaining of the mine attack, the latter protesting the hostile incursion of the minesweepers. After months of inconclusive debate, the Council passed the question to the Court. They used (for the first and only time) Article 36.3 of the Charter, which says, "Legal disputes should as a general rule be referred by the parties to the International Court of Justice." A resolution calling on the disputants to do so passed.

The United Kingdom filed a complaint at the Court about the mine attack. Although not subject to suit (Albania was not a member of the United Nations or a party to the Court's statute) the defendant sent a note to the Court, saying that it "fully accepts the recommendation of the Security Council," but that the complaint was not filed with her agreement and didn't comply with the statute of the Court. It was added that Albania "is prepared, notwithstanding the irregularity of the action taken by the government of the United Kingdom, to appear before the Court." But later, before the case came on for hearing, Albania filed objections to the Court's jurisdiction. After consideration the Court accepted the case: based on the first note the defendant had sent, Albania was precluded from denying the Court's authority.

Albania bowed to the ruling. To prepare the case for hearing on the merits, it entered into a *compromis* with Britain, a formal agreement defining the issues. First, under international law, was Albania responsible for the mine explosions? Second, did Britain violate Albania's sovereign rights when the minesweepers were sent into local waters?

The Court did not confine itself to hearing arguments and reading briefs. Witnesses were heard; a commission of experts was formed, composed of naval officers from neutrals, and went to the channel to investigate and report. The commission found no direct evidence that Albania had planted the mines. But the commission reported that knowledge of the mines' existence in navigable waters was imputable to the defendant state. In the experts' opinion, Albania could have and probably did have such knowledge.

The Court held accordingly that the knowledge presumably held by Albania imposed on it an international law obligation to make known the existence of the minefield for the guidance of shipping. The opinion declared that the obligation was based "on general and well-recognized principles, namely elementary considerations of humanity, even more exacting in peace than in war . . . and every state's obligation not to allow knowingly its *territory to be used for acts contrary to the rights of other states*" (emphasis added). The phrase that was emphasized has become a source of judicial power to protect the environment.

As to the nonhostile passage of the two destroyers that were victims to the mines, Albania's assertion of a right to forbid passage without its consent was rejected.

It is, in the opinion of the Court, generally recognized and in accordance with international custom that States in time of peace have a right to send their warships through straits used for international navigation between two parts of the high seas without the previous authorization of a coastal State provided that the passage is innocent.

The Court's reasoning was reminiscent of the first case of the Permanent Court of International Justice (PCIJ) in which the barring of the SS *Wimbledon* was disallowed, since the Kiel Canal had been given status as an international waterway by the Versailles Treaty. That doctrine of the right of innocent passage was accepted by the community of nations as a standard of international conduct: in the first international conference on the law of the sea it was incorporated almost textually into the treaty resulting.

Britain's subsequent intrusion by minesweepers was quite a different matter. They were not engaged in an innocent voyage through the channel. Their admitted intent to sweep mines and secure evidence was an attempt to exercise self-assumed "police power," an exercise of authority that only the sovereign government was entitled to wield in its territorial waters.

A highly qualified lecturer before the Hague Academy of International Law later declared that the minesweeping was "undoubtedly . . . armed intervention." The speaker was Sir Humphrey Waldock, then editor of the *British Yearbook of International Law,* later a judge and president of the ICJ—and formerly himself counsel for the United Kingdom in the *Corfu Channel* case.

To the argument that the United Kingdom was entitled (in Sir Humphrey's words) "as a strictly limited measure of self-help to investigate the minefield and preserve the evidence," the Court—this time unanimously (the prior points having been by votes of 11 to 5 and 14 to 2)—replied:

> The Court can only regard the alleged right of intervention as the manifestation of a policy of force, such as has in the past given rise to most serious abuses and such as cannot, whatever be the present defects in international organization, find a place in international law.

To this, the Court, comprised in part of judges of every "great power" nationality added:

> Intervention is perhaps still less admissible in the particular form it would take here; for, from the nature of things, it would be reserved for the most powerful states, and might easily lead to perverting the administration of international justice itself.

Continuing in his lecture, Sir Humphrey explained:

> An exercise of rights of passage through territorial waters . . . and of rights of fishing on the high seas would seem to be within the principle admitted by the Court, as would also exercise of a treaty right of passage over land, such as that through the corridor to West Berlin. [The Berlin crisis had ended ten years earlier.] But the dispatch of troops to another State's territory to prevent an unlawful expropriation

of the property of nationals and other acts of a similar kind are altogether outside the principle and are forbidden by Article 2(4) of the Charter.

It should be noted that the Court's ruling on the limits of intervention and self-help was not, in the *Corfu* case, made under the UN Charter subsection referred to by Sir Humphrey. Albania, not yet in the organization, was not bound by the Charter's outlawry of "threat or use of force." But the Court was declaring that the common Law of Nations forbade Britain's forceful action; its holding was a statement of the requirements of customary international law binding on all members of the international community irrespective of the Charter.

When Albania bowed to the Court's first (the jurisdictional) ruling and appeared to defend itself in the second phase of the case, it did not do so as a dutiful member of the United Nations; members were treaty-bound to comply with Court decisions. It did so to participate in Security Council debate to comply with Charter obligations in the controversy as if it were a member. But when the Court directed that a third proceeding was needed to calculate reparations, Albania balked. She claimed that her *compromis* gave the Court power only to determine *if* compensation should be paid, not *how much*. Following a PCIJ precedent in the *Chorzow* factory case, the Court ruled that authority to determine whether compensation should be paid necessarily included authority to determine the amount due. It ordered a hearing on this phase.

As to Britain's liability for illegal use of force in sending in the minesweepers, which neither inflicted injuries nor damaged property, the Court ruled that the holding that Britain was in the wrong and condemning her action was all the compensation called for in the circumstances.

And so a third hearing was held, this time without benefit of Albania's participation. (This was the first such occurrence in the history of the Courts; it was a precedent that unfortunately has been repeated.) After getting a report from the new group of neutral naval officers that were sent there as experts, the Court issued an award of £843, 947. Albania made an offer of £20,000, and doubled it, the equivalent of a shilling to the pound or 5 cents on the dollar. The English contemptuously declined this. Some years later there was an attempt to collect from some Albanian gold that had been seized by the victorious Allies from the Germans who had taken it from Italy. That would have worked, save that the Italians put in a claim for the gold, which could not be litigated, as Albania would not consent.

So the case closed with a state's failure to obey a Court judgment, the first and only one in Court history until the 1980s. Then came the cases of *U.S. v. Iran (Tehran Hostages),* in which there was at least delayed obedience, and *Nicaragua v. U.S.,* in which two rulings were disobeyed by the United States. In the case of the hostages, it was almost a year before Iran settled by releasing the detainees and made a financial deal; Albania took forty-five years: Britain settled with her after the Cold War ended.

FORCEFUL DOWNING OF AIRCRAFT:
RULE OF LAW TEST SELF-DEFEATED

During the 1950s, the Court was relatively active. A variety of contentious (nation versus nation) cases came to The Hague for decision, involving fisheries, rights of nationals abroad, adjudication of conflicting territorial claims, and some commercial matters. None of these presented Cold War issues, though some advisory rulings did (see chapter 8). The major outbreak of violence incident to the East/West conflict, the Korean War, was not brought to the Court by either side: of course the Court cannot reach out and bring in business.

Nor can cases, however suitable, be taken to Court except in accord with the rules. A number of U.S. military planes were forced down or shot down after they had crossed and allegedly violated the borders of a number of East bloc nations. These included Hungary and Czechoslovakia, and in three cases, the USSR itself. In the middle of the decade, an Israeli plane was shot down over Bulgaria. This was a civil transport, and there was significant loss of life, including U.S. and British nationals.

These events were each followed with strong disagreements about the facts and the responsibility. There was exchange of claims about the location of the victim plane at the point where the incident occurred; whether the intrusion was deliberate, or just what the downed plane was up to; whether the plane had been warned before being fired on, or signaled to land. Mingled with these factual questions were legal issues. Apart from the inevitable question of compensation, they included such matters as the rights and obligations of states in case of accidental intrusion by overflight, conduct of interceptors, treaty law, territorial limits, and freedom of airspace.

Such questions of law and fact seem to need and could benefit from international adjudication. But they did not receive judicial examination. That they did not was not the fault of the International Court of Justice. The Court lacks the comprehensive, obligatory jurisdiction that it could have had if the wishes of the majority of the states represented at San Francisco had been respected. Instead, as we have seen, this was blocked by the refusal of the two most powerful nations, the United States and the USSR, to go along.

Nevertheless, the aircraft incidents of the 1950s, in the view of the U.S. State Department, offered an excellent opportunity for making points. In each instance, after diplomatic exchanges brought an impasse, a suit was filed in the ICJ. There was no basis for jurisdiction under the optional clause, nor was there a treaty conferring power on the Court, nor had the parties agreed to submit the particular issue to the Court—nor was it, as in the *Corfu Channel* case, a matter "specially provided for in the Charter of the United Nations." (In the *Corfu* case, the Council sent the parties to the Court.)

The United States, in filing its case, made no claim that it had a right to sue; it simply indicated that the nations involved were called upon to accept the invitation to have a court settle matters between them. There was nothing in the Charter to forbid such an attempt to secure agreement to litigate, although it is obvious, and became increasingly apparent as the cases piled up, that there was great propaganda value in offering to go to Court and challenging an opponent to agree to do so. On one occasion, Moscow protested that the United States had "acted in disaccord" with the statute by so filing; to this the United States responded merely that it was in "profound disagreement" with the Soviet Union. The United States asserted that it was initiating these cases because of respect for the process of international adjudication.

It could be said that to file suit without the slightest basis for expecting the other state would agree to be sued, was a sort of publicity stunt or propaganda ploy. Reviewing the events of this period in 1971 in a study prepared for the Council on Foreign Relations (later published in the *Vanderbilt Journal of International Law*), Professor (by then, ex-judge) Philip Caryl Jessup gently suggested that "the actual applications to the Court must be considered as gestures designed to reveal this country's devotion to the ideal of judicial settlement of international disputes and to expose the undeviating refusal by our adversaries to accept any third party settlement of disputes to which they were parties."

The Bulgaria case presented a different situation. This was a serious effort to go to Court with a good-faith belief that there was a right to sue that did not depend on a new consent by the perpetrators. In July 1955 an Israeli passenger plane, flying from Austria to Israel, strayed off course in its passage from Yugoslavia to Greece. Out of its flight path, it was shot down by Bulgarian aircraft.

Under the PCIJ, prewar Bulgaria had accepted the optional clause, exposing her to suit. It was hoped that its commitment remained effective: the Court's new statute provided that declarations accepting the PCIJ compulsory jurisdiction automatically continued "as between parties to the present statute." But Bulgaria, having joined the United Nations later, was not a party "to the present statute." So ruled the Court, 12 to 4, in the first of three cases that were brought by Israel. Britain, which had lost nationals, then withdrew.

Israel having thus been defeated on jurisdictional grounds, and the United Kingdom having admitted defeat and withdrawn its case, what could the United States do but drop its own case? It might have done so at once, had not State Department lawyers concluded that they had plausible grounds to persuade the Court to reconsider its ruling in *Israel v. Bulgaria*. Even if there was but a slim chance to convince the majority that the four dissenters in that case were right, it was worth the effort to secure a ruling on what Professor Leo Gross called "beautiful issues relating to the rights and duties of states in the event of aerial intrusion and involuntary overflight."

This was not to be. In addition to objecting to the Court's intervention on the grounds on which they had frustrated Israel's suit, the Bulgarian international lawyers realized they had another weapon: one that Senator Tom Connally of Texas, as chair of the Foreign Relations Committee had, in effect, handed to them (see chapter 7). The condition of "reciprocity" required by the Court's statute for optional submission to compulsory jurisdiction gave each state sued under the clause the right to exercise such bars to jurisdiction as the suing state's own commitment contained.

A prediction made by Senator Wayne Morse of Oregon, during the debate on the addition of the words "as determined by the United States" to the domestic jurisdiction reservation, had been fulfilled. When a case called *Certain Norwegian Loans* (*France v. Norway*) came to Court, France was suing for bondholder-citizens rights under a gold clause in their loans. But France had aped the Connally reservation as to exclusion of cases she called "domestic," and Norway invoked as a defense, despite her own unconditional commitment, a claim that (a) reciprocity entitled her to invoke France's privilege of ousting the Court in cases of solely "domestic jurisdiction," and (b) she had determined that mode of payment of foreign bondholders was a purely domestic matter, not to be decided under international law.

Bulgaria's invocation of the Connally clause in the case of the downed Israeli airliner, with loss of U.S. lives, as a purely "domestic" matter was even more absurd. And when the defense filed such an objection, the initial U.S. response was to contend that the exercise of the reservation had to be "reasonable"—a question that would have left it up to the Court.

Second thoughts overcame the State Department's legal staff. If the United States won this, they realized, then it would subject itself to review of the arbitrariness of any invocation of the domestic jurisdiction clause that *the United States* might make in the future. It was thought better to stick to the idea that our one-sided decision—that a subject was "essentially domestic," no matter how arbitrary—should be treated as final and not to be reviewed by a Court: so to protect our "right" to be arbitrary and unreasonable in walking away from a case as solely of domestic interest, the United States filed a brief saying that Bulgaria had that right and dropped the case.

Thus, the forecast by Senator Morse that the Connally words would be "self-defeating," was vindicated; indeed, it had been said diplomatically, if not in so many words, that our 1946 "acceptance" of compulsory jurisdiction, was a fraud on the international community of nations; per Sir Humphrey Waldock, "the professed acceptance of compulsory jurisdiction in the declaration is illusory."

Official public repentance came soon afterward, with the launching of a campaign by President Eisenhower and Secretary of State William P. Rogers, to press the Senate to "repeal" the Connally reservation. This would have been effected by Senate Resolution 94, introduced in 1959 by Senator Hubert H. Humphrey. It received the bipartisan support of such senators as Kenneth B. Keating and Jacob Javits, both of New York. Hundreds of law school deans and law professors joined in the circularization of a statement that:

We believe that repeal of the self-judging reservation would be a forceful and desirable reaffirmation of American concern for extension of the rule of law, and would demonstrate anew our willingness to participate in the settlement of international disputes by persuasive, rather than coercive means . . . it is as objectionable for a state as party to determine the question of jurisdiction as it would be for an individual before a domestic tribunal. We conclude that the self-judging reservation seriously reduces the effectiveness of the International Court of Justice.

Addressing concerns apparently still felt by members of the Senate Foreign Relations Committee on the subject, Senator Keating, during hearings on S.Res. 94, cited experienced observers who agreed "these judges have acted with a high degree of impartiality."

It was all in vain. The Senate never acted, despite many initiatives by Senator Humphrey, who noted and denounced, ten years later, the curious objection that had surfaced: that the United States might have to use its veto power "to override the enforcement of an adverse decision." That, he said, would "be more damaging to our international image than retaining a domestic jurisdiction reservation."

NUCLEAR TESTING:
TRANSNATIONAL ENDANGERMENT

The introduction of nuclear weaponry was a feature of the new world faced by the Court that, while of omnipresent importance, did not seem likely to present the kind of questions that were quite ready for international judicial inquiry. There was to come a time when, as the nature of the danger came to be widely seen, some in the international legal community responded. It was asked whether the use—perhaps even the mere possession—of atomic weapons was in and of itself unlawful. Known in the Law of Nations as *jus cogens,* something so inherently evil that it was an enemy to all humankind, it had been recognized for such offenses as piracy, genocide, and the like, and was to be seen as applicable to international terrorism.

As early as 1961 the UN General Assembly declared in a resolution that "any state using nuclear or thermonuclear weapons is to be considered as violating the Charter of the United Nations, as acting contrary to the law of humanity, and as committing a crime against mankind and civilization." But the Assembly does not have authority by itself to pass legislation that effectively makes international law. Nevertheless that resolution, and its later reaffirmations, represent a growing global consensus. That the Court could help give effect to the consensus (chapter 18) seemed remote.

Not all that remote, however, was the question of the legality of nuclear testing, especially in the earth's atmosphere. As long ago as 1954, it was widely realized that the environmental impact of the experimental denotation of nuclear devices was not (and indeed could not be) confined to the territory of the state engaged in the experimentation. What elevated international concern about nuclear testing to a level that could not be ignored was the disaster that befell the Japanese fishing vessel *Fukuryu Maru* (meaning "Fortunate Dragon") in March 1954. The ship and its crew and cargo had dropped their nets, unknowingly, at a point within a few miles of an area that U.S. authorities had declared closed to fishing because of nuclear testing at the island of Bikini. The Japanese did not realize they had been too close until they returned to port and had sold part of their catch.

They discovered the extent of their exposure and the impact of the radioactive fallout when a crew member died and others began to experience its effects; local consumers suffered to an extent never fully ascertained. From that point onward, there was substantial and ever-increasing agitation about atmospheric testing. This gained further strength when scientific evidence determined that the substance Strontium 90 could contaminate milk and diary products of cattle ingesting affected fodder thousands of miles away from the tests. Then the pressure on the two major nuclear powers became enormous. In 1959, the General Assembly passed resolutions by overwhelming majorities, calling for a moratorium on nuclear testing.

That set the stage for the U.S.-USSR test ban treaty that began a relative truce in the Cold War, facilitated by the Kennedy–Khrushchev settlement of the Cuban missile crisis of 1962. The 1963 Test Ban Pact provided for a halt in tests not only in the atmosphere, but also under water and in outer space. The treaty and an accompanying agreement barring nuclear proliferation were opened to other nations and more than 100 soon signed both. But France and China, probably still not nuclear powers and unwilling to be excluded while far behind or out of the running, refused to sign.

Treaties in which a great majority of nations joined, setting new standards of behavior, stimulated fresh thinking among international legal scholars. They began seriously to discuss the possibility that pacts that brought about widespread obedience to the norm of behavior defined in such agreements might also be considered as bringing nonsignatories into the agreement. Arguably, a customary rule of international law might be considered to have arisen, especially in the context of the aftermath of the *Corfu Channel* ruling. The Court there had defined it to be "every state's obligation not to allow knowingly its territory to be used for acts violative of the rights of other states."

In the early 1960s France—in striving, under influences of Charles de Gaulle, to become an independent nuclear power—had begun testing its weapons and their development in the vast reaches of the Sahara that it controlled as a colonial power. After a few tests there, the experimentation was transferred to the South Pacific, to be conducted over the atolls that were part of French Polynesia. People in Australia and New Zealand became increasingly apprehensive about the radioactive fallout, which they feared would reach them, and France was oblivious to protests. At this point the question of legality, of whether there was an international remedy, was transferred from the desks of scholars and the studies of jurists to the courtroom of the ICJ.

Petitions were filed with the ICJ on behalf of Australia and New Zealand, asserting that the French atmospheric nuclear tests disseminating radio fall-out violated their rights under international law. The legal underpinning of the case was the principle that forbids each state to cause harm to the territory, people, or property of any other. The Court was requested to order "that the French Republic shall not carry out any further tests."

This began a creative and exciting attempt to develop an international remedy for transborder aggression against the environment. It was made possible by the fact that France, New Zealand, and Australia had each agreed previously to the terms of the optional clause, that special arrangement for mutual obligation to submit to suit at the ICJ. In addition, the complaining states invoked a pact promoted by the League of Nations in 1928, known as the "general act" for peaceful settlement of disputes.

In response France became the first major power, a founder-participant in the creation of the Court, to refuse flatly to appear and to deny the Court's authority (prescribed under the statute) to determine if the parties were subject to suit. While so spurning the Court's procedures, the recalcitrant nation made the claim, in a letter sent to The Hague, that her optional-clause commitment was not binding because of a reservation excluding "disputes concerning activities connected with national defense"; France added that the general act of 1928 had become inoperative with the demise of the League of Nations.

The Court's statute provided for an interim remedy, similar to a temporary injunction under local law, called the "power to indicate provisional measures." It was known that France had scheduled a new series of tests of nuclear explosion in the near future. The Southwest Pacific states petitioners requested application of the "provisional measures" clause to prevent further injurious discharges of radioactivity while the case was being considered. France stood on her ambassador's unofficial, irregular letter denying the Court's authority and requesting the Court to strike the case from its list.

After hearing full arguments, but only from the petitioners, the Court made a quick preliminary ruling, as customary in cases where temporary emergency relief was asked. By a close vote of 8 to 6, it refused to dismiss the cases, refrained from passing on its jurisdiction, and ruled "that the provisions invoked by the applicants appear, prima facie, to afford a basis on which the jurisdiction of the Court might be founded." That supported an order to "cease tests." France, again the first major power to do so, disobeyed the order, and continued to disregard the Court, while the case was awaiting further hearing on jurisdiction, to be followed by a hearing on the merits.

But in time the Court was heeded. A communiqué was issued from the office of the president of France on June 8, 1974, followed by a note from the French Embassy in New Zealand on June 10 and a letter from the president of France to the prime minister of New Zealand on July 1. The announcement was repeatedly made that France would cease conducting the tests in the atmosphere at the end of the 1974 series. Meanwhile, the written and oral arguments to the Court on jurisdiction were presented, concluding July 11, 1974.

The announcements resumed. The president of the France held a press conference on July 25; the French minister of defense gave a television interview and another press meeting on August 12 and October 11; and the French foreign minister gave a speech at the UN General Assembly—all to the same effect, that France was abandoning atmospheric nuclear testing.

The Court interrupted its own deliberations on the then-pending question of jurisdiction. Instead of deciding, the Court, taking a note of statements made by France "in systematic and sustained and repeated fashion from June 8, 1974 onwards, to the effect that it was discontinuing atmospheric object and that the Court is therefore not called upon to give a decision," dismissed the case on a vote of 9 to 6. The Court explained that the French announcement that was repeatedly given "conveyed to the world at large, including the applicant, its intention effectively to terminate these tests. It was bound to rely on their being effective. . . . The Objects of these statements are clear and they were addressed to the international community as a whole, and the Court holds that they constitute an undertaking possessing legal effect."

Regardless of absence of agreement by France "that it was bound by any rule of international law to terminate its tests . . . the French government had undertaken an obligation." Good faith among nations requires recognition of "the binding character of an international obligation assumed by unilateral declaration," so that other states may "place confidence in them and are entitled *to require that the obligation thus created be respected*" (emphasis added).

International legal scholars were in disagreement about what the Court had done. The Court itself was divided into a number of groups, not just majority and dissent. Some observers were reminded of the not infrequently fragmented, post-1940s U.S. Supreme Court. They were reminded, too, of the Supreme Court's tradition of not deciding grave or constitutional questions if the decision could be avoided on procedural grounds. Professor Edward McWhinney has argued that the international court did just that in the *Nuclear Tests* case.

Although the mode of decision avoided the merits of the case, it achieved a substantive result. This is evident from the absence of further atmospheric testing by the French, and some others. One student of the Court's dissenting opinions concluded that the judges "opted for a sure and safe course to pin down France to cease the tests by finding it obligatory on her to honor the unilateral commitment made in the matter."

It was doubtful that the principles that would have made testing illegal under customary law had crystallized. Hence, as McWhinney concluded, the Court's solution of the problem was "imaginative and innovatory in the best traditions of World Court jurisprudence."

The breakdown of the various shades of opinion that divided the judges may not be of great interest today. But it is worth referring to one of the dissents, which questioned the technique used by the Court to "impose on France an international obligation to refrain from further nuclear tests." The complaint was that the Court had "exercised substantive jurisdiction without having first made a determination of its existence." Yet this was what France had offered, and what the Court had accepted by dismissing the case.

10

Transnational Force:
Iran and Nicaragua

VIOLATING DIPLOMATIC
IMMUNITY AT TEHRAN

The first of two cases in the 1980s involving the United States at The Hague, one that was to be titled *United States Diplomatic and Consular Staff in Tehran,* was initiated with a petition against Iran saying in part:

> At about 10:30 A.M., Tehran time on November 4, 1979, during the course of a demonstration . . . the United States Embassy compound in Tehran was overrun by several hundreds of the demonstrators. . . . Since the time of the takeover, the Embassy personnel have been held hostage. . . . Embassy records have been ransacked. During the entire time and with the support and assistance of the Iranian authorities, demonstrations have been occurring outside the compound, often quite vociferous.

This opened the case that answered the seizure of U.S. citizens (mainly diplomatic personnel) in the aftermath of the revolution that ended the imperial rule of the shah. Seized by a mob, made up mostly of student protestors, they were held with the acquiescence of the new government for more than a year.

Within a few days after the mob invaded the U.S. Embassy and seized the Americans, the United States filed a suit at the International Court of Justice (ICJ) demanding that they be freed. U.S. lawyers, as a first step, asked for provisional measures, in effect a preliminary injunction, to win their release. Speedily and unanimously, the Court gave the United States what had been requested.

Determining the Court's action, then and as the final judgment in the case, was the principle announced:

> [T]here is no more fundamental prerequisite for the conduct of relations between States than the inviolability of diplomatic envoys and embassies, so that

throughout history nations of all creeds and cultures have observed reciprocal obligations for that purpose and . . . the obligations thus assumed . . . are essential, unqualified, and inherent in their representative character, and their diplomatic function.

When the case was first filed and notice given to the government at Tehran, the Iranians failed to respond in the fashion prescribed by the rules of the Court. Instead, the Foreign Ministry sent a telegram to the registry of the Court, asserting that since the U.S. petition was confined to the question of the hostages, the Court "cannot and should not take jurisdiction of the case." The seizure of the embassy and its occupants could not, they wrote, be "studied separately" from "more than [twenty-five] years of continual interference in the internal affairs of Iran." Special attention was drawn to "the coup d'etat of 1953, stirred up and carried out by the U.S. Central Intelligence Agency (CIA): the overthrow" of the Mossadegh regime and the restoration of the shah.

While of doubtful materiality in the case concerning the hostages, the Iranian complaint was not without justification. Responsible historians agreed with George Brown Tindall, who had written:

Hatred of the United States dated back to the CIA-sponsored overthrow of Iran's Mossadegh government in 1953 [after he expropriated foreign oil properties]. Nor did it help the American image that SAVAK, the Shah's ruthless secret police force, was also trained by the CIA.

After the CIA restored the shah and ousted Mossadegh, 80 percent of Iranian oil production was granted to British and U.S. interests. By 1979, twenty-five years later, all this may have been absent from the historical consciousness of the West. It was not forgotten in Iran.

The Nigerian barrister and scholar Taslim O. Elias, who was elected judge in 1976, said Iran's request "could not be taken at all seriously. . . . An important element in the Court's consideration was Iran's obligation in international law regarding the inviolability of diplomatic envoys and embassies."

The Court did not confine itself to the treaty provisions protecting diplomats. It stressed the human rights issue:

Wrongfully to deprive human beings of their freedom and to subject them to physical constraint in conditions of hardship is in itself manifestly incompatible with the principles of the Charter of the United Nations, as well as with the fundamental principles enunciated in the Universal Declaration of Human Rights.

A close student of the Court's role and the attitude of the United States, Professor Leo Gross, called the case a "landmark in the relations of the United States and the Court." He asked whether "the United States will henceforth demonstrate its devotion to the cause of international adjudication *by deed as well as words*?" (emphasis added).

According to Warren Christopher, President Carter's undersecretary of state, the Court's inclusion of an award of reparation, as well as its order for release, contributed to the settlement of the case. It played an important part in the agreement to create a tribunal that has been quietly judging U.S.-Iran claims for two decades (chapter 14).

While the case was pending at the Court, a tragic mistake was made in Washington. President Carter, no doubt under pressure because of the public's impatience with a superpower's inability to deal with the situation, turned to the use of force. He ordered a commando-type raid to invade Iran, seize the hostages, and return them to safety. Secretary of State Cyrus Vance resigned in protest at this attempt at self-help made while the nation was seeking the aid of an international Court. And the raid failed. Defective helicopters and a crash with a transport plane brought the ill-advised effort to an end with a loss of eight lives.

The president and his advisers had disregarded a principle summarized by the Court's principal founding father, Elihu Root, half a century before: "The parties to a case, when they have submitted their controversy to the Court, might be regarded as having come under an obligation not to destroy the subject matter of the controversy or in any way to anticipate the judgment of the Court by action of their own."

The judges at The Hague were quite familiar with this principle. In the judgment they said that the helicopter raid into Iran could not be "let pass without comment." The Court summarized a sequence of events that began when the case was ready for hearing on February 19, 1980. The U.S. agent requested a postponement, allegedly due to "the delicate state of certain negotiations." Then, on March 11, he informed the Court of "anxiety to obtain an early judgment." Hearings were then held March 18–20, and the Court's decision included the following statement:

> [T]he Court was in course of preparing the present judgment . . . [when] the operation of 24 April [the raid] took place. The Court therefore feels bound to observe that an operation undertaken in those circumstances, from whatever motive, is of a kind calculated to undermine respect for the judicial process in international relations.

To this expression of censure the Court added that the order of December 15, 1979, "had indicated that no action was to be taken by either party which might aggravate tension between the two countries." Two of the judges went further. They voted to deny the application for reparations, in effect as a sanction for the U.S. action.

Writing about this in the *American Journal of International Law*, Professor Ted L. Stein expressed near-agreement with the dissent vote to deny that reparations claim. Sadly he cited the argument made for the United States, early in the proceedings:

This case presents the Court with the most dramatic opportunity it has ever had to affirm the rule of law among nations and thus fulfill the world community's expectation that the Court will act vigorously in the interest of international law and international peace.

NICARAGUA: JUDGING A
WAR IN CENTRAL AMERICA

There arrived while the Iran case was still pending at the Court another opportunity for the judges to (as the United States had asked in the *Hostages* case) "fulfill the world community's expectation that the Court will act vigorously in the interest of international law and international peace."

The next appearance of the United States at The Hague was as defendant. The conflict that led to it began in March 1981, while the debris from Ronald Reagan's inaugural still littered the streets of Washington, D.C. The new chief executive signed a "presidential finding" that gave to the CIA the authority to begin covert actions against the small Central American republic of Nicaragua.

The subject of U.S. relations with Nicaragua is controversial—has been since the early years of the twentieth century—and public discussions, as well as media debate were often intense. The policy pursued, its necessity and morality, and the compatibility of our action with our national interests were widely questioned. In contrast to that concern hardly any attention was paid to the case at the Peace Palace—the Court's decisions were one-day wonders and forgotten the following day.

One of the many subjects that came before the Court for decision was whether the United States had consented to be sued. As was described in chapter 7, the United States had filed a consent under the optional clause and won its privilege and its responsibility: to sue, and to be sued, by nations that had filed similar consents. An exception (added on the Senate floor by Senator Tom Connally of Texas) provided that consent could be withdrawn in cases regarding matters of domestic jurisdiction *as determined by the United States*. U.S. acceptance of the optional clause provided that it may not be terminated, that is, withdrawn, save on six-months' notice to the international community.

The U.S. intervention into Nicaragua began with the introduction of a body of troops, mainly of Nicaraguan nationality, to conduct a guerrilla war against the Nicaraguan state. Logistical, financial, and material support were given by the United States to the insurgent force, called "contras" (composed principally of former militia loyal to the ousted dictator Somoza). These rebels launched raids from Honduras and Costa Rica, which border Nicaragua.

When U.S. support for the contras escalated to the mining of the harbor of Managua and attacks by U.S. planes on oil tanks, Nicaragua filed a complaint against the United States at the ICJ alleging violations of international law. Several U.S. senators—including Republican Barry Goldwater and Democrat Daniel Patrick Moynihan—had also charged the United States government with violating the Law of Nations.

Nicaragua filed suit on April 9, 1984. The world then learned that on April 6, the last business day before Nicaragua's papers reached the Court, there had arrived at the office of the UN secretary-general (with whom the consents were originally filed) a letter from U.S. Secretary of State George Shultz announcing that the U.S. consent, the 1946 declaration agreeing to be sued, "shall not apply to disputes with any Central American State." This provided that it "shall take effect immediately" and ignored the six-months' notice pledge of the original consent. Six days after the Schulz letter was filed, three days after the Nicaraguan petition was filed, the annual meeting of the American Society of International Law began. It had been scheduled long before. Those attending were concerned with and qualified to evaluate the significance of the U.S. announcement, an attempt to revoke an agreement, not labeled as such but intended to have such effect.

The association had been formed in 1907, fruit of an idea that came from one of the meetings at Lake Mohonk. Its first president had been Secretary of State Elihu Root, who had been responsible for creation of the Central American Court of Justice and had, with his fellow members, been an advocate of creation of a world court. When a World Court came into being, its statute was designed in large measure by Root, and the society's members continued for a long time to be activists for international law and international adjudication.

Previously scheduled, well before the Shultz letter and the Nicaragua filing, was a talk by U.S. Ambassador to the United Nations Jeane Kirkpatrick. She departed from her prepared text to insert a defiant defense of the Shultz letter's attempted withdrawal of U.S. consent to be sued. If Kirkpatrick intended to deter discussion and possible action by the American Society of International Law at its business meeting, she failed. At 5 P.M. the same day, the delegates who had heard her assembled. The association's executive council had prepared a resolution addressed to the action of the secretary of state.

Remarking that "taking a position" was "a most unusual event," the society's president began the discussion by citing its most important previous position-taking. That was the 1946 resolution favoring the adoption of the optional clause offer to dispense with consent among states with similar declarations. During the ensuing discussion on the 1984 action, one senior member of the society, Federal Court Judge Edward Dumbauld, quoted a remark by the 1946 president, Frederic R. Coudert: "[I]f we could not support a resolution favoring an international court, what are we here for anyhow?"

Professor Thomas M. Franck, later to be president of the society, after serving as editor in chief of the highly respected *American Journal of International Law,* drew laughter and applause by citing a unanimous 1945 Senate report approving the six-months' notice requirement as having renounced "any intention to withdraw our obligation in the face of a threatening legal proceeding."

By a voice vote it was resolved:

> The Society therefore deplores, and favors rescission of, the recent action . . . attempting to withdraw from the jurisdiction of the International Court of Justice disputes with any Central American State.

The State Department lawyers and the president were not moved. But the attempt to withdraw consent to be sued did not result initially in total refusal of the United States to face the Court proceedings.

There were two separate contests at the Court during which an impressive number of distinguished attorneys argued for the defense in opposition to counsel retained by the complaining Central American state. Most of the latter were lawyers of U.S. nationality, led by Felix Frankfurter Professor Abram Chayes, himself a former deputy legal adviser at State.

The initial legal contest occurred within a few days after Nicaragua's complaint was filed at the Court. This was over a request by the complaining state for protective measures on an emergency basis, the equivalent of a temporary injunction. It was necessary for the Court, in order to grant such relief, to find that a plausible case could be made for the complaint, on jurisdiction and on the merits. The merits presented no problem. It was obvious, it could not be denied, that directly (mining the harbors, and so on) and indirectly (involvement with the so-called contras) the United States had attacked Nicaragua. The only issue before the Court on that was, as a matter of international law, whether the facts met the requirements of the law of self-defense. But the case on self-defense could only be adjudged when and if the United States presented its position.

The defense team took aim primarily at the issue of jurisdiction: whether this case belonged in this Court between these parties. Ingenious lawyers offered quite a variety of reasons to contest jurisdiction. The most important was "admissibility," said Abraham D. Sofaer, who served as State Department legal adviser during the latter part of the Nicaragua litigation. By inadmissible he said he meant that, because the issue of the use of force in self-defense was best handled by the Security Council, "the framers of the United Nations Charter intended to exclude the Court" from passing upon claims of self-defense and legality of use of force.

The argument was offered at a rushed early hearing in opposition to provisional measures. It was pressed with great energy at the second, later hearing, where representatives of the United States again appeared and argued that the Court should dismiss the case.

The position taken by the United States, that the Court was not authorized to adjudicate self-defense/force questions, was rejected by all fifteen judges.

This included judges from the so-called Free World, nations allied with the United States in Cold War combat with the Soviet camp.

The Court also rejected—again unanimously—the U.S. contention that the Court was prevented from acting by Nicaragua's prior application to the Security Council. In a concurring opinion Judge Stephen Schwebel, a former State Department deputy legal adviser, recalled that in the *Tehran Hostages* case, where the United States had gone to the Court after a presentation to the Security Council, U.S. Agent Owen said, "There is absolutely nothing in the United Nations Charter or this Court's Statute to suggest that action by the Security Council excluded action by the Court."

Having found that there was adequate probability that the Court had jurisdiction, the judges directed the provisional measure of ordering the United States to stop attacks on Nicaragua. The Reagan administration continued with total disregard of the Court's order. The Charter provides no express remedy when such an order is disobeyed.

More than a dozen distinguished U.S. lawyers came to the Peace Palace to argue and submit the full-dress hearing on jurisdiction to the Court. It took seven days of argument to present this preliminary phase of the case. More than half a dozen separate objections to the Court even hearing the merits of the case were now presented. All were rejected by the Court, with votes ranging from 10 to 5 to 14 to 1.

Only two objections required serious discussion: First, was the three-day notice, Shultz's letter, effective to withdraw the pledge of six-months' notice? Second, had Nicaragua herself accepted the optional clause, an action required to entitle her to sue? Deciding on Nicaragua's entitlement to sue without consent of the United States should have been very simple: the eligibility to sue depends on the state's own previous agreement to be sued. Did they or didn't they?

The fact was that they did: Nicaragua had, in writing, moreover, given notification that it had ratified the statute of the old Court. All this took place when ratification was supposed to be filed at the League of Nations in Geneva. On November 29, 1939, the secretary-general of the League received a telegram from the Nicaraguan Foreign Ministry confirming that the ratification had taken place, and that a formal document so certifying would be sent. Had the formal document been received? In November 1939, World War II was raging. German submarines prowled the Atlantic. Transatlantic airmail was for the future.

As far as it is known, the formal document did not reach the League of Nations. But neither the parties nor the Court seemed concerned with whether that failure of physical filing could have been dispensed with by the Court in those unusual circumstances. That would have avoided some pettifoggery as to whether the consent, never withdrawn, was "in force" though technically ineffective. The new Court's statute made provision to continue League of Nations consents of original signers of the Charter, of which

Nicaragua was one. Prior consents still in force were carried over to the new Court with no further diplomatic action. Accordingly, for many years the registry of the new Court had treated Nicaragua as one of the states listed as participant in the optional clause. That was sufficiently persuasive to be treated by Nicaragua as dispensing with going through the motions of a new filing, and treated by the United States as making the Shultz letter necessary.

After full consideration and argument, the Court majority held that Nicaragua's status was such as to enable her to sue.

The other major issue was with regard to the Shultz letter. Did the United States succeed in its effort to withdraw consent and to prevent the Court's judgment as to the legality of U.S. military implementation of Central American policy?

Not only international lawyers, as recounted above, were offended by the Shultz letter. Many other lawyers in this country and abroad were dismayed. Even Roberts Owens, whom we have met as legal adviser during the Iran hostage case, was embarrassed. He deplored the impression created that if the United States thinks it will not win "we will pick up our marbles and go home."

The United States vigorously contended that the letter dated April 6 was effective to derail the suit filed on April 9. In the very act of coming to Court to defend it, the U.S. lawyers appeared to be abiding by the provision in the Court statute—a treaty the United States had signed—"In the event of a dispute as to whether the Court has jurisdiction, the matter shall be settled by decision of the Court."

A not-too-serious argument was made to the effect that even if termination required six-months' notice, Shultz had only written a "modification." Not much weightier was the contention that the "reciprocity," previously understood to be required only in matters of substantive content, could apply to the duration. A more bitterly fought contention, which perhaps had been taken more seriously, was that circumstances in international affairs had changed so much since the six-month pledge was made that the United States was no longer bound by it.

By overwhelming votes, the U.S. positions were rejected by the Court and jurisdiction sustained. Only three judges in dissent thought the Shultz letter was effective; five thought that the failure, in wartime, of a ratification to reach Geneva—when notice of ratification had—was fatal.

Back-Up: Commercial and "Friendship" Treaty

Just as the United States had offered alternate or "back-up" positions as a basis for its defense strategy, the Nicaraguan legal team offered a separate basis for the Court to take jurisdiction. They turned to the 1956 Treaty of Friendship, Commerce, and Navigation between Nicaragua and the United States. It had a dispute clause that provided an advance consent to go to the

ICJ if a disagreement about violation or meaning could not be settled between the parties.

The United States argued in opposition that the treaty drafters never intended that a dispute about one state trying to overthrow the government of another should be included in the dispute clause. The suggestion was that creating and financing the contra forces was not the kind of subject that treaty was meant to cover. (After the case was begun, there was a clearly commercial dispute injected: a trade embargo.)

On the availability of the "friendship" treaty as a basis for jurisdiction, the vote in favor of keeping jurisdiction was 14 to 1.

"Disappearance" of the United States

There were not many changes in personnel on the Court between the time that the United States went there and got in 1980 what it wanted regarding the *Tehran Hostages* case and the filing of the Nicaragua case in 1984. The United States nevertheless, after losing the case on jurisdiction with Nicaragua, issued a formal statement denouncing the Court as "politicized" and calling its decision on jurisdiction "contrary to law and fact." The statement went on to say, "With great reluctance, the United States has decided not to participate in further proceedings in this case."

That action has been variously called a "withdrawal" or a "walk-out." There is no provision in the Court's statute or the UN Charter that contemplates such a move. It has long been established in Court doctrine that once a state becomes or has been held to be a "party" to a proceeding, it remains such throughout. Indeed, in his opinion in the 1966 South-West Africa Case, Judge Philip Jessup said that the Union of South Africa had "fulfilled its duty" when it went on to litigate the merits after losing its first (1962) attack on jurisdiction.

In the view of some attorneys, it is quite unconscionable to recognize the authority of a Court to decide a question by appearing there to litigate it and then to disregard the decision. There is no punishment or sanction for failure to fulfill the obligation to appear. The consequence is not a "default" judgment, such as some may be familiar with in domestic litigation. Sovereign states parties to an international Court case could not be treated so. The 1920 founders imposed a duty on the Court to see for itself that the claims of the applicant state were "well founded in fact and law." That remains the rule.

In accordance with its past practice, the Court proceeded to set dates for the briefs of the parties (called "Memorials") and for oral arguments and evidentiary hearings. The U.S. State Department followed an example set by Iceland, the first notable absentee defendant, and filed a comprehensive statement of its factual claims. In the form of a booklet called "Revolution Beyond Borders," it was, of course, pure hearsay, not subject to cross-examination.

That document gave the United States a sort of "shadow" presence at The

Hague. The Court gave it notice of every step in the trial phase of the case. There was a rough equivalent to cross-examination of the witnesses for Nicaragua supplied by Judge Schwebel. He was playing his part in fulfilling the Court's obligation to "satisfy itself" as to the soundness of the claims made by the Applicant.

The Verdict

There had been seven days of public hearings in September 1985. The Court convened to issue its judgment on June 27, 1986. It was a massive document. The joint opinion of the twelve-judge majority required 136 pages. In addition there were almost 400 pages of concurring and dissenting opinions. Two judges, Oda and Jennings, dissented, again on jurisdictional grounds. The single dissent on the merits of the case came from Judge Schwebel, and was in two parts: 128 pages of opinion and an "Appendix," with 132 pages of his factual findings.

The Court's opinion, unsigned as usual, represented the views of all twelve concurring judges. The effort to touch upon and deal with every conceivable issue in the case, necessitated by the absence of a presentation by the United States, covered many points. The breadth and character of the Court's "judgment"—what the unsigned majority opinion is customarily called—was well described by Dean Frederic Kirgis Jr. of Washington and Lee University, a scholar not wholly sympathetic with all that the Court said:

> Every once in a while the International Court of Justice hands down a decision that contains a veritable cornucopia of significant rules and principles of international law. The *Anglo-Norwegian Fisheries* case was an example; so was the *Namibia Advisory Opinion*. The *Nicaragua* decision is another. It is positively loaded with rules and principles, ranging from the specific to the abstract, from self-defense to the humanitarian law of war, from the sources of customary international law to the interpretation of treaties, from jurisdiction and justiciability to aspects of remedies.

One preliminary issue was the effect of a reservation the U.S. Senate imposed on consent under the optional clause, at Senator Arthur Vandenberg's insistence. It was his idea that consent be inapplicable to cases arising under multilateral treaties (such as the UN Charter) unless other states that were party to the treaty and that might be affected by the decision were participants in the case.

The question now was whether El Salvador's absence from the case brought the multilateral treaty reservation into play. The Court upheld the U.S. claim that El Salvador was a state "affected" by the possible outcome of the case, and hence, violation of the Organization of American States' or United Nations' charters could not serve as legal basis for the charges. The vote was 11 to 4 in favor of the U.S. position. After weighing the implications and effect of the ruling, the Court majority decided the result should serve only to prevent Nicaragua from resting its case on the charters.

Both the United States and Nicaragua had agreed that the customary law rules on the use of force and forbidding intervention were similar to the excluded Charter provisions. The ruling meant that these non-Charter principles would govern. The case continued for consideration of the central issues, whether the use of force against Nicaragua was justified or excused because it was employed in legitimate collective self-defense as an ally of El Salvador. After reviewing the evidence in detail, the Court's finding on the first issue was:

> As to the claim that United States activities in relation to the contras constitute a breach of the customary international law principle of the non-use of force, the Court finds that, subject to the question of whether the action of the United States might be justified as an exercise of the right of self-defense, the United States has committed a prima facie violation of that principle by its assistance to the contras in Nicaragua, by "organizing or encouraging the organization of irregular forces or armed bands . . . for incursion into the territory of another State."

On a related issue, the judgment favored the United States. The Court ruled that it had not been clearly proved that the invaders had been under command and control of U.S. officials as to make that nation responsible for all of their individual actions.

The Court went on to deal with the major issue: whether the nature of the aid proved or admitted to have been sent by Nicaragua to the indigenous, preexisting El Salvador rebellion was such that "the action of the United States might be justified as an exercise of the right of self-defense." In this instance, the claim was of "collective self-defense," in that the United States was an ally of El Salvador. On this subject, it has been suggested that Washington had injured its own nation's cause by its deliberate decision to absent itself from the courtroom—which must have prevented El Salvador from attempting to participate, or even to offer proof.

The Court had whatever facts it could glean from its own cross-examination of Nicaragua's witnesses. There was also the material in argumentative self-serving form, which was contained in the sort of "white paper" compendium called "Revolution Beyond Borders," compiled by the U.S. Department of State to answer congressional and other domestic, as well as foreign, critics. Despite the irregularity of the submission of this document, the Court examined it without exhibiting skepticism and Judge Schwebel's factual appendix dipped liberally into it, as if its statements were legally admissible.

The "self-defense" claim offered the Court the opportunity to resolve an issue that had divided international lawyers and scholars. The Court majority went along with the views of the majority of scholars that "assistance to rebels in the form of provision of weapons or logistical or other support is not an armed attack justifying the use of force in self-defense." ("Armed attack" are the key words in this context.) Whatever aid Nicaragua had given those rebelling against the various "death squad" regimes did not amount, according to the Court, to an armed attack.

Since "States do not have a right of 'collective' armed response to acts which do not constitute an 'armed attack,' " the necessary consequence was that the Court, whose authority the United States had agreed by treaty to respect,

> *Decides* that the United States of America, by training, arming, equipping, financing, and supplying the contra forces or otherwise encouraging, supporting, and aiding military and paramilitary activities in and against Nicaragua, has acted, against the Republic of Nicaragua in breach of its obligations under customary international law not to intervene in the affairs of another State.

Judge Schwebel, though articulate and impassioned in his dissent, nevertheless remarked of the majority decision:

> While I disagree with its legal conclusions . . . I recognize that there is room for the Court's construction of the legal meaning for an armed attack, as well as for some of its other conclusions of law.

As in the aftermath of the provisional order to desist, the Congress and president of the United States continued to act in behalf of the contras. Despite that, the judgment was effective and respected to the extent shown in chapter 13.

11

Some New International Law: Namibia and Decolonization

The first century of the World Court saw revolutionary changes in international law. No longer was its principal purpose to define the rules and protect the institution of territorial imperialism. It had a new role. This was evident in the disappearance of some key phrases and the arrival of others unheard of at the time of the first Hague conference. Common in 1900 were concepts such as suzerainty and protectorate, and rules that governed discovery and occupation. A phrase as ancient as it was illustrative was *terra nullius,* meaning unoccupied land—but by no means vacant: merely "up for grabs" because it was inhabited by people who had not organized themselves into a state capable of warfare to back up its independence.

New phrases unimaginable in 1900 are dominant at the start of the Court's second century: self-determination, decolonization, even national liberation. They were not conceived nor were they introduced by the international court, but they became an important part of the business of the Court to consider and apply.

The transformation did not come overnight. The seeds were planted and the direction of international law changed as a result of the leadership of two U.S. presidents, Woodrow Wilson and Franklin Delano Roosevelt. What Wilson sought to achieve was frustrated in large part by unwilling partners abroad and partisan opponents at home. Roosevelt's influence on the form and content of the UN Charter built on what Wilson had begun, and is at the heart of what can fairly be called the international law of liberation of peoples.

FROM THE KAISER'S "SOUTH-WEST AFRICA" TO NAMIBIA

The land now known as Namibia, formerly called South-West Africa, was the last large section of Africa to be subjected to colonial rule by a European power. Its acquisition by the German empire—which came late to imperial expansionism because it had come late to unification under the kaiser—was recognized by its brother European colonizing powers at a Berlin conference in 1885.

The conquered area was about the size of the state of Texas with a population of less than a million. It had not tempted the earlier colonizers because it had limited agricultural potential, with little surface water, not much rainfall, and predominantly sandy or rocky soil. Its rich mineral resources, including diamonds and uranium, have become evident only in recent decades. But after the turn-of-the-century Boer War, from which the Union of South Africa emerged as a quasi-independent member of the British Empire, the Union began to have geopolitical ambitions toward this territory with which it had such a long common land border.

The Last Surviving League of Nations Mandate

The German kaiser's "ownership" and control of South-West Africa lasted for barely thirty years. By 1915, World War I had begun. The Union of South Africa loyally joined the imperial war effort of George V and Britain's devoted Dominions. Its principal contribution—and perhaps principal motivation—was the invasion, seizure, and occupation of German South-West Africa. But the hoped-for reward—annexation and integration of the huge new territory—was frustrated (and as it was thought, temporarily deferred) by U.S. President Woodrow Wilson's input to the Versailles Treaty Conference. Wilson went to Versailles with a viewpoint that he had explained to the Congress in February 1918:

> Peoples are not to be handed about from one sovereignty to another by an international conference or an understanding between rivals and antagonists. National aspirations must be respected; peoples may now be dominated and governed only by their own consent. "Self-determination" is not a phrase. It is an imperative principle of action which statesmen will henceforth ignore at their peril.

Wilson was outnumbered, but could not be ignored at the Versailles victors' peace conference, to which his allies had looked forward as a division of the spoils of war. The outcome was a compromise that created the "mandate" system, whereby the former enemy colonies were to be held under new administration, not as property but as a "sacred trust" of civilization. The immediate consequence to the indigenous inhabitants may have seemed to be little more than a change of ownership. But the success of the compromise in satisfying the adversaries is illuminated by their opposing beliefs, shown by Ralph Zacklin, author of a monograph on Namibia, based on a lecture he gave at the Hague Academy:

Wilson believed that the mandate system represented the universal application of a principle . . . of colonies lifted into the sphere of complete self-government, while Smuts [of South Africa] was convinced that "the relations between the South West Protectorate and the Union amount to annexation in all but name."

The Treaty of Versailles had resulted in the renunciation by Germany of its claim to South-West Africa. Under the mandate system that was part of the League of Nations Covenant, the control of the territory passed to the Union of South Africa. A variety of other mandates over the former enemy (principally German and Turkish) colonies were assigned to other victorious states.

From the long-range point of view, the mandate system may be seen as having had a "bad" side and a "good" side. The bad side varied from case to case; in the instance of South-West Africa, the provision for annual reports of the mandatory regime to the League Council and for advisory supervision by a Permanent Mandates Commission were a paper shield. They did little to safeguard or ameliorate the condition of the inhabitants of the mandated territory. The good side, not much consolation in the short run, was that there was paper protection against annexation. The dream of ultimate freedom was kept alive. Transfer of actual ownership to the Union of South Africa could not take place without the consent of the League Council.

But the League of Nations died with the end of World War II. It had become defunct when the war began, and it dissolved itself April 18, 1946. The UN Charter made provision for a system of "trusteeships" to replace the mandate system but with no automatic transfer or succession. Where a mandated entity had not become independent, it would enter trusteeship under the Charter only after negotiation with a designated UN body.

By 1947, all formerly mandated territories had become independent or transferred to trusteeship arrangements with the United Nations—except South-West Africa. And so the trek to the International Court of Justice began. Aspects of the legal status of the land that was to become Namibia were taken to the Court on six separate occasions.

The Court's First Achievement:
The Mandate Survives

White political leaders in South Africa had always had the view that their neighboring "trust" territory was annexed de facto from the inception of the mandate. They expected to take it over de jure when the right moment came, as a fifth province of the Union. After dissolution of the League, they rejected initiatives looking toward a trusteeship agreement. They said that the mandate had expired. Without public debate, or a vote by secret ballot, they "consulted" (so they said) with the people concerned. They reported to the UN General Assembly that the popular "will" favored annexation. They proposed that the first General Assembly of the United Nations approve legal absorption of the territory—a proposal that was rejected by a vote of 37 to 0, with nine abstentions.

The resolution rejecting the acquisition of the territory included a recommendation for a trusteeship agreement, and again South Africa declined. The Union's white ruling party then submitted mandate-type reports for the next three years. But in 1948, the Nationalist Party, which had just come to power (and was soon to impose apartheid as a legally enforced way of life), repudiated the idea of international accountability, and ceased to make reports on the administration of the territory.

Faced with this rejection of responsibility to the international community, the General Assembly turned to the International Court of Justice for an advisory opinion. Contributing to this decision was the persistent effort of the International League for the Rights of Man (now known as "the International League for Human Rights"), a non-governmental organization (NGO) provided for and functioning under Article 71 of the UN Charter.

Beginning in 1947, its agent, Reverend Michael Scott, a white South African, repeatedly brought to the UN's Fourth Assembly Committee petitions and data from the abused and exploited indigenous population. A monograph by Rutgers professor Roger S. Clark assigns Scott credit not only for conveying detailed information from tribes whose representatives were denied exit visas by South Africa. Clark's study adds:

> The Fourth Committee, following its debate on the item and the hearing of Scott, recommended to the Plenary Session that an opinion be sought from the International Court of Justice as to the obligations of South Africa under the mandate and other relevant documents.

The Assembly voted to ask both a general question and inquiries as to specific aspects. The questions were, generally, What is the "international status" of the territory, and the "international obligations" of the Union? Specifically, are there obligations under the mandate, do the Charter's trusteeship clauses apply, and how can the status of the territory be changed? The intent of the "international status" question was to settle the crucial point, Did the mandate, granted by the League of Nations, survive the League's demise?

Although the decolonization implicitly contemplated by the Charter had not really begun as of 1950, the Court was unanimous in holding that the mandate did survive. It reasoned that, although the League of Nations was gone, its members survived, and it was they who, while associated in the League, had created the mandate and hence continued the responsibility of safeguarding the "sacred trust" of the mandate. Moreover:

> The authority which the Union [of South Africa] exercises over the territory is based on the Mandate. If the Mandate lapsed, as the Union contends, the latter's

authority would equally have lapsed. To retain the rights derived from the Mandate and to deny the obligations . . . could not be justified.

With regard to the specific questions submitted along with the general question of status, as to one the Court was unanimous also: no change in status of the territory would be legal without the approval of the United Nations.

There was a divergence as to the Union's responsibilities. The Court ruled 10 to 2 that a clause in the UN Charter served as the basis for the United Nations to act (even though not technically the successor to the League) to receive the reports the mandate directed and generally supervise. But the vote was 8 to 6 against the idea that South Africa had an obligation to enter a full, formal trustee relationship under the Charter.

The ruling on the continuance of the mandate gave no perceptible benefit to the population of the territory. More frequent complaints came to Reverend Scott—and were passed on—especially as the ultimate indignity of apartheid began to be imposed on the people whose well-being was supposed to be treated as a "sacred trust."

Two additional, relatively minor advisory opinions were prompted by difficulties that followed South Africa's rejection of the 1950 advisory: its continued refusal to make annual reports on administration of the territory, and its refusal to pass on to the General Assembly the petitions of the inhabitants protesting aspects of their treatment. The first of these resolved the doubts in the Assembly with regard to a proposed special voting rule with respect to decisions on Assembly supervision after the 1950 decision. The proposed two-thirds-vote requirement was approved by the Court without dissent, in the face of the contention that League of Nations action had to be unanimous. But in a second case, when advice was sought as to whether the Assembly committee could grant oral hearings to petitioners, the Court divided: a majority voted to so advise; the dissenters preferred to withhold Court intervention on such minutiae and in effect to encourage the Assembly to make such decisions for itself.

These minor rulings could not and did not deal with the more serious problem: South Africa's refusal to accept and perform the obligations of a mandatory as affirmed in the advisory of 1950.

Going for a "Binding" Ruling—and the Court's Self-Reversal

As noted earlier, an advisory opinion, while supposed to be treated as "authoritative," is not enforceable. A contentious case, one brought by one state against another, *can* result in a judgment. If the judgment directs something to be done or not done, then there becomes available the mutual promises of all UN members: "to comply with the decision of the International

Court of Justice in any case to which it is a party." Performance of that promise can be brought about by action of the Security Council, which is equipped by the Charter with power to compel action directed by a judgment, or restrain wrongdoing in violation.

South Africa had refrained, for the time being, from outright annexation. But it was increasingly conducting the affairs of the former German colony occupied under the mandate as a "sacred trust" as if South-West Africa were a mere possession. It denied accountability for its actions, refused to transmit reports, and denied exit visas to those who wished to go to the Assembly's fourth committee to complain of mistreatment; its culminating indignity was the use of the Native Affairs Administration Act of 1954 for the formal introduction of apartheid into the territory.

As for the problem of enforcing obligations declared to exist by the advisory opinions of the 1950s, the solution might be to find a legal tool for transforming them into a judgment in a contentious case. That this should be done was formally advocated by a UN General Assembly resolution in 1957. Corridor discussions at the United Nations had been centered on a contentious case route for some time; as early as 1953, Michael Scott, who had helped precipitate the move to getting the 1950 advisory, distributed a memorandum that explained and advocated the bringing of a case against South Africa.

To pursue this it was necessary to find a plaintiff, a state eligible to bring a suit, and a basis for jurisdiction against an unwilling South Africa. The latter seemed provided by the terms of the original mandate, that "any dispute whatever between the Mandatory and another Member of the League of Nations relating to the interpretation or application" of the mandate could be submitted to the PCIJ. (Article 37 of the International Court of Justice (ICJ) statute provided that any treaty in force that supplied PCIJ jurisdiction would support the authority of the ICJ to take the case.)

What about a plaintiff? Could a former member of the League of Nations qualify, for the purpose of securing status as a state eligible to file and to compel South Africa to appear and defend—and ultimately, if the Court so ordered, to obey?

In 1960, the Organization of African Unity (OAU), formerly a mere handful of states (most of the continent was colonies or protectorates), secured fifteen new members who at the same time became members of the United Nations, and were in a position to influence decisions of the Assembly. The OAU had two members who had been members of the League, Ethiopia and Liberia. These two secured as counsel Ernest Gross, former State Department undersecretary and U.S. delegate to the United Nations. He filed the necessary petition to the Court for them.

By a resolution of December 1960, the UN Assembly declared its approval of the decision of the two African states to ask the Court for a remedy. The resolution stated that the case was being pursued in the interest of the entire international community. Thus it could be said that this new item of Court business was a sort of "class action."

In the first branch of the two states' petition to the Court, they asked that it be declared that South-West Africa was still a territory under mandate and that South Africa was still subject to the obligations to submit reports of administration, to forward petitions, and to submit to supervision by the United Nations. The petition's second branch sought a judgment that the mandatory had violated its trust by introducing apartheid, installing military bases, and creating administrative structures in violation of the mandate's terms. An order to cease and desist was the object of the action.

Since the first branch of the action sought no more than what had been declared in the 1950 advisory, and the second branch was based on facts that could be easily established, there really remained for decision only the question of jurisdiction. In this case, that had several features.

None of the South African objections was a surprise. As expected, the question whether the plaintiffs were still "members of the League of Nations" was raised. Another: was the mandate (the League having been dissolved) still a "treaty in force," another condition required to justify the claim of consent to be sued? Also South Africa questioned whether there existed a "dispute" between plaintiff states and South Africa. Could the issues presented be raised only by the members of the League collectively?

These questions were argued to the hilt by the attorneys representing South Africa. The Court, by a vote of 8 to 7, voted for the plaintiff states.

The question whether the mandate was a treaty still in force, the majority held, was settled by the 1950 advisory. "Membership" in the expired League was held to survive the latter's demise enough to provide an effective mode for the enforcement of the mandate's obligations. The majority had no doubt about the question that some thought the most difficult: whether there was, between Ethiopia and Liberia, as against South Africa, a "dispute" in the sense intended by the mandate's court-reference clause. To dispose of this objection, they said the "language used is broad, clear, and precise. It gives rise to no ambiguity, and it permits of no exception. It refers to any dispute whatever. . . ."

An Australian and a British judge were the lead dissenters. They dissented on all points, particularly the meaning of the word "dispute." The nature of the dispute required to justify Court intervention, they argued, was one in which each side was pressing its own direct claim; the parties who brought the case, Ethiopia and Liberia, they contended, were acting only as agents of the General Assembly, and had no direct, litigable interest of their own (this based on the ICJ statute allowing only states to sue and be sued).

In a separate opinion concurring with the 8-to-7 majority of the Court, Judge Philip Caryl Jessup explained why states could enforce rights that were not specifically their own, that were in the interest of the common humanity of the community of nations.

International law has long recognized that States may have legal interests in matters which do not affect their financial, economic, or other "material," or, say, "physical" or "tangible" interests. One type of illustration of this principle of international law is to be found in the right of a State to concern itself, on general humanitarian grounds, with atrocities affecting human behavior in another country.

(Judge Jessup had prevision of the twenty-first century's principal problems.)

After the objections to jurisdiction were overruled, the hearing on the merits was scheduled. South Africa, frustrated in its attempt to escape judgment, kept the promise made when it signed the UN Charter "to comply with the judgment of the Court," namely to participate in the trial of the merits instead of walking out. South Africa litigated the case with energy. The exchange of written pleadings, answers, replies, and rebuttals did not close until December 1964, two years after the decision on objections to jurisdiction.

Public sittings of the Court were held during two lengthy periods in 1965. Many witnesses were called to testify for South Africa, to defend its conduct of the mandate. As Richard Falk, of counsel for the plaintiffs, has written:

South Africa, with great resources and ingenuity, sought to overwhelm the Court with pleadings, witnesses and arguments that it was acting in good faith as mandatory and that its judgments as to what constituted the well-being of the inhabitants did not unreasonably exceed its discretion under the mandate.

Liberia and Ethiopia did not call "live" witnesses; they did submit depositions and affidavits in support of their case. Then followed a number of lengthy oral arguments.

All this was to result in a stunning surprise. Instead of making a decision on the African states' complaints, the Court dismissed the case on a ground that so closely resembled one of the objections overruled in the 1962 decision that sophisticated scholars of international law procedure declared that they could not tell the difference.

What had happened was that the stubborn dissenters of 1962 staged a coup aided by changes in membership on the Court due to death and disability, and by the statutory rule that gave the Court's president a tie-breaking second vote when the judges divided evenly. They ruled that the applicants had shown no litigable claim or interest, despite the 1962 ruling that they did have "standing" to sue.

The indignation of the 1966 dissenters, led by Judge Jessup and a colleague, Tanaka of Japan, was so strong as to sound nearly unjudicial. This was exceeded in the world outside. The debate in the General Assembly was scorching, and the cause of securing peace via the Rule of Law was injured. The Court was to suffer for years afterward from what can fairly be described as a "self-inflicted wound," of the dimensions and impact of the U.S. Supreme Court's *Dred Scott* decision.

The passion and breadth of the dissents make interesting reading today. Suffice it to say that Judge Jessup quoted (another example of the resort to U.S. constitutional history) Chief Justice (and former PCIJ judge) Charles Evans Hughes's dictum that:

> A dissent in a court of last resort is an appeal to the brooding spirit of the law, to the intelligence of a future day, when a later decision may possibly correct the error into which the dissenting judge believes the court to have been betrayed.

But in this case, the ICJ was not to be the tribunal with the last word, nor was the 1966 word its last.

Council and Court Oust South Africa and Create Namibia

The UN General Assembly provided the "intelligence of a future day," within four months of the Court's startling dismissal of the Ethiopia–Liberia case. Relying on the Court's 1950 advisory ruling that South Africa held the territory only by virtue of the League of Nations mandate and was accountable to the United Nations as successor to the League for performance, the Assembly decided to exercise the right to "revert to itself the administration of the Mandated Territory." On the finding that South Africa "failed to fulfill its obligations," the Assembly resolved that the mandate was terminated and that the United Nations should govern directly. A UN Council for Namibia was created for this purpose.

The General Assembly had no power, by itself, to enforce the resolution it had passed. It turned to the Security Council, which did have the power. That body was at first not ready to act, particularly since France and Britain were not enthusiastic. South Africa inspired further action by starting so-called terrorist trials, under which thirty-seven indigenous inhabitants were prosecuted under ex post facto laws. After the Union spurned the Council's call to cancel the trials, the latter resolved that it was in agreement with the Assembly's termination of the mandate, and that "the continued presence of South Africa in Namibia is illegal." The abstention of France and the United Kingdom made it evident that the power of the Council could be paralyzed by the veto.

Meanwhile, the General Assembly had passed a resolution that named the territory—based on one of its regions—"Namibia." Unwilling to subject further enforcement action to the threat of a veto, the Council used its separate power to request an advisory opinion in which the question was put: "What are the legal consequences for States of the continued presence of South Africa in Namibia, not withstanding Security Council Resolution 276 (1970)?"

In a monograph on the Namibian question, UN legal staffer Ralph Zacklin suggested that it could be "looked upon as an opportunity for the Court to rehabilitate itself following the 1966 decision, an opportunity to place its authority behind the General Assembly and the Security Council in furtherance of the attempt by the United Nations to assume direct responsibility for the administration of Namibia."

The Court had recently seemed to invite a new approach. In the first *Ethiopia/Liberia v. South Africa* case, Judge Philip C. Jessup argued, "States may have legal interests in matters which do not affect their financial [and so on] . . . interests." That view was now accepted by the whole Court (as reconstituted through the normal passage of time) in a dictum carefully included in the decision of *Barcelona Traction Power and Light.*

Barcelona Traction was a case holding that Belgium could not sue Spain for actions claimed to deplete assets of a Canadian corporation whose stockholders were mainly Belgian. The opinion asserted that there were two types of international obligations to be distinguished: those owed to the members of the international community as a whole, and those owed solely to individual states.

> By their very nature the former obligations concerning the community as a whole are the concern of all States. In view of the importance of the rights involved, all States can be held to have a legal interest in their protection. . . . Such obligations derive for example . . . from the outlawing of acts of aggression and genocide, as also from the principles and rules concerning basic rights of the human person, including protection from slavery and racial discrimination.

So much in conflict was this passage with the point of view implemented by the 1966 dismissal that it seemed quite sensible to try the Court out again when an occasion presented itself. And so the Security Council submitted its request for advice on July 29, 1970—six months after *Barcelona Traction.*

South Africa could see that the possibility of a judgment supporting the Assembly and Council orders to "get out" was a danger ominous enough to fight all the way, as they had from 1962 to 1966 against the Ethiopia–Liberia case. South Africa:

- Tried to invoke the *Eastern Carelia* case, which declined an advisory when one of two states in a dispute refused consent to jurisdiction (distinguished here since, unlike the Soviet Union, a nonmember of the League in 1922, South Africa had been a member of the League and the United Nations).
- Challenged the composition of the Court.
- Questioned the Council's request because a veto-entitled member had abstained.
- Tried to block a hearing until they could attempt to win the right to have a white South African designee added to the bench as an ad hoc judge.

These objections and requests were overruled, one by one, the last self-defeated by the 1966 dismissal of the Ethiopia–Liberia case, which necessarily implied that there was no "legal question actually pending between two or more States"; existence of such a question was necessary for the grant of the privilege of an ad hoc jurist.

The question on which advice was asked did not necessarily include the legality of the UN resolutions declaring the mandate ended and ousting the mandatory: these were assumed to be valid by the body passing them. But South Africa raised the question of their legality and the Court responded.

South Africa's lawyers challenged the General Assembly's 1966 resolution terminating the mandate; they also attacked the Security Council's finding based on that action, that South Africa's very presence in Namibia and all actions taken by it that had anything to do with the territory were illegal. Their argument was that the General Assembly and Security Council actions violated the League Covenant under which the mandate was created and the UN Charter under which UN bodies acted.

The objection based on the Covenant, under which the UN body acted as partial successor, was that neither it, nor the specific mandate drawn up to govern South Africa's administration, reserved any right to cancel, that therefore it could only be by mutual consent. The Court's response was that it must be implied that there was power to cancel, even if not expressly provided. This was necessary to control the mandate and make it responsive to what it called a fundamental principle, "that a party which disowns or does not fulfill its own obligation cannot be recognized as retaining the rights which it claims to derive from the relationship." Judge Jessup had by the time of this ruling on June 21, 1971, retired from the Court; but his earlier opinions dealing with the South-West Africa problem had left the leaven that would rise to result in another application of U.S. Chief Justice John Marshall's doctrine of implied powers, the antithesis of strict construction.

Still another challenge, this based on the UN Charter, claimed that the Assembly could make only "recommendations," and hence was powerless to end the mandate. That was a "decision" and the Charter gave the Assembly such power only with regard to the budget.

The Court based itself, in the examination of this question, on the assumption that there must be a body to put into effect the principle that a treaty may be terminated when "an essential provision for the realization of its objects or purposes has been violated." The power was implied, not to make a formal "decision," but to recognize that the mandatory had, by its own conduct terminated its authority.

In a lecture, later published as a book, Nagendra Singh, a former judge and president of the Court, asserted that the Court's contribution to the development of the law on decolonization was to be found in passages in the opinion that he quoted:

[V]iewing the institutions of 1919, the Court may take into consideration changes which have occurred in the supervening half-century, and its interpretation cannot remain unaffected by the subsequent development of the law, through the Charter of the United Nations and by way of customary law . . . . Development of international law in regard to non-self-governing territories, as enshrined in the Charter of the United Nations, made the principle of self-determination applicable to all of them.

In consequence of this view of the matter, he concluded, the Court was resolved that "the ultimate objective of the sacred trust was the self-determination and independence of the peoples concerned." The ultimate outcome of the struggle for Namibia was shaped, if not decisively influenced, by the General Assembly's first visit to the Court for an advisory opinion.

"Just as the Court in 1950 provided the judicial basis for the General Assembly's assumption of supervisory responsibilities in relation to the Mandate," Ralph Zacklin wrote, "the 1971 opinion provided the judicial underpinning for the Council for Namibia as the legal administering authority for the Territory by confirming the validity of the General Assembly's termination of the Mandate. . . ."

Independence was won by Namibia nineteen years later. It was not the fault of the Court that it was so long delayed. And it can be said, in fairness, that the institutional pride of the United Nations in the winning of Namibia's freedom must be shared with the Court.

MOROCCO AND SOME ASPECTS OF
COLONIALISM ADJUDGED

Morocco has been seen in three cases in the two World Courts: two as a passive colony, one as active colonizer. It played a role in a case at the PCIJ, with Tunisia similarly situated, as a powerless protectorate of France, in 1925. Britain went to Court to fight a Paris decree forcing French citizenship on English residents in Morocco and Tunis. After the Court held this to be of more than French "domestic" concern, the case was settled. The relationship of France to Morocco was really a special kind of colonialism not involving seizure, occupation, or annexation. Called a "protectorate," the imperialist power's rule was usually established by express agreement with a reigning monarch of the subject state. Such a ruler's character and integrity would seem to be compromised by her or his willingness to so sign away the nation's liberty and to subject a people to foreign rule.

The next case came after the vicissitudes of World War II, when French prestige and power had been shaken by the 1940 surrender to the Germans and the period of Vichy rule that ended with the Allied landings of 1942. During the immediate postwar period, another case, decided two years after the first South-West Africa advisory, came along that was equally illustrative of Morocco's subjection. This case, *Concerning the Rights of Nationals of the United States of America in Morocco,* marked the first appearance of the United States in any international court as litigant.

The principal dispute had arisen after France, in December 1948, via her resident general in Morocco, issued a decree imposing import restrictions, purportedly to conserve foreign exchange. The decree affected the United States and important commercial interests adversely, as it permitted unlimited imports from France and colonies of the French Union. Two years of fruitless negotiations followed the U.S. diplomatic challenge to the decree, as a result of which other differences emerged over U.S. treaty rights in Morocco, long antedating the establishment of the French protectorate.

France initiated the case in exasperation at U.S. bargaining tactics. The ultimate result was a mixed bag, but on the most important issue, the Court ruling favored U.S. merchants. Morocco's rights, as they might have conceivably been presented under the then-emerging law of self-determination, were not discussed: General Assembly Resolution 1514 (15) on that subject was still eight years away. But there was a promising "aside," an observation by the Court that may have given comfort to the native independence movement. In pressing the U.S. claim that discriminatory treatment could be challenged under the 1906 Pact of Algeciras, which had preceded by six years the formal protectorate, Adrian Fisher of the U.S. State Department had to make an argument that nettled the French. He insisted that despite the protectorate, Morocco still retained a national identity separate from France. The necessary implication would be entitlement of U.S. traders to continued equality.

The litigation was marked by a conflict of views within the State Department on how hard-hitting U.S. advocates could be, due to concern about French sensibilities as the North Atlantic Alliance was being forged. Despite their displeasure with Fisher's argument, as Judge Jessup later was to describe the case in his book, *The Birth of Nations:*

> The French could not deny that, unlike Algeria, Morocco was not a part of France, but they hated to make the admission. Nevertheless in its judgment the Court was able to say: "It is not disputed by the French Government that Morocco, even under the Protectorate, has retained its personality as a State in international law."

In his essay on the work of the ICJ, former Judge Jiménez cited that statement of 1952 "at the very beginning of the anticolonial movement," as the earliest contribution of the Court to the law of decolonization.

In this case, as in the 1925 lawsuit, Morocco had played no part as a state. Then, having attained her liberty from the French after some years of struggle in the 1950s, she was to play a dual, conflicting—even treacherous—role in the major ICJ case that began with the request for an advisory opinion regarding the status of the territory known as *Western Sahara.*

As far north in Africa as Namibia was south lay a territory that was part of the Sahara, fronting the Atlantic Ocean. Spain had ruled there since 1885, her position as an occupying colonial power probably related to her long-held possession of the Canary Islands, off that part of the African coast.

Also known as Rio de Oro, the fairly barren territory is about the size of Colorado. It is inhabited mainly by an indigenous population known as Sahrawis, numbering fewer than 100,000. During the decades that followed World War II, they began to respond to the nationalist tides that were rising among colonial peoples. Speeches and then resolutions in the UN General Assembly responded to the native unrest.

Spain was at first reluctant even to discuss the subject because of its interest in the principal asset of the territory: rich phosphate deposits, valuable in the production of fertilizer. This asset tempted others: Morocco, which had won its own independence in 1956, had, as one element of its population, tribes not unlike the Sahrawis. These were used as the pretext to lay claim not only to Rio de Oro, but also to an adjoining French possession called Mauritania.

While pressing its claim, Morocco at first resisted the French grant of independence to the latter, part of whose population also resembled the Sahrawis. When Mauritania gained her own liberty, it, too, made claims that turned the problem into a four-way fight.

These conflicting claims and the pressure that mounted in the General Assembly combined to induce Spain to begin to prepare a referendum that would enable the population to express its own wishes. The foreign minister of Spain met with Morocco's to seek his cooperation and was told that Morocco would permit a vote only if it were limited to Spain versus Morocco, excluding the idea of independence. And when Spain committed itself to going forward with a UN-sponsored and supervised referendum, Morocco's king held a press conference at which he threatened to use his army "to recover the usurped territories."

When Spain ignored the threat, Morocco maneuvered for delay, proposing to take the case to the ICJ. Despite the argument that in the circumstances, "The people of Spanish Sahara should be the court," put forward by Kenya, the Assembly passed a three-pronged resolution:

- for postponement of the referendum pending the action of the Court;
- to send a UN mission to the disputed territory; and
- to ask the Court (1) whether when Spain declared ownership the land belonged to no one (*terra nullius,* the old international law's concept that people neither armed nor Christian just didn't exist), and (2) what (if the answer to the first question was "no") were the ties in 1884 between

the territory and the Kingdom of Morocco and with the "Mauritanian entity," so called because there was no such state recognized at that time.

The questions presented in the Assembly's resolution had been shaped to some extent by the influence of Morocco and Mauritania among the Third World states in that body—so much so that in a separate opinion adding his own views to the Court's verdicts, U.S. Judge Hardy C. Dillard characterized the questions as "loaded," that is, formulated in a fashion designed to induce a result favorable to the newly freed nations' wish to do some annexation of their own.

The Court was able to resist such manipulation. Spain argued that the request for an advisory opinion was an improper way to settle its dispute with Morocco. Spain's first objection was overruled on the ground that the Court was deciding nothing between Spain and Morocco, giving the Assembly only nonbinding advice to help it exercise its decolonization duties.

The second objection was that:

> [T]he questions submitted to the Court were devoid of purpose or practical effect, in that the United Nations had already settled the method to be followed for the decolonization of Western Sahara, namely a consultation of the indigenous population by means of a referendum.

The Court's response to this preliminary objection was the most significant portion of its opinion, outweighing by far the value of its later discussion and analysis of the historic basis for Spain's claim of title and the fragmentary basis for the modern annexationist claims of the new neighbors. What the Court did was to answer a question it had not been asked, to put the questions it was asked into their proper perspective, namely to inquire into, as Professor Thomas Franck put it, "how important in the final act of decolonization is historic title as compared to the right of self-determination?"

In its answer the Court formalized, and supported with a detailed presentation of the course of General Assembly resolutions, the proposition that "the right of self-determination for non–self-governing territories had become a norm of international law." The Court's action gave judicial confirmation to the General Assembly's 1960 Resolution on Decolonization. What was particularly stressed was that, while there were alternative forms of self-determination (not only independence, for example, but also association or even integration with an existing sovereign state) indispensable to the legitimacy of the process, it should come about as the "result of the freely expressed wishes of the territory's peoples, acting with full knowledge of the change in their status, their wishes having been expressed through informed and democratic processes, impartially conducted and based on universal adult suffrage."

As the Court studied the case, the mission sent by the United Nations under the same resolution that requested the advisory toured the territory. It concluded, after many interviews—and despite potential embarrassment faced by two of the three Third World members of the commission—that a solid majority of the indigenous population favored independence, and "was against the territorial claims of Morocco and Mauritania."

The opinion of the ICJ was released on October 16, 1975, not long after the report of the UN mission. The Court advised the Assembly that the land had not been *terra nullius,* that the nomadic peoples there were socially and politically organized into tribes under chiefs competent to represent them. As to Morocco and Mauritania, the Court by votes of 14 to 2 against the former and 15 to 1 against the latter, concluded that there was no proof of existence "at the relevant period of any legal tie of territorial sovereignty" between either claimant and Western Sahara.

Morocco's rulers were not persuaded by either the report of the UN commission or the findings of the Court. Their interest had been whetted by their learning of the finding of iron ore and the hints of petroleum in the off-shore continental shelf, added to estimates of the value of the phosphate deposits. To give such valuable resources to such a tiny population, some said, would be wrong, and one was reported to have said—this was 1975—"one Kuwait in the Arab world is enough."

There followed the Court's opinion a march into Western Sahara by thousands of Moroccans led by their king, to implement a secret agreement with Mauritania to divide exploitation of the mineral resources. Spain at first resisted, and went to the Security Council, which did not act; then Spain made its own deal for division of the spoils with Morocco. The POLISARIO (Frente Popular para la Liberación de Saguia el Hamra y Rio de Oro) Front, backed by Algeria, began a guerilla resistance that caused Mauritania to back off.

The Security Council's failure to act when Morocco marched in defiance of the Court's opinion was explained later by Daniel P. Moynihan, United States Ambassador to the UN at the time. He wrote in *A Dangerous Place* (Little Brown 1978):

> The United States wished things to turn out as they did, and worked to bring this about. Department of State desired that the UN prove utterly ineffective in whatever measures it undertook. The task was given to me and I carried it forward with no inconsiderable success.

Morocco's occupation continued for years as Polisario's ineffectual guerrilla resistance persisted. The UN finally secured a cease-fire with a promise of a referendum; that never took place, repeatedly postponed because of voting list disputes.

On June 20, 2001, the UN offered a new plan that legitimized Morocco's occupation with "autonomy" for the region. James P. Baker III, former U.S. Secretary of State, drew up the plan, which was reported in *The Economist* for June 30, 2001, under the head "The UN's U-Turn."

12

Contesting Ownership on Land and at Sea

As the twentieth century drew to a close, it was evident that the argument made by U.S. peace advocates at the century's beginning for a standing court was vindicated in one way. Replacement of the rule of force by the Rule of Law often resulted from the Court's handling of border disputes. This was not only seen on land, where strips of border of minor economic significance were disputed, but also at sea.

Cases involving what was called the "Law of the Sea" were more complex, involved increasingly higher stakes, and required more original and creative judicial craftsmanship than other cases. As to these, too, the Court was uniformly successful. The parties came to it with cases freighted with much more than pride or pique, yet they submitted in good grace to its rulings, win, lose or draw. Decisions were made that won respect among scholars and the foreign officers who were "clients" of the Court. Principles it laid down were accepted and used in drafting the global legislation produced at rounds of multilateral treaty conferences.

The earliest land case that came to the International Court of Justice (ICJ) concerned the tiny English Channel islets of Minquiers and Ecrehos. The opposing contestants were France and England. The dispute may well have been the oldest unsettled argument that ever came to any court: by the time the adversaries agreed to take the case to The Hague, their disagreement was more than 300 years old—albeit France's formal claims of sovereignty were asserted in diplomatic communication only in the 1880s.

At stake in the case were more than the two rocky reefs off the coast of the English Channel island of Jersey. Only part of them rose above high tide sufficiently to support occupants of a handful of dwellings. The islands hardly seemed worth the considerable expense of taking the case to Court. But as retired Judge Jessup observed in his book *The Use of International Law,* under the question of disputed sovereignty "one can detect the gear of fishermen behind the papers of the Foreign office."

To tell the story of the case adequately, one would have to begin somewhat as follows: "William, Duke of Normandy, owner of the channel islands off his Duchy's coast, conquered England in 1066. When Normandy was severed from the Norman–English domain in 1204 by its conquest by French King Philip, the English remained in the Islands. . . ." One of the main French arguments—just to illustrate what the Court was confronted with—was that when the conqueror's son granted the Ecrehos islets to a Norman follower who in turn made a grant in 1203 to an abbey on the French mainland, that severed the feudal link of the Ecrehos to England, so that the French seizure of the province of Normandy transferred title to them.

After examining that and similar arguments, and many medieval pacts to which the parties attributed conflicting meanings, the Court ruled all such feudal matters to be unpersuasive and inconclusive. The judges chose to rest their decision in favor of England on the continuous, open, and unchallenged exercise of English sovereignty over the island for centuries.

Two land cases, heard soon afterwards, had overtones much more contemporary in their resonance. There was a disputed border in each where gunfire may still crackle today and tomorrow, although not for reasons left unsettled by their referral to the Court. One was the line to be drawn between Honduras and Nicaragua; the other as to whether a historic temple, object of reverence and tourist attraction as well, belonged to Thailand (Siam, when the argument began) or Cambodia, originally part of French Indo-China.

Each argument had simmered for most of the twentieth century; each was settled in the early 1960s by a decision of the Court; the related principles that the Court applied were subsequently put together and included in the UN International Law Commission's draft of an article in the multilateral "Law of Treaties" compact (Vienna Convention of 1969).

The common border of Nicaragua and Honduras runs from the Atlantic to the Pacific Coast of Central America. The neighbors had agreed to let a binational commission try to settle their differences and to arbitrate those as to which they could not agree. After some wrangling about the choice, they selected the king of Spain as their neutral arbitrator. The king's 1906 decision in favor of Honduras was greeted with congratulations by Nicaragua's president, who wired: "A strip of land, more or less, is of no importance, when the close harmony of two sister nations is involved." A few years later, Nicaragua cited some alleged defects in the award and denied that it was valid or obligatory.

For decades there were verbal fireworks, and some armed conflict over the failed settlement. After the last clash of 1957, the Organization of American States persuaded the parties to go to The Hague. The rights and wrongs of the boundary question itself never got to be considered by the Court. First it had to decide whether, contrary to Nicaragua's long-held contentions, the award of the king of Spain was indeed valid and binding.

Despite the efforts of a battery of distinguished international lawyers from France, Italy, and the United States, including former ambassador and professor, and future judge, Philip Jessup, the Court was not moved by Nicaragua's contentions. While there were points made in the opinions discrediting the specific objections to the arbitrator's award, the essential holding was that Nicaragua's expression of initial satisfaction with the award, and failure for some years thereafter to challenge it, precluded consideration of the objections belatedly made.

On November 18, 1960, the day the ICJ decision was made public, the government of Nicaragua issued the following press statement:

> Nicaragua, as always respectful of its international obligations and commitments, will faithfully comply with the decision of the International Court of Justice and will by common agreement with her sister republic of Honduras carry out the provisions of the decision.

Nicaragua promptly evacuated the disputed territory.

Judge Jessup tells us little about the contested Central American strip of land, save that it was "swampy." He is able to tell us more about the bone of contention between Thailand and Cambodia, from personal observations made when he was consulted by the Siamese about the case:

> As if climbing to heaven, a seemingly endless flight of stone steps leads to the temple of Preah Vihear, one of the great monuments of the Khmer civilization, which created also the more renowned temple of Angkor Wat. Stone columns flank the stairway, pushed askew or knocked down by the wild elephants which still frequent the area in certain seasons. When you reach the temple at the top of the steps, you can look down on the flat stretches of the Cambodian plain more that 500 meters below the top of the escarpment.

The issue between Cambodia and Thailand went back to a treaty settlement between France (then imperial master of all Indo-China, including Cambodia) and Siam, as Thailand was then known, a semi-dependent land wedged between the British and French empires. In that 1904 treaty, the Siamese and the French established the frontier in the Dangrek Mountains (in which the temple's cliff lay) as the line of the watershed running along them. But they provided also that a commission, jointly staffed, was to make a survey and to draw a map based on it, for specific identification of the line. A cartographer, who had been employed by the commission, delivered the map to the Siamese Paris legation. The map was accepted and sent around by the Siamese for many years. It seemed, as the Siamese first claimed in 1935, that if the watershed line were followed strictly, the map was mistaken in placing the temple in Cambodia.

At several conferences on border matters, two held after World War II to straighten out problems left by the Japanese occupation, no claim was made or issue raised about the location of the Temple Preah Vihear, but local Siamese authorities sent soldiers, who took possession of the ruins and policed them.

France protested diplomatically against the stationing of the Siamese guards without success; preoccupied with the Indo-Chinese freedom effort, France did nothing further. Cambodia was given independence in 1953 and, as international law successor to France under the latter's treaties, took the case to the ICJ when further diplomatic efforts proved fruitless. (When the case came on for hearing, Judge Jessup had joined the Court; having been consulted in the preliminary phases of the case by Thailand—he was even taken for a view of the "premises," from which his report is quoted above— he disqualified himself from sitting on the case.)

The Court did not consider it necessary to examine whether the line as mapped did in fact correspond to the watershed line. The 12-to-3 majority found the essential question in the case to be whether Thailand and Cambodia had adopted the 1908 map as a mutually acceptable description of their border, thereby making it a binding instrument, regardless of the claimed defects in its making. The heart of its opinion was:

> Even if there were any doubt as to Siam's acceptance of the map in 1908 . . . the Court would consider, in the light of the subsequent course of events, that Thailand is now precluded by her conduct from asserting that she did not accept it. She has, for fifty years, enjoyed such benefits as the Treaty of 1904 conferred on her—if only the benefit of a stable frontier. France, and through her Cambodia, relied on Thailand's acceptance of the map. . . . It is not now open to Thailand, while continuing to claim and enjoy the benefits of the settlement, to deny that she was ever a consenting party to it.

There was another outcome possible, Judge Jessup argued in his own memoir of the case, admitting that he was a possible "prejudiced commentator" because of his early association.

He cites the dissenting opinion of Sir Percy Spender of Australia, who suggested that Siam at that period might be excused from a standard of sophisticated attentiveness such as a European state, "highly developed," might be expected to manifest. Sir Percy then added, with sensitivity to the impact of imperialism at the turn of the century, "apprehension on the part of Siam as to France's attitude toward her is a factor which cannot be disregarded in evaluating Siam's conduct—her silence, her lack of protest, if protest might otherwise have been expected of her."

Defeat at the Court was harder for Thailand to swallow than it had been for Nicaragua, when that country lost its "swampy" strip to Honduras. The Bangkok government, nevertheless, ordered its small detachment to withdraw. The Thai captain had sworn never to pull his flag down, so he ordered the flagpole dug up, and the pole was carried off with the flag still flying, Judge Jessup reports, admitting the story may be apocryphal.

During the years that followed the Southeast Asia and Central America border settlements by the Court, the UN International Law Commission was preparing a code governing the Law of Treaties. The result, in the form of a multilateral treaty, when ratified by the agreed-on number of nations, becomes the equivalent of an act of international legislation. The *Preah Vihear* and *King of Spain* decisions have been praised for their contribution to the drafting of the now authoritative Vienna Convention.

One recent peace-restoring border settlement achieved by the Court had been preceded by armed clashes between the adversaries. These resumed while the case was being studied by the Court, which promptly helped stop the fighting by the international form of "temporary injunction" known as provisional measures. The opponents were former members of the French colony known as French West Africa, the former province of Upper Volta having taken the name Burkina Faso, and the French Sudan now being known as Mali. After gaining independence, they resumed the laborious process of surveying and establishing the frontier that the colonial administration had begun. Most of their common border was sparsely inhabited and difficult of access. After they had settled about 1,000 of the 1,300 kilometers of their frontier, they could not agree further. Intermittent hostilities broke out. The Organization of African Unity (OAU) intervened as mediator and, when unable to complete agreement on the border, induced the parties to go to the ICJ to resolve their problem. Their agreement to submit their dispute to the Court proposed that the final result should be based on respect for "the principle of the intangibility of frontiers inherited. . . ." To this the judges of the Court sitting on the case agreed. They noted that this was a principle that originated in Spanish America in the nineteenth century as decolonization won out south of the U.S. border, and that the OAU had endorsed "frontiers existing on the achievement of national independence."

The Court's judgment endorsed this as a "general principle to prevent the independence and stability of new states being endangered." At first sight this principle conflicts outright with another one, the right of peoples to self-determination. In fact, however, the maintenance of the territorial status quo in Africa is often seen as the wisest course, to preserve what has been achieved by peoples who have struggled for their independence, and to avoid a disruption, which would deprive the continent of the gains achieved by much sacrifice. Hence the need "to consent to the respecting of colonial frontiers . . . in the interpretation of the principle of self-determination. . . ."

While the case was pending at Court, another outbreak of violence occurred at the disputed border. The Court's panel, uniquely in the history of the provision giving power to "indicate . . . provisional measures," received from both parties to the case requests for a temporary Court order to stop the fighting. Such an order was granted by the Court and was effective.

In dealing with the specifics of the *Burkina Faso–Mali* case, the judges had to address themselves to numerous minutiae. There were many tedious factual details to review—photographs, maps, and old colonial documents, including personal and business letters as well as French decrees—and the job was done kilometer by kilometer, in a painstaking, businesslike way. No noteworthy new legal guidelines were announced for international problem solving. But the very accomplishment of their task, winning the approval of the two ad hoc jurists designated by the adversaries, and the peaceful resolution of differences that had brought several resorts to force, was a triumph for the Court. It stands as a late 1980s omen for constructive future use in the ways envisioned by U.S. peace activists eighty years earlier.

LAW OF THE SEA:
MORE THAN MERE BORDERS

The Court's experience in settling sea-boundary questions (fluid though they are) has been as successful and as gratifying as coping with land border problems. These results have been achieved even though the temptations to use force have been greater, because the material interests at stake have been tremendously more vital and/or lucrative than the mere strips of territory involved in land frontier cases.

Not only involving higher stakes, the problems above and below the waters have been more complex. Their importance was heightened and their difficulties enhanced by developments in technology that were arriving on the world stage just as the ICJ accompanied the United Nations in opening for business: the application of mass production techniques to meet the fishing industry's multiplying needs, and the development of novel, post–World War II capacity to drill for oil and gas below the ocean floor.

The rules and principles that were used for solving the problems presented were part of a not-quite-autonomous, but nevertheless fairly separate division of international jurisprudence called the "Law of the Sea." The nations have respected the logical necessity that there be an international source for law governing waters that owe sovereignty to no one, and through which all must pass if there is to be trade, traffic, and communication.

In the period of the ICJ the questions that arose in the Law of the Sea proliferated so that they became a frequent subject of the business of the Court. Work started with the case of the Corfu Channel, which established a principle—usually called the right of "innocent passage"—that was formally adopted from the Court's ruling and made the basis of what can fairly be called "international legislation" at the first of the three Law of the Sea conferences sponsored by the United Nations in the postwar period.

It was a commonly accepted idea, early on, that a ship using the seas had to have one definitive "nationality." Aside from the special problem created by a collision, as we have seen in the *Lotus* case, only one state can have jurisdiction over a ship on the high seas. The flag a ship flies is determined by its nationality and registration, and that is usually determined by agreement between the owner and the state he chooses. A case decided by the Court in 1955 made possible a multinational treaty clause to curb slippery shifts in ship registry.

Friedrich Nottebohm was a subject of the German kaiser who settled in Guatemala in 1905, and remained loyal to the kaiser, the Weimar Republic, and the Third Reich of Adolph Hitler, while plying a profitable import/export business. Following the start of World War II in September 1939, when Germany invaded Poland, he traveled to Europe, and while there, secured citizenship in little Liechtenstein. He promptly returned to his business in Central America, having secured a waiver of residence requirements from the European ministate. When Guatemala went to war against Germany four days after Pearl Harbor, she ignored his new nationality, seized his property as "enemy alien," and arrested, detained, and expelled him.

After the war, Liechtenstein, on behalf of Nottebohm, brought suit against Guatemala, both states having previously accepted the rights and obligations of the optional clause. The claim was that a citizen had been deprived of liberty and property wrongfully, in violation of international law. Guatemala in response argued that Nottebohm had not validly secured citizenship in Liechtenstein.

The Court concluded that it must determine "whether such an act of granting nationality by Liechtenstein entails an obligation on the part of Guatemala to recognize its effect, namely, Liechtenstein's right to exercise its protection." As the Court viewed the controversy, it did "not depend on the law or decision of Liechtenstein whether that State is entitled to exercise its protection. . . . It is international law which determines whether a State is [so] entitled." Reviewing the facts, the judgment declared that Nottebohm's "actual connections with Liechtenstein were extremely tenuous. No settled abode, no prolonged residence." Indeed, his very application for naturalization was said to show he was only paying a visit there at the time, and was therefore a "transient."

The first of three UN-sponsored international conferences on the Law of the Sea began three years later. Based on comprehensive preparation by the UN International Law Commission, the conferees were drawing up the first code of law to govern the use of the waters. They were impressed by and applied the Court's ruling. While they were providing that "Every State shall fix the conditions" for a ship's "right to fly its flag," they imposed the condition "there must exist a genuine link between the State and the ship." The idea of requiring a "genuine link," as imposed in 1958, was based on the 1955 ruling in *Nottebohm*'s case.

In the land cases it was infrequent that there was more at stake than pride or emotional involvement; cases like the *Temple of Preah Vihear* were the exception. When it was drawing the lines at sea, the Court ruling could have serious consequences, such as when fishing rights were stake, or the wealth and power that came with new sources of petroleum. Such conflicts carried the possibility of triggering war; none came—save for a few shots fired at fishing trawlers in what has been called the "Cod War" and that figures in no military or naval history.

An instructive feature of this aspect of the development of international law has been the interaction among its three principal sources. These, as identified in the Court's own statute, Article 38, have been "international conventions," that is, multiparty treaties, "international custom," the common Law of Nations, and judicial decisions. There have been, as we shall see, interaction and mutuality of contribution in the molding of new principles and clarification of the rules to apply. They were needed in a world where it was no longer possible to say glibly that there were lots of good fish in the sea or to think that there were adequate petroleum and natural gas resources on dry land.

Unique to the process of settlement of maritime disputes are three factors that played little or no part in the period of "classical" (that is, pre–World War II) international law: (a) baselines; (b) the allocation of the continental shelf; and (c) economic zone (that is, fishing, drilling, and so on) monopolization by coastal states. As to each of these, the ongoing work of the ICJ has been valuable and accepted as authoritative.

Baselines

A "baseline," a term much used in sea law discussions, can be defined by its function: to fix the points on the coast of a state from which the width of certain significant zones of the ocean, in which that state has a special interest or rights, is to be measured. The "territorial" sea, for example, was fixed to begin at the coastal baseline. This was a portion of the sea that the coastal state has as much right to rule and to exploit as its home soil, to the exclusion of all, save for the right of innocent passage for ships of nations with which it is at peace.

In classical times it was pretty much the consensus—but never the rule, because of enough holdouts to prevent it becoming a customary law principle—that the territorial sea was three miles wide. That now-forgotten measure was picked centuries ago, it being thought to be the maximum distance shore-based guns could reach. (It may still be familiar to those who recall U.S. liquor prohibition and tales of rumrunners slipping in from or escaping to points beyond the three-mile limit.) When fish supplies seemed endless and there was no worry about oil, "there was virtually no need for precision in claims to authority over ocean areas, much less in the criteria and techniques of ocean boundary-making," as Douglass M. Johnson has written. The baseline then was sometimes the high-tide mark, sometimes the low. In time, the low-water mark was so widely accepted that it came to be recognized as the line fixed by customary law.

The geography of the globe is not so simple as to let that be the end of the story. Baselines among many familiar coasts can be drawn easily by simply following their natural curves. A different case was presented by Norway's Atlantic Coast:

> Very broken along its whole length, it constantly opens out into indentations, often penetrating far greater distances inland. . . . To the west, the land configuration stretches out into the sea: large and small islands, mountainous in character, the islets, rocks and reefs, some always above water, others emerging only at low tide.

This graphic description is from the judgment of the ICJ, in one of its great cases, brought to it by Britain after repeated seizures of British fishing boats that had been caught because of straight baselines drawn and announced by Norway in 1933. They ran between the headlands of fjords or around the outside of the outermost reefs or islands. The running diplomatic argument had been interrupted by World War II, but resumed immediately afterward, and the 1951 decision was the Court's second contentious case, immediately following *Corfu Channel*. (Jens Evensen, who worked on the case as a young Norwegian lawyer, was elected a judge of the Court in 1984.)

The Court upheld the legitimacy of the straight baselines that disregarded the tidal margins, approving (for the most part) the straight lines from point to point that had been drawn by the Norwegians—not, however, with a total blessing or carte blanche for other nations that might feel entitled to use the case as a precedent. The Court accompanied the ruling that permitted Norway to protect local fishing with the admonition that "Although . . . the act of delimitation is necessarily a unilateral act, because only the costal state is competent to undertake it, the validity of the delimitation with regard to other States depends upon international law."

As a guide to the nations in application of its ruling, the judgment remarked pointedly that "the drawing of baselines must not depart to any appreciable extent from the general direction of the coast." Future chart makers were warned that a question always to be kept in mind was "whether certain sea areas lying within [such lines as might be drawn] are sufficiently closely linked to the land to be subject to the regime of internal waters." (The use of straight baselines for jagged coasts is not mandatory; for example, the United States has opted not to take advantage of them in mapping Alaskan waters.)

The UN International Law Commission recommended, and its 1958 code on territorial waters drawn up by that year's Law of the Sea Conference accepted, the Court's reasoning and practically copied the relevant language of the opinion as it drafted the conventional (treaty) Law of Nations on baselines.

The Continental Shelf: New Subject of the
Law of Nations

Although home heating and automobile use are heavily dependent on it, the general public is only dimly aware of the "continental shelf." It can be defined as a relatively shallow, submerged extension of most continents, extending from the shoreline to a point of usually sudden, deep descent to the ocean floor. The average depth is about 200 meters and the extension from dry land ranges between 30 and 300 miles.

During World War II, U.S. Interior Secretary Harold M. Ickes aroused the interest of President Franklin Delano Roosevelt's wartime cabinet about two points. One was not a new discovery: great reserves of oil and gas lay beneath the continental shelves. The other was that the technology for drilling and gaining possession of the undersea treasure had been developed. Action was delayed until the war's end, and hence until after President Roosevelt's death.

It was in September 1945, not many weeks after Japan's surrender ended World War II, that the "continental shelf" entered the annals of the law. The initial step was taken by U.S. President Harry S. Truman, who asserted by proclamation that "the natural resources of the subsoil and seabed of the continental shelf . . . contiguous to the United States" were its property. The formal announcement made no secret about motive: there was a "long-range world-wide need for new sources of petroleum and other minerals" that expert opinion had held could be found in "parts of the continental shelf off the coasts" of the United States.

The immediate sequel was not merely acquiescence, a necessary but not sufficient basis for customary law to come into being. There was also emulation, as time went on. Over the next decade, a number of states made similar claims. Assertions of maritime jurisdiction far beyond any previously made were announced. At the same time, new claims to fishery jurisdiction and control up to 200 miles from shore were asserted.

Exploitation of the new resource could not begin overnight or indeed for years. During the interval, the UN International Law Commission was, as we have just noted, engaged in preparatory work for the first Law of the Sea international conference, scheduled for 1958. The commission had been aware of the developments with regard to shelf claims.

Responding to the uniform acceptance of the principle laid out in the Truman declaration, commission staff, within a decade, agreed that it could and should be incorporated into the Law of Nations. The commission suggested, and the Law of the Sea Conference accepted for inclusion in a widely agreed-to treaty, the formal recording and codifying of the sovereign rights of the coastal state to explore and exploit the natural resources of the continental shelf.

But the widely varying character of coastal regions, and the relation of adjoining or nearby states to what might be the "same" continental shelf, made it impossible to solve or settle in the words of a single piece of international legislation, in advance, all the problems that might arise. And this is where the Court came in. Since no set of rules could be drafted that would be fair if applied to each of the variations of shelf contour that might come up, the treaty, by using broad and general language, left difficult cases to the Court. The division, they directed, should be at the median (equidistant) "unless another boundary is justified by special circumstances."

Numbers of shelf delimitation agreements were negotiated, until a knotty problem arose that stumped the diplomats involved. What interrupted the ongoing negotiating process was a quite stubborn disagreement between Germany (Federal Republic, as it then was) on the one hand, and its coastal neighbors, Denmark and the Netherlands, on the other. It arose, in part, from the nature of the North Sea as one single, continuous (except for a trough near Norway) continental shelf, facing a curved coastline shared by three neighboring states. It had to be divided like a pie, with a wedge for each of the contenders.

How to slice the pie was the problem. The difficulty came with the bulges in the coasts of Denmark and the Netherlands flanking a deep concavity in the German shoreline. Application of the suggested equidistance rule would have given the Netherlands and Denmark pieces of the North Sea pie much larger in area than would be left for Germany. Yet the length of coastal frontage of each on the North Sea was roughly similar. As the geographical complication was later summarized in a statement by the International Court of Justice:

> In the case of a recessing or concave coast . . . the effect of the equidistance method was to pull the line of the boundary inwards, in the direction of the concavity. . . . If the curvature were pronounced [the lines would] inevitably meet at a relatively short distance from the coast, thus "cutting off" the coastal state from the area of the continental shelf outside.

The case that would be known as *North Sea Continental Shelf* (Federal Republic of Germany/Denmark; F.R.G./Netherlands) came to the Court in February 1967. It was submitted under the terms of an agreement negotiated among the contending states. Instead of putting the case to the Court as a request for the fixing of specified maritime borders, or as a "win/lose" issue, they asked the Court "to declare the principles and rules of international law applicable."

The central dispute, as to whether the "equidistance" method of delimitation mentioned in the Geneva pact confined Germany to the tiny wedge it rejected, was disposed of by ruling that equidistance had not become a compelling criterion under the relevant customary law. In its final summing-up, the Court laid out the following guidelines for the parties:

> [D]elimitation was to be effected by agreement in accordance with equitable principles and taking account of all relevant circumstances, in such a way as to leave as much as possible to each party all those parts of the continental shelf

that constituted a natural prolongation of its land territory, without encroach-
ment on the natural prolongation of the land territory of the other.

This three-party case was but the first of a number that were to come to the
Court in which potentially oil-rich underwater areas were marked off, sometimes with gravely disappointing results, and yet in each case peacefully
accepted. The North Sea ruling and its successors likewise assisted other
states in the resolution of their own disputes.

Litigation concerning the continental shelf came before the Court over the
years on several more occasions. Despite dissatisfaction that was voiced by
some dissenters over the rejection of equidistance as a legal principle (it was
always permissible as an agreed-on or possibly appropriate method), the ruling of the Court in its North Sea decision has worked. "Most lawyers still look
upon that decision as a landmark," wrote D. Johnson in the comprehensive
monograph, "The Theory and History of Ocean Boundary-Making."

What this means is that in the negotiating process—agreements arrived at
without having to go to Court—enough direction has been given by the
Court's disposition in the North Sea and later cases to facilitate the arrival at
ultimate agreement. The Court majorities over the years have been aware of
this and have stuck pretty much to the North Sea approach, as expanded in
the successful conclusion of a difficult contest between Libya and Malta:

> [T]here is to be no question of refashioning geography, or compensating for the
> inequalities of nature . . . all States are equal before the law . . . [but] "equity does
> not necessarily mean equality" . . . nor make equal what nature had made unequal.

Expansion of Exclusive Fishing Rights

The scientific advances that made it possible to locate and drill offshore for
oil gave, at least for the short run, some promise of new sources of supply.
Technology applied to deep-sea fishing (sonar location of schools, factory
ships with freezers aboard, and so on) brought a threat of depletion of living
resources of the seas.

Iceland as a nation was sensitive to the danger. A glance at a globe will
show why her people and her commerce were vulnerable. As grave depletion loomed, the customary law limit of three or four miles for coastal state
control faded away. With the coming of the era of the continental shelf, her
legislature took the first of a number of actions in response. The island's initiatives brought on four phases of conflict with people fishing who were not
from Iceland. These were primarily British; trawlers from other lands—West
Germany, Denmark, Netherlands, and Belgium—were also involved; all but
the Germans acquiesced in Iceland's increasingly expanding limits.

New troubles began in 1958, leading to the first of three separate periods
of "low intensity" conflict at sea, called the "Cod Wars" by the media and in

most popular references. Combat was only economic at first. In hostilities that erupted, two dozen ships of Her Majesty's Royal Navy skirmished with the six vessels in Iceland's Coast Guard. Only a few shots were fired, but there was much aggressive maneuvering, deliberate ramming, and cutting of underwater lines that trailed great fishnets. Protests were taken to the United Nations, including an unheeded plea by Iceland to the Security Council. NATO was troubled by incidents involving U.S. ground crews at an air base from which the islanders were excluding British planes.

This ended with an agreement by the British to accept a twelve-mile limit, and by both parties to submit to Court jurisdiction of any disputes under the pact.

Iceland's economic realities and the international legal landscape had changed sufficiently by 1972 for that nation to announce extension of the fishery limit to fifty miles, and to declare the 1961 agreements "no longer applicable and consequently terminated." Viewing the agreement to submit any dispute to Court as quite as obsolete as the twelve-mile limit, Iceland declined to participate in the Court's proceedings that were instituted by Britain and Germany. They claimed that the Court now had jurisdiction by treaty under the 1961 agreement.

Article 53 of the Court's statute provides that "The Court must," if a party fails to appear, satisfy itself "not only that it has jurisdiction . . . but also that the claim is well founded in fact and law." There was no formal appearance, but Iceland's foreign minister sent communications to the Court claiming variously that the 1961 agreement had expired, was no longer binding because of changed circumstances, and was void for duress because "the British Royal Navy had been using force at the time."

The Court ruled against the objections. Guatemala had abstained, at first, from appearing in the Nottebohm affair but won on the merits after an adverse ruling on jurisdiction; Iran ignored interim protection orders when Britain's suit tested oil nationalization in 1953 but nevertheless contested jurisdiction and won. By defiance even after a ruling that it was subject to the Court, Iceland did what even South Africa had not, and set a bad precedent.

A full presentation on Iceland's case contending that coercion voided the agreement might have prevailed. As it was, Judge Padilla Nervo, a Mexican national (who had dissented from an order granting interim protection because many Latin states had already declared 200-mile limits), pointed out, "The Royal Navy did not need to use armed forces. Its mere presence on the seas inside the fishery limits of the coastal state could be enough pressure."

Even so, when the Court came to decide the case, the majority showed awareness of the turbulent, ongoing changes in the Law of the Sea. The ultimate ruling reflected, rather than affected, the ongoing development of the law. The fifty-mile zone was not held illegal against all comers; Britain and Germany's treaty objection to a limit greater than twelve miles was sustained, but that was a nominal circumstance, as the adversaries had already, in 1973 made a two-year interim settlement agreement.

In his book of lectures on the Court's work, Judge Nagendra Singh, who had been president of the Court in the late 1980s, said that the Court had been attentive to the "the fluid and developing state of the law at the time." Despite Iceland's default in failing to appear, "the Court was contributing to the development of international law by its restraint; it was taking great care not to check such development or put any obstacle in its way."

He cited the remark of his colleague, Judge Hardy C. Dillard of the United States: "[B]ecause of the Third Conference on the Law of the Sea it would be imprudent for the Court to attempt to pronounce on the issue . . . in a state of such acknowledged and political flux." But, Judge Singh added:

> This is not however to say that the *Fisheries Jurisdiction* (title of the Iceland cases) did nothing positive to develop the law. The Judgment defined the concept of preferential fishing rights of the coastal state, as well as the principle of "due regard to the interests of others" when dealing with problems arising out of assertion of national interests in the exploitation of natural resources which have come to be regarded as falling in the category of the "common heritage of mankind."

There was a quickly won third Cod War, as Iceland moved to join the many states who had made it clear at the third sea law conference that they backed a 200-mile exclusive fishing zone. That consensus was embodied in the 1982 Law of the Sea Treaty.

Customary international law's acceptance of a 200-mile fishing zone brought to a head a long-standing conflict that had been as restrained as the Iceland/Britain struggle had been disorderly. The contestants were the United States and Canada, and the principal prize was a valuable scallop fishery known as the Georges Bank. There had been fishing rivalry and feuds from time to time, ever since the United States became independent and Canada was "British North America," with a variety of treaty settlements from time to time. Now the problem that needed solution was that both Cape Cod and Nova Scotia were within 200 miles of the Georges Bank.

Even before Canada and the United States—each in 1977—followed the path taken by Iceland in declaring an exclusionary rule over waters within 200 miles of their coast, they had had a low-key continental shelf debate about rights in the great single ledge bordering the Gulf of Maine and seaward from there. Viewing the intersecting arcs from 200-mile radii, the opponents agreed that a decision about the division of the overlap was necessary.

Legal teams from the neighboring countries chose to go to the ICJ for a decision. With so many people in New England and Nova Scotia vitally concerned in the outcome and looking over their shoulder, they needed, as legal adviser Davis Robinson, one of the U.S. lawyers, later wrote, a judicial result that "must be fair, not only in substance as a matter of law, but in perception as well" (*American Journal of International Law* 95: 582).

Being aware of 1972 amendments to the Court rules to facilitate use of Chambers of the Court, that is, specially chosen panels of less than a full bench, the adversaries agreed they had an ideal case to innovate the long-unused procedure. Their plans for presentation of their positions on the case included such a complex of historical, geographical, biological, environmental, and other data that both sides concluded that a smaller body of judges than the full Court's fifteen would more readily cope with the mass of materials and the problems raised by the subject matter. This case was the first to use the chamber procedure. It was also the first time the newly developed concept of the 200-mile exclusive economic zone was considered and applied by the Court. Another "first" was the appearance of the concept of a "single maritime boundary," chosen as suitable for division of both the rights to the continental shelf below and the exploitable resources of the waters above.

The legal teams proved to be correct in their estimate of the bulk of the material to be put forward to support their arguments. Some 10,000 pages of written and oral presentation with 300 maps and diagrams fill a three-foot shelf. The adversaries were at the Peace Palace for weeks, each using eight 2.5-hour sittings for initial advocacy and four for response/rebuttal. A carefully worked out schedule for this was put in disarray by one interruption: in April 1984, under the Court's rules, priority had to be given to Nicaragua's request for emergency measures of protection.

Canada's claims were based on alleged proximity, economic dependence, and past acquiescence. The United States asserted its "predominant interest," plus the existence of a suggested "natural boundary" that was offered by an existing navigable channel; in addition there was emphasis placed on the Maine coast's parallel position to the great scallop bank, and the greater mileage of the U.S. shoreline in the vicinity. Most of the claims made by both sides were rejected by the Court, save for the argument of proportionately larger coastline.

Looking at a map, the Court split the difference. When the result was announced, there were protesting newspaper headlines on both sides of the border; arguably this was evidence that the result was as fair as could be achieved. In any event the parties have complied and lived with it.

13

Some Unfinished Business

There are many who do not take international law very seriously. It is often said that powerful states disregard the law when they please. There is a similar attitude taken with regard to the World Court, manifested by the inevitable cliché accompanying the rare references to it by the media: "It has no way to enforce its judgments."

It is painfully evident that some states, like some very powerful individuals, disregard the law when they choose. But no one argues that what such law-defying people do proves that laws governing social and economic behavior are nonexistent or meaningless. The law does catch up with outlaw individuals, however powerful, most, if not all the time, later if not sooner.

Almost all of the decisions of the Court at The Hague have been accepted and complied with, with neither gloating by the winner nor disregard by the loser. In international relations (as in labor relations, where hotly contested differences are settled by arbitration) the parties know that they must live with each other after the dispute is over. Hence they will ordinarily receive a judgment and act as it directs, with an awareness of the necessity to continue to relate as fellow participants in a planetary community.

In some cases, even after initial defiance or disregard, the verdict of a court will have survival value, a life-after-rejection that will enable it to accomplish its purpose. Two relatively recent cases affecting the identical region but with different issues presented, show the survival value of an international judgment. Each dealt (one indirectly) with the relation of a powerful state to a much weaker one: the United States with Nicaragua.

A SOCCER WAR AND
THE WATERS OF A BAY

The functioning and the abrupt end of the Central American Court of Justice were described in chapter 2. A treaty on canal construction rights between

Nicaragua and the United States was successfully challenged in the Central American Court by El Salvador, which claimed equal rights in the Gulf of Fonseca. Based on the colonial and postcolonial history of the adjacent lands and their relation to the waters of the gulf, the holding was that ". . . the legal status of the Gulf of Fonseca . . . is that of property belonging to the three countries that surround it." There was a shared interest, what we would call now a condominium.

That decision of the Central American Court remained in limbo for half a century. The issues that it settled arose anew and came to the International Court of Justice (ICJ) in 1992. It was brought there as incidental to a border dispute that provoked the so-called Soccer War.

Honduras and Nicaragua had disagreed about their border early in the last century (1906; see chapter 12). They took that dispute to arbitration then; it was settled by an arbitration award rendered by the king of Spain that was reconfirmed by the World Court in 1960.

Thereafter tension mounted between El Salvador and Honduras over a similar issue that had been simmering for some time. Because of much heavier population density in the far smaller El Salvador, and the ownership of a grossly disproportionate part of its land by a few wealthy families, its people had commenced migrating or commuting to Honduras in ever-greater numbers in the 1960s. Honduras tried to halt this by passing harsh anti-alien laws. In this context, long-standing boundary disputes grew more urgent, and led to a variety of harassments in disputed zones.

Finally, in the summer of 1969, with teams from the two nations competing for the finals of the World Cup soccer championship, violence erupted at the playoff games. When El Salvador triumphed, Hondurans began indiscriminately attacking and sharply harassing Salvadorans who had migrated there for survival. Bombs fell in El Salvador, apparently from Honduran planes. Troops from El Salvador then crossed the border and carried the war, with many civilian casualties, to within seventy miles of the Honduran capital. Finally the Organization of American States (OAS) secured a cease-fire. Years of hostility followed, but the truce basically held. An agreement was reached to take the dispute to the ICJ for ultimate resolution if negotiations and mediation failed.

In the mutual agreement taking the case of the border dispute to the Court, two additional issues were submitted. It was agreed to submit the status of the islands in the Gulf of Fonseca, and to bring to the World Court the problem that the Central American Court had adjudicated and Nicaragua under pressure of the United States declined to accept. As the new case began, the Sandinista government was still in office in Nicaragua. As the contra danger began to recede, memories were brought to the surface by the El Salvador–Honduras lawsuit, about their predecessors' failure, seven decades before, to settle the status of the Fonseca Gulf's waters.

Having satisfactorily concluded all but one phase of litigation with the

United States and its neighbors concerning the contra war (to be discussed later in this chapter), Nicaragua chose to petition the Court to intervene and be allowed to participate in the Honduran–Salvadoran lawsuit over the waters of the gulf. Honduras and El Salvador had chosen to submit their case to a panel of five judges instead of the full Court, a "chamber," which permitted Nicaragua to intervene as adjoining coastal state on the gulf.

While the application to intervene was being considered by the Court, Nicaragua's 1990 election had taken place and the new administration of Violeta Chamorro replaced that of Daniel Ortega. But the national interest of Nicaragua in a proceeding that would pass on its rights in an adjoining bay was nonideological. The Chamorro administration agreed, in effect, to have the Court pass upon whether an earlier grant to the United States was, as the 1917 Court had held, a wrongful giveaway of its neighbor's interests: Nicaragua's intervention was limited to the Gulf of Fonseca aspect; the "soccer war" border question took greater effort and detail to decide.

As to the maritime question, the Court held that the entire body of water outside the three-mile limit in the gulf was under joint sovereignty, that is, it was held in condominium by the three adjoining states. El Salvador's paper victory of 1917 was now reaffirmed, with Nicaragua's participation and concurrence; the United States, culprit then, was on the sidelines and silent.

The 1917 opinion of the Central American Court was quoted with approval; the gulf was "property belonging to the three countries that surround it." What had been decided by the Central American Court was, contrary to what Nicaragua had claimed in 1917 under U.S. influence, "a valid decision by a competent court" and entitled to respect as such: this completed that unfinished business.

To decide the border dispute between Honduras and El Salvador, the Court was obliged first to study in detail the history of Central America, and the relation between what were first administrative units of Spanish territory, then states of a Central American republic embracing them all. Detailed evidence of where the borders ran at the time independence was won was examined. Six pockets of disputed territory along the contested line of demarcation required close examination of documents and deeds. When the ruling was announced, the agent for El Salvador at The Hague expressed disappointment but pledged his nation to obey.

On October 6, 1992, in an article titled "A war sparked by a soccer game makes headlines, but not its epilogue in the World Court," the *New York Times* commented on the contrast between newsworthiness of peaceful resolution by the Court and the opposite:

> Few noticed the other day when The Hague jurists settled a bitter dispute over the land, island and maritime boundaries between El Salvador and Honduras. The pacific outcome underscored the court's potential for resolving scores of disputes that now embroil new states in Europe and Asia.

THE CONTRA WAR, CONTADORA, AND
HOW THE COURT PREVAILED

As to effectiveness of a Court decision, we return to the holding that the contra war (see chapter 10) was a "breach of the [U.S.] obligation under customary international law not to intervene in the affairs of another state." The Court decision included a reiteration of its earlier orders directing the United States "immediately to cease and refrain" from "supporting and aiding military and paramilitary activities in and against Nicaragua."

When the UN Charter was signed and ratified by the United States, it became a treaty "made under the authority of the United States . . . the Supreme Law of the Land" (Article 6 of the U.S. Constitution). As a founding member of the United Nations, the United States agreed that it "undertakes to comply with the decision of the International Court of Justice in any case to which it is a party" (Article 94, UN Charter).

Despite this commitment, the administration in power in 1986—President Ronald Reagan's—continued to behave with respect to the subject matter of the ruling just as it had for the previous five years. There was one change, and it was for the worse: The Congress had midway in those five years of contra support, supply, and resupply, enacted a law forbidding it. Now, in June 1986, as the Court was making its ruling, the Boland restriction (as the law was called) was repealed as if to make continued support of the contras legal under domestic law just as it had become illegal under international and treaty law.

When the Law of Nations was thus defied, one would expect that there would be some remedy. As it was before the adoption of the UN Charter, self-help was the only way to make a Court ruling effective; no enforcement scheme was available. In such a state of affairs, only in large, that is, powerful, states was there a way to secure satisfaction.

The Charter provided the possibility of an international judicial enforcement system. It enabled the Security Council to "make recommendations or decide upon measures to be taken to give effect to the judgment." But there was a hitch. The newly created power of enforcement always faced the possible check of the "veto." According to the UN Charter, such an action could be stopped by the negative vote of any one of the "Permanent Five," the major power founders of the organization, which included, of course, the United States.

A limit to the use of the veto was possible in the Charter's provision that "a party to a dispute shall abstain from voting in Chapter VI decisions." (That was the legal way of saying, as the ancient maxim dictates, that "No one shall be judge in her own cause," a maxim that the U.S. Supreme Court has held an essential part of "due process of law.")

The Council vote to take action in the case was 11 to 1. But the single vote against was that of the United States, voting in and thereby acting as judge in its own case. Professor Keith Highet, distinguished scholar as well as popular attorney at The Hague (now deceased), suggested that the Council should and could have ignored the U.S. vote there. No Security Council member raised the question. And so the U.S. veto prevented the imposition of sanctions or other enforcement action. The result was that there was no remedy available within the United Nations to enforce its own Court's judgment.

In the United States, most scholars of the Court either approved the Court's verdict, or asserted that it was inevitable after the United States failed to appear in the Court to defend the legality of its own actions. It seemed to most U.S. citizens that the impact of the Court's action was negligible. There was some scattered, but rapidly decreasing, media concern in the United States about the government's refusal to pay attention to the Court's decision. The *Los Angeles Times,* referring to "the determination of President Reagan to shoot his way to peace in Nicaragua" as responsible for the veto, headlined its editorial of August 3, 1986, "World Scofflaw." Richard Bilder, a distinguished Midwest professor of international law, in a guest column in the *St. Louis Post-Dispatch* on August 7, 1986, titled "In Contempt of Court," called the Nicaragua decision "the most significant international court judgment ever rendered," and told his readers (as the unfolding story was to prove) that "the fact that the United States could thwart enforcement by the Security Council does not mean that the [C]ourt's decision does not continue to be legally binding."

In October 1986, the issue came before the Security Council a second time; again a lone U.S. veto prevented that body from taking any enforcement action. Soon thereafter (and annually through 1989) the General Assembly—which has power only to recommend—took up the question of U.S. behavior. By a vote of 94 to 3, with 47 abstentions, the General Assembly called for "full and immediate compliance with the judgment" of the Court in the Nicaragua case. By now the press had lost interest in this law-and-order issue. The General Assembly resolution made no impression on Washington, and was not considered fit to print anywhere in the United States.

Nevertheless, the Court decision, as a cogent statement of the applicable Law of Nations, played a decisive role in relations among the Central American states whose people were doing the dying. It contributed much to the ending of hostilities. This was not revealed until the publication in 1992 of an obscure work of scholarship by a Costa Rican attorney and diplomat. What Joaquin Tacsan described in his book, titled *The Dynamics of International Law in Conflict Resolution,* has not been as yet understood or recorded in North American journalism or historical writing.

Dr. Tacsan was, until his 1996 death in a plane crash, a close aide of former President Oscar Arias of Costa Rica. He was an official of a peace-serving foundation that had been originally funded by the Nobel Prize cash grant made to President Arias for a Central American plan for peace that bore his name.

Dr. Tacsan was a first-hand witness of the influence of the World Court decision in bringing peace to Central America. His role as a participant is

described in his book: "The author witnessed a substantial part of the deliberative process in the Costa Rican Ministry of Foreign Affairs, where he
worked as a member of the Costa Rican team of legal advisors."

In his book, a work of jurisprudential scholarship, he describes the role that
the World Court decision played in the peace process. The book concentrates,
at first, on a discussion of two divergent, somewhat competing, schools of
legal doctrine, followed by his proposal to synthesize them. His knowledge of
how peace came to Central America is used to illustrate his theory as to the
function of international law in conflict resolution among states.

In consequence, convincing evidence of the contribution of the Court to
the Central American peace process is disguised, so to speak, as an international law dissertation. This has prevented it from having the educational
effect it deserved. In a world greedy for war memories, peace memoirs have
a hard enough time as it is. What follows is a summary of the factual presentation whereby Tacsan explains the Court's effectiveness and impact.

Since the contra's assault on Nicaragua was not an internal, indigenous
rebellion, it was conducted in the early stages, and for a good part during the
entire period, from bases in the neighboring countries of Costa Rica and Honduras. The consequence was a series of back-and-forth cross-border incidents
that raised tensions locally and threatened wider conflict.

Serious concern was raised among other Latin American states not directly
involved, such as Mexico and Venezuela. They feared that a provocation of
some sort would provide a pretext for full-fledged entry of U.S. armed forces
into the region. To head off what they thought would be a disaster, the concerned nations (known as the Contadora Group, named for an island off
Panama where they first met) launched a mediation effort, a project to bring
about a comprehensive local peace settlement.

The Contadora Group's project constituted a pioneer local effort by Central American leaders, with the aid of their neighbors, to shape their own des-
tiny, and to bring a peace free from external meddling. Contadora's object,
as Tacsan tells us, "was to prevent the development of a new hegemonic
(read: U.S.) intervention in the region."

Initial difficulties were due to the willingness of Costa Rica, Honduras, and
El Salvador (whom he often refers to as "U.S. allies,") to agree with the U.S.
program of military pressure on the Nicaraguan government to force "a more
pluralistic and representative government." While it turned out that during
the Contadora period they never relented in this, there came a time when the
"allies" were willing to meet with the Contadora mediators and Nicaragua
(with Guatemala) to discuss an agenda including an item "outside military
assistance, actions aimed at disrupting internal order of countries."

Initial success in bringing the parties together made "Contadora the *de
facto* exclusive mediator for the whole of Central America." The mediators at
one point prepared a draft treaty that Nicaragua accepted but that the United

States persuaded the allies to reject. There followed drafts and counter drafts that diverged principally with regard to an initially proposed protocol that would call on the United States to cease funding the contras.

What kept the group in existence during a three-year period was mutual acceptance of the principles of "self-determination and non-intervention," which Tacsan called "weak links" because of their lack of definition. The additional concepts of "collective self-defense" and "human rights" shared with these the distinction of providing a "highly principled environment" but with an intolerable level of "abstraction."

> A series of stalemates that occurred between 1984 and 1986 evinced the group's lack of conceptual consensus on the basic expectations it needed . . . the contending parties felt free to interpret the leading normative principles in their own ways.

In consequence there persisted a lack of a "unified stance on the legitimacy of U.S. military pressure against Nicaragua." As Tacsan viewed it, this had to be attributed to the failure of the Contadora group "to generate consensual legal criteria . . . [resulting] mainly from its symbolic use of a few abstract and indeterminate principles."

Against the foregoing backdrop, the author–lawyer and diplomat who was serving one of the "U.S. allies" during the time in question tells us what revived the failed mediation: "Nicaragua's resort to the International Court of Justice on April 9, 1984, provided the consensual normative expectations and the authoritative knowledge that the parties needed to resolve the conflict." His summary-analysis of the Court's opinion and its reasoning is tersely recapitulated: "the Court disposed of and rejected all of the U.S. bloc's normative expectations." But, he asks, reminding the reader of the main argument of his book, "the question arises as to how to appraise a judgment that, like this, cannot realistically be enforced."

He undertakes the burden of demonstrating—by examination of "the judgment's impact on the goals and negotiating styles of main participants within the post-Contadora Central American peace process (1987–1989)"—the unsoundness of "the traditional idea that international law must be enforceable to be effective."

We are introduced to his promised evidence with a statement of a proposition that no historian or journalist discussing the success of the Arias plan for peace of 1987 has grasped: "The events in Central America that followed the June 27, 1986, ICJ judgment on the Nicaragua case took a remarkably different direction from that of the Contadora years." To this he adds a comment understandable from his point of view as a Latin American—but tragically inapplicable to the people and leaders of the United States: "Between July 1986 and August 1987 all participants and the international community focused their attention on the International Court of Justice and the possible impact of its rulings."

That "focus[ing] of attention" was helped along by the filing by Nicaragua at the ICJ of two new applications: against Costa Rica and Honduras. Following only by a month the June judgment of the Court against the United States, "they significantly contributed to a change of attitude in Central America." While the two cases differed somewhat—that against Honduras charged direct involvement of its army in raids on Nicaraguan territory, "Both applications complained about Costa Rican and Honduran intervention in the internal or external affairs of another state, violation of another state's sovereignty, and injury (killing, wounding, and kidnapping) of another state's citizens."

The new cases were barely noticed in the U.S. media and caused hardly a ripple among the citizenry, unlike what Tacsan reports as "the convulsion that Nicaragua's application generated within the Costa Rican public." He explains:

> Costa Rica, a country that itself possesses a sophisticated judicial system, grants courts of law a significant place in daily life. Since the Costa Rican constitution places international law above ordinary legislation, Costa Ricans naturally view the ICJ with great respect. . . . The Arias administration could not afford to get entangled in international litigation without being assured of a favorable decision. Such assurance, however, was not clearly available, especially in the light of the rumored double standard assumed by the previous Monge administration toward the Contras.

And so, the author tells us, "the Arias administration saw negotiation as the only way out." The writer of those words has the credibility justified by his having been one of the new negotiators. He added that it was understood that the shift in diplomacy had to recognize as criteria "the kind set forth by the I.C.J. . . . new negotiations outside the Contadora context needed a complete redefinition of issues and bargaining strategies."

There *had* been negotiations for years. But the new "way out" that President Arias now envisioned—knowing that "he could not afford to get entangled in international litigation," Tacsan wrote—would have to include agreement to refuse to allow each country's territory to be used as a base for attacking its neighbors, coupled with a joint plea for cutoff of further aid to the contras.

He went to work on a draft of plan that he chose to present (six months before the famed Arias plan was announced) to a separate meeting of the "allies" to get them to agree first so that they could show the Nicaraguans unity on this point. He persuaded them to concur that "since the U.S.-sponsored Contras were not a significant—or a legitimate—mechanism . . . Nicaragua had to be democratized by diplomatic rather than military means."

Agreement on this point by the four other presidents, offered by Arias, convinced the Nicaraguan president to sign on August 7, 1987, an agreement that became known as Esquipulas II, the embodiment of the Arias plan. On the same day, Nicaragua withdrew its case against Costa Rica.

Peace is a "process," as President Arias said in accepting the Nobel Peace Prize for 1987; it is not won overnight. International peace in Central America took years to come; the promise of internal peace through reconciliation is taking longer. It is obvious from its timing that the Nobel Prize must have been awarded to help bring about the Arias plan's success, which it did; the eyes of the prize committee might well have been turned to the moving force behind the making of Arias's plan and its ultimate success, the teachings of the International Court of Justice.

Honduras had signed the Esquipulas II accord, "officially committing itself to discontinue aid" to the contras and "to restrict the use of its territory," so that it would no longer be used as their base. But unlike Costa Rica, it refused at first to accept the jurisdiction of the Court and forced a separate hearing on that issue. Only after the Court, late in 1988, issued its decision overruling the objections and confirming its jurisdiction did effective steps begin to curtail the activity of the contras. Within weeks afterward, Honduras agreed to accept verification of compliance with the accords "from outside the region." That is what made it possible to bring a UN peacekeeping mechanism into the region.

As part of its ruling in the Honduras case, the Court cleared the way for the entry of other agencies into the peace process, and its decision was followed by an invitation and offer from UN Secretary-General Perez de Cuellar. In response, the Esquipulas II process took a giant step forward. The five presidents, now feeling free to resort to international organizations for verification and implementation of the Esquipulas accords, agreed at their next meeting, at Costa del Sol, El Salvador, to "formulate within a period of no more than ninety days a Joint Plan for the voluntary demobilization, repatriation or relocation of" the contras. Nicaragua agreed to develop a process of democratization and national reconciliation, with elections no later than February 1990. Tacsan wrote:

> With renovated normative expectations—as authoritatively determined by the Court—the strong leadership of the 1987 Nobel Peace Prize Winner, Oscar Arias, and a fresher attitude, the five Central American Presidents undertook new and similar bargaining styles to change the configuration of alliances within the region.

The peace process had undertaken a life of its own that could not now be stopped, and while not accepting or agreeing with the Court decision, the United States "adapted" to it, after having initially criticized it as "unsound." At first it voted in the Security Council for the resolution to support a structure for verification and compliance that the Central American presidents had requested, then, after some resistance and delay, even to support the introduction of UN military observers as a peacekeeping force.

It is of interest to read Dr. Tacsan's view as to how ICJ decisions win regard—as they did in Central America among initially opposed contenders—as "authoritative determinations." To begin with he cites a striking concept, now widely accepted, that was originated by a Columbia University Law School professor Oscar Schachter. He was the first to suggest that the global community of international lawyers constitute "a kind of *invisible college* dedicated to a common intellectual enterprise," as Tacsan wrote, although widely dispersed and engaged in diverse occupations.

The ICJ judges at The Hague had been and continue to regard themselves as being members of that community. In their work they use the leading problem-solving techniques utilized by the larger community of international lawyers, argues Tacsan:

> This linguistic and technical interconnection between the Court and the larger community of lawyers enables the Court to lead and unify that larger commu-nity; it makes it very likely that the normative expectations that prevail at the Court will become consensual within the epistemic community of international lawyers. To strengthen the possibility that Court judgments will become con-sensual in the larger community, Court judges generally work out a high degree of consensus among themselves on most decisions they render.

His own case study—made in the course of serving his client, the Republic of Costa Rica—showed that the ICJ decision in Nicaragua's case "passed the test of truth" of international lawyers and became consensual knowledge among all actors except the United States, for the most part.

> [T]he community of international lawyers, U.S. Members included, welcomed the several clarifications of conventional and customary international law that the Court conveyed through its decision of the Nicaragua case. At a number of conferences, workshops and universities in the United States, domestic con-stituencies echoed international lawyers' remarks that overall the U.S. violated international law as determined by the 1986 ICJ judgment.

Nevertheless, as we have seen—and are to see again in the discussion below of the subsequent proceedings in Nicaragua's case—the United States stead-fastly declined to recognize the validity of the Court's judgment. The United States persisted (though it had participated in full-dress litigation of the point and lost) in its contention that the Court had lacked authority to take cog-nizance of the Nicaraguan application.

Writing now as an attorney who had represented and negotiated for Costa Rica during this period, Tacsan tells us that his client (and Honduras) "evinced greater concern [than the U.S.] about the lawfulness of their respec-tive foreign policies." The process following the Nicaraguan application against its neighbors was twofold. First, top-notch international lawyers were hired to advise the local legal teams. Second, the decision of the Court in the Nicaragua case provided the basis for legal argument and litigation strategy. Tacsan here enumerates some of the knotty problems that he, his colleagues, and local government officials debated, such as, "What are the differences in jurisdiction and admissibility between the new cases Nicaragua brought against Costa Rica and Honduras and the original Nicaragua case" against the United States?

As for the gist of the legal advisers' discussions, and the impact on foreign policy in Central America:

> [T]he Court's findings [in Nicaragua's case] were closely examined in order not to make the same mistakes as had the United States' legal team in the earlier case. Both the opinions of local and international counsels and the prevailing and surviving expectations from . . . the Nicaragua case informed, guided and restrained the Tegulcigalpa bloc's [Costa Rica, Honduras and El Salvador] foreign policy. For Costa Rican and Honduran political leaders, losing a case in Court would have brought great embarrassment; it would have meant the end of their political futures.

With Honduras as well as Costa Rica being "guided and restrained" by the law made in the Nicaragua case, the "business" of the contra war was finished. Under the observation of UN peacekeeping troops, the contra forces were demobilized. To the extent that the United States had ceased violating international law by supporting military actions against Nicaragua, there was compliance with the Court decision, even if not immediately. But the Court had also held the trade embargo illegal, and that did not cease until after the election of Violeta Chamorro—and may have contributed to her margin of victory.

Peace had been restored on the borders and internally, and Dr. Tacsan's evidence is that the Court's decision played a far greater part than has been recognized. The reparations aspect of the case needs a separate discussion, which supporters of international law and order will find less satisfying than the above.

14

Reparations: Nicaragua and Iran

After it became known in 1986 that profits from illegal sales of arms to Iran had been financing the Nicaraguan contras, the words "Iran" and "contra" were coupled. The Iran and contra cases of the 1980s at the World Court involved the United States as the accuser in the former and the accused in the latter. The Court held in the contra (Nicaragua) case, as it did in Iran's, that a prior complaint at the UN Security Council did not bar judicial proceedings.

In each case, the Court's ruling on the merits did not itself end the matter. The Court held in both—in identical language—that "an obligation to make reparation" existed; the parties were invited to agree about the amount that, failing agreement, would be settled by the Court.

NICARAGUA VERSUS UNITED STATES: PROMISES AS REPARATIONS

Toward the end of the Court's discussion of Nicaragua's case in its opinion, it remarked that the United States, in accepting the Court's jurisdiction, agreed that the Court should determine "the nature or extent of the reparation to be made for the breach of an international obligation." It was also noted that Nicaragua's attorneys had correctly assumed that only at a later hearing could the full amount of damages payable be assessed; they nevertheless requested an immediate allowance on account to be paid for "the minimum amount of direct damage sustained." This the Court declined, postponing consideration of the reparations claim to a later hearing. But by a unanimous vote the Court directed that the parties be reminded of "their obligations to seek a solution to their disputes by peaceful means in accordance with international law."

After having been informed that the United States had not accepted invitations to negotiate, the Court requested the parties to meet on November 17, 1987, to discuss the future proceedings. The United States refused to attend, citing previous expressions of opinion that the Court lacked authority to proceed. The Court then unanimously—with concurrence of the three dissenters from the judgment, including Stephen Schwebel, the judge of U.S. nationality, who had expressed vigorous disagreement with the Court's findings against the United States—directed that the proceedings in the case be resumed and set time limits for the filing of the respective positions.

Nicaragua filed its statement of claim, citing several recent cases involving the United States. In the most recent of them, the "hostages" case with Iran, Washington had said: "The U.S. holds it has the right to full reparations for the damages suffered by the United States as a state and by its citizens as victims of the illicit actions of Iran." Preceding the itemization of its claim, its "bill of particulars," Nicaragua asked for $12.2 billion in damages.

Little press or other attention was paid to this phase of the Court's proceedings. This writer pointed out in the *Los Angeles Times* that, contrary to popular belief, the case was still very much alive. While Security Council enforcement of a ban on contra aid could be prevented by a veto, a money judgment could be enforced in other ways: by applications to local courts, attachment of assets, and so on. This analysis was confirmed some months later in a study published in the *Virginia Journal of International Law;* its author, Professor Mary Ellen O'Connell commented, "The better the enforcement, the more effective the system, and, perhaps, the greater the extent the system will be used in settling disputes peacefully."

From 1988, when the U.S. response to Nicaragua's claim was due (and never came) until June 1990, the Court took no steps that have been recorded. In the summer of 1990, Court President José Maria Ruda invited the parties to discuss and set a date for a hearing to determine the amount due to Nicaragua.

By then, Nicaragua's 1990 presidential election, which was promised during diplomacy following the Arias plan, was over. The incumbent, Daniel Ortega, was defeated by a coalition led by Violeta Chamorro, and she had been peacefully inaugurated as president. The United States again failed to show up; the Nicaraguan representative said, "[T]he instant case is very complex and. . . there are special circumstances that would make it extremely inconvenient for it to take a decision on what procedure to follow in this case during the coming months."

Behind that terse paragraph were events that need not be discussed in detail in this study of the Court and its case handling. The election itself had been overtly influenced by the United States. Millions of dollars had been funneled to the opposition to the incumbent regime. President Bush publicly promised to lift the U.S. embargo (a promise that was to take unreasonably long to fulfill) if Ms. Chamorro should be elected.

The National Assembly at Managua, after the election but before the new regime's inauguration, passed a Law of Protection of Rights of Nicaraguans in the International Court of Justice. This forbade the government, or any successor, from dropping the case without payment of the reparation claim in full—describing it as "the inalienable patrimony of all Nicaraguans." Soon after this action the United States, during a visit of Special Envoy Thomas Pickering, began diplomatic initiatives to bring about just that: the dropping of the case. Pickering's visit was followed by a visit by U.S. Ambassador Henry Schlaudeman. Each sought to induce the new administration to withdraw the case and renounce its claim, despite the local law.

After these efforts became known a serious national debate followed, during which there emerged opposition from a substantial element of the press and public that had not otherwise been identified with the outgoing Ortega regime. All this, together with concerns about "Law 92," the supposed freeze on dropping the case, accounted for the "inconvenience" in making a decision that was mentioned to the Court at the meeting. The debate in Managua was enlivened by the aftermath of the Mideast war with Iraq over Kuwait, during which spirited and quite stubborn demands were made on Iraq to be sure to pay the reparations declared due by the Security Council.

There was, for a long period, an impasse within Nicaragua. Evidence of what had built up behind the scenes emerged in an apparently well-informed report on September 30, 1990, to the *New York Times:*

> With hundreds of millions of American aid hanging in the balance, the Bush Administration has begun exerting sharp new pressure on President Violeta Barrios de Chamorro to abandon a judgment of as much as $17 billion. . . . the American pressure runs counter to a strong nationalist sentiment among Nicaraguans of all political backgrounds who believe the Court decision was an important international victory.

The final chapter of the Court aspect of this story begins with a debate in the National Assembly in June 1991 to repeal Law 92. Ultimately the ban on dropping the case was ended. With that done, a settlement was agreed upon.

Instead of total abandonment of the reparations claim as earlier demanded, the case closed with a letter, dated September 12, 1991, to the Court by Nicaragua requesting discontinuance in the light of "agreements [with the United States] aimed at enhancing Nicaragua's economic, commercial and technical development." The U.S. comment, requested by the Court before acting, confirmed without further particulars an "agreement . . . to take steps to enhance their friendship and mutual cooperation."

The president of the International Court of Justice (ICJ) accepted this exchange of letters as the basis for an order terminating the case on September 26, 1991. The Associated Press reported this from The Hague in a dispatch, stating, "[T]he United States agreed to economic aid for the democratically elected government of Violeta Chamorro," as the basis for the case's ending. That was not contradicted by either government.

Indeed, even before the Court acted, the press in Managua quoted the Foreign

Ministry as having asserted that accords terminating the case had been "reached to stimulate economic, commercial and technical development to the maximum possible extent for the benefit of Nicaragua." Thus, despite long resistance to accepting the authority of the Court to decide the case, the United States made a settlement in lieu of reparations, under which some $500 million in aid (albeit some of it in the form of debt relief) was granted or promised to Nicaragua. That partial compliance with the U.S. reparations obligation was marred by defaults in the form of "suspensions" at the random behest of some members of Congress.

IRAN: A TRADE FOR REPARATIONS?

There were other serious disputes between the United States and Iran pending before the seizure of the hostages in Tehran (see chapter 10). That these were settled at the same time that the hostages were freed was not a coincidence, and their nature and origin demonstrate that the delay in freeing the hostages should not necessarily be taken as evidence of the ineffectiveness of international law.

For years before the hostage crisis began, the shah of Iran had used that country's swollen oil revenues to fuel a rush program of modernization and westernization. This push was marked by force-fed economic development and military expansion. The U.S. economy was almost the sole beneficiary. Literally hundreds of businesses and thousands of individuals were enlisted and well paid. At the peak, 45,000 Americans were engaged in providing an enormous variety of goods, services, and installations. There was, as John Westberg, a Washington attorney, put it, "every kind of business transaction known to man."

As 1978 dawned, at the height of this oil-for-gold rush, President Jimmy Carter (based on U.S. intelligence reports) toasted the "island of stability" that the shah's Iran stood for in the Middle East. Within a few months it all came to a sudden and shocking halt. A revolution overthrew the shah. Many of the 45,000 U.S. nationals left Iran before he did; most were gone soon after.

The immense and ongoing U.S. business entry into Iran was a principal target of the Iranian revolution. In consequence, cancellations and confiscation, seizures, and takeovers were widespread. Much new court business then began in the United States. As lawsuits proliferated, attachments were levied on the billions of dollars held in the name of Iran and nationalized entities. Because of the international law doctrine of "sovereign immunity," the outcome of this mass of litigation was not at all predictable.

When the U.S. Embassy was raided and its people seized as hostages on November 4, 1979, the U.S. government's response created a new, multibillion dollar distraction: all Iranian assets were frozen, immunized to suit. Soon a new complication appeared to confront all the U.S. claimants who had suffered economic loss. Their lawsuits could not produce any results: the "freeze" prevented collection.

This generated another international legal problem. The order was aimed at and purported to reach all Iranian deposits and gold holdings, not only in U.S. banks at home but also in their branches abroad. Litigation challenging the U.S. action was begun in London and Paris. Overall, it was "like the mutual taking of hostages," in the estimate given by U.S. State Department Legal Adviser Roberts B. Owen.

There might have seemed a simple solution. Could Iran have bid for its badly needed funds—the seizure had crippled her foreign trade—by a reverse ransom: offering to release the fifty-two U.S. citizens held in Tehran, to buy freedom for their $12 billion (as it turned out)? Such a deal could not have been offered or accepted by the United States because of the catastrophic impact of the Iranian revolution on U.S. business: the billions frozen supposedly to create pressure to free the hostages was to be held as security for U.S. business interests' claims.

There is some evidence that Iran would have been willing to obey the Court's order to free the hostages if it could find a way to win freedom for its $12 billion. While the crisis continued, the Embassy of Iran at The Hague exhibited some respect for the Court. In September 1980, as was later disclosed in a book on the Court's work by its then-president, Nagendra Singh, the embassy sent a note to the Court "presenting its compliments." Iraq under Saddam Hussein had just begun what was to be a ten-year war by raids on Iranian airports, and the note asked that the Court condemn them. Lacking jurisdiction, the Court wasn't free to act.

It had not been the Iraqi attack that put Iran in a mood to settle and to obey the Court order to free the hostages. Three months earlier—within weeks of the Court's decision—the chief of Iran's central bank had given an unmistakable signal that showed why obedience had been delayed. He invited the United States to free the $12 billion by announcing that Iran was ready to arbitrate all U.S. claims that arose from the revolution. There was no immediate follow-up on the arbitration idea. Lloyd Cutler, shortly after leaving the White House where he had served as counsel to President Carter, ruefully remarked, "Iran did not form a government with enough internal control to be capable of acting until the fall of 1980."

Even when Ayatollah Khomeini, the new leader of Iran, signaled willingness to obey the Court order on four stated conditions, meaningful bargaining was for a time prevented. He had prohibited face-to-face dealing or any direct contact with Great Satan's (as his faction termed the United States) people. The logjam was broken in November 1980, when the Parliament ("Majlis") was finally organized. After confirming Khomeini's ascendancy and reiterating his September proposals, they asked the leaders of decolonialized

Algeria to act as mediators. The Algerians were to fulfill this role with fairness and commitment to get the results.

The ayatollah's conditions included one that called for the United States to drop all claims against Iran for losses sustained by U.S. and business interests due to the revolution. Recalling the bank head's hint in June, U.S. Deputy Secretary of State Warren Christopher replied via the Algerians, as real bargaining got under way:

> There will be serious legal obstacles in releasing your assets from judicial attachments unless we show our federal courts that some sort of reasonably fair remedy is going to be provided for the claimants. . . . The U.S. government will bring about cancellation of all commercial claims if Iran agrees to let the claimants present their claims to an international arbitration tribunal and guarantees to pay any awards that are made.

This would have freed the hostages, except that the Iranians persisted in demanding that reparations for the hostages be dropped, and the victims themselves be precluded from suing Iran in U.S. courts. Christopher, lead U.S. negotiator, resisted this demand at first. Then, according to the State Department legal adviser's report—published in a book, titled *American Hostages in Iran: The Conduct of a Crisis,* in which Christopher had written an opening essay—after taking soundings among the hostages' families, they concluded that they preferred to give in to the Iranian demand that reparations be dropped, rather than delay the release.

Many other questions, large and small, were to be ironed out between the Iranians and the Algerians, then between the Algerians and Christopher's team. Along the way, on Christmas eve of 1980, Radio Tehran announced that Iran had accepted the U.S. proposal for international arbitration of all claims except for the hostages; in addition they agreed to the creation of a fund out of which payment of claims as adjudicated would be paid. In the final flurry of exchange of drafts on the eve of the release in January 1981, there was created a novel instrumentality of international law that will be described in some further detail later in this chapter.

The seizure of the hostages was a criminal violation of international law. It was illegal to fail to free them after the Court's order to do so. But it cannot be ignored that the U.S.-supported reinstatement of the shah in 1953 was a violation of the Law of Nations that was better remembered inside Iran than outside, as were the bitterly detested reign and its results. Two wrongs do not make a right, but the persistence of the effects of one cannot be ignored in remedying the other.

When litigation between two domestic factions is addressed to only one of a number of issues in contention, compliance with the court's order may not come overnight. The verdict may be put "on hold" to gain a broader peace. Deferred obedience does not mean the court has been disregarded. Its work may well have moved the parties along to address other simmering issues. Some of the judicial outcome may be dropped as part of a trade-off. What is not taken as a sign of law's ineffectiveness on the domestic scene should not be taken as such in the international arena.

This is what U.S. Deputy Treasury Secretary Robert Carswell meant when he said the World Court's action against Iran had served a useful purpose. He also could have been aware of the effect of the Court's action on continental lawsuits that challenged the extraterritorial effect of the freeze on U.S. banks' holdings of Iranian deposits. This component of U.S. leverage, which helped bring the successful final result, was sustained when the decision at The Hague deferred a rush to judgment in London and Paris that might have weakened U.S. bargaining power in Algiers. Hence, international lawyers understood what Carswell meant when he said, "The successful action brought by the United States against Iran in the International Court of Justice" contributed to the successful result.

THE IRAN–U.S. CLAIMS TRIBUNAL: PROMISE FULFILLED

The Court's decree freeing the Tehran hostages did not direct reparations to the individuals who had suffered seizure and detention. It ordered "reparation to the Government of the United States for the injury caused to" it by the seizure of November 4, 1979, and "what followed." The U.S. government was free to agree to drop that claim, leaving it as a domestic matter whether any compensation was to be paid to the detainees. Instead of reparations for the fifty-two embassy people, there was a trade-off: the United States preferred to obtain restitution for the many hundreds of firms and many thousands of stockholders whose investments were lost or impaired.

The transnational dispute procedure that was established at Algiers was not only for claim disposition. It extended also to adjudication of any dispute as to the meaning or performance of the settlement terms. (This, in effect, subcontracted the work of the World Court itself.) Never had a successful revolution, while its effort to complete its aims was continuing, agreed to compensate in this manner those who had suffered losses as a result of takeovers, seizures, confiscations, or cancellations.

To do the work of judging the validity of claims, and of resolving disputes arising under the agreements, there was to be established a new body to be called the Iran–United States Claims Tribunal. Under that name, individuals chosen by the two states have functioned as an independent international organization. While the treaty calls it an "arbitral tribunal," it has been in most respects more like a court. It has established and occupies premises of its own. There is a continuity of adjudicative personnel on the bench, an administrative and clerical support staff, annual reports, and a separately published and bound set of "Law Reports," containing opinions—including dissents—and other documentation regarding its work.

Accompanying its creation was an advantage—for U.S. claimants only—that is unique. Collection of their verdicts is backed by a fund, established out of the Iranian assets that the United States had held hostage by the freeze order. For securing payment for U.S. claimants, $1 billion was set aside; Iran pledged to replenish the fund if it ever fell below $500 million, and that promise was repeatedly kept.

In consideration of creation of the tribunal and the fund, the United States agreed to check all litigation the claimants had started in U.S. courts, and to nullify all attachments of Iranian funds. Presidential power to do this was litigated. A hearing at the U.S. Supreme Court was expedited to make possible the inception of the tribunal's business. The Supreme Court held that the president's action directing suspension of the lawsuits was a lawful exercise of foreign affairs power, since the tribunal provided an adequate alternative remedy.

The general impression of the claimants and their attorneys (as described by Professor Lori F. Damrosch of Columbia University) was that they were apprehensive of judgment by an "unknown tribunal, which was to sit in a foreign country, under unfamiliar procedural rules, and to apply an amorphous body of substantive law." Doubts were, over the years, to be dispelled.

The Algiers settlement offered as seat of the tribunal The Hague, where the World Court and its Peace Palace were located. It was thus hoped to minimize the impact of the persistent hostility between the participating states. As a further pacifying influence, there came an invitation from the Permanent Court of Arbitration (PCA), the first tenant of the Peace Palace, to share space in the house that Carnegie had built, to provide a home for the court of peace. Initial secretarial assistance was furnished by the PCA bureau. Even after the tribunal was given a rent-free home of its own near the Peace Palace by the Netherlands government, it would continue to use the PCA courtroom when a case required more space for parties and attorneys.

The new tribunal was to consist of nine members, of whom three each were to be appointed by the participating powers; the other three were to be neutrals, selected by the six party designees as a group. The first six U.S. and Iranian tribunal members met at the Peace Palace in May 1981 to discuss the first three neutrals; to their surprise they were able to agree on all three. Gunnar Lagergren, who had been a judge in Sweden, was chosen from the neutrals as first president of the tribunal.

A picture of one of the early days in the functioning of the tribunal was furnished by Stanton Belland, Los Angeles lawyer for some U.S. claimants, who went to The Hague to look into the remedy his clients would have to replace the California lawsuits that had been aborted by presidential order. He went to the Peace Palace one rainy morning in October 1981, one of many anxious and competitive U.S. lawyers jostling for position, and speculating on the acceptability of their claims. Claims were filed at a temporary counter set up in the anteroom of the PCA hearing room, under the great jasper loving cup presented in 1913 to the World Court by Czar Nicholas II.

The number of claims that were filed was surprising. About 450 lawsuits had been filed against Iran or its agencies when proceedings in U.S. courts were halted. Judge Nils Mangard, another one of the first three neutrals, told of their consternation when 4,000 claims were counted after the closing date for filing had passed. They "had expected to serve only for a limited period and without too heavy a caseload," according to Nils Mangard.

The third of the initial group, Judge Pierre Bellet of France, chose not to stay very long. He decided a caseload ten times greater than anticipated was too much. In his 1982 resignation he wrote, "I cannot continue at the risk of endangering my health and my family life."

A provision in the "Claims Settlement Declaration"—the agreement setting up the tribunal—made it possible to reduce the burden somewhat. It said that "claims may be decided by the full Tribunal [of nine] or by a panel of three members as the President shall determine." Judge Lagergren must have anticipated the flood of cases that was to come in. He divided the tribunal into three chambers. Each was to be presided over by a neutral, and to have one each of the designees of the state parties. Cases were to be divided by lot among the chambers, which were to have final decisional authority. (Members too were to be distributed by lot.) Reserved for the full tribunal were major cases, complex issues of law, and disputes between the two governments about the meaning or application of the terms of the claims or other declaration.

Despite the overload, and many other handicaps and obstacles from without and within, the tribunal functioned with only one brief interruption. It dealt with numerous claims for breach of contract and for losses due to nationalization that destroyed, directly or indirectly, the value of U.S. investments in Iranian enterprises that the shah had invited. The skeptics about international law and adjudication should look at this record, which the media have ignored.

By the end of 1999, the tribunal had distributed more than $3 billion, the major share of which went to the United States or its nationals as claimants. This was the product of adjudications in 300 separate cases and 250 more that were settled before hearing by the tribunal. One major pretrial agreement terminated more than 2,300 claims at once. These had been grouped as asking damages of less than $250,000. The tribunal approved by formal order an agreement between the parties for payment of a lump sum of $105 million into a fund to be distributed among the many claimants as may be determined by a U.S. agency, the Foreign Claims Settlement Commission.

Charles Brower, who said that the "initial perplexity [of claimants] will not soon abate," had a different view seven years later. Lecturing at the Hague Academy of International Law as a former member of the tribunal, he described it as "a remarkable institution that successfully met the substantial challenges it faced and managed both to apply and advance principles of international law in the context of international arbitration."

"Remarkable" is a word that can be fairly applied to the mere fact of the tribunal's survival, serving two adversaries who were as hostile as any could be in the absence of actual belligerence. It began when echoes of the cry "nuke 'em," provoked by the long-drawn hostage crisis, still echoed in the land. It functioned throughout in the total absence of diplomatic relations between the United States and Iran.

The continuing hostility was accompanied with provocations and flare-ups incidental to the actual war between Iraq and Iran. There was also supposed support by Tehran of militant Lebanese patriots who fought intermittently to drive out U.S.-allied Israeli invaders and their cooperative Lebanese allies. Iran was believed to be behind a bombing in Beirut that killed more than 300 U.S. Marines. The Reagan administration was almost brought down when the laws of the U.S. forbidding the sale of arms to Iran and enacted to stop the arming of the contra rebels in Central America were violated in transactions in which the White House and probably the president himself were deeply involved. In two violent episodes, U.S. war planes attacked and destroyed Iranian oil platforms in the Persian Gulf, and naval gunners shot down a civilian Iranian airbus, bringing death to almost 300 people.

Iran's response was peaceful, suing for each of these events at the World Court, as the United States had in 1979 for the taking of the hostages. One suit charged that the naval attack on the civilian flight violated a multinational treaty of Montreal designed to safeguard peaceful civilian travel. The other separate suit charged that destruction of the oil platforms violated the bilateral pledges of amity contained in a treaty made long before the Khomeini revolution. The United States had succeeded in convincing the World Court that the treaty of friendship remained in force despite the revolution and the overthrow of the shah. (That decision of the World Court was, naturally, followed in rulings by the Tribunal, as were others from time to time.)

Acts of violence and use of force between nations draw big headlines. Media attention to threats and boycotts always helps increase the concern and inspires incessant comment. Peaceful dispute resolution gets neither attention nor very much respect. The Iran–U.S. Claims Tribunal has functioned at The Hague in the shadow of the Peace Palace. Its story is possibly the least covered event of its time in international affairs. So far as the writer has seen, it was the subject of only one news item of consequence: An item in the *New York Times* for September 7, 1984, tells of an account by an unidentified diplomat. He reported an incident at the tribunal's chambers, during which two Iranian arbitrators pushed and shoved Nils Mangard, the Swedish judge who was one of the three neutrals. The incident required and received appropriate remedial treatment. The U.S. agent at The Hague promptly made a formal challenge to continued service by the disorderly pair.

There was no argument about the challenge by Iran. There was no evidence or claim that the weaponless and mildly violent assault by two judicial officials and their colleague was inspired or approved by the Tehran authorities. Tehran simply gave notice that the U.S. challenge to continued service by the two shovers was not contested. Two new arbitrators from Iran were named in November and business was resumed in January 1985.

Judge Brower told his audience at the Hague Academy half a dozen years later,

> While the attack on Judge Mangard and its aftermath were disruptive, they marked in some sense a turn-around in the tribunal's work. The difficulties were overcome and the tribunal was not permanently impaired. Significantly, when work resumed, its pace increased; while only eleven hearings had been held in 1984, in 1985 there were thirty-three, signaling a welcome end to an era of tribunal sluggishness. . . . At the same time the atmosphere of the tribunal became more businesslike and cordial.

After he looked back at his period of service with the tribunal, Judge Mangard was to write his own memoir of his service in a fifty-five-page essay describing the history and work product of the tribunal. He did not mention the minifracas with Shafeiei and the other Iranian. Instead, he simply noted tersely that there had been decisions "felt by Iran to be unfair and unjust [that] have contributed to the hostile and inflammatory atmosphere which during certain periods has prevailed in the tribunal."

The flash point, the ruling that really triggered the unrestrained anger and unacceptable behavior of the arbitrators who attacked Judge Mangard, was a full tribunal decision on a facet of the often-intriguing problem of "dual nationality." When two states each claim (or accept) an individual as a citizen, a situation exists that is pregnant with possible conflict and sometimes danger. Even in the situation that is familiar to some, of dual nationality in two closely allied nations such as Israel and United States, there is a potential for a clash. The Iran–U.S. relationship during the shah's invitations to and patronage of U.S. business and military involvement tended to produce acceptance of U.S. citizenship and retention of Iranian nationality, for the special convenience of having both.

What made dual loyalty acceptable as long as the shah ruled is precisely what made it repellant to the new leaders after the revolution that was aimed at the shah's relationship with Washington as it developed: double citizenship was an irritating reminder of the shah's relationship with and dependence on Washington. Not only that, but it also created a situation at the tribunal that put into play a rule of international law of long-standing that had been confirmed by a "Convention on Conflict of Nationality" developed at a

1930 conference held at The Hague: a person of dual nationality could not invoke the aid of one of the states to which he or she belonged, to make a claim on the other.

What provoked the ire of the Iranians was the attempt of people they viewed as their own citizens to avoid that rule by disclaiming the nationality they had never renounced, to enable suit against their own country as if they were now U.S. citizens only. There were among the claimants at the tribunal more than 150 such hyphenates with 300 or more claims. When the first such case came up the conflict was sharp. The Iranian arbitrators insisted that these people, who had used their Iranian passports to come and go freely, could not sue the country of which they had enjoyed the benefits of citizenship, albeit they are also U.S. citizens. The drafters of the claims settlement agreement in Algiers had not anticipated the problem.

Presented with the hard choice between allowing all the hyphenates to sue— or none—the tribunal went across the street to the decisions of the ICJ for guidance. They found it. The World Court had dealt in the Nottebohm case of 1955 with a relevant question. Herr Nottebohm had lived in Guatemala for years, making a fortune, but retaining German citizenship. When World War II loomed in 1939, he hastened to Liechtenstein, a European ministate, and became a citizen. When the war came and Guatemala seized his property on grounds that he was an enemy alien, Liechtenstein presented a case on his behalf at the ICJ.

The World Court rejected the claim made by Liechtenstein. They inquired into Nottebohm's "real and effective nationality." The Nottebohm case, as shown in chapter 12, was deemed useful in setting guidelines on "flags of convenience": now it was to be a useful precedent when nationality disputes hit the tribunal. The Iran–U.S. Claims Tribunal acted just as a good lower court should. It ruled in favor of some claimants and against others, basing the decision on interpretation and application of the principles outlined in Nottebohm's case.

This decision, which for a time angered the Iranians and briefly halted the coworking in the tribunal, was but part of many rulings it made. For present purposes they need not be reviewed in detail. The consensus of practitioners was that other important commercial issues were satisfactorily handled, principally aspects of effects of nationalization.

The tribunal is an example of how international law can work when there is a will that it should.`

15

Court versus Council

AT COURT FOR DEFENSE OF
TREATY RIGHTS: LIBYA'S CASE

On July 3, 1988, the *USS Vincennes,* a guided-missile cruiser on patrol in the Persian Gulf, shot down an Iranian civilian airliner. None of its 290 passengers and crew survived. Iran, charging U.S. violation of a 1971 Montreal convention "for the Suppression of Unlawful Acts Against the Safety of Civil Aviation," took the case, as mentioned in chapter 14, to the World Court.

On December 21, 1988, Pan Am Flight 103 was destroyed over Lockerbie, Scotland, by a bomb explosion. Nearly 260 passengers, mostly civilians, and some civilians on the ground were killed. This tragedy also became the subject of a World Court case, filed under the Montreal Convention. Libya, accused of state terrorism that resulted in the crash, initiated the case.

Late in 1991, after a joint U.S.–UK investigation, a District of Columbia grand jury indicted two Libyan nationals, described as state employees, on charges of having placed a destructive device aboard the Pan Am flight, a device that caused the plane to explode while flying over Lockerbie. Simultaneously, a Scotch prosecutor issued warrants of arrest of the same individuals on a similar charge.

Having been notified of the indictments, Libya announced four days later assignment of a judge to investigate and its readiness to cooperate. A week later, the United States and United Kingdom jointly demanded surrender of the accused for trial. Libya in response assured the two countries that the request would be investigated and dealt with seriously; the Libyan judge requested the assistance of the U.S.–UK authorities and offered to visit them to review the evidence they had collected.

More or less simultaneously, Libya offered to submit the entire matter to the International Court of Justice (ICJ), or to an international commission of investigation, or any other type of impartial international proceeding. The World Court does not have criminal jurisdiction and cannot pass on the guilt or innocence of individuals. An international criminal court did not then exist. Libya's assurance of investigation and request for evidence, followed by the arrest of the accused, were seemingly in consonance with Libya's obligations and rights under the Montreal Convention. Britain and the United States were also signatories to this treaty to combat international terrorism.

All of Libya's proposals were unofficially rejected and officially ignored. After a few weeks, Libya's Foreign Office, on January 17, 1992, sent notices to the complaining states, calling attention to the Montreal treaty, and to Libya's actions and statements that seemed to comply with the pact's requirements. These communications concluded with a notice of intent to submit the controversy to arbitration, as provided in the Montreal Convention. Pursuant to the UN Charter, the Security Council was also notified.

The United States and United Kingdom ignored Libya's request for arbitration. With Britain's Sir David Hannay as president for the month, in the customary rotation, the Council took no action on the request for arbitration. Instead, at a meeting on January 21, 1992, the Council adopted a resolution (No. 731) that urged instead of ordering, as the complaining powers had sought, Libya to respond "effectively" to the "requests" made in November for surrender of the accused—and (as if they'd been found guilty already) for compensation.

The Montreal pact provided that should the parties be unable to agree on arbitration, any one of them could take the case to the World Court, which presumably could order arbitration, or decide it was unwarranted. Libya accordingly filed with the Court a petition for a ruling that it was in compliance, and that the U.S.-British team was not, with obligations under the treaty. Also requested were orders for its adversaries to "cease and desist" from noncompliance, that is, to participate in an impartial arbitral tribunal's consideration of the issues. The Libyan petition also sought an order directed against threat or use of force. To bring the case to Court for hearing many months in advance of the usual time, Libya filed, simultaneously with its basic petition, an application for an "indication" similar in purpose and effect to a temporary injunction.

When the first hearing in Libya's case began, on March 26, 1992, the Court's consideration of the case would not necessarily have been complicated by the Council's previous action. Court and Council are both "established" in the same section of the Charter as "principal organs" of the United Nations.

Nothing in the Charter treats or classifies the Council or the Court as superior or more authoritative to the other. There *is* a provision in the text instructing the Council that "legal disputes should, as a general rule, be referred" to the World Court. But the Council is explicitly given "primary responsibility for the maintenance of international peace and security." The Court *has* ruled, from time to time, with the apparent acquiescence of the Council that the fact that a case was taken to the Council, and is being acted on there, does not preclude the Court from adjudicating whatever legal aspects it may have. Such a ruling *was* made at the explicit instance of U.S. counsel in the case of the Tehran hostages.

The situation was tense when the Court opened its hearing. Threats were in the air to use force to compel Libya to comply with demands that it was not legally obligated to obey. There were questions presented by Libya's pleading that the Court seemed to be the appropriate tribunal to answer:

- Was Libya's invocation of the Montreal Convention against terrorism an "effective response" to the demands that Britain and the United States had made for surrender of the alleged culprits, and so on?
- Were the United States and Britain violating the treaty they had signed and the international law it made?

When counsel for the United States, the United Kingdom, and Libya arrived at the Peace Palace to present and to oppose the case for indication of provisional measures, the Court gave careful attention. There were several days of long and learned arguments. There was a sense among the counsel for the British–U.S. allies after the argument concluded that the Libyans had made a plausible case. Seeking Court assistance for enforcing the Montreal treaty, they had shown that the necessary steps had been taken by them in a case contemplated by the pact's requirements.

If this had been the full trial, that would have entitled Libya to a judgment declaring that it had the right to choose between bringing the alleged culprits to trial in its own courts or giving them up for trial abroad. And if the Court found that they were being interfered with and coerced in an attempt to implement that choice by the defendants, the latter would be subject to an order to cease and desist. The likelihood that they would win that right would be enough to justify the temporary measures of protection that were sought against Britain and the United States.

An outcome favorable to Libya's claim, to be able to ask compliance with the Montreal antiterrorism pact, would have been acceptable to enlightened public opinion. That was a message given by a *New York Times* editorial dated March 30, 1992:

> Now the slippery Colonel pleads for delay until the World Court has ruled on Libya's claims that its promise to try the suspects complies with aviation treaties. . . . But advocates of sanctions need to make a plausible case for denying Libya's request for a World Court ruling before the Security Council acts. Doubts and suspicions are apt to linger until Washington finally divulges everything it knows about Lockerbie.

But the day after that editorial appeared, three days after the hearing at the World Court concluded, another UN organ suddenly stepped into the affair. The Security Council acted again, led by the United States and United Kingdom, which sensed that Resolution 731, "urging" Libya (in effect) to give up its rights under the Montreal Convention, might be frustrated by the Court decision that was in the making. A new resolution (No. 748) was adopted, denouncing Libya for failure to yield to the requests endorsed, but not commanded, in the earlier Resolution 731. Declaring that Libya's failure was a threat to peace and security, the Council ordered Libya to "comply without any further delay" with what Resolution 731 had merely "urged." There were five dissenters; the earlier Council action had been unanimous.

The Court now had to take into account an obscure article (103) of the UN Charter. That provided that in case of a conflict between a state's obligations under a treaty and obligations under the Charter, the latter must control. Since it was a Charter obligation to obey the order of the Council, Libya's rights under the Montreal pact were, so to speak, "trumped." If the resolution was a valid exercise of the Council's authority to keep the peace, treaty rights that stood in the way could not be enforced.

Only the Court could decide whether the action of the Council was valid, and only if it had the authority to do so. The question of its authority had to be deferred until the full-dress trial of the case. The pending motion for emergency relief had not initially presented that question: it came up only after the arguments on the temporary stay were concluded. And in any case, for the purposes of the application, the action of the Council would have to be assumed to be valid.

Libya's effort to seek treaty enforcement was deferred. The result was serious, since the later resolution carried a threat of sanctions if it were not obeyed. To win a test of her rights, Libya chose to decline to surrender the two alleged perpetrators and to undergo sanctions, which were promptly imposed. (There were negotiations initiated in an effort to avoid the sanctions, one offer being to surrender the prisoners if and only if they were guaranteed a fair trial in a neutral country. The allies declined.)

There were five dissenters who, while agreeing that the new resolution could not be immediately tested, advocated that the Court fashion a form of temporary relief of another sort than enforcement of the treaty rights. Indeed, Libya had the right to appoint an ad hoc judge, who joined in the dissent and proposed that the remedy should be trial in a neutral country.

The other dissenters deferred to the necessity of giving to Resolution 748 the presumption of validity at that point. Nevertheless, they would not disregard the threats of the use of force implied in such statements from allied officials as "we do not rule out any measures." One of them did take the trouble to say that the Court's deference for the time being was "not the result of the imposition of superior authority—there is none" superior to the Court.

This was the opinion of Judge Mohamed Shahabuddeen, a keen-thinking native of Guyana. The judge articulated best what was on the mind of some of his brethren on the bench, both in dissent and in concurrence with the Court's denial of Libya's petition. The questions are, he explained, "whether a decision of the Security Council may override the legal rights of states"; whether there are any "limitations of the power of the Council to characterize a situation," that is, calling it a situation threatening peace and security; "and what body, if other than the Security Council is competent to say what those limits are?"

As if to answer his colleague, the great Judge Manfred Lachs declared in a separate nondissenting opinion, "the Court is the guardian of legality for the international community as a whole."

Denial of Libya's initial application neither ended the case nor answered the question implicit in the judges' discussion: Would the case ultimately have the impact that *Marbury v. Madison* had in U.S. constitutional history? The question left open was not answered in the Charter, just as in the *Marbury* case, where the U.S. Constitution had not mentioned judicial review.

The international lawyers' and scholars' debate began soon after the text of the Court's opinions became available. In June 1992, the World Federalist Movement sponsored a so-called "Experts' Roundtable," one of a series initiated by the UN's Sixth (legal affairs) Committee and the American Society of International Law. Begun to mark the otherwise almost forgotten UN Decade of International Law (1990–1999, the latter date the centenary of the first Hague conference), the group's meeting on June 22 addressed the subject of "politics and law" at the Security Council.

The session was chaired by Professor Louis Henkin and led off by Professor Oscar Schachter, both of Columbia Law School. Present were other scholars and thirty or so members of member-nations' missions to the United Nations, usually the delegates active in the Sixth Committee. No minutes were taken; the rapporteur's notes (the usually reliable B. G. Ramcharan of the Secretariat) included:

> [T]he general issue raised was whether the council was bound by law. . . . There was a discussion of the recent decision of the International Court of Justice on the request for provisional measures in the Libyan case. The general sense of the meeting was that the International Court of Justice should assert its right to review the legality of decisions of the Security Council.

The debate ranged over both hemispheres, and in law journals, classrooms, and foreign offices. On one side was an editorial comment from Professor Thomas M. Franck, then editor in chief of the *Journal of the American Society of International Law*. He began with a heading that asked, "Who Is the Ultimate Guardian of UN Legality?" As a student of UN functioning for decades, Professor Franck warned:

> In extreme cases the Court may have to be the last-resort defender of the system's legitimacy if the United Nations is to continue to enjoy the adherence of its members. . . . In the inevitably rough spots ahead, it is reassuring to note that

the Court has carefully, and quietly, marked its role as the ultimate arbiter of institutional legitimacy.

Not all agreed. Professor Reisman, quoted on the questionable timing and motivation of Resolution 748, pitched in on the other side. He urged the need of the Council for flexibility in "discharging its primary Charter responsibility . . . for the maintenance of peace and security," arguing that the Court should have been prepared "even to decline the exercise of well-founded jurisdiction when, in its view, the larger purposes of the United Nations requires it." Yet withal, he did concede, in the final analysis that there might be a rare need to "review Security Council action." This, however, he contended, should be done only when the Council asks the Court via advisory opinion.

Limiting review to instances where the Council takes the initiative could not remedy cases where its action is predicated on its declaration of a nonexistent threat to the peace. It could have been argued that was so in Libya's case. In dissent, Judge Bedjaoui noted that Lockerbie had occurred three years before the Council acted.

In 1993, at a joint conference of U.S. and Netherlands scholars at The Hague, a panel of experts assembled to discuss "U.N. Checks and Balances," during which were voiced strong statements pro and con on the question of the Court's authority. A third cautionary view was expressed by Dr. Nico Schrijver of The Hague. Doubtful as he was, he recalled an observation by an outstanding British scholar, who would become the first woman to be elected to the Court:

> Of course, the Security Council is bound by the purposes and principles of the [United Nations] and it cannot, as Rosalyn Higgins put it, "declare any situation, no matter how calm it looks to the average man's eye, as a threat to peace."

(He was referring to a conclusion suggested by then-professor, now International Court Judge Dame Rosalyn Higgins, in her book *The Development of International Law through the Political Organs of the United Nations* [1963].)

The denial of Libya's application for interim relief did not prevent the case from going forward. Meanwhile, as threatened in Resolution 748, drastic sanctions were imposed on Libya. Having declined to extradite its nationals so as to preserve the right to contest the legality of the resolution, Libya nevertheless entered negotiations looking to settlement.

It was because of the perceived necessity of guaranteeing a fair trial—considered impossible in Britain or the United States because of public anger about the act of terrorism—that Libya had suffered sanctions. Negotiations were aimed to secure the result proposed by ad hoc Judge El Kosheri, an arrangement for trial in a neutral nation as a concession to win an end to sanctions. The allies declined.

The case went forward after 1992 with pleadings and replies over a stretched-out time period. The delay over a period of several years was granted by the Court on joint application of the litigators, presumably to facilitate efforts to settle.

Ultimately, in 1997, the case came on for another hearing. The subject was the validity of objections filed by the allies to jurisdiction and admissibility. After several days of hearing, the objections were overruled by the Court. Dame Higgins, now a judge, recused. This may have been because of the opinion expressed in her book, referred to above, that there could be a legal objection to the Council's acting on a "finding" that there was a "threat to peace," when it was perfectly clear that there was none. That was a central issue in the case.

When the Court's decision was disclosed, there was a rare instance of (1) appropriate media attention and (2) correctness of analysis. The *Washington Post* of February 27, 1998, got it right: "Libya Wins a Round in Pan Am 103 Case."

The decision brought on the ominous perception in the allied foreign offices that the props under the sanctions might be knocked out. Added pressure came with the appearance of a number of neutral states at the Security Council to call for a lifting of the sanctions. There was a common theme that the settlement of the dispute could be obtained only through agreement on holding the trial in a neutral place. The protest was led by members of the Non-Aligned Nations and the Organization of African Unity. The latter group announced that it would ignore the sanctions in the future.

Negotiations were revived. Britain took the initiative in giving new life to the Libyan proposal: for trial in a neutral country. Finally (to quote a recapitulation in the *New York Times* for April 6, 1999) "The deadlock was broken when Washington and London took up an old Libyan offer to have the suspects face trial in a neutral country." (Characteristically in a tabulated list of significant dates in the saga, the *Times* omitted the dates of both Court decisions, although it was the second one that opened the way to the settlement that brought the lifting of sanctions.)

CAN THE GENOCIDE TREATY BE STRETCHED?: BOSNIA'S CASE

In Libya's case, the Security Council brought on the potential clash with the Court: the Council acted in response to the African state's resort to a treaty against terrorism to bar pressure for a result that would bypass the treaty. While Libya's case was pending, the Council was induced by defendants in its Court case to frustrate the purpose of the case. Bosnia's case sought to persuade the Court to correct an action of the Council that the latter had failed to change when it had become inappropriate. The embattled little Balkan state attempted to use the Genocide Convention to accomplish this.

The Council had initially acted to impose an arms embargo against all Yugoslavia in 1991, when the civil wars resulting from secession of other states began. The purpose of the embargo was to lower the level of conflict among Serbs, Croats, and Slovenes as they contested borders after secession. Bosnia-Herzegovina ("Bosnia") had been a Yugoslavian province in 1991, and did not become an independent state until 1992.

After Bosnia declared her independence and was recognized as such at the United Nations, internal conflict began. As a mere province, Bosnia had been a place where a Muslim majority had coexisted peacefully with Roman Catholic Croatians and Greek Catholic Serbians. All had been content to coexist as "Bosnians." Serbians, now that Serbia had become most of what was left of former Yugoslavia, were persuaded to conclude that they should in turn secede from Bosnia to form a ministate, probably with an aim to merge with a "greater Serbia." Croatians, too, decided that they did not want to live under Muslim rule.

In the three-way civil war, the Yugoslav (really Serbian) army aided the Bosnian Serbs both with supplies and personnel. They were ruthless as they sought to eliminate Muslim inhabitants from areas they chose to occupy, and were responsible for civilian deaths on a tragic scale. The Security Council resolved against this, forbade it, and so on, but took no effective action. Its role was viewed as negative by the Bosnian government: the Council was ineffective in countering what was coming to be seen as genocide; yet the arms embargo was kept in place, impacting mainly on the Bosnians in hampering their efforts at self-defense.

Faced with continuing civilian losses, the state of Bosnia-Herzegovina acted. Claiming that Yugoslavia was responsible for genocide, as defined in the multilateral Convention on the Prevention and Punishment of Genocide, the victim sued in the World Court. The defendant was Yugoslavia and jurisdiction was based on the Serb-Montenegrin state's assumption of the treaty obligations of the former state.

The suit had two branches. One was to "convict" the Serbian state, condemn it as violating the Genocide Convention and obtain a remedy. In the other branch, a product of creative thinking by the lawyers for Bosnia, the Court was asked to enable Bosnia to combat the genocide, and to adjudge and declare that it retained the right of self-defense, including the right to seek and receive military assistance from other states. To implement that, the Court was asked to find that Security Council Resolution 713 must be "construed" so as not to be used to impose an embargo on arms to Bosnia.

Were the Court to agree to that request, it would be in confrontation with the Security Council again. The Council had been requested, after fighting in Bosnia broke out and its character became evident, to lift the embargo by itself, amending the resolution, and it refused.

The issues came before the Court twice in 1993 (in each instance by application for emergency relief only), the second time because of the worsening of the tragedy during that summer. The Court granted orders as requested against the actual perpetration of genocide, seemingly without effect, a point that troubled the judges the second time around. But they held, almost unanimously, that there was a bar in the Court's jurisdictional limits to even considering the requested modification of the embargo. The point that had been consented to, when Yugoslavia signed the treaty, was litigation as to whether the defendant was guilty of the international crime. The state had not consented to the Court's review of the conduct of other states or the actions of the Council itself.

The maxim "hard cases make bad law" may not be exactly applicable. What the Court confronted was a challenge to its capacity to be "activist" and to reach out to mold the law in a fashion that bent it pretty far. And after getting around the jurisdictional point, the question of the unappetizing notion of a conflict with the Security Council would have to be faced. But the Court does have great respect for the limits on its jurisdiction and, in a case against Yugoslavia, could not act to defy the Security Council.

The *Denver Journal of International Law,* in 1988, criticized the Court for failure to enforce the genocide treaty. But the Court only adjudicates: it is for the other organs of the United Nations to "enforce."

Obviously, the end of the story of "Court versus Council" is some way off. It would not be wise to make a prediction, but an opinion may be offered, in the words of Bosnia's ad hoc judge, Elihu Lauterpacht, son of one of the Court's great early judges, Sir Hersch Lauterpacht, and himself an esteemed scholar:

> But the Court, as the principal judicial organ of the United Nations, is entitled, indeed bound, to ensure the rule of law within the United Nations system and, in all cases properly before it, to insist on adherence by all United Nations organs to the rules governing their operation.

16

Was It "Worth the Trouble"?

During the meetings of the advisory committee that designed the first World Court in 1920, Bernard Loder, the Dutch representative, was insistent on one point: he wanted to make it possible for any state that wished to litigate to be able to do so "without any previous consent." He asked:

> Otherwise, why create this? . . . To continue a deplorable state of affairs and administer justice between two contesting parties only after having obtained their mutual consent and their agreement on the wording of the complaint and on the choice of judges? That is not worth the trouble.

It was the unanimous view of his colleagues, including the U.S. member, Elihu Root, that the requirement of consent be taken out of international law. This was approved by a solid majority of states members of the League of Nations. However, Britain and France, the then-dominant victorious powers, prevented its implementation (see chapter 3).

Loder accepted election to the new Permanent Court of International Justice (PCIJ). Its charter member judges chose him to be their first president and he served until 1925. He was to watch the opening years, and see how the Court helped settle difficulties among states peacefully (chapters 4 and 5). He saw the beginning of decades of the development of increased stability and certainty in the Law of Nations (sadly interrupted from 1939 to 1945). He might have thought that creation of a multilateral standing Court, although weakened by reservation of the states' privilege to decline consent to be sued, was worth some trouble.

As important as its dispute resolution achievements and the legal advice given the International Labor Organization (ILO) and others was the Court's magnificent demonstration of the very fact that it could function. It must have been an exciting, innovative period as the members of the first international court (save for the tiny Central American bench; see chapter 2), each from a different country and trained in a variety of legal systems and traditions, worked together to create a new and collegial organization.

They had to fashion modes of working intimately with each other, despite coming from disparate backgrounds and speaking in a variety of tongues. They learned to manage the participation of advocates who appeared as emissaries of sovereign states. Their triumph was the creation of an organic entity, with a developing tradition and esprit de corps, united with a mutual commitment to the purpose that brought them together.

This was recognized repeatedly by judges who served sixty years later. Hardy Cross Dillard, the former U.S. Army colonel and University of Virginia law dean, served as a judge on the modern Court from 1970 to 1979. He encountered and appreciated the collegiality and mutuality of respect among jurists from so many nations and different continents. He told his U.S. audiences how helpful their spirit was in avoiding "subjective preference" and in resisting "extraneous influence."

The Court, he said in one lecture, was "an institution most of whose members are animated and sustained by common aims and a sense of pride and tradition." In agreement was Sir Robert Jennings of Britain, who took office as a judge in 1982, on the eve of the period when people in Washington began to call the Court "politicized," and biased against the West.

Sir Robert, who had been a distinguished Cambridge professor of international law and became president of the Court, devoted an entire essay to making the point expressed in its very title, "The Collegiate Responsibility and Authority of the International Court of Justice."

As to Judge Loder's question, "Was it worth the trouble?": Measured by the enthusiastic expectations of Andrew Carnegie and others in the peace movement earlier in the century, one might answer "no." The Court did not by its mere existence abolish war. It did not prevent one that was worse than the tragic conflict that preceded its creation. It lacked the asset that Root and Loder felt that a Court worthy of the name should have: the capacity to offer to states the sovereign right to ask, in a time of trouble, whether international law was on its side. This was prevented by the survival of the state privilege to decline to be judged.

As he led the commemoration of the "international judicial system's" fiftieth anniversary, the Court's president in 1972, Sir Muhammad Zafrulla Khan, pointed out how it happened that the Court was deprived of the universality needed to make it effective. "The responsibility is not on the tools designed to preserve peace but on the hands that shaped them, only to lay them aside."

The purpose to prevent war cannot be accomplished by any one method— not by the Court alone, not by arms reduction alone, not by trade, not by student exchanges, not by respect for and attention to the needs of the underdeveloped, or any other mode of doing unto others as a nation would have itself treated. All must play a part and neither law nor Courts alone can keep the peace. But observance by states of the Rule of Law, of the norms of conduct required by the Law of Nations, can play an important part. In case of disagreement, judicial guidance as to the law's requirements can be of considerable value when diplomacy fails.

That being so, it should be evident that a court would be far more useful if the courthouse doors were open, regardless of an adversary's unwillingness to appear. The battle for that was lost again in 1945, when the emergent superpowers—the United States and the Soviet Union—reserved the "right" to avoid adjudication to settle disputes.

We have discussed the value of abolition of the privilege of refusal to consent to be sued. The term that is usually applied is "compulsory jurisdiction." It is not entirely accurate—no real coercive measure is applied—and it puts the case for changing the rule requiring consent at a disadvantage because compulsion, generally speaking, is suspect in a free society.

Unhindered freedom to seek legal rulings should not bear that burden; the moral disadvantage belongs to the other side. As put by U.S. Senate Foreign Relations chair, Utah's Elbert Thomas, in 1945, "Why should any nation be afraid to take its case before the bar of international justice?"

There is no principled reason for holding the "sovereign" privilege of refusal to be judged to be of greater importance than a sovereign right to seek justice from a judicial body representing the international community.

The case for resisting change is based on a belief that states will doggedly hold onto things as they are. It was so put by Judge Guy Lacharrière of France, who served at The Hague from 1982 until 1987. When asked by an interviewer if the Court was not weakened by the absence of so-called compulsory jurisdiction, Lacharrière said, "No, it is a fact of international life. To say it is a 'defect' would imply that something better was possible."

Was it a "necessary handicap" or a condition to the existence of an international court, that some be allowed to decline to have the legality of their action adjudicated? Not in the opinion of the majorities who appeared at the two postwar conferences and who considered the shape of international organization for peacekeeping. Twice these majorities offered to accept what had for so long been the U.S. plan: that jurisdiction be universal and compulsory.

Concerning those who vetoed that idea, no comment seems more apt than that of Leonard Woolf, the husband of Virginia Woolf, and a writer, thinker, and student of world affairs. While World War I was decimating Europe's young men, Britain's socialist Fabian Society asked Woolf to devise a plan for safeguarding peace by international organization. A response he prepared was called "The Framework of a Lasting Peace." In it, Woolf described the establishment of a court to pass on the legality of national conduct as a "first step" to the creation of the necessary plan.

As to consent to be sued, he said, the "refusal of a nation to bind itself to submit [its] disputes to the decision of an international tribunal is tantamount to a declaration that it proposes to regulate its relations not by right and law, but by the pure frightfulness of force."

There are many treaties between and among states that provide for referral of disputes as to their meaning or application to the international Court. Such clauses dispense with the need for consent. Many cases that arose from the Versailles settlement came to the PCIJ without specific consent. These included the cases showing the international Court's capacity to protect human rights (see chapter 5).

The ICJ's role as successor to the PCIJ is helped and illuminated by a clause in its statute to the effect that existing treaties calling for referral to the PCIJ be construed as automatically consenting to referral to the ICJ.

There is also the dispensing with consent provided by the optional clause, an arrangement the Court's statute offers that provides for standing agreement to consent to be sued by states that have made similar commitments. (Chapter 7 tells how this was created as a consolation for the majorities frustrated by the "Great Powers" denying full abolition of consent.) The usefulness of this provision was affected adversely when the United States nullified its acceptance via the Connally amendment (see chapters 7 and 9, and below).

In the first decade of each of the Courts, the treaty consent and the optional clause gave the Court the opportunity to fulfill its creators' purposes to a modest extent. The number and variety of cases that were handled, their aid to peaceful relations, their usefulness in the development of international law, will surprise many otherwise literate and well-informed citizens.

Our histories say little and explain less about the transnational affairs in which Courts played a role. On viewing the volume of cases and the compliance record, one may think that one is visiting another planet. Only two events involving the PCIJ survive in American historical consciousness. One was the Court's advice on the Austro-German customs union (see chapter 5); the other was the final U.S. Senate rejection in 1935 of President Roosevelt's request for approval to participate in the Court. That is more often mentioned because of the despicable character of the opposition incited by Huey Long, Father Coughlin, and the Hearst press.

Much less attention has been paid to the contemporary episode involving and affecting the ICJ that was the functional equivalent of that 1935 defeat. Few outside of the community of international lawyers and scholars have been aware of the significance of the two features that marked the history of the Connally amendment's vitiation of the optional clause acceptance. These were, independently, its adoption and the later abandonment of the effort to repeal it.

Unconditional agreement by the United States to consent to be sued under its terms had been unanimously approved by the responsible Senate committee. That had been supported at hearings by a diverse group of civic organizations. These included the National Council of Catholic Women, National Education Association, American Veterans Committee, League of Women Voters, Federal Council of Churches, General Federation of Women's Clubs, American Association of University Women, and a number of associations of lawyers. No witness testified in opposition (see chapter 7). Despite that showing, Senator Connally engineered a reversal of the committee vote by the full Senate, which acted without hearing or inquiry.

The message to the foreign offices, parliaments, and people of the world was that the United States repudiated the objective so well stated in the unanimous Senate committee report:

> The ultimate purpose of the Resolution is to lead to general worldwide acceptance of the International Court of Justice in legal cases. The accomplishment of this result would, in a substantial sense, place international relations on a legal basis, in contrast with the present situation, in which states may be their own judge of the law.

When the Senate voted to reject that purpose, as it did when accepting the Connally amendment, the world could not have been expected to ignore the message: The world's greatest power did not propose to "place international relations on a legal basis."

Even less well remembered than the rejection of the 1935 Roosevelt request to join the old court, the 1946 action had a far more serious effect. By 1935 the world had become used to the absence of the United States from The Hague. That adverse vote may, as some historians have contended, been an encouragement to Hitler by its reconfirmation of the strength of U.S. isolationism. But the Court was no more seriously affected than it was by Nazi Germany's nearly simultaneous withdrawal.

What has been underestimated, underreported, and all but forgotten is the double impact of the Connally amendment story: "double" in the sense that it twice caused a dismaying and debilitating shock to the international legal system. First, when the Senate reversal took place; second, when it became quite evident, after years of home-front campaigning to repeal Connally, by a bipartisan galaxy, that the effort had failed.

Every president, from Eisenhower to Carter, had expressed support for the "repeal Connally" campaign. Senate Democratic leader Hubert Humphrey was active and articulate. Support was given by an impressive legal committee, whose honorary chair was the revered U.S. Appeals Judge Learned Hand. They secured endorsement by eighty-one law school deans and hundreds of professors to the view that repeal was essential "to demonstrate our willingness to participate in the settlement of international disputes by persuasion rather than coercive means."

Richard M. Nixon argued that the United States should show by repeal "that the rule of law is the one system that all free men of good will should support." Hubert Humphrey asked that we cease "token allegiance to the Court," which has hampered its effectiveness.

Despite the very impressive presentation made in its behalf, the repeal-Connally movement failed. While it flickered on until the 1970s, what really amounted to defeat came in 1960, when the U.S. Senate committee in charge of Senator Humphrey's resolution to terminate it voted, 9 to 8, to refuse to let it go to the Senate floor.

The world, which was watching and listening and heard and understood the arguments of the repeal-Connally supporters, got the message. Perhaps the chancelleries and foreign offices abroad understood it better than the American people: it was a negative expression of the policy and attitude of the United States to the idea of a thoroughly workable international legal system and to the Court itself.

The history of the ICJ is marked and marred by a period from 1960 to 1980, during which it became much less useful in world affairs. For the first decade or so after it began to work, it was busy and productive, making history by making law, in contentious cases (such as *Corfu Channel* [Britain versus Albania]) and advisory cases that taken together did for the UN Charter as an international constitution what John Marshall's Court had done for the U.S. Constitution. From 1960, the Court's business steadily decreased. By 1970, when Judge Hardy Cross Dillard began his term as an international judge, the former dean and JAG officer found not a single case on its docket as he was sworn in. He tells how he was greeted at home by a headline: "Prestige Ranks High, Influence Low, As World Court Opens 25th Year."

Judge Dillard's successor—also a former U.S. Army officer—Richard Baxter, who became a Harvard professor of international law, was likewise greeted by a lack of business. Only one case was on the docket in 1979. Recalling that he'd been the butt of jokes about what a soft job he would have, he told a bar association audience, "It is not the Court or judges who are responsible for the present situation, but nations themselves. The Court stands ready."

He had met his colleagues, whose work he had followed as a professor of international law, and called them "an admirable group of jurists, under the presidency of Sir Humphrey Waldock." He added praise for the three new judges elected with him "who came to the Court with a wealth of experience."

To this should be added the view of Sir Humphrey himself, as given to a group of English lawyers visiting The Hague in 1980. "Do not be deceived by the somewhat theatrical mise-en-scène," he said. "It conceals a thoroughly professional Court . . . and a markedly efficient staff and organization."

This was the Court that stood ready for the decade of the 1980s, during which the United States brought to it the case of the Tehran hostages, and Nicaragua brought the case against the United States charging that it had armed, trained, and supported the contra movement. With these decisions a great change took place.

At the beginning of the 1990s, President Sir Robert Jennings addressed the UN General Assembly on the Court's work. "After decades of underuse," he began, "the Court now has a full docket of important cases, with parties ranging from Scandinavia to Australia and from Central America to the Gulf. . . .

Their docket of cases is an impressive list compared with any other time in the history of the court."

WHAT HAD HAPPENED?

For a period of twenty years, following the defeat of the repeal-Connally movement in the United States, activity at the Court had been relatively limited. There were some years when the Court had no cases on its docket. Somehow, the media, which had ignored the Court and its work—including some important achievements during its first fifteen years—began to poke fun at the institution and its judges, to call election to the Court a sinecure.

A variety of efforts were begun in the U.S. State Department and among international lawyers and bar groups to remedy the situation, to find business for the Court. Obviously, such artificial pumping up, the creation of pseudo-situations, is not the way to demonstrate the value of an intergovernmental arrangement, an international institution.

The Cold War has been blamed for the lack of interest in the availability of the Court. But that did not affect it in the first fifteen years. Other reasons given were a lack of faith in a "Western" Court by an Eastern bloc, and a lack of faith in a "Northern" Court by the Southern, developing nations, and former colonial possessions.

Each, of course, played a part. However, one factor has been underestimated, and in some quarters ignored: the implication that the world drew from the failure of the movement to repeal the Connally reservation. Senator Connally's intervention had reversed his own committee's choice, as stated in its unanimous report, to act to "place international relations on a legal basis," and to promote "general worldwide acceptance of the International Court of Justice."

It is completely understandable that this was taken to mean that the United States did not want international relations on a legal basis, or to see worldwide acceptance of the Court. Moreover, some states in their own acceptance of the optional clause aped the Connally idea. If the U.S. attitude toward the Court and the Rule of Law was half-hearted at best, why be better?

As the 1980s went on, a great change took place in the rest of the world. The Iran hostages' case first focused attention on the Court. The spotlight shone brighter with the Nicaragua case. There was consciousness as the Arias plan won the Nobel Prize, even before Tacsan's book's disclosures (see chapter 13) that the Court had some effect in movement toward peace in Central America. The successful functioning of the Iran–U.S. Tribunal, fruit of the Court's hostages decision (chapter 13) was no secret, except in the United States.

By 1986 and increasingly thereafter, the Court was busier than it ever had been, entrusted by nations on five continents with the peaceful settlement of their disputes. The Court was no longer the butt of the media's jokes, no longer "moribund." You would not know this from U.S. media coverage.

One Indian writer called the case brought by Nicaragua the "catalyst" that sparked a "renaissance" of the Court. Not alone was the judgment of a distinguished West German scholar, J. A. Frohwein, sometime visiting professor at Michigan and the Sorbonne. He lectured in 1994 at the Hague Academy on aspects of third-party (that is, nations not directly involved) states' reactions to international events such as Court decisions affecting others. On the point in question:

> The importance of that [Nicaragua case] judgment by the International Court of Justice on the international legal system can hardly be overestimated. The sudden understanding in the whole world that the United States is also subject to judicial control had an enormous impact, particularly in countries of the then Eastern bloc.

This was recognized at home by international law scholars of integrity—but totally ignored by the media that had so often poked fun at the Court. But in the *Catholic University Law Review,* Richard Bilder, Burrus-Bascom Professor of International Law at the University of Wisconsin, wrote, "despite dire United States predictions that the Nicaragua decision would broadly discredit the World Court . . . the Court has never been busier." Also, Professor Thomas M. Franck, longtime editor of the *American Journal of International Law*— and one of the best-known scholars in the field—wrote that the decision, in the world outside, "was welcomed as an example of judicial independence in the face of a super-power's defiance . . . accounts at least in part for the frequent use now made of the Court."

The Connally reservation, subject of so much debate for so long, came to the end of the road in the Nicaragua case. In the beginning there was a bizarre twist: Theoretically, the Connally language, excluding subjects "essentially within [U.S.] domestic jurisdiction . . . as determined by" the United States, could have been invoked to dismiss the case, by calling Reagan's Central American policy a matter within domestic jurisdiction. It was not.

Professor (and Ambassador) Richard N. Gardner asserted that the United States was "ashamed" to do so. Davis Robinson, the legal adviser in charge of the case, said that he was afraid that if it were invoked, the Court would invalidate it. Whatever the reason, it was waived.

The Connally clause ended the wrong way, for the wrong reason. After having litigated the first round of the Nicaragua case and lost, the United States failed to appear to defend the case and carried out its threat to withdraw its consent to the application of the optional clause. When that was done, the Connally clause sank with the vessel to which it was hooked. What should have been separately repealed, as so many had urged, was "thrown out with the bathwater," to use one observer's phrase. While that termination of consent on six-months' notice was perfectly legal, there was an intense but brief protest. It was understandable, even if what was lost was illusory.

Two subsequent developments deserve attention. One was from Vatican City, a papal message ignored by most and quickly forgotten, which still deserves close attention. What must have been carefully crafted at the Vatican was a wasted exercise in papal diplomacy. The head of the Roman Catholic Church—in 1985 Pope John Paul II—plays a part in international affairs that is alert to and informed by a dual role. He is chief of state in a quasi-sovereign, statelike entity; he is also leader of a global religious body with communicants in every country. Consequently, the papacy has an abiding concern for peaceful international relations.

At the very start of the century, the czar's call inspired Pope Leo XIII to attempt to take part in the first Hague conference, and although excluded, to publicly support its aims. Pope Benedict XV, in an initiative that lacks adequate attention in histories of World War I, attempted to end the slaughter by proposing a cease-fire and establishment of a form of international organization that would include "the institution of arbitration with its high peacemaking function."

These facts were recited by John Paul II in an address given in the Great Hall of the Peace Palace on May 13, 1985. As part of a pastoral visit to the Netherlands, he was addressing the members of the ICJ, standing at the barristers' bar of court. At the moment the speech was given:

1. Nicaragua's case against the United States (chapter 10) was *pendente lite,* actually before the Court, which had only a few months previously decided over U.S. objections that it had jurisdiction and scheduled a hearing on the merits;
2. Prior to even the first prejurisdictional hearing in that case, on an application for a temporary restraint—at a time when the United States should have been satisfied with the Court in the hostages case and the decision in the Canada fishing case—a campaign was begun in the United States to discredit the Court. The campaign was led by UN Ambassador Jeane Kirkpatrick, who charged it with being biased against the West and "not a court at all."
3. Following the adverse jurisdictional ruling and a few weeks before the pope came to The Hague, the United States attacked the ruling intemperately, charged the Court with having been "politicized" to such an extent that it was unfit to pass on the case, and announced it would decline to defend its conduct at the merits hearing.
4. The foregoing was followed by a threat to cancel, for all purposes, against all nations, the partial acceptance of compulsory jurisdiction filed by President Truman with Senate approval.
5. The pope had just visited Nicaragua in 1983 and may have precipitated the

worsening of tensions between the local Catholic Church officialdom and the Sandinista regime.

6. After lengthy and delicate negotiations, the Vatican had recently won diplomatic recognition recently by the United States, an achievement long sought by the Holy See.

It was with this background that the head of the papal state stepped up to the barristers' bar to address the Court. It was a special sitting of the full Court with the royal family, the diplomatic corps, and the press in attendance.

The pope began with something more than the usual perfunctory expression of respect: he spoke "with a profound sense of respect and esteem . . . honored to have this opportunity to speak." After outlining the support of his predecessors for peaceful judicial settlement and international organization, going back to Hague I of 1899, he expressed approval of their purpose to aid in the evolution of a world legal system. To this he added a brief summary of Vatican support for the United Nations since its founding in 1945, and its affiliated organizations.

Stressing the continuing danger of total war, he deplored the effect of a diplomacy based on self-interest rather than the common good, as having an inhibiting influence on the Court. He went on to say that the ICJ "had an *extremely important role* to play" (emphasis in original papal text). To this he added:

> The International Court of Justice has intervened in difficult areas and has managed to do more than simply apply existing law. It has also *contributed to the development of law*. The decisions of the Court have not infrequently had a wide-ranging scope because they are to be seen in the framework of the rules of international law and legal principles. (Emphasis in original text.)

(There had been no rulings except the Nicaragua jurisdiction decision since 1980 save for the U.S.–Canada fishing rights case, a Tunisia–Libya continental shelf dispute, and review of the grievance of a UN staff member, each case narrow in scope.)

The pontiff continued with an expression of approval of the "impartiality and objectivity" of the two judicial bodies. "Their members have included many eminent lawyers [and] . . . constitute an *international center of distinguished legal activity*" (emphasis in original text). To help it become a totally effective judicial authority, he suggested ways in which "the judicial element can play a wider role in international relations," including more intensive use of the Court, and a wider acceptance of the so-called compulsory jurisdiction of the Court. To this he added applause for "extension of the role of the international court . . . for advisory opinions" and explicit recognition of "the *need to develop a world legal system*" (emphasis in original text).

In the words delivered by the pope in the Peace Palace, he was addressing the fifteen judges, but obviously in his praise and all other aspects of this address, the target audience was not in the Peace Palace. At that very moment there was pending the threat, made only a few weeks before by the U.S. State Department, to *narrow,* by withdrawing, what had passed for U.S. consent. As to that threat—the only form of pressure recorded as having been attempted in relation to the Court for many years—the pope warned that the Court "comes under *pressure* designed to prevent it from transcending ideologies and interests." After a tribute to the "independence and integrity" of the judges, he said, "They must resist such pressures and must be assisted in their efforts to do so."

In the light of the pervasive efforts of the Reagan administration to discredit the Court at the time, it is entirely fair to say the papal peroration went beyond the necessities of mere courtesy:

> Above all, I commend the efforts of the Judges of the International Court of Justice. . . . I pray that God will strengthen you in your efforts to be just and promote justice. May he bless your work abundantly, so that it may help bring forth greater harmony in the world, and strengthen the foundations of a true and lasting peace.

A spectacular endorsement of the work of the Court and a frustrated attempt to initiate widening of its compulsory jurisdiction soon followed from a most unexpected quarter. Almost as the pope was addressing the Court, Mikhail Gorbachev became chief of the USSR. It had been a Communist Party doctrine for seven decades that the Court was a biased capitalist and/or imperialist tool. Typically a Moscow paper called the Court's *Peace Treaties* ruling "self-exposure of international reactionary and aggressive forces."

After two years in office, devoted to beginning a series of domestic reforms, Gorbachev turned to foreign policy. In September 1987, at the opening of the UN General Assembly, he published in the principal Soviet newspapers a statement recognizing the world's interdependence, endorsing the United Nations and calling for "unconditional observance of the United Nations Charter." He expressed appreciation for the potential of the ICJ and recommended it as a frequent resort to advisories, and its mandatory jurisdiction should be recognized by all on mutually agreed upon conditions. The permanent members of the Security Council were to take the first step.

Coming from a state that had been dared, challenged, and needled on the subject of the Rule of Law in transitional relations, Gorbachev's statement on the Court and international law could not be ignored. The United States, the nation that, more than any other, had given the world the Court and then insulted and defied it, faced a problem. It could not allow itself to be embarrassed by spurning the offer from Moscow.

The United States responded to the offer of a great power pact for leading the nations to agree to mandatory jurisdiction with a counterproposal. Its terms drained the idea of real content and ultimately frustrated it. Two conditions were imposed on U.S. acceptance. One was that there be specifically excluded from the consent to agreeing to go to court when challenged any issue that might concern the legality of use of force by a state. The second condition was that the consent be limited to the hearing of a case by a "chamber" (usually five judges) agreed upon by the parties. This gave the state agreeing to it the power to blackball judges deemed to be hostile; it reduced the Court to the status of an arbitration tribunal in effect.

For reasons that need not be dwelt on, the Soviets seemed inclined to accept the U.S. limits. Leaders of the U.S. international law community did not: they thought their country was proposing a step backward. Great Britain rejected it and France condemned it. The idea died as the Soviet Union and Gorbachev's tenure did.

There was an instructive sequel at a special, 1992 supersummit meeting of the UN Security Council, called for the purpose of discussing ways and means of keeping the peace in the new, post–Cold War world. The "summit" sobriquet came with the special invitation to the head of state of each member of the Council. Concerned Americans who knew their nation's role in the creation of an international court might have been embarrassed.

In formal statements made at the start of the sessions, Moscow's new chief executive, Boris Yeltsin, who had ousted and had mutually intense hostile relations with Gorbachev, called (as the latter might have been expected to) for enhancement of the prestige of the Court to facilitate peaceful settlement of disputes, "to consolidate the rule of law throughout the world." Similar expressions were made by Venezuela, Austria, Japan, and Zimbabwe. But U.S. President Bush was silent.

There has been no public explanation of the persistence of the United States in the hostility to the Court and in its distrust of the tribunal's capacity to pass on the legality of forceful actions by states—especially with the end of the Cold War, and the end of pretextual or plausible reasons for noncompliance with the Charter limitations on transnational use of violence by states.

A clue will be found in the strict condition put on U.S. acceptance of the now-defunct Gorbachev initiative, for permanent members of the Security Council to lead in securing by treaty the wider acceptance of compulsory submission of disputes. That condition has been that states should be exempt from having the Court pass on the legality of unilateral use of force.

The law laid down unanimously on the point, with the concurrence of Judge Stephen Schewebel of the United States, who had previously been a U.S. State Department official, was that the Charter that the United States signed at San Francisco, and the Court's accompanying statute, did not intend to exempt force from being judged.

Should the United States continue to assert and insist on the stance that its use of force transnationally, whether for self-defense or otherwise, be immune from judgment, the question that will again arise is, "Was it worth the trouble" to create the Court?

17

Rounding Out the Century

"After decades of underuse," as Court President Sir Robert Jennings reported, "the Court now has a full docket of important cases." Has the Court shown the capacity to deal with its unprecedented caseload, serving the goals of peace and justice?

It will be useful to look at some of the cases that were disposed of during this active period—and some that may still be pending. What we will see may illuminate further the relevance of the Rule of Law to the maintenance of peace.

The attempt, reported in the close of chapter 16, to withdraw the authority with which the Courts have operated to consider "force" cases suggests a look at some recent adjudications settling territorial disputes. Some came after force was used, but that did not impair the Court's effectiveness. One was the Burkina Faso-Mali case, discussed in chapter 12. Another was the post-Soccer War case of Honduras-El Salvador, which figures in chapter 13.

An African case resolved a problem that followed a military action that resulted in occupation and administration of a large segment of neighboring territory. The case of Chad and Libya came in 1990 after mediation by the Organization of African Unity. The Court ruled that Libya and Chad were bound to accept a border that had been fixed in a 1955 treaty between Libya and France, the colonial ruler of Chad at that time. What was at stake was a land corridor called the Aozou Strip, which was said to be a rich source of uranium.

The treaty in question provided that it was to be of only twenty years' duration. But that was no problem, Sir Robert said on behalf of the Court's ruling. "When a boundary has been the subject of an agreement, the continued existence of that boundary is not dependant on the continuing life of the treaty," he said.

Those accustomed to media references to the loser as a "rogue state" will be interested in the compliance as reported to the Court. An agreement was made between the parties after the Court ruling, calling for prompt withdrawal of the Libyan forces and administration from territory held to be Chadian. Libya complied promptly and cheerfully with the Court's decree.

Another case of interest had a "David versus Goliath" character, as well as presenting some important questions of postcolonial international environmental law. Nauru is a Central Pacific island of about 8.25 square miles, with a population of less than 10,000. Australia is an island too, of 3 million square miles and a population of 15 million.

Nauru had the temerity to take Australia to the ICJ. Damages and restitution were sought for actions that occurred while Australia was in control of Nauru under a League of Nations mandate, followed by a UN trusteeship. The island, a German colony prior to 1914, was occupied by Australian troops as World War I began. At Versailles, the mandate was nominally given to "His Britannic Majesty," still ruler of an empire, but in practice shared by Australia, New Zealand, and Great Britain. But Australia was the dominant partner, the actual ruler.

Why were partners needed to supervise such a tiny place? Because a valuable resource was there for the taking. In 1900, when the Germans were still in occupation, a British company obtained the right to extract phosphate rock, an extremely useful source of fertilizer. The agricultural interests of several parts of the British Empire wanted to share in it. They did, to the hilt, for half a century.

When Nauru obtained independence during the peak of the decolonization period, the new self-governors saw their island in good part in ruins. About a third of the plateau that constituted the bulk of the arable land was unusable and uninhabitable. This was the aftermath of the mining and export of 35 million tons of phosphate, without any repair of the land. Profit was immense: just a bit of the revenue was used to pay for the island's administrative costs. The bulk was shared by the partners.

The leaders of the newly independent ministate appointed a commission of experts to assess the responsibility for what had been done and to seek a remedy. An expert in international law was needed to chair the commission. One was found in Christopher Weeramantry, a well-reputed professor in Melbourne, Australia, who would later become a World Court judge. He will figure as such in another case in this chapter, and he was to be a potentially significant participant (concurring and dissenting in part) in the historic decision concerning legality of nuclear arms in chapter 18.

After studying the commission's report, Nauru's new government used the optional clause to enable it to sue Australia, a state that had accepted the privileges and responsibilities that accompany the clause. Suit was filed at the World Court on May 19, 1989, demanding reparations for the resources carried off.

Basically, the theory of the suit was breach of trust, a familiar concept in Anglo-American law, but revolutionary and novel in international litigation.

All that was sought was to make genuine the "trusteeship" that was supposed to be the legal basis of the League mandate, and responsibility enacted in the very name of a UN trusteeship.

The Court heard first the preliminary procedural objections filed by Australia. All but one were disposed of by votes of 12 to 1. (One nonvoting judge was Weeramantry, self-disqualified for his previous role in the case.)

The principal Australian objection to the suit, which split the Court 9 to 4, was based on the same argument that was later to derail East Timor's suit (as brought by Portugal). It was the failure of Nauru's counsel to include as defendants New Zealand and Great Britain, who had shared the proceeds of the island's exploitation. The "Monetary Gold" case (discussed below) was invoked to suggest the suit was faulty for having failed to include defendants that might be affected by a judgment as to liability for the same set of actions.

That effort failed, as nine of the judges joined in an opinion accepting the distinction argued by Nauru's counsel: that the claim that Nauru might have against the two other states was, while similar, not the "very subject matter of the suit," the formula used in the earlier decision.

Now it was more than the international law community that looked forward with interest to the next stage of the case: the assessment of responsibility. The diplomatic world, the colonial and ex-colony states, and the Third World were eager to learn what the outcome would be. The question of betrayal of trust, as charged by one state against another, for environmental damage and deprivation of resources was novel, serious, and intriguing.

But the case never came up for final a hearing. Australia's leaders agreed to settle Nauru's claims, just as one large enterprise in domestic litigation will settle a suit by an adversary, large or small, after the first round is lost. Payment of more than $150 million was to be made.

That settlement has a significance not limited to the parties concerned, or to the legal issues in the case. It was but one of several, in the post-Nicaragua case period, that was disposed of by agreement between the parties after a round in Court. That a higher level of maturity and usefulness has been attained by the Court in this respect was noted in a talk to the American Political Science Association in 1993 by Professor Keith Highet, who was the U.S. attorney most frequently at the Court, with clients the world over:

> What are the implications of the fact of these settlements? One must infer that the Court is now obviously filling a role that is important for the judicial settlements of international disputes. . . . That role should not be limited to handing down decisions and judgments; it is also to present an available forum for the negotiations of settlements of cases that have been brought to the Court. It is a credible role that may assist in the larger process of dispute resolution.

It is not only that the very existence and prestige of a fully functioning Court will make more likely the settlement of cases brought or on the verge of being brought to it; the very role of peacemaker is fulfilled better by a settlement, in that a "win" must be accompanied by a "defeat," which can leave an after-effect of resentment.

Other examples of these post-Nicaragua settlements are worth touching on briefly as illustrative of the process in action. There was a case brought by Denmark against Finland given the title *Passage Through the Great Belt.* The belt is a strait that is both an international waterway, connecting the Baltic and North Seas, and a part of Danish territory through which two major centers of population are connected only by ferry.

As the flow of people and trade between two parts of the nation increased in the postwar era, the ferry link became increasingly unsatisfactory, intermittently impeded as it was by the local weather. Denmark announced plans to build a bridge. Finland protested because a sixty-five-meter-high bridge would prevent passage of what had become Finland's valuable export of 170-meter-high oil rigs. Denmark argued that it was only obliged to make possible the passage of "normal" vessels, of which none would be affected by a sixty-five-meter-high bridge.

Two rights in conflict, sovereignty and passage, and a touchy question of interpretation. When agreement proves to be impossible, a Court can be helpful. It was. After one round at The Hague, on an application for a temporary restraining order ("indication of provisional measures," in the Court's language), the parties, after sessions with the president about future proceedings, resumed negotiations and settled their case.

In chapter 14, describing the tensions between Iran and the United States, and how they did *not* prevent the Iran–U.S. Claims Tribunal from carrying on with its conflict-resolution functions, two ICJ cases between those nations were mentioned. One presented to the Court the claims for reparations made by Iran resulting from the shooting down of an Iranian commercial passenger plane, which caused 290 deaths (see also chapter 15).

Hearings were set on preliminary objections to the Court's jurisdiction, and submissions in writing were made by both sides. A final hearing on jurisdiction was set for September 1994. That was postponed by joint request of Iran and United States. They were not only able to agree on that—as harsh words on other subjects were traded between the two governments—but also sat down to begin serious negotiations.

The bargaining came to fruition in February 1996 with a settlement. The United States agreed to pay $132 million to be divided among the victims' families. No payment would be made to the Iranian government itself. This proved to be a "package" deal, settling some seriously contested claims between the two governments that were pending at the Iran–U.S. Claims Tribunal.

But the settlement did not include the other ICJ case between the same nations, resulting from U.S. destruction of two Iranian oil platforms that were functioning in the Gulf.

EAST TIMOR'S CASE:
A MISSING DEFENDANT?

The island known as Timor lies about 300 miles north of Australia, somewhat east of the group of islands that used to be known as the Dutch East Indies, but which now constitute the Republic of Indonesia. Between Australia and Timor Island is an area called the "Timor Gap," which geologists have said contains one of the world's richest oil reserves, with possibly as much as 5 billion or 6 billion barrels of untapped resources.

During the colonial era, Timor's western portion had been part of the Dutch Indies; the east was occupied by Portugal, one of the few remnants of a global empire. A liberal revolution displaced a long-ruling dictatorship in Portugal in 1974, and the change brought a heightening of the independence movement in East Timor. Portugal was now tolerant to this, and prepared to face the process of decolonization.

There was a split in the Timorese independence movement, a minority making overtures to Indonesia and influenced by agents of the latter since it was aware of the gap's oil resources. Indonesia had made a deal with Australia about the adjoining areas that were part of its continental shelf.

But a majority of the Timorese freedom movement desired full independence, rather than affiliation with Indonesia. As it seemed evident that their rivals were intriguing with the latter, the native movement, called by the acronym Fretilin, declared independence.

An invasion and occupation by Indonesian troops followed. Portugal, which had withdrawn its own forces rather than fight Fretilin, protested and won, from both the UN General Assembly and the Security Council, denunciation of Indonesia's move as illegal. They demanded that Indonesia withdraw to enable completion of the UN decolonization process, with Portugal as administrative authority as is customary, in its capacity as former colonial power.

The Indonesian ruler was not moved. A purported annexation followed, amid harsh, allegedly genocidal, repression. This came to a head with a brutal massacre in 1991 at Dili, which brought the scandal of an ex-colony's colonialist conduct to global attention. Oil-consuming powers prevented effective UN intervention. Australia, as one of them, actually gave formal recognition to the annexation, and entered into a treaty with Indonesia for division of the contestable portion of the continental shelf in the Timor Gap. Its effect was to allow Indonesia to appropriate, with Australia, valued assets of the Timorese indigenous people.

Both Portugal and Australia were subscribers to the ICJ's optional clause, with its agreement to consent to be sued. Indonesia was not. Until the Timorese could obtain nationhood, Portugal, as the former colonial power, was the only party under international law qualified to sue, if a legal remedy could be sought. But Indonesia could not be sued without its consent.

As described in chapter 16, the jurists who were founding drafters of the Court's statute had twice wanted to do away with the "sovereign immunity" that made consent to suit necessary in international litigation. But the Great Powers blocked that each time. Here was a good example of the crippling effect on international justice of the requirement of consent.

But even though Indonesia could not be sued—and directed under order of the Court enforceable by the Security Council to leave East Timor—what about Australia? Had not the island continent done a wrong to both Portugal and to the Timorese people? A suit against Australia for wrongfully making a treaty affecting Timorese rights could not undo the wrong that Indonesia had done; it could impede exploitation of Timorese resources and thus aid in gaining a negotiated solution. The UN secretary-general had, from time to time, sought to bring this about.

On the foregoing basis, Portugal began a suit against Australia in the World Court. While nominally claiming damages for itself, as well as the reparations that the East Timorese were entitled to for the injury to their unrealized rights, Portugal was in a sense acting pro bono, litigating in the international public interest, having no economic or power incentive of her own. But this was the least that could be done, and the people of Portugal approved, even, it is said, demanded it, in view of a sense of remorse at having been a colonial power to the detriment of the Timorese.

There was a problem suggested by one of the Court's early rulings, and it served as a precedent that ultimately derailed the case and brought it to an end. It is worth looking at.

In the aftermath of the case of the Corfu Channel (see chapter 9), Albania declined to pay the damages due Britain for mining (or at least not warning of the mining) of the channel. Early on in the nonpayment period—the matter was settled by a new regime after the Cold War was over—an attempt was made to secure payment from some monetary gold (that became the name of a new case) of Albania, seized from an Italian bank and carried off by the Nazis to Berlin.

In the case of the monetary gold, the victorious allies holding the gold had agreed they would use it to pay Britain the Corfu case damages, unless Italy could prove that Albania owed the gold to it; Italy filed a case at the Court to establish its claim, which the allies consented be litigated. But Albania wouldn't consent. The Court held that it could not take jurisdiction of the case without Albania's consent. To pass on the validity of Italy's claim against Albania, for the purpose of deciding whether the gold should be used to pay Britain or Italy, could not be done without Albania's participation. There the requirement of consent in determining the interest of an absent party blocked the Court from passing on Italy's claim.

While the ICJ does not have as strict an obligation to abide by the governing status of precedent as is common in Anglo–American law, it will usually treat principles decided in earlier cases as a preferred source of international law rules. The obvious interest of Albania in the outcome of the *Monetary Gold* litigation that it had disdained to join seemed to resemble Indonesia's interest in a contest between Portugal and Australia.

The cause and struggle of the Timorese people had gained worldwide attention and concern after the massacre at Dili in 1991. It become known that the Dili tragedy was but the tip of an iceberg that represented a genocidal course followed by Indonesian troops on the island. Sympathetic volunteer organizations came into being in civil society, publicizing and seeking financial aid. They followed with keen interest the suit that Portugal had begun. They joined in an international scholarly conference in London in 1992. Papers submitted on the historical, legal, and political aspects of East Timor's plight, later published, included contributions by Australian scholars of distinction, unafraid to criticize their nation when they thought it to be in the wrong. Among papers giving attention to the issues in the Portuguese ICJ case were expressions of caution concerning the obstacle that the *Monetary Gold* precedent might become.

The outcome showed the concern to have been warranted. In June 1995, Portugal's case against Australia was dismissed on the basis of the interpretation given in *Monetary Gold* to the principle "that [the Court] cannot decide a dispute between states without the consent of those states." The case could not proceed, ruled the Court, because it could not be decided without passing on the legality of Indonesia's invasion and occupation of East Timor.

Disappointment was slightly mitigated by assertion in the Court opinion that the legal status of East Timor was a "non–self-governing territory"—a phrase having a definite technical meaning under the UN Charter. Such lands are entitled to have an occupying power "develop self government . . . and assist them in the progressive development of their free political institutions" (Article 73, UN Charter). And, added the Court, "the people has the right to self-determination." This would not necessarily be a defeat, it could be argued, were not the Security Council in a state of paralysis due to entanglement of some states in the politics of Indonesia, including the United States.

An aspect of the case that should not be ignored is the remarkable sixty-six-page dissenting opinion filed by Judge Weeramantry. The Court should have granted full satisfaction to Portugal, he contended. It constitutes an instructive essay on the several principles of international law involved and concludes, without disputing *Monetary Gold*'s ruling on its special facts, by showing how the case can be decided separately from and without passing on Indonesia's guilt or innocence.

All that had to be considered, Judge Weeramantry argued, is the legality of Australia's separate obligation and its individual actions, "without any need for an examination of the conduct of another state."

Space does not permit a fuller summary and analysis of Judge Weeramantry's dissent in the East Timor case. But it is worth adding a few words about him. He is a native of Sri Lanka, and began his legal education at the

University of London. He practiced and taught in Australia, and held visiting professorships in Pennsylvania, Florida, South Africa, and Japan. In a brief sketch of the judge in a book about the Court, its librarian, Arthur Eyffinger, tells how the judge has "been inspired by Eastern and Western sources of law, letters and wisdom alike. He draws from Plato, Stone or Cardozo as readily as from Hindu or Buddhist sources." Nevertheless, when Judge Weeramantry's nine-year term ended, he was not reelected to the Court.

The struggle by and on behalf of the people of East Timor continued. It seemed possible that it would come to a "happy ending" when new rulers of Indonesia consented to allow the United Nations to conduct a referendum as to the wishes of the Timorese in the occupied portion of the island.

Despite some alarming episodes of brutal intimidation in the prevoting period by so-called militias aiming to defeat independence, the people of East Timor voted in overwhelming numbers for their freedom. There followed a holocaust, inflicted by the militias under the observation of complaisant and probably complicit Indonesian troops. The only logistically possible rescue effort could be maintained from Australia. But, tragically, help did not arrive in time to avert destruction of Timor's capacity to function as a state. Those in the media who were unable to explain its "pointlessness" would have understood, if they were familiar with the subject matter and aim of the Portuguese suit against Australia, a case not mentioned once in the aftermath.

KOSOVO: NO COURT DECISION

In one of the last cases filed in the twentieth century, the Court faced a new and troublesome issue. Can the use of force contrary to the clear mandate of the Law of Nations be held legitimate if claimed to be justified as "humanitarian intervention"?

After the first few weeks of intense, sustained, and widespread bombing in regard to the Kosovo controversy, Serbia (in the name of Yugoslavia) instituted proceedings in the ICJ against the United States and nine of its NATO allies. The charges were (1) variations of a claim of illegal use of force, and (2) genocide against the Serbian people. Separate cases were begun against each member of NATO; with the filing, Serbia applied for provisional measures pending trial, to stop the bombing at once.

What could have ultimately been presented at trial and to some extent at the preliminary application were two great questions:

1. Can the use of force, hitherto clearly illegal, be permitted where constituting "humanitarian intervention"?

2. Was the manner in which force was used so unreasonable as to disallow a claim of "humanitarianism"?

The Court did not reach or discuss either question.

As in U.S. law, when a preliminary "stay" is asked, there are two preconditions: Does the applicant have a reasonable probability of success? And would there be injury considered irreparable if the injunction were denied? Important as a requirement to show "probability of success" in a World Court case is that there be a reasonable likelihood that the Court has jurisdiction: Did the defendant state give its consent to have its conduct judged by the Court?

Yugoslavia had contended that consent was given, first because signers of the Convention Against Genocide, by their acceptance of the treaty, thereby consented to have charges under it decided by the Court. Also invoked was consent via the optional clause; this was available only as to six of the defendants, not including the United States.

The Court refused to order the bombing to be suspended. It expressed deep concern "with the human tragedy, the loss of life, and the enormous suffering in Kosovo [and in all parts of Yugoslavia]." But it could not find a likelihood of a final showing of jurisdiction sufficient to justify stepping in with a preliminary drastic remedy.

As to the genocide charge, the Court majority held that a necessary element of the offense was actual intent by the use of force to eliminate members of a group for their very membership in the group, and that however widespread the destruction, such an intent was not likely to be proven. Nevertheless, as to eight of the defendants, Serbia was allowed to proceed in order to have a chance to prove that intent. The United States and Spain were dropped because, in reservations to acceptance of the pact, they had declined to be sued without specific consent in each case.

The optional clause basis for jurisdiction against Canada and three others, and against the United Kingdom and Spain, was also rejected. Yugoslavia had never been a participant in the scheme of suing and consenting to be sued under the clause; suddenly, a few days before filing its case Yugoslavia accepted it; but with a tricky provision that backfired: because Yugoslavia was wary of suits based on earlier conduct in Bosnia and others, its acceptance of the optional clause excluded any acts prior to the day before its agreement.

The Court's view (against which there were several dissents) was that the bombing itself had started before the exclusionary date; dissenters argued that each bombing created a separate new grievance and "dispute," arising after Serbia's acceptance of the option.

With the case likely to be ended without merits decision, there will be no answer to the nagging question of the legality of using abominable means for humanitarian ends. That question is raised sharply by the compressed portrait of the bombing campaign in its entirety, given by correspondent Steven

Erlanger in the *New York Times Sunday Magazine* in an article titled "Beneath the Falling Bombs" and dated June 13, 1999:

> What began as a campaign against the Yugoslav military, to get Slobodan Milo-sevic to capitulate quickly over Kosovo, veered, perhaps out of frustration, into a psy-op war aimed also at civilians, at their electrical and their water and their heating plants.

GUARDING HUMAN RIGHTS
UNDER TREATY

In the *LeGrand* case, a suit by Germany against the United States, the Court settled three important points on June 27, 2001:

- A country's treaty right of consular access to its nationals may be enforced not only on behalf of the state, but by the state for its national as the latter's human right.
- A local rule of "procedural default" may not under international law bar a claim by one unaware of her right at trial.
- An indication of provisional measures temporarily issued to keep a case from being futile is "binding" and enforceable when disobeyed.*

These holdings came too late to save the life of a German who was executed in Arizona in disregard of such an order. The same fate had been suffered in Virginia by Angel Breard, a Paraguayan, after a provisional measure granted in a similar suit; the suit was dropped without follow-through after the execution. All but one of seven commentaries by Law of Nations scholars in a symposium in the October 1988 AJIL agreed that a version of "federalism" presently in vogue did not immunize states from the world's law.

Nevertheless the State Department in LeGrand's case informed the Arizona governor that the ICJ's action was not binding, as it had with Viriginia in Breard's case. The ICJ ruling in *LeGrand* implicitly rebuked Secretary Albright for this, as it did the U.S. Solicitor General who had helped induce the Supreme Court to abstain by a similar assertion.

The ICJ ruling in *LeGrand* will be helpful to Americans traveling abroad; the treaty right vindicated was important, as the Secretary of State herself said, for America's "ability to ensure Americans are protected when traveling abroad."

---

*At pages 43, 74, 124, 127, 132, 159, 196, and 220 of this work the Court's power to "indicate provisional measures" was analogized to a U.S. "temporary injunction."

18

To Court to Ban the Bomb?

In the aftermath of nuclear bombings at Hiroshima and Nagasaki, findings of commissions and the like were not required for humankind to conclude that it was confronted with a threat more serious than any in recorded history. Fire, flood, or famine, plague or pestilence, none, or even a combination of any, could match the threat of nuclear weapons. The horror was not only in the developing capacity of some on earth to destroy most of the rest, to make earth uninhabitable. It was also in our seeming incapacity to do anything about it.

Not that the components of civil society did not try. The scientists themselves, without whom the generals would not have had this "advanced" weaponry, were horrified at what they had done; some organized and spoke out. Others in academia, business leaders, professionals of all kinds, and religious leaders each protested after their fashion.

The smaller nations, becoming more outspoken and independent in UN circles as their numbers increased with decolonization, sought to act in self-defense. The effort began in the council of nations. Debates in the UN General Assembly culminated with a resolution declaring nuclear and thermonuclear weapons contrary to the UN Charter, to international law, to the "laws of humanity" (1961).

Nothing changed. The mutual dance toward possible self-destruction proceeded with the amassing of tens of thousands of weapons that came to be sufficient to destroy the world several times over. Even a few of the non-aligned nations, fearful of or unduly hostile to some regional foe, participated in the proliferation.

The 1961 vote of the General Assembly declaring the weapons "contrary to international law" was not merely a "political" vote; it was supported by respectable legal authority. Two books had already been published confirming an opinion that had been expressed by Albert Schweitzer, humanitarian par excellence, in a letter saying it was "elementary," and "obvious . . . that international law prohibits weapons with illimitable effect, which cause unlimited damage . . . no government can deny that these weapons violate international law."

One of these books, *Nuclear Weapons and International Law,* coauthored by McWhinney, had unusually distinguished jurisprudential credibility. The author was Nagendra Singh, whose standing and authority to speak were authenticated by his later election as a judge and later president of the ICJ. In agreement was a treatise by George Schwarzenberg, long a respected professor of international law, *The Legality of Nuclear Weapons.*

In the light of the horror and indescribable worldwide fear produced by nuclear weapons, it might seem to have taken unduly long for a movement to develop in civil society to validate as official doctrine the teaching of these jurists. But for that to occur, their message had to become better known. An early advocate was Professor Richard Falk of Princeton University. Perhaps his first contribution was to report in the pages of the *American Journal of International Law* the decision of a Japanese court in the *Shimoda* case, holding in effect what was implicit in Nagendra Singh's work, that the very first use of nuclear weapons against civilian population centers was illegal.

Then came the first visit of an aspect of the question to the ICJ. In 1973, Australia and New Zealand sued France at The Hague, in the case that is described in chapter 9. Not long afterward, Falk, together with two colleagues, wrote an essay further developing Singh's thesis of the intrinsic illegality (that is, not requiring the legislative support of an international treaty) of nuclear weapons.

The Falk-Meyrowitz-Sanderson essay, "Nuclear Weapons and International Law," was rejected by all major U.S. law reviews. It appeared first in 1980 in the *Indian Journal of International Law.* (Later the Center of International Studies of Princeton University republished it as an "Occasional Paper.")

The early 1980s saw the apex of the growing antinuclear movement, in its incarnation as the "freeze" cause. The contribution of Falk's writing was to add a legal dimension to the effort to end the nuclear weapon's danger to the earth and its inhabitants.

In late 1981 or early the following year, Robert Boehm, a New York attorney and president of the Center for Constitutional Rights, is said to have inspired, with some of his colleagues, the creation of the Lawyers Committee on Nuclear Policy (LCNP). Its aim was to find a way to apply the ideas Falk and others had been developing, based on Singh's work. The members of LCNP included able legal scholars who began the publication and distribution of both legal and lay-directed papers to further the cause. Similar activity developed in New Zealand, after a visit by Falk in 1986. That nation had been a successful plaintiff in the suit against atmospheric testing by France; its sensitivity was enhanced by the effect of its rejection of the entry into its harbors of warships equipped with nuclear weapons.

These efforts and others—including an unofficially constituted tribunal in London—culminated with a multinational meeting of lawyers at The Hague. Its outcome was the formation of the International Association of Lawyers Against

Nuclear Arms (IALANA). Its leaders included lawyer-scholar Peter Weiss, who had become head of LCNP, and vice chair Saul Mendlovitz, Rutgers Law School professor and head of a peace-oriented think tank called World Order Models Project. In action to take a major step to fulfilling IALANA's aim, they conceived what came to be called the "World Court Project." For this they began a joint venture with the International Physicians for the Prevention of Nuclear War, which won the 1985 Nobel Peace Prize for dedicated work against nuclear disaster. The century-old International Peace Bureau (IPB), a coordinating organization based in Geneva, also joined the campaign.

The object of the World Court Project was to seek an advisory opinion on the legality of nuclear weapons from the International Court of Justice, in the hope that it would confirm the conclusions that they had been advancing. This is more easily said than done. As the yearbook of the ICJ regularly reports, "Private persons frequently apply to the Court . . . [they] are informed that only States may be parties in cases before the Court." Likewise, the Court's advisory opinion process is available only to the UN General Assembly and Security Council, or to UN organs authorized by the Assembly to apply.

What had to be done was to lobby for and gain the agreement of such an official agency to request the Court's opinion.

It was a daunting job for outsiders to win Assembly action. Inertia and the powerful opposition of the nuclear states had to be overcome. It was thought that a better target at first would be the World Health Organization (WHO). It was a qualified UN affiliate and directly concerned with the health and environmental effects of nuclear explosions.

It had become known that the WHO had recently commissioned reports on the public health effects of a nuclear war, so that it could advise nations how to prepare to mitigate the effects. A principal response had come from Joseph Rotblat, a nuclear physicist who had worked on the bomb and who many years later won a Nobel Prize for a long fight to ban it. He advised the WHO that there was no adequate way a public health system could respond, and that the only possible "therapy" would be total nuclear disarmament. It was not long before the WHO agreed to address the Court to seek an opinion on legality of the bomb.

But the main objective was to win action by the United Nations' principal deliberative body, the General Assembly. A worldwide campaign was launched. The organizations united in the venture sought allies in every state. They began by publishing two books, one by LCNP, the other by IPB, explaining the project, its aims, and the legal arguments available. One volume was aptly titled *From Hiroshima to The Hague.*

An extraordinary effort followed that cannot fairly be summarized. There were meetings, regional, international, and local; circulation of a Declaration of Conscience; solicitation of endorsement by individuals and organizations of civil society. Energetic individual campaigns were conducted in many venues.

One who visited them all, and was a leading figure in meeting with state delegations to the UN Assembly, was Alyn Ware, former school teacher from New Zealand, first a volunteer then a staff worker for LCNP.

On May 8, 1993, the World Health Assembly voted to ask the Court whether, "in view of the health and environmental effects," use of nuclear weaponry would be a "breach of [a state's] obligations under international law." The momentum from this helped the continuing effort with the Assembly, which voted December 15, 1994, to ask the Court whether threat or use of the weaponry is "in any circumstances permitted under international law." The two requests for advice appeared on the Court's list as separate cases, but they were consolidated for a single set of hearings. These began on October 30, 1995, and continued through November 15.

In theory, no advocacy is strictly necessary at the Court when it is sitting to consider a request for an advisory opinion. Such factual material and commentary as the requesting organ sees fit to submit can be adequate. Under the Court statute, the registrar gives notice of the submission of the question to all states, and they may appear to argue or submit views in writing.

In the nuclear weapons case, the response was unprecedented. Forty-five nations, from Australia to Zimbabwe, presented positions, twenty-two of them orally. As part of Japan's presentation, the mayors of Hiroshima and Nagasaki addressed the Court. The Marshall Islands of the South Pacific offered a statement by Joseph Rotblat (too ill at the time to appear in person).

In a remarkable departure from the usual absence of media interest in proceedings at the Court, there was Court TV coverage of all of the hearings in the Great Hall of the Peace Palace. A television documentary produced from this by Kevin Sanders for the War and Peace Foundation was shown on PBS channels. The subject matter justified the phrase "Trial of the Century," used by Peter Weiss, at The Hague as a spokesman for LCNP and IALANA, and in Court as counsel for Malaysia.

Weiss added, in the same review of the proceedings, "Whatever way the opinions go, it's a safe bet there will be more than one opinion." When the Court's judgments in the two cases came down on July 8, 1996, there were twenty-two: the cases were separately decided, each with an official opinion expressing the judgment of the Court; six separate or dissenting opinions in the World Health Organization case; and fourteen, one for each sitting judge, in the General Assembly case.

In the WHO case the Court decided it lacked power to offer an opinion on the grounds argued by the United States and others, that the constitution of the WHO did not authorize it to deal with questions of legality. That had been raised by WHO's own legal counsel at the Assembly that voted to ask the question, and he repeated it in his presentation to the Court. Three judges dissented, including Weeramantry, who with his colleagues argued that a health agency must be as concerned with preventing threats to health as with a cleanup.

In its decision on advice to the General Assembly, the Court did hold, despite arguments by the nuclear powers, that it should use its discretionary power to grant an opinion; its central holding was two-fold:

a. that "the threat or use of nuclear weapons would generally be contrary to the rules applicable to armed conflict and in particular the principles and rules of humanitarian law";
b. the Court could not "conclude definitively" about legality "in an extreme circumstance of self-defense in which the very survival of a State would be at stake."

The two were voted on as a single package, creating some problems for some of the judges and all of the commentators; as reflection of the difficulty within the Court, the vote was evenly divided, 7 to 7, one judge having died just before the ruling. In the Court's practice, as will be recalled from the pre–World War II Austro-German customs union ruling and one of the Namibia rulings, the Court's president gets a tiebreaker second vote so the decision stands as judgment of the Court.

In a spontaneous—in the sense of not having been a point raised by the General Assembly's request—added paragraph in its decision, the Court unanimously told the nations united in the Assembly that "There exists an obligation to pursue in good faith and bring to a conclusion negotiations leading to nuclear disarmament in all its aspects under strict and effective international control."

Just what did the Court *do* by its decision, what did the quoted words mean? Applying the title of chapter 16 to the effort made in so many places by so much advocacy on behalf of the "World Court Project"—was it worth the trouble? The answer cannot be determined by the instant response of the media, or on the continuing returns from scholarly studies. It is being seen in the variety of actions that the advisory opinion has inspired and the ongoing actions that it has spurred on.

Although the world press, particularly the U.S. press, did not cover the fortnight's daily proceedings at the Court (compare the attention given to another so-called Trial of the Century—the O. J. Simpson murder trial), its reporters were at The Hague for decision day July 8, 1996. Instant analysis was offered by headline writers on July 9: "Use or threat of nuclear weapons 'unlawful'," *Financial Times;* "World Court Condemns Use of Nuclear Weapons," *New York Times;* "Outlawing the Unthinkable," *Toronto Star.* These are samples of one batch.

On the other hand there was doubt: "World Court: Nuclear Arms Mostly Illegal," *International Herald-Tribune;* "Court says Nukes *should* be outlawed" (emphasis added) with subhead "But the International Court of Justice waffle . . . ," *New Zealand Evening Post;* and, from the *Manchester Guardian Weekly,* "International Court Fudges Nuclear Arms Ruling."

The first round of expert opinion—law journals and articles by international scholars—was also divided. The *Australian Law Journal* called the Court's opinion "fatally ambivalent," headlining the piece "Court Judges Nuclear Weapons Unjudgeable." Commander Ron Neubauer, a scholarly U.S. Navy attorney who was detailed from his judge advocate duties to work on the case for the U.S. Department of Defense, said of the first part of the central holding ("generally unlawful") that it was consistent with the views of the United States, but that the second part ("self-defense in the extreme circumstance") was a little bit troublesome.

Roger S. Clark, distinguished professor at Rutgers Law School, gave his verdict in one of his letters from The Hague to some colleagues (1996). (Others are cited in "Sources and Suggestions: A Bibliography"). As counsel for states whose representation he shared, he said that his clients "got more from the Court . . . than expected . . . but less than might have been hoped for" in terms of absolute illegality of the weapon. In his essay for the book *The Case against the Bomb,* Clark points out, as did others, that the seven judges who concurred in the judgment of "general illegality," together with the three who dissented on the ground the seven did not go far enough, made up a majority against the legality of the bomb.

Richard Falk, who had contributed so much to the effort, offered an evaluation in political terms of the decision that condemned the bomb so thoroughly even though leaving a "loophole": In the heart of his essay in the editorial section of the January 1997 *American Journal of International Law,* he wrote:

> The language and the reasoning of the decision of the Court provides strong encouragement to antinuclear social and political forces to push for abolition. . . . Whether international law will develop in accordance with the advice given, namely in the direction of nuclear disarmament, depends on the reception of the decision in various areas of influence, including those within government, the United Nations system, civil society, academia and the media."

Attorney Peter Weiss, principal creator and leader of the "court project," as a mode of enabling civil society to use international law for self-protection, naturally had a few words to say. Agreeing with some comments of the majority and minority, that the 7-to-7 decision of the Court "is not perfect," he stressed its great importance and called it "close to perfect in that it affirms that the threat and use of nuclear weapons are subject to humanitarian law, environmental law and human rights law . . . subject to an extremely narrow and highly speculative *possible* exception"—"specifically" so narrow that it would not have justified the bombing of Hiroshima and Nagasaki.

He pays special tribute to Judge Weeramantry's dissent, in which the judge states that the Court's opinion takes "the law far on the road to total prohibition." In a separate essay, Professor Mendlovitz and Merav Datan seem to agree.

IMPLEMENTATION AND COMPLIANCE

More important than the opinions of international law scholars in evaluating the impact of the Court's action as to whether the tremendous effort that went into it was worthwhile are tangible *results*. No one in his or her right mind could have eagerly anticipated (no matter how eloquent and decisive the Court's ruling turned out to be) that it would serve as a magic broom to sweep away the clutter of nuclear weapons that threaten humankind. That no miraculous disappearance took place cannot to a rational mind have been disappointing.

What was it all about? In an advisory proceeding there is no judgment or finding on whether one state or another has violated a "norm," a standard of conduct internationally accepted, or has complied with an obligation, self-created by entering into a treaty or signing a multistate convention. The Court is asked to give *advice* to an entity authorized to ask for it, to help it judge how to deal with a subject of concern. Having received the advice, what did the UN General Assembly do with it or about it? One only has to look at the performance of the body at its next regular session after the Court gave its advice.

The General Assembly, after receiving the decision and debating it, adopted three resolutions. Two were general in wording: one welcomed the Court's action, and urged that there should be an international convention on the subject. Another called on the Conference on Disarmament to establish a committee to act accordingly.

There then followed real action. On motion of twenty-three UN members, there was passed a much more specific resolution. In words described as underlining the Court's unanimous ruling that there existed an obligation "to bring to a conclusion negotiations looking to nuclear disarmament," the Assembly pointedly said that it:

Calls upon all states to fulfill that obligation immediately by commencing multilateral negotiations in 1997 leading to an early conclusion of a nuclear weapons convention prohibiting the development, production, testing, deployment, stockpiling, transfer, threat or use of nuclear weapons and providing for their elimination.

The vote was 115 to 22, with 32 abstentions. Of the nuclear powers, Russia, the United Kingdom, the United States, and France voted "no." Israel abstained, and China, Pakistan, and India voted "yes."

All that the Assembly could have done to comply with and to implement the Court's recommendation has been done. But that is not all that happened. Other activities outside the UN have looked to civil society's compliance with the recommendations of the ICJ. For example, in cooperation with several states, lawyers led by the LCNP prepared a draft ("model") nuclear weapons convention to start the action. While the case was being argued, Australia, in preparation for any outcome, announced its government's initiative to form an independent international panel of experts from all nuclear states and all continents, to design procedures that would address the problem of nuclear weaponry. Known as the Canberra Commission, the qualified group in its report "noted with satisfaction" the advisory opinion of the ICJ and declared of the Court's finding of an obligation to pursue and conclude negotiations leading to nuclear disarmament that it was "precisely the obligation the Commission wishes to see implemented."

In the aftermath, a member of the Canberra Commission, General George Lee Butler, retired U.S. Air Force commander who was general in charge of deployment of thousands of nuclear weapons, led a group of generals and admirals to "call on the five declared nuclear powers and three undeclared to begin moving toward abolition by negotiating new treaties and removing nuclear warheads from missiles."

It is now up to the members of civil society to act so their respective governments, regardless of how they voted on the last General Assembly resolution would comply with it and with the admonitory direction in the Court's judgment, by entering into an abolition (nuclear disarmament) convention and proceeding to fulfill its mandate.

It would not be accurate to say, meanwhile, that apart from the action of the General Assembly and the circulation of a draft, the Court's advisory has been disregarded. Domestic courts in a number of nations (Germany, Russia, and Scotland, for example) have been presented with and considered the defense of illegality of the weapons, as declared by the ICJ, in trials involving civil disobedience aimed at manufacture or installation of atomic weapons. Saul Mendlovitz and John Burroughs have prepared a survey and analysis of the cases, available from LCNP, that is constantly being updated on its Web site.

Sources and Suggestions: A Bibliography

The following is presented with the dual objective of listing principal sources and helping readers who wish to know more about the Law of Nations, its Court, or specific subjects, such as early twentieth-century peace movements, and U.S. contributions to the Court idea and its realization—and the reverse.

BRINGING THE COURT INTO BEING: THE FIRST CENTURY

This book discusses two interrelated themes:

- Americans have long striven for and ultimately succeeded in helping to create a World Court.
- There *is* a World Court, a going concern, an able institution of which we should be proud.

The U.S. effort to create the Court marks, for the most part, the first part of this book; the reality of the Court is portrayed in the second. A third subject that lurks throughout is the United States' intermittent undermining of the Court.

Background: International Law; Peaceful Dispute Settlement

It is not necessary for the reader to "know" international law and it is not this book's purpose to teach it. One should, as a literate person, accept that there is a body of law in the world, a set of principles and rules governing the relation of states and the interaction of inhabitants of states with each other and with states other than their own. That "most educated people [*formerly*] knew quite a lot about International Law" was observed by Haskell Fain in *Normative Politics and the Community of Nations* (Temple University Press, 1987).

There are many books about international law for international lawyers, teachers, diplomats, and other consumers of the Law of Nations. Several books are especially accessible to the lay reader:

M. B. Akehurst, and Peter Malanczuk, *Akehurst's Modern Introduction to International Law,* 7th ed. (London: Routledge, 1997)

J. L. Brierly, *The Law of Nations: An Introduction to the International Law of Peace,* 6th ed. (New York: Oxford University Press, 1963)

Martin Dixon, *Textbook on International Law* (London: Blackstone Publishers, 1996)

Helpful in understanding the relation of international law to interstate dispute resolution are:

Louis Henkin, *How Nations Behave,* 2nd ed. (New York: Columbia University Press, 1979)

Arthur Larson, *When Nations Disagree: A Handbook on Peace through Law* (Baton Rouge: Louisiana University Press, 1961)

Brief and readable as their titles imply are Thomas Buergenthal and Harold G. Maier's *Public International Law in a Nutshell* (St. Paul, Minn.: West Publishing, 1988), and Louis B. Sohn and Kristin Gustafson's *Law of the Sea in a Nutshell* (St. Paul, Minn.: West Publishing, 1984). (Professor Buergenthal has been elected a judge of the World Court.)

Recommended for the lay reader eager to get something more than an introduction are two scholarly books:

Rosalyn Higgins, *International Law and How We Use It* (Oxford: Oxford University Press, 1994). Professor Higgins was the first woman to be elected a judge of the World Court.

Ingrid Detter De Lupis, *The Concept of International Law* (1987)

For history, the following are recommended:

Arthur Nussbaum, *A Concise History of the Law of Nations* (New York: Macmillan, 1962)

A valuable one-volume book, *The International Court of Justice* (Arthur Eyffinger, with T. H. Witteveen), was published in 1996 by Kluwer Law International, a company that publishes, in English, more books on international law and related subjects than any other. The book is meant for the lay reader. It provides an informative history of the Court; a broad outline of international law; a comparative study of the world's various legal systems; a summary of the work of the Court and its predecessor; and a really valuable and unique summary of the life, style, and character of each of the eighty-two judges who had sat on the Court up to 1996. It is illustrated with a generous supply of photos of the Court, the judges, incidents in its history, subjects of principal cases, and memorabilia. It is an oversized book to accommodate the photographs, and is not within the financial means of students or most lay readers, but deserves to be in every college and most secondary school libraries.

Shabtai Rosenne, a former Israeli ambassador and an international law scholar, has an impressive record of scholarly books and essays about the

Court. Of special interest is his *The World Court: What It Is and How It Works* (Dordrecht: Martinus Nijhoff, 1989).

The current state of government and public opinion in the United States regarding International Law has been the subject of many scholarly articles. Their essence was given in a report of ASIL, published in its newsletter of March–April 1999, submitted by an ad hoc committee on effectiveness and outreach: "International law is today probably less highly regarded in our country than at any time since ASIL's founding. It is . . . arguably given short shrift by all three branches of the U.S. government." A relevant episode is the Breard case, see the chronology April 3–12, 1998, and see Henry J. Richardson, "The Execution of Angel Breard by the United States: Violating an Order of the ICJ," *Temple Journal of International Law* 12 (1998): 121–131. And see *LaGrand* ICJ decision (Germany v. U.S.) June 27, 2001, p. 226 this volume.

The "American" Plan for a Court
(Prologue; chapters 1 and 2)

The references to the *Diary of Gideon Welles* are excerpted from the four-volume text as published by W. W. Norton (1966). The best sources on the *Alabama* claims arbitration is Adrian Cook, *The Alabama Claims: American Politics and Anglo-American Relations* (Ithaca, N.Y.: Cornell University Press, 1975). See also Thomas A. Bailey's *A Diplomatic History of the American People*, 9th ed. (Englewood Cliffs, N.J.: Prentice-Hall, 1970); and William McFeely's *Grant* (New York: W. W. Norton, 1982).

Jay's Treaty, 1794, is recognized everywhere (except in U.S. history texts) for its unique and valuable contribution as a spur to arbitration among the nations as explained in Arthur Larson, *When Nations Disagree* (1961) and, of course, in every international law casebook. It is also described in detail in J. B. Moore, *History and Digest of Arbitrations to which the United States Had Been a Party* (Washington, D.C.: Government Printing Office, 1898). In a brief address on the Court, one of its presidents, Sir Arnold McNair, said, "one of the main contributions, if not the main one, made by the United States to international law since [1794] has been the impulse, frequently repeated, towards arbitration and the judicial settlement of disputes between States." This was published in 1949 by the Holdsworth Club of the University of Birmingham.

Merle Curti's classic, *Peace or War: The American Struggle* (New York: W. W. Norton, 1936), tells how Jay's Treaty, the effect of which was enhanced by the Grant presidency's successful *Alabama* claims arbitration, inspired and provided a goal for peace activists, who became arbitration advocates. Curti includes Senator Charles Sumner's 1845 "The True Grandeur of Nations," cited in the text with quotation from Charles Sumner, *Orations and Speeches* (1850).

Warren F. Kuehl's *Seeking World Order* (Nashville, Tenn.: Vanderbilt

University Press, 1980) is a valuable and comprehensive account of the century-long effort in the United States to achieve international organization, ending with defeat of the Versailles Treaty by the Senate on March 19, 1920. On p. 105 is reported Scott's comment on Hague II on "The recognition of the idea makes the ultimate realization a certainty."

Other books and essays on this subject include:

Charles DeBenedetti, *The Peace Reform in American History* (1980)

Roland Marchand, *The American Peace Movement and Social Reform 1898-1918* (1972)

John Whiteclay Chamber II's *The Eagle and the Dove* (Syracuse, N.Y.: Syracuse University Press, 1991) has a useful collection of documents and an introductory essay that includes reference to the paltry budget of the American Peace Society.

Charles Chatfield's *Peace Movement in America* (New York: Schocken Books, 1973) includes an essay by David S. Patterson, "An Interpretation of the Peace Movement 1898-1914." See also Patterson, "The United States and the Origins of the World Court," *Political Science Quarterly* 91 (Summer 1976).

The published *Annual Reports* of the twenty-two meetings held at the Mohonk Mountain House, from 1895 to 1916, are primary materials. Excerpts from talks there of Edward Everett Hale and Justice David Brewer appear in Edwin D. Mead, ed., *Mohonk Addresses* (Boston: Ginn and Co., 1910). At the 1914 (twentieth annual) Lake Mohonk meeting, John Bassett Moore gave a talk later published as "International Arbitration" in his book *International Law and Some Current Illusions* (New York: Macmillan, 1924).

Lucia Ames (who married Mead after a Mohonk meeting) offers what amounts to primary evidence in her books *Patriotism and the New Internationalism* (Boston: Ginn and Co., 1910); *Swords and Ploughshares: Supplanting the System of War by the System of Law* (New York: Putnam, 1912); and *Law or War* (Garden City, N.Y.: Doubleday, 1928).

The National Arbitration and Peace Conference of 1906, chaired by Andrew Carnegie, published *Proceedings,* on which part of chapter 2 was based. Ms. Mead's address was a major event.

Michael A. Lutzker's study of the early years of the CEIP appears in Jerry Israel, ed., *Building the Organizational Society* (New York: Free Press, 1972).

Published *Proceedings* of the 1910 meeting of American Society for Judicial Settlement of International Disputes provided the talk of John Foster and other events cited.

The early volumes of the *American Journal of International Law* (AJIL), published by the American Society of International Law, are peppered with items recording the 1907-1921 period. The January 2000 (vol. 94, no. 1) issue has a useful symposium of ninety-eight pages on "The Hague Peace Conference."

Calvin DeA. Davis, *"The United States and the First Hague Peace Confer-*

ence" (Ithaca, N.Y.: Cornell University Press, 1962) and "*The US and the Second Hague Peace Conference*" (Durham, N.C.: Duke University Press, 1975).

Some of the relevant material is provided in Frederic L. Kirgis, "The Formative Years of the American Society of International Law," *AJIL* 90 (1996): 559. There is a comprehensive roundup of this material in Alfred Zimmern's *The League of Nations and the Rule of Law* (New York: Dutton, 1953).

The not-too-serious contest between "two hosts who disputed each other's honour to grant hospitality" to the PCIJ at the Peace Palace (as well as the inventory of gifts of members of the community of nations [see chapter 6]) are from Arnoldos Lysen, *History of the Carnegie Foundation and the Peace Palace at The Hague,* vol. 28 of Bibliotheca Visseriana Dissertationum Ius Internationale Illustrantium Lugdvni Batavorum, 1934.

Central American Court (1907–1917)

An essay by PCIJ Judge A. S. Bustamente, "The First Court of International Justice and the Causes of Its Dissolution," is included in Norman Bentwich et al., *Justice and Equity in the International Sphere* (London: Constable & Co., 1936).

Other sources consulted include the chapter "The Central American Court" in Helen Cory's *Compulsory Arbitration in International Disputes* (New York: Columbia University Press, 1932).

The United States Backs Off As Its Plan Succeeds (chapters 4 and 5)

Philip C. Jessup's biography *Root* describes how the draft statute produced at Hague II in 1907 was made acceptable for the PCIJ in 1920. In *AJIL* 15 (1921): 2–10 was published the text of Root's statement to the League's advisory council that offered the plan to solve the impasse.

The most recent study of the pre-Court and early Court years is Michael Dunne, *The United States and the World Court 1920–1935* (New York: St. Martin's Press, 1988).

Books titled *The World Court* by Manley Hudson (New York: Macmillan, 1943), Alexander Fachiri (London: Oxford University Press, 1932), and Alexander Bustamente (1925) provide information on the early days.

See also:

Edward Lindsey, *The International Court* (New York: T. Y. Crowell, 1931)

Wheeler-Bennett and Fanshaw, *Information on the World Court* (London: Association for Universal Understanding, 1924)

A volume titled *Essays on International Law from the Columbia Law Review* (New York: Columbia University Press, 1963) contains John Bassett Moore, "The Organization of the International Court of Justice." (In somewhat different form is Moore's *International Law and Some Current Illusions,* [New York: Macmillan, 1924].)

The Effort for the Court until Rejection

Dunne's *The United States and the World Court* (1988) is the most complete version. The standard source until his publication was Denna Frank Fleming, *The United States and the World Court: 1920–1966* (New York: Russell & Russell, 1968).

More recent and inclusive is Michla Pomerance's *The United States and the World Court As a "Supreme Court of the Nations"* (The Hague: Martinus Nijhoff, 1996).

Robert H. Ferrell's *Peace in Their Time: The Origin of the Kellogg-Briand Pact* (New Haven, Conn.: Yale University Press, 1952) tells how the initiative of Salmon Levinson to win "outlawry" of war succeeded. Unmentioned is the use of the "outlawry" movement to hamper progress for the United States joining the Court. For that, biographies of Senator William E. Borah are useful.

Other books:

J. Chal Vinson, *William F. Borah and the Outlawry of War* (1957)

Thomas A. Bailey, *A Diplomatic History of the American People,* 9th ed.(1974), has a nine-page summary of the 1922–1935 Court effort.

Selig Adler, *The Isolationist Impulse* (London: Abelard Schuman, 1957), has much of the story.

Philip C. Jessup tells the story of the 1920s diplomatic effort in *Root.* See also his *International Security* (New York: Council on Foreign Relations, 1935) and a reprint of earlier essays in *The United States and the World Court* (Worcester, Mass.: CEIP, 1929).

Lucia Ames Mead, *Law or War* (1925)

R. P. Anand, *Studies in International Adjudication* (Delhi: Vikas Publishing, 1969)

Biographies of Eleanor Roosevelt, such as that by Blanche W. Cook (New York: Viking Press, 1992), tell of her efforts in the 1920s. Feminist efforts appear in Jacqueline van Voorhis's biography of *Carrie Chapman Catt* in a chapter titled "The Cause and Cure of War" (New York: The Feminist Press, 1987).

The role of Charles E. Coughlin, Huey Long, and William Randolph Hearst is described in Alan Brinkley, *Voices of Protest* (New York: Knopf, 1982). They made the difference in the 1935 rejection, says this author.

Partial Success of a Part World Court
(chapters 5 and 6)

Manley O. Hudson's *The Permanent Court of International Justice and the Question of American Participation* (1925) includes a lively description of the first election of judges for the PCIJ. See also James Brown Scott, "The Election of Judges for the PCIJ," *AJIL* 16 (1921): 556.

The Court's initial success is that it was able to function at all. How, despite the language, cultural, and national differences of a body of jurists who met as strangers, they developed a collegiality and esprit de corps has been remarked upon but not recorded. Hints appear in Akè Hammarskjöld, "The Early Work of the PCIJ," *Harvard Law Review* 36 (1923): 704; and his "Sidelights on the PCIJ."

To see the Court's work as described in chapters 5 and 6, its officially published decisions are available. Another source is *World Court Reports,* an unofficial series of volumes edited by Manley Hudson.

Most convenient and useful is a series of annual essay roundups on the Court's work, contributed to *AJIL* by Manley Hudson. These begin in volume 17, with "The First Year of the Permanent Court . . ." and continue diligently until the "Twentieth Year . . ." opens, taking note of "the cataclysm that has come upon the world."

The decisions of the PCIJ in summary-digest form are contained in a pair of books by Hudson that were successively updated during the Court's tenure. They ended with *International Court of International Justice 1921-42* (New York: Garland Publishing, 1972) in the scholarly version; the World Peace Foundation, *The World Court 1921-1938* (Boston: World Peace Foundation, 1938) is a popularized version.

Summaries of decisions are also available in:

J. H. N. Verzijl, *The Jurisprudence of the World Court, a Case by Case Commentary,* vol. 1 (Leiden: A. W. Sitjhoff, 1965)

Alexander P. Fachiri, *The Permanent Court of International Justice* (1938), contains brief summaries.

Max Planck Institute, *Encyclopedia of International Law,* vol. 2 (1991–1992). (This and Verzijl's have commentaries, too.)

The section titled "Extra Dividend: Human Rights" in chapter 5 is based, in addition to the judgments themselves, on the following:

John T. Humphrey, *No Distant Millennium: The International Law of Human Rights* (Paris: UNESCO, 1989)

Julius Stone, *International Guarantees of Human Rights* (London: H. Milford Oxford, 1932)

Urmila Haksar, *Minority Protection and the International Bill of Rights* (Bombay: Allied Publishing, 1974)

The description of the Court's decision-making process is based in part on remarks of four judges: Charles Evans Hughes as offered in *American Bar Association Journal* 16: 157; Sir Robert Jennings, *British Yearbook of International Law* 59 (1988); Stephen M. Schwebel, *Suffolk Transnational Law Journal* 13 (1996): 543; and Mohammed Bedjaoui, *Pace Yearbook of International Law* 3: 29.

Judge (and recent president of the ICJ) Stephen M. Schwebel's "verdict" that the PCIJ was a "marked success" came in an address he gave to students at the University of Washington, published in *University of Washington Law Review* 61 (1986): 1061. The Hogarth Press (Leonard and Virginia Woolf) published Katherine E. Innes's *The Reign of Law: A Short and Simple Introduction to the Work of the PCIJ* (1929).

The Second Coming (chapter 7)

The new national mood is best described in Robert A. Divine's *Second Chance: The Triumph of Internationalism in America during World War II* (New York: Atheneum, 1971).

The 1944 London "Report of the Committee on the International Court of Justice" is recorded in *AJIL Supplement* 39 (1945): 1.

The refounding of the Court was the fruit of two meetings: one of a committee of jurists that met at Dumbarton Oaks was reported in volume 3 of the multivolume *United Nations Conference on International Organization,* called UNCIO. The second, at San Francisco, mainly the work of a special committee on legal affairs, is in volume 13.

Summaries used were:

The first *Yearbook of the Court* itself (1947) (these appear annually) contains a substantial opening chapter titled "Historical Outline of the Composition of the Court," adequately summarizing the documents referred to above.

AJIL 39 (1946) contains a report by Manley Hudson of these founding events, titled "The Twenty-fourth Year of the World Court."

The added chapters of D. F. Fleming's *United States and the World Court,* covering events up to 1966, also tell the story.

The Connally Clause: Torpedoed before Sailing

Sources for the narrative in the section titled "Undermining Our Own Creation with an Illusory Commitment" in chapter 7, and the narrative in chapter 16, concerning the adoption and subsequent failed campaign to repeal the clause:

Primary evidence is contained in the *Hearing* on S. Res. 196 Senate Foreign Relations Comm., 79 Cong. 2d Sess., and the Report with the unanimous agreement of the senators that in accordance with the UN Charter Article 36.6 in cases of contested jurisdiction, the Court should decide the question.

The Congressional Record 79 Cong. 2d Sess., pp. 10695–10697, reports the chair's (Senator Connally's) reversal to reserve "veto" rights and full Senate vote overruling the committee.

Sen. For. Rel. Comm. *Hearings*, initiated by President Eisenhower and Vice President Nixon, contain the testimony delivered January 27 and February 17, 1960.

Summarizing and explaining the events of 1946 is Lawrence Preuss's "The

International Court of Justice: The Senate on the Matter of Compulsory Juris-diction," *AJIL* 40 (1946): 720.

Ernest A. Gross's *The United Nations: Structure for Peace* (New York: Harper, 1962) has a chapter titled "The Rule of Law." Ambassador Gross called the result, "Keeping the key to the courthouse door in the United States' own pocket."

The most comprehensive and up-to-date collection of references to and description of the failed repeal-Connally effort can be found in Michla Pomerance, *The United States and the World Court as a Supreme Court of the Nations: Dreams, Illusions, and Disillusion* (1996).

WHAT A WORLD COURT DID
AND CAN DO

What can a World Court do? For a clue, look at what it has done. The several subdivisions of this section deal with the material on which most of the last eleven chapters of this book were based.

Generally: Overview of the Record

In the same fashion as the U.S. Supreme Court, the World Court makes the text of each ruling available at once to the press, libraries, and the public. The decisions are collected on an annual basis in a bound volume. Official texts (just as with the PCIJ) are published in both English and French. All are now available on the Court's Web site: www.icj-cij.org. Likewise, as in the fashion prevalent with regard to U.S. Supreme Court decisions, there are commer-cially published "unofficial" volumes of the decisions, the principal one being called *World Court Reports*.

Information about the "bare bones" of the decisions—a summary of the facts and an outline of legal content—is provided by the Court's registrar's office. These will mention dissents as well.

These summaries are made available in the first instance in "communiqués" issued from the courthouse. They are useful enough to justify their being pub-lished in collected groups annually. This is done in two forms: the *Annual Reports* of the Court that are submitted to the General Assembly and pub-lished as documents by the United Nations, and the annual *Yearbook* of the Court, published at The Hague, each containing a variety of information about Court affairs, proceedings, and personae.

The United Nation has published a one-volume collection of all the summary-digests, from 1948 to 1991 inclusive, in the same form as originally issued. There is also a supplement 1991–1996.

In 1986, on the occasion of the Court's fortieth anniversary, there was published the third edition of a "handbook" on the Court, prepared by the Registry. Its purpose is to prepare "without excessive detail" facts about the Court, its composition and its work, and it includes excellent briefer summaries of the decisions up to the date of publication, not quite as well circulated was a new edition of 1996 for the fiftieth anniversary. Difficulties with this and other publications include delays caused by the UN financial crisis, precipitated by default in meeting legal obligations by several states, including the United States.

An important resource—an analytical study of each case—is provided by the *AJIL*. A section headed "International Decisions" is led by the summary of Court decisions provided by qualified scholars.

Judges or former judges of the Court, working as individual scholars, have put together partial collections of the Court's case law. Most accessible to the American lay reader, witty and anecdotal, are the groups offered by former Judge Philip Caryl Jessup, whom we met earlier as a Root biographer: *The Price of International Justice* (New York: Columbia University Press, 1971) and *The Use of International Law* (Ann Arbor: University of Michigan Law School, 1959).

Other reviews of the Court's case law by its judges include:

Nagendra Singh, *The Role and Record of the I.C. of J.* (Dordrecht: M. Nijhoff, 1989) (book-length study)

E. Jiminez de Aréchaga, "The Work and Jurisprudence of the I.C. of J. 1947–86," *British Yearbook of International Law* 58 (1987)

Jose Maria Ruda, "Some of the Contributions of the I.C. of J. to the Development of International Law" 24 *NYU Journal of International Law* 24 (1985)

Jens Evenson, "The I.C. of J.: Main Characteristics and Its Contribution to the Law of Nations," *Nordic Journal of International Law* 57 (in English, 1985)

Manfred Lachs, "Some Reflections on the Contribution of the I.C. of J. to the Development of International Law," *Syracuse Journal of International Law and Commerce* 10 (1983)

T. Olewale Elias (books): *New Horizons in International Law*, rev. ed. (Aalpen an den Rijn: Oceana, 1979); *United Nations Charter and the World Court* (Lagos: Nigerian Institute of Advanced Legal Studies, 1989); and *The I.C. of J. and Some Contemporary Problems* (The Hague: M. Nijhoff, 1983)

Except for Judge Evenson, each of the forgoing authors was for a period president of the Court.

Commentaries on the Case Law

Commentaries and critiques on the case law of the Court have been persistently and continuously produced. Taken together they should refute clichés denigrating the value of the Court, or asserting that international law is "not really law."

Strangers to the Law of Nations—in the United States including almost all of the most literate laypeople and a surprising percentage of members of the bar—would be staggered if browsing for the first time in a well-stocked international law library. The variety and sheer volume of treatises, monographs, and the like are impressive. Having consulted many, the writer is hard pressed to select a few that the general reader should consult.

Special value was found in one of the earliest modern works and one of the most recent.

Sir Hersch Lauterpacht, *The Development of the Law by the International Court* (London: Stevens, 1958); Lauterpacht, a writer and professor, served as a member of the Court from 1955 to 1960. He was a visionary, not dated.

A recent book by a nonlawyer is highly recommended: Thomas Bodie, *Politics and the Emergence of an Activist International Court* (Westport, Conn.: Praeger, 1995).

Mention should be made of some of the monographs that deal with special aspects of the Court's jurisdictional law and practice. (There are others; these were helpful.)

H. W. A. Thirlway, *Non-Appearance before the I.C.J.* (Cambridge: Cambridge University Press, 1985)

Jerzy Sztucki, *Interim Measures in the Hague Court* (Deventer, Netherlands: Kluwer, 1983)

Ijaz Hussain, *Dissenting and Separate Opinions of the World Court* (Dordrecht: M. Nijhoff/Kluwer, 1984)

Michla Pomerance, *The Advisory Function of the International Court in the League and UN Eras* (1973) (including a study of failed attempts to formulate and submit requests)

Recent scholarly symposia marked the fiftieth anniversary of the ICJ:

Lowe and Fitzmaurice, eds., *Fifty Years of the International Court of Justice* (Cambridge: Cambridge University Press, 1996)

A. S. Muller et al., eds., *The I.C. of J. Its future Role after Fifty Years* (The Hague: M. Nijhoff/Kluwer, 1997)

D. W. Bowett et al., *The International Court of Justice, Process, Practice, and Procedure* (London: BIICL, 1997)

Also quite helpful were the following more general scholarly studies, ranging across the work of the Court:

Leo Gross, ed., *The Future of the International Court of Justice* (Dobbs Ferry: Oceana, 1976) a compendium of scholarship about the Court and in large part about its decisions.

Lori Damrosch, ed., *The International Court of Justice at the Crossroads* (Ardley on Hudson: Transnational Publishers, 1987). Not attempting to be a complete update of the Gross-edited work above, this came from an ASIL-initiated study panel created "in the wake of the *Nicaragua* case."

Edward McWhinney of the Queen's Court and a member of Parliament (Canada), *Judicial Settlement of International Disputes* (Dordrecht: M. Nijhoff/Kluwer, 1991). This insightful and helpful study was developed from lectures the writer delivered at the Hague Academy, and celebrates as well as explains the sea-change from a Court that John King Gamble in 1976 called "least successful and most disappointing" (*The International Court of Justice: Analysis of a Failure* [Lexington, Mass.: Lexington Books, 1976]) to one McWhinney praises highly.

The Advisory Opinions

The role of the Court's cases in decolonization, primarily by advisories, is in the subsection below titled "The New International Law: Decolonization" (see p. 250). Usually instructive analyses have come from Professor Leo Gross of the Fletcher School of Tufts University. Scattered through the pages of a variety of publications, these have been gathered in a single anthology, *Essays in International Law and Organization* (Irvington on Hudson: Transnational Publishers, 1993), with relevant sections identical under subject head as with Thomas Franck, *Nation against Nation: What Happened to the UN Dream and What the U.S. Can Do about It* (New York: Oxford University Press, 1985). What follows is a classification after the chapter-by-chapter presentation in this work.

Admission to Membership

Gross, *Essays,* "Election of States to UN Membership" and "Progress toward University of Membership in UN"
Pomerance, *Advisory Function* (pp. 89–93)

Reparations ("Constitution We Are Expounding . . .")

Discussed in most Law of Nations books and:
M. Rama-Montaldo, "International Legal Personality and Implied Power of International Organizations," *British Yearbook of International Law* 44 (1970): 123
Manfred Lachs, "Some Reflections on the Contribution of the I.C. of J. to the Development of International Law," vol. 10, *Syracuse Journal of International Law and Commerce* 10 (1983)
Pomerance, *Advisory Function* (pp. 93–98)
Franck, *Nation v Nation* (pp. 97–100)
Eduardo Jiminez de Aréchaga, "Work of the ICJ 1947–1986," *British Yearbook* 58 (1988).

Human Rights Treaties

Gross, *Essays,* "The I.C.J. and the United Nations" (pp. 860–869)
Pomerance, *Advisory Function* (pp. 98–103, 117–125, and passim)

Protection of Staff Rights

F. Amersingh, "Cases of the I.C.J. Relating to Employment in International Organizations," in Lowe and Fitzmaurice, *Fifty Years of the I.C.J.* (1996) (pp. 193-209)
Pomerance, *Advisory Function* (pp. 125-130)
Franck, *Nation v Nation* (pp. 97-103)

Peacekeeping and "Certain Expenses"

Gross, *Essays,* "Expenses of UN for Peacekeeping" (p. 753 ff.)
J. F. Hogg, "Peacekeeping Costs and Charter Obligations," in *Columbia Law Review* 62 (1962): 1250
Stanley Hoffman, "A World Divided and a World Confused: The World Court's Advisory Opinion in UN Financing," in Lawrence Scheinman and David Wilkinson, *International Law and Political Crisis*
Pomerance, *Advisory Function* (pp. 140-148)
Evaluations of certain expenses cited appear in Wolfgang Friedmann's "Hague Lecture" (General Course) vol. 127 (1969), p. 171; and Judge Eduardo Jiminez de Aréchaga's essay on "The Work and Jurisprudence of the ICJ 1947-1986," in *British Yearbook* (1988).

Adjudication and the Use of Force
(chapters 9 and 10)

The case of *Corfu Channel* (1949), the first covered in chapter 9, is discussed in many articles; intriguing because he was counsel for the United Kingdom is the Hague Academy lecture by Sir Humphrey Waldock, later judge, in volume 106, collected lectures (1962) and see Roosevelt and Hopkins (New York: Harpers, 1948).

On the effort of the United States to complain to the Court about violence in shooting down planes for border intrusion, see the overall discussion in Michla Pomerance, "Seeking Judicial Legitimation in the Cold War: U.S. Foreign Policy and the World Court, 1948-1962," *Indiana International and Comparative Law Review* 5 (1995): 305; and compare the view of Professor Philip Jessup in "The Development of a United States Approach toward the International Court of Justice," *Vanderbilt Journal of Transnational Law* 5 (1971): 6 . Also, in Gross's *Essays* (pp. 717-752), "Bulgaria Invokes the Connally Amendment."

Tehran Hostages

The important case of *Tehran Hostages,* described in chapter 10, is covered well by:

Gross, "The Case Concerning U.S. Diplomatic and Consular Staff in Teheran," *AJIL* 74 (1980): 395–410

George Brown Tindall, in *America: A Narrative History,* vol. 2 (New York: W. W. Norton, 1984), was one of the first post-crisis historians to record CIA activities in Iran and the reaction of the population.

Falk, "The Iran Hostage Crisis: Easy Answers and Hard Questions" (editorial comment), AJIL 74 (1980): 411–417 (followed by the text of U.S. pleadings in the case and the text of the decision)

Ted L. Stein, "Contempt, Crisis, and the Court: The World Court and the Hostage Rescue Attempt," *AJIL* 76 (1987): 498

Oscar Schachter, "International Law in the Hostage Crisis: Implications for Future Cases," in *American Hostages in Iran: The Conduct of a Crisis* (New Haven, Conn.: Yale University Press, 1985), a single volume collecting essays on all aspects

Michael P. Malloy, "The Iran Crisis: Law under Pressure," *Wisconsin International Law Journal* (1984): 15–97

The UN Charter outlawed the use of force by states without Security Council consent, except in cases of self-defense. This restates the customary international law on the subject. The propensity of some states to resort to force persisted. Many articles, anthologies, even single-issue books have been devoted to the discussion of the legal problems that might or did arise.

Discussions Prior to or Independent of Nicaragua *Case*

Goodrich and Hambro, *Charter of the UN, Comments and Documents* (Boston: World Peace Fund, 1949). Commentary on Articles 2, 42, and 43.

C. H. M. Waldock (later Sir Humphrey and judge of the Court) in a published version of the Hague Academy lecture, chapters 3 and 4 on "The Charter of the UN and the Use of Force," and "Self-Defense and Self-Protection under the Charter," *Collected Hague Academy Lectures,* vol. 81, pp. 487 and 495

McDougal and Feliciano, "Aggression and Self-Defense," in *Law and Minimum World Public Order* (New Haven, Conn.: Yale University Press, 1961) (p. 245 ff.)

Philip C. Jessup, "The Legal Regulation of the Use of Force" and "Rights and Duties in Case of Illegal Use of Force," chapters 7 and 8 of *A Modern Law of Nations* (1948)

Rosalyn Higgins, "The Legal Limits to the Use of Force by Sovereign States," *British Yearbook of International Law* 37 (1961): 269–319

Thomas M. Franck, "Who Killed Article 2 (4)?" (Charter provision outlawing force or coercion), *AJIL* 64 (1970): 8

James P. Piscator, "Law and Peace in American Legal Thought," in Booth and Wright, *American Thinking about Peace and War* (1978) (pp. 135–154)

Edward Miller, "Self-Defense, International Law and the Six-Day War," *Israel Law Review* 20 (1985): 49–73

Oscar Schachter, "The Legality of Pro-Democratic Invasion," *AJIL* 78 (1984):645; "The Right of a State to Use Armed Force," *Michigan Law Review* 82 (1984); and "In Defense of the International Rules on Use of Force," *University of Chicago Law Review* 53: 113

Discussions in Light of or Affected by Nicaragua

The *AJIL* 81 (1987) carried a symposium of scholars and others on the merits decision in the *Nicaragua* case. They cannot all be listed here; special attention should be given to: Herbert W. Briggs (regarded then by many as "dean" of international law scholars), "The International Court of Justice Lives Up to Its Name"; Richard Falk, "The World Court's Achievement"; Tom J. Farer, "Drawing the Right Line." Several others disagreed.

Articles on the first (jurisdiction) decision in the case do not deal with the use-of-force question, which the United States refrained from litigating. Of special interest were essays on the decision not to defend the use of force:

Abram Chayes, "Nicaragua, the United States and the World Court," *Columbia Law Review* 85 (1985): 1445. Harvard professor Chayes, former State Department deputy legal adviser, was an attorney at the Court for Nicaragua.

Thomas M. Franck, "Icy Day at the ICJ," *AJIL* 79 (1985): 375. Franck was then editor of the *AJIL*.

Edward McWhinney summed up these and other first-level reactions in "Historical Dilemmas and Contradictions in U.S. Attitudes to the World Court; The Aftermath of the *Nicaragua* Judgment," in Y. Dinstein, ed., *International Law at a Time of Perplexity* (Dordrecht: M. Nijhoff/Kluwer, 1989).

Another view, likewise in the Dinstein anthology, came from an alternate "dean" of U.S. scholars, Louis B. Sohn, "The International Court of Justice and the Scope of the Right of Self-Defense and the Duty of Non-Intervention" (p. 868).

D. W. Greig, Australian scholar, produced two careful studies: "Nicaragua and the United States," *British Yearbook of International Law* (1991); and "Self-Defense and the Security Council: What Does Article 51 Require?" *International and Comparative Law Quarterly* 40 (1991): 366.

R. St. J. MacDonald, "The Nicaragua Case: New Answers to Old Questions?" *Canadian Yearbook of International Law* (1986): 127

Oscar Schachter, "Self-Defense and the Rule of Law," *AJIL* 83 (1989): 259

Professor Keith Highet (president of ASIL, 1985–1990) wrote two important commentaries: "Between a Rock and a Hard Place—the United States, the International Court, and the Nicaragua Case," *International Lawyer* (ABA) 21 (1987): 1083; and " 'You Can Run but You Can't Hide'—Reflections on the

U.S. Position in the Nicaragua Case," *Virginia Journal of International Law* 27 (1987).

M. Akehurst, "Nicaragua v. United States of America," *Indian Journal of International Law* 27 (1987): 357

W. Michael Reisman, "Old Wine in New Bottles: The Reagan and Brezhnev Doctrines in Contemporary International Law and Practice," *Yale Journal of International Law* 13 (1988): 171

Richard B. Bilder, "Judicial Procedures Relating to the Use of Force," *Virginia Journal of International Law* 31 (1991): 249 (Bilder's most useful paper appears in slightly varied form in the Damrosch-Scheffer book, *Law and Force in the New International Order*, referred to below.)

Josef Mrazek, "Prohibitions of the Use and Threat of Force: Self-Defense and Self-Help in International Law," *Canadian Yearbook of International Law* (1989): 81

J. A. Frowein, in *Hague Academy Lectures* (1994) vol. 4, p. 427

Mary Ellen O'Connell, "Enforcing the Prohibition on the Use of Force," *Southern Illinois Law Journal* 15 (1991): 453

Published Symposia

Henkin, Hoffman, et al., *Right v Might, International Law and the Use of Force* (New York: Council on Foreign Relations, 1989)

Damrosch and Scheffer, eds. *Law and Force in the New International Order* (Boulder, Colo.: Westview Press, 1991)

Why the pros and cons? A tenable theory comes from Professor J. Patrick Kelly in "The Changing Process of International Law and the Role of the World Court" (*Michigan International Law Journal* 11 [1989]: 129 at 148): ". . . it is clear that the U.S. government's position on a broad range of law of force issues is at variance with those of most nations of the world, and is a minority view even within the U.S. international law community."

The New International Law: Decolonization
(chapters 11 and 17)

For cases such as Namibia, Western Sahara, Nauru, and East Timor, one source that should be kept in mind is the UN Charter Articles 1 (20;55(c) and chapters 11, 12, and 13.

The five cases in which the Court grappled with the relation of South Africa to Namibia tell much of the story in their judgments.

Advisory cases: *International Status of South Africa* (July 11, 1950); *Voting Procedures Concerning the Territory of Southwest Africa* (June 7, 1983); *Admissibility of Hearings of Petitioners* (June 1, 1983); and *Legal Consequences of the Continued Presence . . . of South Africa* (June 21, 1991).

Contentious case: South West Africa: *Ethiopia and Libya v. South Africa* (two judgments, December 21, 1962, and July 18, 1966)

Other References

To begin with, dealing not so much with the actions of the Court as with the credit for initiating the major series of cases:

Roger Clark, "The International League for Human Rights in Southwest Africa; the Human Rights NGO as Catalyst in the International Legal Process," *Human Rights Quarterly*

As to legal issues and judicial proceeding:

Ralph Zacklin, *The Problem of Namibia in International Law* (1981) (text as published of a *Hague Academy* lecture, vol. 171)

Solomon Slomin, *Southwest Africa and the United Nations: An International Mandate in Dispute* (Baltimore, Md.: Johns Hopkins University Press, 1973)

Edward McWhinney, *The World Court and the Contemporary Legal Process* (Aalpen an den Rijn: Sitjhoff, 1979), chapter 2, "Judicial Law Making, Judicial Self-Restraint and Judicial Activism" (primarily 1966 decision)

There was commentary written before South Africa's compliance that was sympathetic to the purpose of the litigation, yet seeming to doubt its utility:

Milton Katz, *The Relevance of International Law* (Cambridge, Mass.: Harvard University Press, 1968)

Richard Falk, *Reviving the World Court*, chapters 2, 3, and 4 (Charlottesville: University Press of Virginia, 1986). Falk was counsel in the case.

Regarding the 1952 Morocco case, in which the United States was involved, the writer is indebted to the interpretation in a subchapter at p. 120 and following of Philip C. Jessup, *The Birth of Nations* (New York: Columbia University Press, 1974).

For chapter 11's story of the case of Western Sahara, see Thomas Franck, "The Stealing of the Sahara," *AJIL* 70 (1976): 694. A confession of a sort appears in Daniel P. Moynihan, *On the Law of Nations* (Cambridge, Mass.: Harvard University Press, 1990), p. 3.

In the case of *Certain Phosphate Lands in Nauru* (1972), the Court rejected preliminary objections. For that, see the commentary "Recent Decisions," *AJIL* 87 (1993): 282. This helped bring about the settlement of the case discussed in Roger Clark (book review), "Nauru/Environmental Damage under Trusteeship," *The International Lawyer* 28 (1884): 186.

For extensive study of the case see the article by Anthony Anghie, "The Heart of My Home: Colonialism, Environmental Damage, and the Nauru Case," *Harvard International Law Journal* 34 (1993): 445.

East Timor's case was discussed before the decision in a book offering scholarly papers on the case: *International Law and the Question of East Timor* (London: Catholic Institute for International Relations, 1995).

See also Roger Clark, "Timor Gap: The Legality of the Treaty on the Zone of Cooperation in an Area between the Indonesial Province [*sic*] of East Timor and Northern Australia," *Pace Yearbook of International Law* 4 (1994): 69.

C. M. Chinkin, "The Merits of East Timor's Case Against Australia," *University of New South Wales Law Journal* 15 (1992).

A pamphlet containing essays and reports on the reaction to the Court's ruling with the text of all the opinions, including dissents, has been distributed by the publisher, East Timor Actions Network / U.S. of White Plains, New York 10602.

Drawing Border Lines on Land and at Sea
(chapter 12)

A simplified statement of the Law of the Sea as a whole appears in Louis B. Sohn and Kristin Gustafson, *The Law of the Sea* (1984), self-styled as "law 'in a Nutshell.' "

More complex (and professionally useful) books, such as R. R. Churchill and A. V. Lowe, *Law of the Sea* (Manchester, U.K.: Manchester University Press, 1983); and Douglas M. Johnson, *The Theory and History of Ocean Boundary-Making* (Montreal: McGill-Queen's University Press, 1988) were consulted. The latter discusses the leading ICJ case in some detail. Other sources include:

Clyde Sanger, *Ordering the Oceans, The Making of the Law of the Sea* (Toronto: University of Toronto Press, 1987)

Horace R. Marshall, "Law of the Sea and the New US Oceans Policy," *New York State Bar Journal* (April 1983)

Taslim O. Elias, "The New Law of the Sea—an Outline Report," in his *New Horizons in International Law* (1979)

Essays and commentaries on particular cases consulted include:

Wolfgang Friedmann, "The North Sea Continental Shelf Case—a Critique," *AJIL* 64 (1970): 229

C. H. M. Waldock, "The Anglo-Norwegian Fisheries Case," in *British Yearbook of International Law* 19 (1938): 114

Hannes Johnsson, *Friends in Conflict: The Anglo-Icelandic Cod Wars and the Law of the Sea* (London: C. Hurst, 1982)

D. N. Hutchins, "The Seaward Limit to the Continental Shelf Jurisdiction in Customary International Law," *British Yearbook of International Law* 46 (1975): 1

Mark B. Friedman, "The Tunisia-Libya Continental Shelf Case: Geographic Justice or Judicial Compromise," *AJIL* 77 (1983): 219

Ted L. McDornman, "The Libya-Malta Case: Opposite States Confront the Court," *Canadian Yearbook of International Law* (1986): 335

E. D. Brown, "The Libya-Malta Continental Shelf Case," in *Contemporary*

Problems in International Law: Essays in Honour of George Schwarzen-berger (London: Stevens, 1988) (p. 3)

Jan Shrieder, "The Gulf of Maine Case: The Making of an Equitable Result"; and Robinson et al., "Some Perspective on Adjudicating Before the World Court: The Gulf of Maine Case," *AJIL* 79 (1985): 539 and 575

Treaties Must Be Respected:
Justification by Compliance

The eyewitness account that supports the second part of chapter 13 comes from Joaquin Tacsan, a legal officer in the foreign ministry of the Costa Rican Republic, in his book *The Dynamics of International Law in Conflict Resolution* (Dordrecht: M. Nijhoff/Kluwer, 1992).

Oscar Schachter's seminal "The Invisible College of International Lawyers" appeared in *Northwestern University Law Review* 72 (1977): 217.

Reparations: Nicaragua and Iran (chapter 14)

Nicaragua v. United States: Promises as Reparations: The "secret" that the reparations phase of the *Nicaragua* case was still pending two years after the 1986 merits decision was the subject of the writer's "U.S. Snub of World Court Won't Avert Day of Reckoning," *Los Angeles Times* (September 29, 1988), republished in the *Congressional Record* (October 21, 1988), and awarded the Project Censored prize as an underreported story of 1988.

The enactment in Managua of "Law 92" and events surrounding it are reported as part of "The World Court Case: A Historic Decision," in *Envio* (October 1991), a quarterly publication of Georgetown University's Central American Historic Institute.

Legai aspects of a collection of World Court judgments are discussed in Mary Ellen O'Connell, "The Prospects for Enforcing Monetary Judgment of the International Court of Justice," *Virginia Journal of International Law* 30 (1990): 291.

Iran: A Trade for Reparations

The acceptance by the United States of the Iran–U.S. Claims Tribunal as reparations was made clear in several of the essays in *American Hostages in Iran*, a work cited above in support of the narrative in chapter 10.

Nils Mangard, "The Hostage Crisis, the Algiers Accords, and the Iran–U.S. Claims Tribunal," in *Studies in International Law, Festschrift Hjerner* (1990) (pp. 363–417)

Richard W. Edwards, "Extraterritorial Applications of the U.S. (1981) Iranian Assets Control Regulations," *AJIL* 75 (1981): 870

Rahmatullah Khan, *The Iran-United States Claims Tribunal: Controversies, Cases, and Contribution* (Dordrecht: M. Nijhoff/Kluwer, 1990)

Stephen J. Toope, "The Iran-United States Claims Tribunal," in his *Mixed International Arbitration* (Cambridge: Grotius Publications, 1990)

John Westberg, *International Transactions and Claims Involving Government Parties* (1991)

Aida Avanessian, *Iran-United States Claims Tribunal in Action* (London: Braham & Trotman, 1993)

Richard M. Mosk, "Lessons from the Hague—An Update on the Iran–U.S. Claims Tribunal" (1987), *Pepperdine Law Review* 14 (1997): 819

Lloyd Cutler, "Negotiating the Iranian Settlement," *American Bar Association Journal* 87 (August 1991): 99

Concerning Court versus Council: Libya's Treaty Rights (chapter 15)

José E. Alvarez, "Judging the Security Council," *AJIL* 90 (1996): 1. In his third footnote, Alvarez identifies the number and variety of legal discussions already generated by then, including:

Thomas Franck, editorial comment, *AJIL* 86 (1992): 519

W. Michael Reisman, "The Constitutional Crisis in the United Nations," *AJIL* 87 (1993): 83

Mohammed Bedjaoui (Court president), *The New World Order and the Security Council, Testing the Legality of Its Acts* (Dordrecht: M. Nijhoff/Kluwer, 1994)

Edward McWhinney, "The International Court as Emerging Constitutional Court," *Canadian Yearbook of International Law* (1992): 261

See also: R. St. J. Macdonald, "Changing Relations between the I. C. of J. and the Security Council," *Canadian Yearbook of International Law* (1993): 3

Bosnia's case against Serbia and Montenegro (Yugoslavia), also discussed in this chapter, is another case of (partial) universal jurisdiction, as provided for by the multilateral treaty on genocide.

WHAT KEEPS THE COURT FROM DOING MORE?

Making It "Worth the Trouble" (chapter 16)

The quotation from Judge Bernard Loder that supplies the title for chapter 16 is cited from the original records of the 1920 Advisory Committee of Jurists in Helen Cory's *Compulsory Arbitration of International Disputes* (1932), p. 121.

The Court's creation of a collegiate body is described in an essay by Akè

Hammarskjöld, the Court's first registrar, in the *Harvard Law Review* 36 (1923): 704. To similar effect is his "Sidelights on the Permanent Court," *Michigan Law Review,* 327. See also Judge Moore's view in the essay "Fifty Years of International Law," *Harvard Law Review* 50 (1937): 412–419.

Tributes to the continuing collegiality of the members of the Court appear in Judge Dillard's article in *American Law Review* 27 (1978): 205; and in Judge and President Sir Robert Jennings's essay of Dinstein (pp. 342–353).

The Court's 1972 *Yearbook* contains President Sir Muhammad Zafrulla Khan's speech on the fiftieth anniversary of judicial settlement of transnational disputes.

Senator Elbert Thomas's observation on willingness to be judged was recalled by Representative Jim Leach at a House subcommittee hearing on the Reagan termination of the consent to be sued (91st Cong. 1st Sess.; House Comm. For. Aff., October 10, 1985).

Judge Lacharrière's interview was published in Sturges and Chubb, *Judging the World* (Sidney: Butterworths, 1988), p. 468.

Leonard Woolf's *Framework of a Lasting Peace* was initially published in 1917 (London: Allen & Unwin); Garland Publishing Co. reissued it in 1971. Historian Alan Brinkley in *Voices of Dissent* (pp. 131–135) described the role of Huey Long, Father Coughlin, and the Hearst papers in the 1935 defeat by the Senate.

References to the U.S. Senate Committee on Foreign Relations' unanimity on approving acceptance (to the full extent) of the optional clause are in *Hearing & Report,* S. Res. 94 86th Cong. 2d Sess.

The extent of support for repeal of the Connally self-judging provision is fully laid out in Michla Pomerance, *The United States and the World Court as a Supreme Court of Nations: Dreams, Illusions and Disillusion* (1996), pp. 264–325.

The Committee for Effective Use of the International Court, a group whose honorary chair was Judge Learned Hand, published a pamphlet with their findings; it's on file in law libraries. ABA bodies published advocacy studies in August 1959 and 1960 (the latter from the Special Committee on World Peace Through Law). Last of the many statements for repeal was from Hubert H. Humphrey in *Virginia Journal of International Law* 11 (1971): 21.

Remarks from Judge Dillard on the 1960–1980 decrease in Court business are in the previously cited *American University Law Review* 27 (1978): 208; Judge Baxter's praise for the 1981 Court is in *Journal of American Bar Association* (1981). Sir Humphrey Waldock's view of the Court appeared in *British Yearbook of International Law* 54 (1984): 1.

The post-*Nicaragua* increase in the Court's business was first noted publicly in an editorial comment by Professor Keith Highet in *AJIL* 85 (1991): 646. It was restated and also applauded in a letter to the *Journal* from J. J. Quintana, Legation of Colombia to the United States, *AJIL* 86 (1992): 542.

Court President Sir Robert Jennings's confirmatory remarks to the UN General Assembly were published in the Court's *Yearbook* for 1991–1992.

That the *Nicaragua* decision "catalysed the renaissance of the Court" was an observation made by Yogesh K. Tyagi, an Indian scholar, in a *Festschrift* (p. 237) in tribute (and memory of) Nagendra Singh, Court president. Characterization of the Court as "moribund" was made by Secretary of State William P. Rogers as he addressed the annual meeting of the ASIL, published in *Proceedings* for 1969 (p. 205).

The phrase "invincible ignorance" as applied to the "man in the street's" knowledge about the Court was coined by Sir Robert Jennings, later president of the Court, *British Yearbook of International Law* 59 (1988): 31.

Professor Frohwein's remarks about the effect of the Nicaragua ruling on other nations appears in *Hague Academy Lectures*, vol. 248 (1994) (p. 427).

Professor Bilder's observation about the positive effect of *Nicaragua* on the Court's business and prestige was made during his delivery of the Brendan Behan Lecture at Catholic University, and published in *Catholic University Law Review* 40 (1990): 251 ff. Professor Franck's phrase "welcomed as an example of judicial independence" was stated during his Hague Academy lecture of 1993, published in volume 240 (p. 306).

Ambassador Gardner's suggestion that the United States "was ashamed" appeared in *Columbia Journal of Transnational Law* 24 (1986): 421; the contrary assertion was made by legal adviser Davis Robinson in *AJIL* 79 (1985): 423. The "baby/bathwater" metaphor was used by Professor Anthony D'Amato during a workshop on the future of the so-called Compulsory Jurisdiction, reported in the published *Proceedings* (1985) (p. 142).

The address of Pope John Paul II to the Court at the Peace Palace was published in an anthology of papal talks called *Paths to Peace* by the Holy See's Permanent Mission to the United Nations (1987). It was also published in *l'Osservatore Romano* (English edition) on June 3, 1985.

Ambassador Kirkpatrick's opinion that the body of judges was "not a court at all" appeared in *Time* magazine on April 23, 1984. The U.S. State Department's statements, derogatory to and threatening the Court, were distributed as official State Department documents, and published *inter alia* as an Appendix to Lori F. Damrosch, ed., *The ICJ at a Crossroads* (1985).

The standard pre-1985 Soviet critique of the Court as a tool of "international reactionary and aggressive forces" has been cited often. It was quoted in Neri Sybesma-Knol, ed., *The Compulsory Jurisdiction of the ICJ: A Turning Point?* (Brussels: Vrije University, 1990). That book includes a discussion of the Gorbachev initiative for Great Power consent to jurisdiction in a record of the proceedings of a Belgian academic roundtable in honor of the presentation of a degree *honoris causa* to Professor Louis B. Sohn.

That the U.S. counterproposal to the Gorbachev initiative for Great Power acceptance of universal jurisdiction for the Court was accepted by the Soviet Union was reported by Paul Lewis in the *New York Times,* Aug. 7, 1989 (p. A-5). A comprehensive oral discussion of this ill-starred venture, held as part of "International Law Weekend" (November 3, 1989), was not published. It was transcribed by the writer and the tape and copy of the forty-nine-page transcript are in his possession.

The "Supersummit" Security Council meeting of February 1992, attended by chiefs of state and/or government of the current members of the Council, was recorded and published by the UN Divisions of Information.

LITIGATING THE ILLEGALITY
OF NUCLEAR WEAPONRY

Nuclear Testing

A comprehensive critical discussion appears in:

T. O. Elias, "The I.C. of J. and the Nuclear Test Cases," in his *The I.C. of J. and some Contemporary Problems* (1983)

Edward McWhinney, "International Law Making and the Judicial Process: The World Court and the French Nuclear Test Case," *Syracuse Journal of International Law & Commerce* 3 (1975): 10–46

W. K. Ris Jr., "French Nuclear Tests in Court," *Denver Journal of International Law* 4 (1974): 111

Ban the Bomb?

The literature on this problem and case are best divided into items published preceding and following the 1996 advisory.

Preceding the 1996 Advisory Opinions

The subject demanded and received a good deal of attention before it came before the Court. Much came from activity of the World Court Project, a movement organized in civil society to eliminate nuclear weapons; its first step was to get it to Court. The debate had begun long before the project's leaders went into action, in an effort to bring before the Court a question that could be raised there only in litigation between states or by a request for an advisory opinion by an authorized UN body.

George Schwarzenberger, *The Legality of Nuclear Weapons* (London: Stevens, 1958)

Negendra Singh with Edward McWhinney, *Nuclear Weapons and Contemporary International Law* (Dordrecht: M. Nijhoff/Kluwer, 1984)

Richard Falk, "The Shimoda Case: A Legal Appraisal of the Atomic Attack on Hiroshima and Nagasaki," *American Journal of International Law* 59 (1963): 759

Richard Falk, Lee Meyrowitz, and Jack Sanderson, *Nuclear Weapons and International Law* (Princeton, N.J.: Woodrow Wilson School of Public and International Studies, 1981)

F. A. Boyle, A. P. Rubin, B. H. Weston, et al., including Peter Weiss, *In re: More Than 50,000 Nuclear Weapons; Analyses of the Illegality of Nuclear Weapons Under International Law* (1991)

D. Schindler and J. Toman, *The Laws of Armed Conflict* (Dordrecht: M. Nijhoff, 1988)

In 1987, the U.S.-based Lawyers Committee on Nuclear Policy published a booklet, *Statement on Illegality of Nuclear Warfare*, citing five treaties and dozens of law review articles, policy journal articles, and the like, on the subject.

Dewes and Green, "The World Court Project: How a Citizens Network Can Influence the United Nations," *Pacifica Review* 7: 17–37, tells the New Zealand group's version of the story of events leading up to the General Assembly Request for an Advisory.

Christopher Weeramantry, *Nuclear Weapons and Scientific Responsibility* (Wolfeboro, N.H.: Longwood Academic, 1987)

The arguments to be presented to the Court, as proposed in a draft brief form, are in a document published in advance in *Transnational Law and Contemporary Problems* 4 (1994): 721–825. Peter Weiss (founder of the "Project"), Falk, Burns Weston, and Saul Mendlovitz jointly sponsored publication.

Mendlovitz and Weiss wrote for *Arms Control Today* (February 1996) a description of the proceedings at the Court in summary form. A transcript is available from LCNP, 211 East 43rd Street, New York, N.Y., covering fifteen days of the hearing.

Following the 1996 Advisory Opinions

The period since the Court's advisory opinions has been marked by a veritable cornucopia of books and international law journals. Not so the general media of civil society. Books include:

Roger Clark and Madeleine Sann, *The Case against the Bomb* (New Brunswick, N.J.: Rutgers University Press, 1996)

Charles J. Moxley Jr., *Nuclear Weapons and International Law in the Post-Cold War World* (Lanham, Md.: University Press of America, 2000)

John Burroughs, *The (Il)legality of the Threat or Use of Nuclear Weapons* (Munster: Die Deutsche Bibliothek, 1997)

Laurence B. de Chazournes and Philippe Sands, eds., *International Court of Justice and Nuclear Weapons* (Cambridge: Cambridge University Press, 1999)

Ved P. Nanda and David Krieger, *Nuclear Weapons and the World Court* (Ardsley: Transnational Publishers, 1998)

Ann Ginger, ed., *Nuclear Weapons Are Illegal* (New York: Apex Press, 1998) (contains the full text of the ICJ judgment and opinions)

Symposium, *Transnational Law and Contemporary Problems* 7:1 (Fall 1997) (includes essays by Weiss, Falk, Mendlovitz, and Datan et al.)

Other articles:

Review of de Chazournes and Sands, above, by Weiss, October 2000

Falk, "Nuclear Weapons, International Law, and the World Court: A Historic Encounter," *AJIL* 91 (1996): 69

Jill M. Sheldon, "Nuclear Weapons and the Laws of War," *Fordham Journal of International Law* 20 (1996): 1818

Sean M. Howley, "Legality of Threat or Use of Nuclear Weapons," *NYU Journal of International Law* 10 (1997): 237

Lawyers Committee on Nuclear Policy published a pamphlet with draft "Model Nuclear Weapons Convention on the Prohibition, etc., of Nuclear Weapons and Their Elimination" (1997). Contains an essay on the draft, and two resolutions of the UN General Assembly, as well as text of ICJ judgment (one resolution adopts and accepts Court advice to the General Assembly).

At the 2000 review conference of the parties to the Non-proliferation of Nuclear Weapons Treaty, there was agreement on an unequivocal undertaking "to accomplish the total elimination of their nuclear arsenals." Text in *AJIL* 94 (2000): 706.

The Mendlovitz-Burroughs paper dated July 2000 is available from LCNP; its Web site with updated cases is www.lcnp.org/wcourt/casessurveyand-analysis.htm.

Chronology

PRELUDE: SOME LANDMARK DATES
BEFORE THE HAGUE CONFERENCE

1794   **May 19.** Serving as President Washington's special envoy, Chief Justice John Jay makes a treaty with Britain that will settle remaining disputes by joint commission. This is now regarded as launching a modern movement for third-party dispute resolution among nations.

1832   **July 21.** The United States rejects and declines to comply with an arbitration award in a dispute submitted to the king of Netherlands that arose after the 1814 Treaty of Ghent.

1840   William Ladd, founder of the American Peace Society, publishes a pioneer plan for an association of nations that would sponsor an independent court to settle disputes between and among them.

1845   **July 4.** Charles Sumner (later an abolitionist U.S. senator) is selected to deliver the Boston Independence Day talk and focuses on denouncing war as a foolhardy "mode of litigation" among nations; calling it an "international lynch law," he urges the settlement of disputes by peaceful tribunal.

1856   **February.** European nations at the Paris Peace Conference that followed the Crimean War approve and recommend acceptance by all nations of a proposal by New York Judge William Jay, son of John Jay (above), that future treaties embody an agreement that disputes under them be arbitrated.

1872   **September 14.** Serious questions of warfare and obligations of neutrals are settled in the Geneva-based arbitration of the *Alabama* claims case that had almost brought war between the United States and the United Kingdom. Despite dissent by a British arbitrator from the award, Britain complied and paid. An enormous lift is given to peace movements and other groups advocating an arbitration system to end war.

1887   **October 31.** Ongoing peace-by-arbitration movement is marked by the U.S. visit of Randal Cremer, British M.P. and labor leader who had secured 234 signatures in Commons for an arbitration pact with the United States for all issues; Andrew Carnegie introduces Cremer to President Cleveland.

1889   **March 4.** At the centennial of Washington's inaugural, keynote speaker Edward Everett Hale predicts that the twentieth century will bring a permanent court of international arbitration that will result from U.S. initiative.

1890   **April 28.** Inter-American multinational arbitration pact is signed after the first Pan-American Conference, chaired by Secretary of State James Blaine, with no ratifications, however.

1895   **June 5.** At a Lake Mohonk, New York, hotel, the first of twenty-two annual conferences on international arbitration assembles. There begins a persistent and increasingly influential campaign for arbitration for peace and a permanent tribunal to facilitate it with incidental networking that results in such side products as the formation of the American Society of International Law.

1896   **April 16.** New York State Bar Association's special committee to draw a plan for a permanent tribunal for arbitration of all questions between the United States and the

261

United Kingdom, rejects bistate limitation as too narrow, then proposes a permanent world court of nine judges to deal with cases of all nations.

April 22. Three hundred delegates, including many notables, attend the first National Arbitration Conference at Washington, D.C., to advance the peace cause.

1897 **May 5.** The Olney-Pauncefote Treaty providing for the general arbitration of all disputes with Great Britain, which had been signed on January 11 and celebrated thereafter, was defeated by the U.S. Senate, beginning a long course of such obstruction/declination.

THE CHRONOLOGY OF THE CENTURY OF THE HAGUE COURTS

1898 **August 24.** The peace movements, disheartened by the defeat of Olney-Pauncefote Treaty, hear of the proposal of Czar Nicholas II of Russia for a meeting of nations to discuss "the most effective means of ensuring to all peoples the benefits of a real and lasting peace."

1899 **January 11.** The czar's formal invitation is amended/supplemented by addition of topic, "the use of good offices, mediation, and voluntary arbitration . . . with the purpose of preventing armed conflicts between nations." The Hague is selected as the place to meet and the peace movements' interest is doubled.

February. Native groups in the Philippines, objecting to a denial of independence after they aided United States in its war with Spain, begin a tragically doomed insurrection.

May 18. The First Hague Peace Conference begins in response to the invitations of Czar Nicholas.

July 29. Hague I closes, the nations having agreed to establish a "Permanent Court of Arbitration."

October 12. The Boer War begins in South Africa.

1900 **January 8.** U.S. Supreme Court declares, "International law is part of our law," and applies it to free an unarmed fishing vessel from Cuba; U.S. forces must bow to a Law of Nations rule that such shipping is immune from seizure as "prize."

February 5. U.S. Senate ratifies a Hague convention to set up a "permanent" arbitration court, responding to a combined pressure of the administration, peace forces, and a lobby of international lawyers and other internationalists.

June. "Boxer Rebellion" against foreign domination begins in China; it will be crushed by joint forces of U.S. and European imperialists and the Japanese.

September 4. The required number (seventeen of twenty-six signatories) having ratified the Hague Convention, the "permanent court" comes into being, ready to offer arbitration services.

1901 **April.** The Permanent Court of Arbitration (PCA) rents space at The Hague for its secretariat.

1902 **May 22.** The first international arbitration to be handled by standing facility, the PCA, is initiated by pact between the United States and Mexico (the "Pious Fund").

In a historic inter-American arbitration, but outside of the PCA, Chile and Argentina submit a long and troublesome border dispute for a third-party decision by King Edward VII of Britain.

October 14. The Pious Fund case results in a ruling against Mexico in favor of California Catholic bishops, regarding money held for their sees when the territory was Mexican. It is promptly paid.

1903 **January 1.** As petitioned by the American Peace Society, the Massachusetts legislature calls on Congress to support international peace parleys every seven years; the ultimate result is a calling of the Hague II conference for 1907.

April 22. At the urging of movement colleagues, Andrew Carnegie pledges funds to build a home at The Hague for the PCA; the building was to become known as the Peace Palace.

1904   **February 8.** A sneak attack by imperial Japan on the czar's force at Port Arthur, Siberia, begins the Russo-Japanese War.

February 22. PCA arbitration settles the Venezuelan debts case. The agreement for this hearing ended a near-war condition with the United States threatening Euro-creditors who were blockading a debtor. Germany, Italy, and Great Britain, who had initiated the blockade, were given assignment of customs revenues to secure payment and priority over other claimants.

September 24. The Interparliamentary Union, meeting in the United States gets a pledge from President Roosevelt to initiate Hague II.

October 21. Secretary of State John Hay keeps pledge with note.

November 25. First Commission of Inquiry, an alternative to arbitration provided by the 1899 Hague convention, is set up to get facts on why and how Russian warships (on the way to fight in the Pacific) fired on British fishermen at Dogger Bank.

1905   **February 13.** U.S. Senate vitiates President Roosevelt's plan for improving the effectiveness of arbitration for peace. This was done by an amendment requiring a separate treaty for proceeding with each case. This would force separate Senate ratification for each proposed arbitration, with a risk each time of delay by filibuster or amendment.

April. As a "peace education" initiative, state school boards in Massachusetts and Ohio direct local districts to plan informative commemoration exercises for May 18 (opening day of the Hague Conference) with special attention to the nature and meaning of the arbitration "court" that was created. This initiative spreads to other states.

May 22. PCA arbitration results in a ruling against Japan in the "House Tax" case; land held under perpetual leases by foreigners may not be taxed at a rate higher than the lease.

May 31. The Tenth Lake Mohonk Conference on International Arbitration is the setting for the first meeting to initiate the American Society of International Law. The society's goal is to organize and unite international lawyers for peace.

July 19. Elihu Root begins a new phase of his career, as secretary of state. His efforts will be concentrated on advancing peaceful international relations by promoting third-party resolution of disputes; his work will continue to the late 1920s when, at age 82, he joins an effort in Geneva to make World Court statute more acceptable to the United States.

August. President Roosevelt, having been secretly offered the chance by Japan, assumes the role of mediator to settle and end the Russo-Japanese War; he wins the Nobel Prize.

1906   **April.** Invitations to the second Hague conference (Hague II) are quietly arranged by the United States under Root's leadership, to be issued in the name of Czar Nicholas II. This done in courteous recognition of Russia's 1898 initiative. Backers hope and plan to transform the PCA into a real court, a standing body of independent jurists, as proposed in 1896 by the New York Bar.

1907   **April 14–17.** The "Great" (as it immediately came to be known) National Peace and Arbitration Congress is held at Carnegie Hall, drawing nationwide media attention. Andrew Carnegie acts as president, and there is an impressive concentration of top-ranking political and community leaders of the day, typified by New York Governor Charles Evans Hughes (a Republican, and later to be a judge at The Hague); William Jennings Bryan; and long-time American Federation of Labor leader Samuel Gompers.

May 31. Secretary of State Root instructs U.S. delegates to Hague II "to bring about . . . a development of the tribunal into a permanent tribunal composed of judges who are judicial officers and nothing else."

June 15–October 18. Second Hague conference is held and closes with unanimous agreement to create a permanent court with compulsory jurisdiction, as soon as a major stumbling block is overcome: failure to reach agreement on a method of selecting judges, with limitation to a practical (that is, fewer than one for each nation) number. A draft statute for the Court is composed; the content and structure closely resemble the statute ultimately created for the first World Court, the Permanent Court of International Justice.

1908   The American School Peace League is formed as a genuinely national organization, headed by Fanny Fern Andrews, and is publicly endorsed and aided by the National Education Association and the U.S. commissioner of education. Its efforts for widening peace education efforts achieves wide recognition of May 18 as "Peace Day" to mark the opening of Hague I.

February. Secretary of State Root attempts to persuade the U.S. Senate to let him negotiate a new round of treaties to replace those on which Roosevelt had been beaten, "to get the arbitration business on its legs," he says.

April 2. U.S. Senate ratifies Second Hague Convention.

May 25. Inspired by Root at the November 1907 Pan-American Conference held in Washington, D.C., Central American states create and participate in a Central American Court of Justice, the first of its kind in world history, with compulsory jurisdiction. Woodrow Wilson, as president of Princeton University, joins and becomes speaker/advocate for the American Peace Society's campaign for peace through arbitration.

October 17. A Peace and Arbitration League is formed by Haynes Davis; its slogan, "The Practical Program for Peace Is Adequate Armament and Effective Arbitration." While other peace groups object, this reflects breadth of sentiment for arbitration among nations.

1909   **May 22.** A PCA panel by arbitration ruling peacefully closes a Casablanca incident. A crisis erupts over French obstruction to a German rescue attempt directed at German deserters from the French Foreign Legion.

1910   **February 25.** Carnegie's New York Peace Society calls for regular, periodic Hague conferences, and the framing of a "universal obligatory arbitration treaty."

March 10. President William Howard Taft urges nations to adopt a new approach to arbitration that will not exclude, as most past treaties had, "matters of national honor."

March 22. Taft, addressing the American Peace and Arbitration League, argues that all disputes without exception should be settled by arbitration and goes on to negotiate such treaties with Britain and France.

May. Former President Roosevelt, in his Nobel Prize address, advocates arbitration for all but national honor disputes. He suggests strengthening an international tribunal along the lines of the U.S. Supreme Court.

September 7. A PCA panel makes an award that brings peace to the United States and Britain after an increasingly bitter conflict over fisheries jurisdiction off Canada's coastline.

December 14. Responding to publisher Edward Ginn's grant of $1 million to World Peace Foundation for arbitration advocacy, Andrew Carnegie gives an endowment of $10 million to the Carnegie Foundation for International Peace.

December 17. The American Society for Judicial Resolution is formed and, per peace historian Merle Curti, did more than any other single organization to make the first World Court a reality.

1911   **February 24.** A PCA panel settles a British–French dispute over Saverkar, a Hindu prisoner who had escaped; recapture had been impeded by French police.

May 30. President Taft, speaking at Arlington National Cemetery on Memorial Day, says "the best method of securing disarmament is establishment of an international court . . . which nations will recognize as affording a better method of settling international controversies than war."

June. Following the National Arbitration and Peace Conference, peace societies endorse and agree to fight for Taft's treaties providing unlimited arbitration. Former President Roosevelt and Senator Henry Cabot Lodge oppose.

August 3. Secretary of State P. C. Knox concludes broad-scope arbitration treaties with Britain and France; Carnegie is enthusiastic and a *Los Angeles Times* editorial hails it as the "greatest act of statesmanship since the Emancipation Proclamation."

1912   **March 5.** U.S. Senate vote seriously impairs Taft's treaties, and he drops them.

September. In advance of the presidential election, both Democratic and Republican parties endorse broad arbitration of international disputes; Roosevelt's "Bull Moose" Party does not.

November. The Nobel Peace Prize is given to Elihu Root for his key role in establishing the Central American Court of Justice.

1913   **May 6.** A PCA panel of arbitrators settles a dispute between France and Italy over an episode in which the Italian Navy seized some French ships. Italy is held liable and pays damages.

New Secretary of State W. J. Bryan, Wilson's appointee, commences negotiation of a series of treaties over a two-year period, providing for fact-finding commissions in case of threatening disputes, conciliation efforts, and a "waiting period" before a war starts. These the Senate ratifies.

August 28. The Hague Peace Palace is dedicated as the home of the arbitration court, under the Dutch and U.S. flags. The cornerstone expresses gratitude to Andrew Carnegie, who says historians will call the "world court" the greatest step forward ever taken by man.

1914   **June 25.** A PCA panel ends a long dispute between Portugal and the Netherlands as to the border dividing their colonial possession of Timor Island.

August. The Austrian archduke is assassinated at Sarajevo. Various demands by Austria are embodied in an ultimatum. The Serbs agree to most of them, and propose arbitration of the rest by the PCA. Austria, backed by Germany, declines and war begins.

August 4. President Wilson offers mediation as the war begins. It is accepted by none.

1915   **February.** The Massachusetts legislature calls on the U.S. Congress to initiate the establishment of an international court.

February 27. A National Peace Federation meeting, presided over by celebrated social worker Jane Addams, calls for "an international court for the settlement of all disputes between nations."

April 9. A convention of peace groups, initiated by the New York Peace Society, urges "the United States to form a league of all the great nations in which all justiciable questions between them shall be submitted to a judicial tribunal."

May 12. With former President Taft and former Secretary of State P. C. Knox present, the International Peace Forum holds a "World Court Congress" in Cleveland and formally organizes a "World Court League."

June 8. William Jennings Bryan resigns in protest from his post as President Wilson's secretary of state; his principal objection is to the nonconciliatory, hostile character of communications with Germany.

1916   **May 17.** Former President Taft, now head of a newly formed League to Enforce Peace, presides at the twenty-second and final Mohonk Conference for Arbitration. He says the first objective of all participants and sympathizers should be a Permanent Court of International Justice.

August. Congress, in a rider to a naval appropriations bill, suggests an international conference to form a "true world court."

1917 **January 22.** The American Institute of International Law, meeting in Havana, recommends a multinational "court of justice" for arbitration between and among nations.
March 9. In its tenth, and what is to be its last, case, the Central American Court of Justice upholds the objections of El Salvador and Costa Rica to Nicaragua's entry into the Bryan-Chamorro Treaty, granting canal rights and a naval base to the United States, because it affects U.S. interest in the Gulf of Fonseca.
Under U.S. influence, Nicaragua fails to comply with Court ruling and the Court ceases functioning as its members decline to renew its charter.

1918 **July 16.** Colonel Edward House, a longtime Wilson chief adviser, after hearing Elihu Root's arguments begins an effort to induce the president to include a Court in his peace plans, which were focused solely on a league of states and political power.

1919 **January 31.** Wilson, at Versailles, agrees to accept the idea of a Court, after persuasion by South Africa's Jan C. Smuts and especially Lord Robert Cecil.
April 28. The League of Nations Covenant, as included in the Treaty of Versailles, directs the League Council to formulate plans for creation of a Permanent Court of International Justice.
July 10. Senate debates ratification of the Versailles Peace Treaty. Objections center on the League; no senator expresses objections to (or offers reservations undercutting) participation in the Court.

1920 **March 19.** The final Senate defeat of the Versailles Peace Treaty leaves open the question of participation in the Court.
June 16. The advisory council of jurists of ten nations—including Root, despite U.S. treaty avoidance—meets until July 24 to prepare a governing statute for the coming Permanent Court of International Justice (PCIJ).
September 4. A Permanent Court of Arbitration panel sits for the first time at Peace Palace. The case awards damages at the instance of Britain and France, against Portugal, for destruction or damage inflicted on religious properties during the 1910 revolution.
October 20. PCIJ statute is amended and adopted as amended by the League Council.

1921 **March 30.** Panel of PCA decides a dispute over the sinking of a Netherlands vessel.
April 20. Colombia seeks arbitration damages from PCA for U.S. intervention during Panama revolution of 1903, which had made the canal possible. Bryan had settled the case in 1914, but payment was deferred because it was not ratified by the Senate. The Senate ratifies a treaty to pay a $25 million indemnity.
June 13. Denmark becomes the first nation to ratify the protocol (treaty in effect) establishing PCIJ statute. The ratification process is completed by September 1, 1921.
August 6. Netherlands is the first nation to accept the so-called optional clause of the PCIJ statute; this provides obligatory jurisdiction among states that also accept that clause.
August 21. As nominations for first set of judges begins, five member nations nominate Root, although United States is not (and never will be) party to Court's protocol. He declines due to age (75).
September 4. Initial election of first full bench of judges to serve on the PCIJ is held. League Council and Assembly vote separately, under a procedure devised by Root, to avoid an impasse similar to that of 1907. A U.S. national is included, John Bassett Moore, long a preeminent scholar and writer on international law and arbitration. Also elected, and most equally distinguished, R. Altamira of Spain; D. Anzilotti of Italy; R. Barbosa of Brazil; A. Bustamente of Cuba; Viscount Finlay of the United Kingdom; H. M. Huber of Switzerland; B. Loder of Netherlands (first president of Court); D. Nyholm of Denmark; Y. Oda of Japan; and C. A. Weiss of France (vice president).
November 29. The Carnegie Foundation, landlord of the Peace Palace, accepts the PCIJ as cotenant with existing PCA.

1922   **January 30.** The first session of the PCIJ opens with Bernard C. J. Loder of Holland elected first president; the Court statute allows for three-year terms. Akĕ Hammarskjöld is named first registrar.

March 24. The Rules of Court, as drafted by the first bench, are adopted by the judges.

May 17. A League Council resolution opens the Court statute for acceptance and participation by nonmembers of the League, a direct invitation to the United States to join the Court in aiding peace by support of rule of law.

June 15. The Court opens its first public session.

July 21. The PCIJ renders its first decision: an advisory opinion at the request of the League Council to solve a problem of the International Labor Organization. A group of independent unions that outnumber the Central Netherlands Federation of Labor may be treated collectively as the largest, for purpose of sending a delegate to the ILO's International Labor Conference.

August 22. The Court's second advisory opinion is rendered: "Labor," as mentioned in title and mandate of the ILO, is construed to include agricultural labor and its working conditions. (French farm employers had objected but agree to comply.)

October 13. Arbitration panel of PCA (original Hague tribunal) settles, in Norway's favor, a dispute about the price to be paid for ships seized for wartime (World War I) use. Secretary of State Hughes sharply protests the decision and method of calculation, but directs payment of amount assessed for the sake of maintaining respect for the principle of international third-party resolution of disputes.

1923   **January 10.** "League of Nations Nonpartisan Association" is formed; its prime objective is to win "adherence of the United States to the Permanent Court of International Justice."

February 13. Senator William E. Borah, opponent of the League and of the PCIJ, offers a resolution to establish a court on the basis that "a judicial substitute for war should be created"—but not the "League" Court.

February 1. Secretary of State Hughes sends a letter to the Senate recommending U.S. agree to adhere to PCIJ, followed by a letter from President Warren G. Harding, to the same effect, dated February 23. This initiates a conflict that will last through four presidencies, ending in defeat in 1935.

August 17. PCIJ issues a decision in the case of the S.S. *Wimbledon,* the first contentious—that is, two or more party-litigated—case (as contrasted with advisory opinion to the League body). The ship was chartered to carry munitions to troops fighting the new Soviet Republic. Despite a Versailles Treaty rule that the Kiel Canal across peninsula between North and Baltic seas is to be kept open, German Republic bars a ship from the canal for the sake of its own neutrality. The Court rules against Germany, for countries of shippers. Treaty requirement results in the law of "natural straits," stating that canals are open to all except when the owner itself is at war.

August 21. In the case of *Eastern Carelia* the PCIJ declines to render a requested advisory opinion that would pass on merits of territorial dispute (Finland versus Soviet Union). Since the Soviet Union is not a member of League, the judges treat the case as subterfuge to get a ruling against a nation not consenting to jurisdiction.

September 10. PCIJ interprets a treaty that protects German nationals in former Reich territory given to Poland by the Versailles Treaty. The new Polish state may not oust from title to land those who had leases before the creation of Polish sovereignty.

December 6. President Calvin Coolidge, who took office on the death of President Harding, calls for affiliation with the Court, as had a November 23 resolution of the U.S. Chamber of Commerce.

1924   **February.** Max Huber is elected president of the Court at expiration of first president's three-year term.

1925 **February 4.** Implementing an important treaty function often exercised by the Court's president—named as such for the purpose of avoiding impasse in selection of neutrals—the president appoints the chair of the mixed tribunal set up to deal with postwar disputes between Greece and Turkey.

February 21. A PCIJ advisory opinion deals with a dispute arising from compulsory exchange of Greek and Turkish inhabitants of land affected by a territorial adjustment. The effect is an exception being made in the treaty for Greeks "established" in Constantinople; it is accepted by both parties.

March 3. Responding to continued delay in Senate Foreign Relations Committee, chaired successively by Henry Cabot Lodge Sr. and William E. Borah, the House of Representatives records by a big margin its "earnest desire" that the United States accept the protocol for affiliation with World Court (PCIJ).

July 24. Four hundred fifty delegates, said to represent 5 million women, attend the first of Conferences on Cause and Cure of War, and adopt a resolution asking immediate action to affiliate with the PCIJ.

August 30. In the case of *Greece v. Britain* (as Palestine mandatory) Mavrommatis's claim under Turkish concession—as predecessor sovereign to Britain—is upheld; the Greek state, in pursuing his claim, "is in reality asserting its own rights." (Court statute limits it solely to cases between states.)

1926 **January 27.** U.S. Senate advises and consents to Court's protocol by vote of 76 to 17, which would have meant ratification save for five reservations. Four were negotiable; a fifth, intended to be a "killer" reservation, prevented U.S. membership by unacceptable conditions on advisory cases.

May 25. PCIJ, in a case called *German Interests in Upper Silesia*, rejects a threatened Polish confiscation of factory conveyed by Reich to private interests before a land transfer.

League Council calls meeting to negotiate Senate's reservations that block U.S. membership. Coolidge administration declines to attend the Geneva talk.

1927 **September 7.** The PCIJ decides the historic case of the *Lotus*. A French vessel rams and sinks a Turkish ship on high seas. The French captain proceeds to his Turkish destination, and is held for trial there. France claims that a trial under Turkish law would be illegal; Court rules for Turkey's jurisdiction on the basis that the ship is an extension of the nation whose flag she flies (part basis for current laws permitting the trial in the United States of alleged terrorists for assault on U.S. nationals abroad). Tie vote in Court resolved under statute with second vote for president.

December 8. In an advisory (No. 14) the PCIJ upholds jurisdictional claim of the European Commission of the Danube, set up by a treaty to regulate multinational navigable inland waterway, against limits argued by Romania.

1928 **February.** Judge Dionisio Anzilotti, Italian first elected before the fascist era, is elected president of the Court.

February 29. The German Republic, permitted now to join the League and accept Court protocol, becomes the first of the "great" powers to file a consent to compulsory jurisdiction of the Court, under the optional clause. (This clause permits mutually effective consent-in-advance to be sued, among states accepting it.) Britain (February 1930) and France (April 1931) follow example.

April 4. United States accepts as arbitrator in a Hague case Dr. Max Huber, then president of PCIJ, in the case with the Netherlands, for the Dutch East Indies, over whether Isle of Palmas was part of the Spanish Philippines the United States had taken in 1899. A ruling for Dutch was accepted.

August 28. The Briand-Kellogg multinational pact "renounces" war as an instrument of national policy. The fruit of movement was begun in United States by Chicago lawyer Levinson, and used by some as a gambit against Court adherence. Franklin D. Roosevelt, former Wilson Cabinet member and future U.S. president, says the treaty fails in two ways: "It leads to a false belief we have taken a great step forward. It does not contribute in any way to settling matters of international controversy."

September 8. Charles Evans Hughes, former secretary of state and associate U.S. Supreme Court justice, is elected judge of PCIJ, replacing Judge Moore after the latter's resignation. Hughes serves until his appointment as chief justice of the U.S. Supreme Court.

September 13. The oft-returning case of Chorzow factory meets its final ruling: Poland must pay reparations to Germany.

September 26. General act for "Pacific Settlement of International Disputes" culminates a movement begun by a Geneva protocol of 1924 that could have been the League's greatest achievement. It provides for effective, permanent PCIJ compulsory jurisdiction among signatories, which reached twenty when there were fewer than sixty nation-states. It was not used before World War II, but was held to be sufficiently alive when the International Court of Justice succeeded PCIJ, to support claimed jurisdiction.

November 22. In a rare (for that Court) case with a non-European party, China is sued by Belgium, the latter claiming wrongful termination of a treaty for special privileges. China denies Court jurisdiction, although both had signed optional clause permitting mutual obligatory submission. The Court "indicates" a provisional measure (international name for temporary injunction), and China settles the case by signing a new treaty.

1929   **March 4.** President Herbert Hoover announces in first inaugural that he will revive efforts to induce the Senate to accept the Court.

March 11. At age eighty-two, Elihu Root agrees to attend a meeting of the newly constituted jurists' committee, sponsored by the League, to try to amend the Court statute to satisfy, somewhat, the Senate's fifth reservation.

July 12. In case of Serbian and Brazilian loans from French bondholders, PCIJ rules that the "gold clause" is enforceable.

September 10. As in an earlier Danube case, the PCIJ rules in the case of the Commission of the Oder River that that body's authority (for regulating international use and navigation) extends to condition in harbors that are mere Polish villages.

September 14. The protocol that Root helped to draft, to amend PCIJ statute to adjust to demands of the Senate reservation regarding advisory opinions, is opened for signature.

1930   **November.** Second (and last, for either Court, in view of ICJ statute change to direct triennial elections of one-third of judges) election of full membership of the Court. Reelected were Altamira, Anzilotti, and Bustamente, "charter" members of the Court. Also reelected were Sir Cecil Hurst, Frank B. Kellogg, chosen in 1929 and 1930 elections to replace Findlay, Hughes, and Weiss. New were M. Adatci, a Japanese lawyer and diplomat who had helped draft the statute (president 1931–34); W. J. M. Van Eysinga, Dutch diplomat and professor of public and international law; J. G. Guerrero of El Salvador; D. Negulesco of Romania; and the first German judge, as a Reichstag member in Weimar Republic, Walther Schucking. He was a local leader of Interparliamentary Union for Arbitration and Peace.

December 9. The revised protocol to meet U.S. objection is agreed to by President Hoover and sent to the Senate. But the economic depression, signalled by the October 1929 stock crash, is such a distraction that consideration is put off until revived by Franklin D. Roosevelt in 1935.

1931   **June 9.** A suit is filed at World Court by France against Britain on behalf of a widow whose husband had been detained in Iran by British occupation troops, then deported to India. Damages of £ 2,100 are allowed and paid.

September 5. PCIJ advisory opinion makes history in a ruling against a proposed customs union of Austria with Germany, holding that this would violate the Versailles Treaty pledge against "compromising" Austria's independence. A tie vote broken by the president's second vote plus Europe's economic problems result in a stormy reception to the ruling, embarrassing Court supporters.

September 16. In Advisory Opinion No. 21, the Court rules that Lithuania is obliged to negotiate or arbitrate its action in barring Polish rail traffic from passing through its territory.

1932   **June 7.** The Court rules for Switzerland in a "free zones" case brought to test France's claim on an old treaty that gave local Swiss merchants free trade near border within France. The Court held that the old pact was not abrogated by the Versailles Treaty; France, following some suspense, submits.

July 18. The United States participates in and wins an arbitration case at the Hague Tribunal of PCA. Sweden claims the detention of its ships by the United States during World War I was illegal, but loses.

August 11. German Baltic Port of Memel was needed both by Poland and Lithuania, each newly given statehood in the Versailles settlement. The case arose after Lithuanian troops took control, followed by a compromise with limited autonomy for the Polish majority. In a flare-up, the Lithuanian military governor dismissed the elected local board. Interpreting the Memel statute, the Court rules that only local chairman can be dismissed.

November 15. Advisory opinion is given for the ILO on whether the 1919 convention regulating night labor for women extends to nonmanual labor. Continuing its liberal tradition in labor rulings, the Court says that it does.

1933   **April 5.** The legal status of Eastern Greenland is settled in a dispute with initial military confrontation between Denmark and Norway. Compulsory jurisdiction under the optional clause is seen here at its best as both countries had signed. Denmark, as initial owner whose people had settled in west, seeks ouster of the new Norwegian settlers in the East. The Court rules that Denmark is the rightful owner of all Greenland; Norwegian troops leave.

1934   **March 17.** France sues Greece to enforce the effectiveness of Turkish grant, issued before the territorial switch of a harbor, of a lighthouse-operating concession to a French national. PCIJ holds Greece bound by Turkish grant.

June 16. The Congress, by joint resolution (bypassing the Senate's two-thirds), gives requested authority to President Roosevelt to accept membership in the Versailles-created International Labor Office.

1935   **January 29.** The Senate inflicts a final defeat on the hopes of four successive U.S. presidents—and generations of peace advocates—for U.S. ratification of the World Court treaty. There is a majority in favor but less than the constitutionally required two-thirds; immediate victory is for its shrillest opponents, Father Charles Coughlin, pro-fascist priest, and Huey Long, demagogic senator from Louisiana.

December 4. In Advisory Opinion No. 27, the PCIJ scrutinizes an action of the internationalized "Free City" of Danzig (now Gdansk) that had come under Nazi local control by democratic process. The Court declares as unconstitutional a decree conforming penal law to a Nazi-style decree permitting local judicial tyranny.

1936   **March 7.** With the United States seeming neutral, as was inferred from the final rejection of the Court by the U.S. Senate, the inexorable march to war begins. Hitler, in flat and defiant violation of the Versailles Treaty, sends a newly, now openly, reconstituted Wehrmacht into the Rhineland. Britain and France fail to act. The road to war continues when Hitler and Mussolini aid an insurrection against the Spanish Republic, which will fall as a result of embargo of arms to both sides, freely and continuously violated by the fascist states.

1936– The Court is reduced to a purely nominal role on the reoccupation of the
1938 Rhineland in 1936.

1937 **June 28.** Belgian and Dutch claims and counterclaims regarding the diversion of waters from River Meuse are dismissed on a finding by the PCIJ that both sides are guilty.

1938 **March 12.** The Court's 1931 ruling in the Austro-German customs union case is effectively overruled as Hitler marches into Austria and merges it with Third Reich, to achieve the "Anschluss," a union of Germany and Austria.

1939 **September 1.** World War II begins as France and Britain declare war in response to Hitler's invasion of Poland. On the same day, by coincidental arrangement, a League of Nations memorial to Woodrow Wilson is dedicated at Geneva.

November 18. The Court's last case: Belgium files claims against Bulgaria on behalf of Belgian-owned Electric Company of Sofia. Bulgaria notifies the Court it is unable to appear and defend itself because of wartime obstacles. The case peters out.

1940 **May.** A Nazi motorized column drives up to the decorative iron gates given to the Court by Germany, as Hitler's forces sweep through Holland. Judge Van Eysinga, the last judge left in residence at The Hague, comes to the gate and orders the Nazi colonel to stop and not to invade "international" territory, Court premises. The Peace Palace is not molested and the war goes on.

1942 **January 13.** St. James Declaration of European governments-in-exile, based in London, announces the intention to punish, through channels of organized justice, the crimes of Germans in occupied territories.

1943 **October 30.** Moscow Declaration of Roosevelt, Churchill, and Stalin tells the world that the major war criminals will be tried and punished by a jointly arranged tribunal; minor criminals will be returned for trial to the lands where the atrocities took place.

November 5. After a long debate, the U.S. Senate passes a resolution committing the United States to postwar international cooperation. It is generally understood to be a pledge to reverse the course of action that opposed and defeated Wilson's plans.

1944 **February 10.** After a series of meetings over a nine-month period, a Committee of Jurists meeting in London proposes a plan for the reorganization and revival of the Permanent Court of International Justice.

October 9. The "Dumbarton Oaks" plan emerges from consultations of the "great powers" meeting from August through September. The draft outline for a general international organization will include an International Court of Justice, whose statute will be attached to the charter and based on that of the PCIJ. All members of the new organization will automatically become members of the Court.

1945 **April 20.** Conclusion of eleven days of meetings by Committee of Jurists from forty-four nations, chaired by Green H. Hackworth of the U.S. State Department. They have drafted a statute for an International Court of Justice, which they take to the San Francisco conference founding the United Nations. The conference will determine whether to set up a "new" court or to continue the PCIJ with new statute as its amended basic law.

June 14. A San Francisco conference subcommittee, during meeting begun May 4, decides a "new" court will be more practical and draws sections of the UN Charter dealing with the Court and statute for the Court to be annexed as an integral part of the charter. The latter will follow the PCIJ statute, section by section, as amended.

June 26. The Court statute is adopted as part of the UN Charter at the founding conference in San Francisco. Opposition to compulsory jurisdiction by the United States and USSR forces its removal from a Court plan agreed on by jurists.

July 28. The U.S. Senate ratifies the UN Charter and with it the statute of the International Court of Justice (ICJ), the new World Court that effectively continued the old.

August 8. The United States, Great Britain, France, and the USSR complete an agreement that was worked on from June 26 (when the UN Charter was adopted) for prosecution of major war criminals. The Charter of International Military Tribunal that will meet in Nuremberg is the result.

October. PCIJ judges meet and agree to hand over its archives and case files to the ICJ, to whom it recommends its staff for employment.

October 24. As the twenty-ninth ratification, the minimum needed for adoption, is filed, President Harry S. Truman announces that the UN Charter is in force as the "fundamental law for the peoples of the world."

1946   **January 31.** The PCIJ judges transmit their resignations to the last secretary-general of the League of Nations.

February 6. Commencement of the term of office of the first fifteen judges of the ICJ, elected by the first General Assembly and Security Council of the United Nations on this date and Feb 9. Two judges, Guerrero and de Visscher, had been members of the PCIJ. Also elected:

- Alejandro Alvarez Joffre of Chile, long an eminent jurist and expert on international law, professor, and representative of his nation at international conferences from 1901.
- Jules Basdevant of France, professor at several universities and at the Academy of International Law at The Hague; delegate to law codification conferences and others; member PCA.
- Arnold D. McNair of the United Kingdom, Whewall Professor of international law at Cambridge, and professor at The Hague Academy; also a delegate to law codification conferences; member PCA.
- José Azevedo of Brazil, judge of the Supreme Court, professor and adviser to the Foreign Ministry
- Isidro Fabela of Mexico, judge, ambassador, and one-time foreign minister; professor of international law and president of the Mexican delegation to the League of Nations.
- Green H. Hackworth of the United States, a Department of State legal adviser from 1925 to 1946, delegate at a variety of international conferences in legal capacity, and chair of jurists' commission that drafted statute of ICJ.
- Helge Klaestad of Norway, judge of Supreme Court for fifteen years; member of the PCA and often a sole arbitrator.
- Sergei B. Krylov of the USSR, professor, dean, and legal adviser to Commissariat of Foreign Affairs, and delegate to various conferences. He fought in defense of Leningrad in 1941–1942.
- Bohdan Winiarski of Poland, legal adviser to the Polish delegation at the peace conference of 1917–1920; professor of public international law at Poznan University since 1922, and dean from 1936 to 1939; attended numerous international conferences.
- Milovan Zoricic of Yugoslavia, judge and legal adviser to the Croatian state; League of Nations official in Saar control; member PCA and ad hoc judge at PCIJ.
- John Read of Canada, professor of law and dean; counsel for Canada in international litigation; member of jurists' committee.
- Hsu Mo of China, professor of international law and dean of humanities at Tientsin University. He wrote about Chinese diplomatic history, and was a counselor in ministry of foreign affairs.
- Abdal-Hamid Badawi of Egypt. Chief legal advisor for his state 1926–1940, Minister of Foreign Affairs; diplomat active at 1945 San Francisco UN Conference.

Since the ICJ statute provided for triennial elections of one-third of the Court, lots were drawn to determine that Alvarez, Azevedo, Basdevant, Guerrero, and McNair had nine-year terms; Fabela, Hackworth, Klaestad, Krylov, and de Visscher, six years; and Badawi, Hsu Mo, Read, Winiarski, and Zoricic, three years. Guerrero was elected first president and Basdevant, vice president.

March 14. Outgoing registrar of PCIJ places premises at the Carnegie Peace Palace at disposal of ICJ.

April 18. The ceremonial inaugural sitting of the ICJ with the Dutch royal family is held. Initial UN General Assembly President Spaak states the hope that compulsory jurisdiction for all countries and all cases will come.

July 24. Senate Foreign Relations Committee (to which the question of optional clause acceptance was referred—although the president could have decided this himself) favors the unconditional acceptance of the clause. No witnesses testify against that recommendation by the American Bar Association and American Society of International Law.

August 2. The Senate refuses unconditional acceptance, and votes for two private John F. Dulles ideas. One, which became known as the Vandendberg reservation, excludes consent in treaty cases unless all parties to the treaty are in case; the other ("Connally") reservation excludes cases about domestic policy, and states that the United States is to be the sole judge of what is "domestic." The "self-judging" reservation had a negative effect on the value of the optional clause as a tool for enhancing obligatory jurisdiction.

October 1. A verdict handed down at Nuremberg holds twenty-four German leaders guilty of war crimes.

December 11. Standards of guilt are laid down by a four-nation tribunal in convicting major war criminals. The so-called Nuremberg principles are approved by the UN General Assembly.

UN General Assembly grants its Economic and Social Council authority to seek, on its own, advisory opinions from the Court. This is later extended to the Trusteeship Council, ILO, UNESCO, and Food and Agriculture Organization.

1947   **February.** American Bar Association House of Delegates votes to recommend a repeal of the Connally "self-judging" reservation.

April 9. UN Security Council, confronted with Corfu Channel incidents—British ships damaged by mines in natural strait, followed by warships forcing straits for minesweeping operation—recommends, under a specific UN Charter clause, that the issues be referred to the ICJ.

November 14. UN General Assembly Resolution 171 (II) calls it "of paramount importance that the Court should be utilized to the greatest practicable extent in the progressive development of international law."

November 17. In its first advisory opinion to the General Assembly, the ICJ is asked if it was inconsistent with the Charter veto purpose to use it as a reprisal to exclude membership of otherwise eligible states sponsored by states that had vetoed candidates believed to be ineligible. It is an ineffective ruling, due to the "Cold War" setting blocking new members.

November 21. The General Assembly creates the International Law Commission to codify international law as believed to exist or as declared in Court rulings.

1948   **March 25.** ICJ rules in *Corfu Channel* case that Albania had consented to jurisdiction as sought by Britain under call of the Security Council (see April 9, 1947). The issue is whether Albania is liable for damage by mines; Britain is ruled wrongful in invading to sweep mines, even though it claimed mines were needed as evidence.

May 28. In its first advisory (see November 17, 1947), the Court rules (9 to 6) that a conditioning veto as a reprisal is not consistent with the Charter.

July 28. Switzerland, although not a UN member, accepts Court statute to become eligible to bring or defend cases.

October 22. On prospective expiration of their thee-year terms, ICJ members Badawi, Hsu Mo, Read, Winiarski, and Zoricic are reelected by the Security Council and General Assembly.

1949   **April 9.** Court issues *Corfu* ruling No. 2: Albania is liable for damage from mines that it should have known about, even if it is not guilty of laying them; also Britain wrongfully invaded to get them.

April 11. Historic advisory is issued on "Reparations for Injuries Suffered in the Service of the United nations." The United Nations is held to have legal capacity to sue after UN mediator Count Folke Bernadotte is murdered by alleged Israeli terrorists. The UN is held to have sufficient legal personality as an entity under international law, as effected by Charter, to sue. Israel quietly pays, without waiting to be sued.

December 15. In the reparations phase of the *Corfu* case, heard separately, the Court awards damages of £ 843,947. Albania fails to pay; it arrives at settlement with Britain in 1992.

1950   **March 3.** A new advisory is sought, in an attempt to get around a Cold War deadlock in Security Council vetoes on new members. Does the Charter requirement of a Security Council "recommendation" prior to the Assembly vote to admit mean a favorable one? Answer: "Yes."

March 29. Settlement of a case filed in Court by France against Egypt. France sued for damages due to Egyptian reprisals against its citizens, who had aided Jewish settlers' victory after 1947, the end of the mandate for Palestine. Filing the case produced a settlement.

Liechtenstein, non-UN member, joins the Court.

March 30. In the Peace Treaties Advisory, first phase, the Court holds it may advise the Assembly, over objections of states (Bulgaria, Hungary, Romania) accused of treaty breach by human rights violations, whether the latter are obliged to appoint their sides' arbitrators as treaties require; answer is that they must appoint.

July 18. In the second phase of *Peace Treaties*, the Court is asked if objecting states have failed to appoint their arbitrators, may a third member of the tripartite panel be appointed by the secretary-general, who had the right to appoint if parties' arbitrators impassed. Answer is "No," because two-member panel could not act.

July 11. NOTE: On this date there is issued the first of four separate advisories over a twenty-one-year period that deal with the status of the land, now known as Namibia, that began this period as a "Mandate" of South Africa. Also presented to Court were two phases of a "contentious case." All are discussed in chapter II of this book.

The Court holds unanimously that South Africa is still under obligations of the League's 1920 mandate, may not unilaterally change the status of a territory, and must account to UN General Assembly for management, but is not obligated to place the territory under the United Nation's new trusteeship system.

November 27. In the first "Right of Asylum" case, Colombia's legation in Peru offers sanctuary to Haya de la Torre, failed uprising leader, classifying his offense as "political," which the Court rejects under a Havana Convention.

1951   **May 28.** Court advises, first, a reservation does not impair the benefit or effect of a treaty if it is compatible with its purpose; second, in a multilateral treaty, no state is bound by a reservation to which it has not consented.

June 13. In the second phase of Haya de la Torre asylum case, the Count rules that even though Colombia could not unilaterally classify the fugitive as "political," automatic surrender is not compelled; the state is entitled to negotiate about terms.

December 6. Election for a judge is necessitated by the death of Judge Azevedo.

Another Brazilian, Levi Fernandez Carneiro, is elected. He had been scholar and writer; participant in international conferences; member PCA; legal adviser to the Foreign Ministry, and principal author of Brazil's new Constitution. There is also held on this date the regularly scheduled triennial election. Judges Hackworth and Klaestad are reelected. New judges (for term 1952–1955) are:

- Eugene Armand-Ugon, former chief judge of Uruguay, attendant at international conferences, and chair of delegation to Assembly.
- Sergei A. Golunsky, foremost Soviet legal expert, professor and chief of legal division, Foreign Ministry.
- Sir Benegal N. Rau of India, judge of Calcutta High Court, chair of commission for internal interstates dispute, and writer.

December 18. Major Law of the Sea ruling is made in fisheries case between Britain and Norway. The especially jagged nature of coast and high dependence on fishing are considered in the ruling, permitting baselines, as drawn by Norway between headlands and, in some cases, islands.

1952 **July 1.** In the first phase of *Ambatielos* case, a Greek shipowner's claim from 1919 against British government is pressed for him, but the Court finds no jurisdiction to decide merits; it does rule under Treaty provision that it can direct arbitration.

July 22. In a case of the Anglo-Iranian Oil Company, Great Britain sues over nationalization of oil properties. Iran contests jurisdiction and wins a dismissal. The optional-clause agreement excluded cases under treaties of prior date, as this was.

August 27. First World Court case with United States as litigant is heard. France sues because of U.S. resistance to curtailment of treaty-granted privileges dating prior to French authority in Morocco. The United States won protection against discriminatory taxes, but must yield on some discrimination in Moroccan courts for its nationals.

1953 **May 19.** In the second phase of *Ambatielos,* the Court directs arbitration.

August 20. The first complete draft of statute for International Criminal Court is completed by a special UN committee. No further action is taken for forty years.

November 17. In the case of the Channel Islands of Minquiers and Erechos, the Court decides an 800-year old ownership dispute in favor of Britain.

November 27. Special election is held because of the death of Judge Golunsky. Fedor I. Kozhevnikov is elected to succeed him; the new judge had just been on the UN International Law Commission; had been a law professor at Moscow State for many years; and was the author of international law works.

1954 **April 2.** Japan, though still under veto as a UN member, agrees to accept the statute of the Court.

June 15. The case of Albania's "Monetary Gold," which had been taken to Berlin, is held in non-Court arbitration among powers to be subject to British claim for Corfu unpaid reparation award. Italy takes the case to ICJ, claiming a part owed to it; the Court declines to act since Albania is not a party to litigation.

July 12. An attempted case is filed against Hungary concerning treatment of U.S. aircraft crew shot down there; USSR is also named. Filing the case is an invitation to accept jurisdiction for which United States knew there to be no legal basis. It was declined and dismissed (first of six).

July 13. Behind case titled "Effect of Awards Made by Administrative Tribunal" is rejection, somewhat, of McCarthyism in the United States. The ICJ upholds decision of a Tribunal set up by the United Nations for general review of staff dismissals, which rejected the firing by Trygvie Lie of staffers who had taken the Fifth Amendment in a congressional inquiry. The Court directs a reluctant Assembly to budget payments.

July 29. In the *Electricité de Beyrouth* case, France complains of Lebanon's treatment of a French-owned company. The case is settled.

October 7. In a regular triennial election, Judges Guerrero and Basdevant were reelected. Three new judges were elected:

- Roberto Cordova of Mexico, career foreign service officer and in 1938–1943 counselor to the embassy at Washington; attended Chapultepec Conference and other international conferences.
- Sir Hersch Lauterpacht of Britain, long a world-class international law scholar and student of the Court.
- Moreno Quintana of Argentina, lawyer, foreign affairs ministry officer, professor of international law, and faculty director.

Also elected, in special vote to replace Sir Benegal Rau, deceased, was Muhammad Zafrulla Khan of Pakistan, a jurist and religious philosopher who led every Pakistani delegation to the United Nations.

1955   **April 6.** Nottebohm was a German with substantial holdings in Guatemala who had assumed Liechtenstein nationality to avoid World War II alien property seizure. Guatemala challenged his new nationality as spurious. The Court establishes a doctrine of a need for a genuine connection to defend any new nationality, found lacking here.

June 7. (Second Namibia advisory) Rule of Assembly on voting procedure is not incompatible with a 1950 advisory defining surviving obligations under a League of Nations mandate.

1956   **June 1.** (Third Namibia advisory) General Assembly's special Committee on South-West Africa may bring to the United Nations petitioners from the Namibia territory.

October 23. In an advisory opinion review of an ILO Administrative Tribunal's review (as vested in it) of a complaint against UNESCO's firing of an employee for failure to appear before a U.S. "Loyalty/Security" Board, employee-grievants are upheld.

1957   V. K. Wellington Koo is elected to replace Hsu Mo, deceased. He holds a doctorate in international law from Columbia University, is a diplomat and scholar, and was active in League of Nations affairs and at the San Francisco conference and War Crimes Tribunal.

July 6. In the case of the *Norwegian Loans,* French claimants sought enforcement of the "gold clause" in bonds. France had copied the U.S.-conceived Connally reservation (self-judging as to whether a matter is one of domestic jurisdiction) and Norway, entitled to reciprocity, successfully invokes it as to bond liability, even though transnational. (This proves how self-defeating the U.S. Senate's idea is.) A notable opinion by Sir Hersch Lauterpacht asserts the invalidity of the reservation.

October 1. A regular triennial election results in the reelection of Judges Badawi, Koo, and Winiarski. New judges are:

- Sir Percy Spender of Australia, barrister, statesman, at the cabinet level, and ambassador to the United States; also, chair and member of various international conferences.
- Jean Spiropoulos of Greece. Professor of international law, diplomat, and member of 1945 Commission of Jurists that drafted Court Statute.

October 24. The *Switzerland v. United States* suit claims Interhandel Company was Swiss and should not have been seized as alien property. A request for interim protection is denied on a promise by the United States not to sell, pending decision, General Aniline shares.

November 26. In a case brought because of a blockade of Portuguese enclaves in the Indian subcontinent (Right of Passage), Indian objections to jurisdiction are overruled.

1958   **November 28.** Ruling in a transnational contest over guardianship of an infant, the Court interprets the Convention of 1902 on the subject and leaves custody undisturbed (*Netherlands v. Sweden*).

1959   **March 21.** Interhandel case goes to Court again on U.S. objections, including a Connally reservation claim that confiscation of possible Swiss property is a "domestic" matter. Case is dismissed on the ground that the Swiss had failed to exhaust their available U.S. remedies. Judges Lauterpacht and Spender denounce the reservation as a vitiating U.S. clause entirely.

March 24. Senator Hubert Humphrey (at President Eisenhower's initiative) introduces a resolution to repeal the Connally self-judging amendment.

May 26. Israel (and the United States and Britain) sue Bulgaria on the shooting down of Israeli aircraft, using a claim of jurisdiction on prewar, PCIJ optional clause. Court rules it was not perpetuated by the Charter because Bulgaria was out as an enemy when it was drawn.

June 20. The Court considers and settles a century-old controversy between Netherlands and Belgium over certain frontier lands. Decision is in favor of Belgium.

July 7. U.S. Department of State, discussing the various cases filed concerning the shooting down of aircraft, affirms the "well-established policy of the United States to resolve such disputes . . . in the International Court of Justice . . . the appropriate international tribunal in which such cases can be heard and decided."

August. Attorney General William P. Rogers recommends the repeal of the Connally reservation.

September 29. An election is held to replace Judge Guerrero, who died. UN bodies elect Ricardo J. Alfaro of Panama, a lawyer, former president of his country, author of many works, and a specialist on U.S. affairs.

October 10. Another invitation to litigate shooting down of aircraft is declined and the case marked off the list (USSR).

1960   **January 7.** President Eisenhower's final State of the Union message urges the repeal of the Connally self-judging reservation. If done, "I intend to urge similar acceptance of the Court's jurisdiction by every member of the United Nations."

April 13. On merits of "Right of Passage" case brought by Portugal regarding communication with enclaves in India, the Court holds (1) right of passage is sustained for private commercial and civilian traffic, (2) not for military. Later, the entire affair is rendered academic by India's seizure, ending Portuguese enclaves.

May 8. Judge Sir Hersch Lauterpacht, who left his mark as a great judge, despite a relatively short tenure, dies.

June 8. The Constitution of Maritime Safety Committee is interpreted in an advisory opinion: determination of eight largest ship-owning states is to be based on total tonnage, and nominal registry; Court rejects exclusion of "convenience" flag lands.

July 26. In a Security Council debate on the downing of the U-2 plane by the USSR, the United States proposes ICJ referral, but USSR rejects it.

November 16. Special and regular triennial elections are held, and Sir Gerald Fitzmaurice is elected after the death of Lauterpacht. He is a lecturer at The Hague Academy; author of many international law articles; and legal adviser to many U.K. international delegations and at the Foreign Ministry.

At regular election, new judges elected are:

- José Luis Bustamente of Peru, teacher of archaeology and geography before law; judge, prosecutor, and minister of justice; was in foreign service and then was engaged in various international law posts.
- Philip Caryl Jessup, longtime teacher of international law at Columbia University, with visits elsewhere; a widely active diplomat, especially at UN bodies; president of the American Society of International Law, 1954–1955, and then honorary president; author of scholarly and popular writings in transnational law.
- Vladimir Koretsky of USSR, scientist and legal scholar; professor of law at Kharkov and Tashkent; legal adviser to Soviet delegations to the UN; member PCA; editor on legal matters in Ukrainian Encyclopedia.
- Gaetano Morelli of Italy, professor of international law at various universities; delegation member to Hague conferences and various diplomatic assignments; PCA member; author.
- Kotaro Tanaka of Japan, professor of law for more than twenty years, then law dean; educator and minister of education; chief justice of the Supreme Court for ten years.

November 18. Court settles fifty-year-old controversy over an arbitration award on a boundary question given in the name of the king of Spain in 1906. The award is held unexceptionable and entirely clear (*Nicaragua v. Honduras*).

1961   **January 27.** A poll of 500 U.S. law deans and professors of international law results in a vote of 305 to repeal the Connally reservation and 5 against repeal; 194 do not reply.
March 23. The Security Council rejects a request by Cuba to refer to ICJ the legality of Punta del Este OAS "quarantine" decision.
May 26. In the first phase of a dispute between Thailand and Cambodia concerning the ownership of land on which the historic Temple of Preah Vihear is located, the Court holds it has jurisdiction despite Thailand's wish to renege on its acceptance of the optional clause.

1962   **June 15.** The case of the Temple of Preah Vihear is heard. The dispute is between Cambodia and Thailand, whose soldiers had seized land where the ancient showplace was situate. Dispute is traced back to border fixing when both nations were French-influenced or controlled; map then drawn shows that Siamese (Thais) had acquiesced. That feature controlled, and the land was awarded to Cambodia. Thai troops obey.
July 20. An advisory opinion on *Certain Expenses of United Nations* legitimizes the Assembly's actions in setting up "peacekeeping" forces, which are not specifically provided for in the UN Charter. The Court broadly construes "expenses of the organization," holds these may be assessed (though France and USSR refuse) but rules that peacekeeping—as against a collective force to halt warmaking—is voluntary.
December 21. South Africa as mandatory, in disregard of prior rulings, begins introducing apartheid into former South-West Africa (Namibia). To win judgment that Security Council can enforce (advisories hold no power) a contentious case is begun with Ethiopia and Liberia as plaintiffs (they hoped to qualify as sole former League members with a consequent interest in mandate enforcement). The Court rejects South Africa's objections to jurisdiction.

1963   **October 21.** Regular triennial election is held. Sir Gerald Fitzmaurice is reelected and Zafrulla Khan, whose previous term ended in 1961, is returned to the Court after a two-year absence. New judges are:

- Isaac Forster of Senegal, a graduate of Paris Law Faculty; general counsel, French West Africa; judge at other French colonies; secretary-general of Senegal government; and Supreme Court judge.

- André Gros of France, full professor at various universities; taught at the Hague Academy of International Law; legal adviser of Foreign Ministry; vice chair of the International Law Commission.
- Padilla Nervo of Mexico, a law graduate and later ambassador at various major embassies; permanent representative at the United Nations, 1946–1952; vice president, International Law Commission.

December 2. The case of the Northern Cameroons is heard. Kaiser's colony of Kamerun in Africa was divided into several mandates, two British and one French. After they became UN trusteeships, independence was gradually won, two in the Republic of Cameroon. The latter was not permitted to sue to protest assignment of third part to Nigeria.

1964   **July 24.** In phase one of a suit by Belgium against Spain, Barcelona Traction Company makes a claim for losses sustained by Belgian shareholders of a Canadian corporation that operated street car lines and electric utilities in Catalonia. Preliminary objections are rejected. The case is to be heard on merits and objections are held needing consideration with merits.

1965   **November 16.** On the death of Judge Badawi, Fouad Ammoun of Lebanon is elected; he earned a doctorate at Lyon, was a judge in a Lebanese Court of Appeal, and later professor of international law, legal adviser to Foreign Affairs Ministry; fifteen-year participation in UN Assembly.

1966   **July 18.** In part two of a case brought by Ethiopia and Liberia to test South Africa's mandate violation, the Court rejects earlier 1962 decision that the Court had jurisdiction under the mandate as treaty with League members (8–7); after two membership changes, the Court rules by tie (with tiebreaker second vote by President Spender) that the nations suing lack standing to receive a verdict, if any.

October 27. Reflecting wave of anger and disappointment with the Court's July 18 decision, the UN General Assembly votes 114 to 2 that South Africa has broken the mandate and it is ended.

November 2–3. Regular triennial election of judges is held. Only Ammoun is reelected. New judges are:

- Cesar Bengzon of the Philippines, lawyer, appeals and then Supreme Court judge; dean and law professor; one-time representative to the UN General Assembly.
- Manfred Lachs of Poland, a law graduate and doctor of laws at Nancy (France) and Moscow; chair of the UN Subcommittee on Outer Space Law; PCA ; chair Sixth (Legal) Committee of UN General Assembly IV, VI, and X; Curatorium, Hague.
- Charles Onyeama of Nigeria, London legal education, Lincoln's Inn, barrister-at-law; Chief Magistrate of Supreme Court of Nigeria.
- Sture Petren of Sweden, lawyer and appeals judge; director of the legal department of Foreign Affairs Ministry; member and president, European Commission on Human Rights; member PCA; arbitrator in case between France and Spain; author.

1969   **February 20.** North Sea Continental Shelf case is really two: one between West Germany and Netherlands, the other between Germany and Denmark, asking Court in each case for principles to apply; parties promised to apply details. The Court answers that uniform equidistance rule must be varied equitably when concave coast adjoins a convex, where straight-line equidistance would have an unfair result.

October 27. Five new judges are elected:

- Federico de Castro of Spain, doctor of literature, philosophy, and laws; professor

at various universities; editor of Spanish international law text; author and leader of Spanish delegation to Law of Treaties.
- Hardy Dillard, professor and dean, Virginia Law School, University of Virginia, and West Point; lecturer at the Hague Academy of International Law.
- Louis Ignacio-Pinto of Dahomey, advocate at the Paris Court of Appeal; senator from Dahomey to France; ambassador to the United States and elsewhere; president of the Supreme Court; member of a great number of UN bodies, including ILC and Reorganization of Secretariat.
- Platon D. Morozov of USSR, Leningrad Legal Institute; counsel in Tokyo War Crimes trials; deputy director of legal affairs, Foreign Ministry; various UN and diplomatic posts.
- Eduardo Jimenez de Arechaga of Uruguay. Professor, diplomat lecturer at the Hague Academy; officer of UN Secretariat for Security Council affairs.

1970   **February 5.** Final decision in Barcelona Traction case is dismissal: Belgium cannot bring suit for losses to its nationals, shareholders in a Canadian corporation made worthless by post-Franco Spanish government acts. Only Canada could have brought the case. Judicial opinion is rich in statements on international human rights.
September. Secretary of State William P. Rogers calls for greater use of the Court (as it suffers from loss of respect and caseload after second South Africa decision).
October 24. UN General Assembly, in an important and oft-cited "Declaration on Principles of International Law Concerning Friendly Relations among States," endorses judicial settlement as valuable.

1971   **June 21.** In the fourth and final advisory on the status of former mandate (by then officially called by ancient African name, Namibia), the Court rules that the mandate was lawfully terminated by the United Nations as South Africa had broken treaty obligations to the League and people of Namibia; its continued presence there (troops and administrators) is illegal. All UN members must recognize this illegal status and decline to aid or participate.
September 15. As U.S. Ambassador to United Nations, George H. W. Bush, in one of the responses to a secretary-general's questionnaire on Court, replies, "The United States firmly believes that a strong and active international Court is a central and indispensable element of an international legal order."

1972   **April 17.** The sitting of the Court marks the fiftieth anniversary of the International Judicial System, as dated from the first sitting of the Permanent Court of International Justice.
May 10. In first revision of the Rules of Procedure, Court directs more expeditious handling of preliminary objections, and permits more frequent use of chambers (panels of less than the full Court) and expedited action on advisories.
August 17. The first of several appearances in Icelandic fisheries cases, one each with Great Britain and West Germany, results from a unilateral extension of fishing zone beyond limits agreed on. Interim measures are granted by the Court, ignored by Iceland.
August 18. Court rules in favor of Pakistan's referral to the Council of the International Civil Aviation Organization of a complaint against India's exclusion of Pak overflights for peaceful passage, in reprisal for the hijacking of an Indian aircraft.
October 30. Forster and Gros are reelected at regular triennial vote. New judges are:

- José María Ruda of Argentina University of Buenos Aires faculty; master of laws (international law, New York University); various international law associations; Hague Academy lecturer; Sixth (Legal) Committee, United Nations; International Law Commission.
- Nagendra Singh of India, professor of international law at various universities;

cabinet official; delegate, General Assembly; vice chair of International Law Commission; PCA; Law of Sea Conferences.
* Sir Humphrey Waldock of Great Britain, professor of public international law, Oxford; counsel at ICJ for United Kingdom, India, Spain, Denmark, and Netherlands; PCA; judge and president, European Court of Human Rights.

December 15. Case is brought by Pakistan to complain of India's threat to send prisoners who fought against its secession to the newly independent Bangladesh. It results in a settlement.

1973 **February 2.** In two Icelandic fisheries cases, jurisdiction is upheld by the Court, Iceland not participating.

June 22. Australia and New Zealand file under optional clause to challenge legality of France's use of South Pacific waters for nuclear testing. The Court, voting 8 to 6, grants an order to temporarily restrain testing. France declines to participate but schedules no tests beyond those already planned; revokes future optional clause consent.

July 12. In Iceland fisheries jurisdiction cases, the Court continues Aug 17, 1972, interim measures, but declares they do not exclude an interim arrangement that may be agreed upon by the parties.

July 12. Administrative tribunal's rejection of an appeal of one Fasla, protesting nonrenewal of employment contract, is sustained.

1974 **July 25.** Final decision made in Iceland fishing case. Court notes that progress in case has been parallel with changing attitudes toward exclusive coastal states limits, but they have not hardened in law and so Iceland must be restrained; the parties are directed to negotiate nevertheless.

December 2. Court, on the basis that France in nuclear test cases issued notices that it was discontinuing testing, treats that as a basis for dismissing the case, as binding agreement not to resume, thereby eliminating "object" of the litigation.

1975 **October 16.** An advisory opinion is sought by the General Assembly in the case of Spain's relationship to Western Sahara colony. Questions as framed by the Assembly about precolonial history are bypassed as the Court works on the basis that self-determination in the present is more important than fragmentary historical ties of the past.

November 17. Judge Lachs is reelected and four new judges are elected at regular triennial:

* Taslim Olewale Elias of Nigeria, professor of law at various universities including Lagos, and dean; attorney general of Nigeria and chief justice of Supreme Court; participant in various international law associations; author.
* Shigeru Oda of Japan, professor of international law, Tohoku University; delegate at several Law of the Sea conferences; counsel for Germany in North Sea shelf cases.
* Hermann Mosler of Germany, professor of public law, Frankfurt and Heidelberg; director of Max Planck Institute; member PCA; judge of European Court of Human Rights; lecturer at the Hague Academy.
* Salah Tarazi of Syria, French school of law at Beirut; associate professor of law at Damascus University; Hague lecturer; secretary-general, Ministry of Foreign Affairs; ambassador and various UN posts.

1976 **April 12.** A Court resolution on its judicial practice covers times for meeting/conferring concerning arguments; questioning counsel; president's role in formulation of issues; and mode of opinion writing, including drafting committee.

September 11. In a case between Greece and Turkey about their common continental shelf, Greece asks for demarcation, Turkey denies the basis for jurisdiction.

Pending a hearing, Greece asks for an order of provisional protection against various activities. The Court denies, on ground there's no evidence there will be irreparable loss.

1978   **April 12.** Revised and simplified rules of the Court are adopted, completing a process that began in 1972. Special attention is given to reducing litigation costs, with so many new, smaller states as possible litigants.

October 31. Regular triennial election is held. Judge Morozov is reelected. New judges are:

- Richard R. Baxter of the United States; was with JAG in military; attended Harvard Law and Cambridge to study international law with Lauterpacht; was international law professor at Harvard; president ASIL; editor *American Journal of International Law*; Department of State consultant.
- Roberto Ago of Italy, chairman of Hague Academy Curatorium; professor of international law at several universities; member and chair of International Law Commission; PCA.
- Abdullah El-Erian of Egypt, faculty of law at Cairo University, doctorate in international law at Columbia University; professor and legal officer, Ministry.
- José Sette-Camara of Brazil, diplomat and ambassador to major states; permanent representative, UN; member International Law Commission; chair of UN Conference on State Representation.

December 19. Aegean Sea Continental shelf (*Greece v. Turkey*) case is dismissed for lack of jurisdiction. It is excluded from 1928 General Act by Greek reservation; Turkey's oral offer is not sufficient in nature.

1979   **March 7.** New staff regulations are adopted by the Court that reaffirm the status of Court personnel as international civil servants.

October 17. Court President Elias appoints an impartial arbitrator to serve in a dispute between Kuwait and an oil company.

December 15. United States appeals to Court, charging Iran with international law violation due to its complicity in the seizure by so-called militant students of U.S. personnel. A provisional measure unanimously orders their release and the restoration of the embassy and consulates to the United States. Parties are directed to take no action that may aggravate tension.

1980   **April 24.** U.S. helicopter-borne armed contingent enters Iran in an effort to free hostages forcibly. Attack fails.

May 24. The Court unanimously directs release of hostages and the return of the embassy and other U.S. property. Also orders, by vote of 12 to 3, the payment of reparations by Iran. (One dissenter, Morozov, is moved by unlawful action by the United States, including forcible rescue attempt.)

December 20. Advisory opinion requested by the Assembly raises questions about removal or transfer of the World Health Organization office from Egypt. The Court clarifies and defines the notice and other obligations that should have preceded transfer.

1981   **January 15.** Judges Baxter and Tarazi have died within a few days of each other. Both elections are held this day. New judges are:

- Abdallah F. El-Khani of Syria, lawyer and graduate of the American University of Beirut, lecturer at Syrian University School of Law; holder of various diplomatic and ministry offices; and UN representative.
- Stephen M. Schwebel of the United States, professor of international law at Harvard University, Johns Hopkins School of International Studies, and Hague Acad-

emy; assistant legal adviser, State Department; four years on International Law Commission; other UN posts.

January 20. After prolonged negotiations in Algiers, with host nation's good offices, all Teheran hostages are released within hours of the inauguration of U.S. President Reagan.

April 6. Completion of negotiations between the United States and Iran, as a result of which pending ICJ case for reparations for the hostage-taking is dropped by the United States as part of a comprehensive agreement to create a new Iran-U.S. Claims Tribunal, to be conducted at The Hague. The tribunal is charged to settle many questions between the United States and Iran resulting from a revolution that overthrew the shah and the events following.

April 14. In a pending litigation concerning the continental shelf division between Tunisia and Libya, Malta's request to intervene and take part is denied. Malta had not shown "an interest of a legal nature" that might be affected, the Court says.

November 5. Regular triennial election is held. Judges Singh and Ruda are reelected. New judges are:

- Sir Robert Jennings of the United Kingdom, a Whewell professor of international law; sometime president of Jesus College, Cambridge; counsel in important international litigations; special counsel to a number of states; member PCA; and eight-year editor of the *British Yearbook*.
- Guy Ladreit de Lacharrière of France, who held various diplomatic posts; taught law at the University of Paris and at Hague Academy; author of numerous works on international law; head of French delegation to third UN Law of the Sea Conference; participant in international arbitrations.
- Keba Mbaye of Senegal, eighteen-year president of Supreme Court of Senegal; lecturer in law at University of Dakar and Senegal; member of various UN bodies; member PCA; and legal author.

1982   **January 20.** Using right under rules, Canada and the United States have agreed in pending Gulf of Maine dispute submitted to Court to have the case heard by a panel ("Chamber") of five judges. The Court votes to approve a procedure wherein the parties select (rather than the Court genuinely and freely elect) the judges to compose the Chamber. Two judges, Morozov and El-Khani, dissent, objecting to an interference with Court's independence.

February 24. In Libya–Tunisia continental shelf dispute, the Court responds to a request jointly made by parties to give guidance about international law principles and rules to be applied to divide the offshore area in which some oil rights had already been granted. The Court does so, specifying the equitable principles to be applied based on geological evidence.

March 19. In a special election held because of the death of Judge El-Erian, Mohammed Bedjaoui of Algeria is elected. He holds a doctorate of laws at Grenoble (France), is an avocat at Court of Appeal there, and was legal adviser to Provisional government during the independence struggle; dean of faculty of law at University of Algiers, minister of justice; ambassador and eight-year permanent representative to UN Law of the Sea Conference.

July 20. On application to review action of UN Administrative Tribunal, the Court holds (in case of one Mortished) no error was made.

December 17. U.S. House of Representatives adopts a resolution, based on hearings, to support the expansion of Court's advisory role.

1983   **July 6.** Court President Elias appoints former president of French Cour de Cassation as arbitrator to act in a dispute between Libya and Mobil Oil Company.

October 14. African states of Upper Volta (later Burkina Faso) and Mali check a border conflict by agreeing to submit to the Court the drawing of a frontier.

1984   **March 21.** In the *Libya v. Malta* case on continental shelf, Italy makes an application to intervene, which is denied.

April 6. U.S. Secretary of State George Shultz (without prior notice as promised in Truman acceptance) files paper, the terms of which exclude from U.S. commitment to consent to suit in any Central American case for two years.

April 9. Nicaragua suit under optional clause against United States (presumably on the way April 6) alleges various forms of aid to contra forces.

April 12. Annual meeting of the American Society of International Law "deplores and strongly favors rescission of" Shultz's action of April 6.

May 10. In the Nicaragua case the Court holds unanimously there is sufficient probability of jurisdiction to justify provisional measures (temporary injunction) against laying mines in Nicaragua harbor; the Court votes 14 to 1 (Judge Schwebel dissenting) against any U.S. intervention against Nicaragua.

October 4. Court votes 14 to 1 against permitting intervention by El Salvador in the Nicaragua case at the jurisdictional phase; nevertheless six judges dissent from denying hearing on the same.

October 12. Chamber of Court in case between United States and Canada draws maritime boundaries in Gulf of Maine.

November 7. Regular triennial election is held. Judges Lachs, Elias, and Oda are reelected. New judges are:

- Jens Evensen of Norway, director general of legal department, Ministry of Foreign Affairs; ambassador for trade agreement, European Communities; minister for Law of the Sea; and counsel in major ICJ cases.
- Ni Zhengyu of China (first from People's Republic, after some delay since recognition at UN), juris doctor, Stanford University; lecturer on public international law and other subjects at Soochow University and others; dean of law faculty at Soochow; legal counsel Ministry of Foreign Affairs; member of International Law Commission.

November 26. Court in Nicaragua case holds that it does have jurisdiction, as contested by United States, under both the optional clause and Treaty of Friendship; some judges dissent from each; Judge Schwebel dissents from both.

1985   **January 18.** U.S. State Department sharply criticizes the Court decision of November 26, 1984, holding the Court has jurisdiction, and announces it will not appear in merits phase of the case to defend U.S. conduct. The State Department claims the Court is "determined" to rule for Nicaragua and that defense evidence is too "sensitive" to show to the Court with two "Warsaw Pact" judges. State Department predicts change in acceptance of compulsory jurisdiction generally.

May 13. Pope John Paul II, in visit to the Court, praises it and urges "wider" acceptance of compulsory jurisdiction via the optional clause, just as the United States threatens to drop it.

June 3. The Court renders its decision in the continental shelf dispute between Libya and Malta. While dissents reflect possible infirmities in the method used (including Judge Schwebel's suggestion that the Court, though denying Italy's intervention attempt, seemed to grant what Italy sought). Despite this, Libya and other Mediterranean adversaries, in these contests about oil resources, strictly comply with the decision.

October 7. Secretary Shultz, this time giving the six-months' notice, terminates the

Truman declaration that had given consent to suit generally under optional clause, and says the United States will accept Court "whenever appropriate."

Companion statement announces agreement with Italy to submit U.S. claims for losses by Raytheon subsidiary to a Chamber of the Court ("ELSI case").

October 30. Most witnesses at a House hearing on H.Res. 208 deplore U.S. decision to withdraw; Representative James Leach of Iowa says it is "deeply troubling for a society committed to the rule of law."

December 9. In special election after the resignation of Judge Morozov, the sole candidate, Nikolai K. Tarassov of USSR, is elected. He is a consultant to the legal department of the Supreme Soviet; head of department, Foreign Affairs Ministry; representative to various UN bodies; frequent General Assembly delegate; and member of the International Civil Service Advisory Board.

December 10. On application by Tunisia for revision and/or clarification of February 24, 1982, shelf judgment, the Court grants clarification, but denies revision. The first woman judge appears: Suzanne Bastid of France, ad hoc jurist for Tunisia.

1986   **January 10.** The Chamber considering a case presenting the border dispute between Burkina Faso and Mali orders provisional measure that directs a cease-fire and withdrawal of troops to end an outbreak of violence. Both states comply with the Court order.

April 29. The fortieth anniversary of first ICJ sitting is marked, with a greeting from the Security Council: "There [can] be no peace without respect for law."

June 27. Lengthy opinion is delivered on the merits of the case of *Nicaragua v. United States*. U.S. training, financing, and supplying of contras violates international law, the Court votes, 12 to 3. The Court also decides the embargo as imposed violates Treaty of Friendship, Commerce, and Amity (14 to 1), U.S. sustained in objections to consideration of violations of multilateral treaties (11 to 4), and in objection to immediate consideration and computation of reparations to be awarded, a question is deferred to a later date, if parties cannot agree, after negotiating.

July 31. In first veto by a party to a case of Security Council enforcement of a Court judgment, the United States votes "no" at the Council on enforcement of Nicaragua judgment.

November 3. General Assembly, by vote of 94 to 3 (47 abstaining), "urgently calls" for U.S. compliance with Nicaragua ruling.

December 11. El Salvador and Honduras agree that the Court should decide land and sea dispute between them and ask for a Chamber of the Court to be constituted to act.

December 22. Court's Chamber in Burkina Faso–Mali case gives its decision on what the disputed border should be.

1987   **January 10.** Mali and Burkina Faso both agree to respect and to obey the Court's decision and thank the Chamber for its ruling.

March 2. The Court grants the United States and Italy joint request for the formation of a Chamber in Raytheon (ELSI) claims case.

May 8. A Chamber is granted in Honduras–El Salvador case.

May 27. A review, via an advisory opinion, of the decision of the UN Administrative Tribunal in Yakimetz case is held. Tribunal is upheld.

September 14. After death of Judge de Lacharrière, a special election is held, at which the only candidate is Gilbert Guillaume of France, who is elected. He is a professor at various institutions and lecturer at the Institute of Advanced International Studies; member PCA; designated arbitrator ICAO; director legal affairs, Foreign Affairs Ministry; delegate to General Assembly; heads the French group at Law of the Sea.

September 18. In a historic reversal of Soviet policy, President Gorbachev declares the compulsory jurisdiction of the Court should be accepted by all states on a mutually agreeable basis.

November 11. Regular triennial election of judges is held, with reelection of Judges Ago, Bedjaoui, Schwebel, and Tarassov. The new judge elected is Mohamed Shahabuddeen of Guyana, who holds various London University degrees; public service as Crown counsel, solicitor general, attorney general, and minister of justice; acting foreign minister from time to time; a participant in numerous international conferences; and author of various books and articles.

November 12. UN General Assembly, in the second of four annual overwhelming votes, calls on the United States to comply with the Court ruling in Nicaragua case.

November 18. Court fixes time for submissions on future steps in Nicaragua case, the hearing on and evidence on the reparations to be awarded. United States does not appear in Court.

1988   **April 26.** To meet a crisis expected as a result of the U.S. antiterrorism law that seems to require a violation of the "host country" headquarters agreement to permit observers recognized by the United Nations to be there, the Assembly asks the Court for an advisory opinion as to the U.S. obligation to arbitrate in case of dispute with the United Nations. The Court rules that the United States must submit to arbitration the question whether the law purporting to close the PLO observer mission violates the headquarters agreement.

June 29. U.S. District Judge Edmund Palmieri rejects and dismisses suit by the United States aimed to force the closing of the PLO office at the United Nations. He holds it is not the intent of Congress to require this. The arbitration demand upheld by the April 26 advisory opinion is thereby rendered academic.

September 6. UN Secretary-General Perez de Cuellar, speaking at The Hague ceremony on seventy-fifth anniversary of Carnegie's Peace Palace, describes as "a development which gives rise to considerable concern" decision by any state not "to take part in the Court's proceedings or to ignore its decisions."

October 14. In case in which U.S. citizen groups sought domestic court enforcement remedy for the U.S. violation of international law by nonconformity with ICJ Nicaragua decision, the District of Columbia U.S. Appeals Court holds the character of violation is insufficient to give plaintiffs "standing" to sue, but rejects previous judicially invented "political question" exclusion of such cases.

November. For the third time, the annual UN General Assembly calls on the U.S. government to comply with the Court rulings in the Nicaragua case.

December 20. In case brought by Nicaragua against Honduras on charges of latter's aid and support for the contra war, the Court holds the Latin American pact of Bogota supports the claim of compulsory jurisdiction.

1989   **February 10.** Presidium of Supreme Soviet of USSR directs the withdrawal of previously made reservations to compulsory jurisdiction of the ICJ in cases charging the violations of human rights treaties; genocide, women's rights, racial discrimination, and torture.

April 18. The United Nations elects a new judge, R. S. Pathak, to replace President Nagendra Singh, who died December 11, 1988. He is a participant in numerous international conferences, editor in chief of the *Indian Journal of International Law,* and was India's chief justice.

May 17. Iran, claiming jurisdiction under treaties/conventions for civil aviation safety protection, brings suit against the United States for damages in the shooting down of its airliner by the U.S. warship *Vincennes* on July 3, 1988.

May 22. South Pacific islet of Nauru—a former German colony, then an Australian trusteeship under the League and United Nations—having recently gained independence, sues Australia at ICJ for exploitative neglect and abuse of its prime resource: phosphate deposits.

July 20. A Court panel (Chamber) is chosen to hear and decide U.S. claims against Italy in Elettronica Sicula (ELSI) and issues a decision. The Court's essential holding (U.S. citizen Schwebel agreeing with much reasoning but not on some facts) is that Raytheon Corp., owner of local ELSI, because feasibility of an orderly liquidation of a losing business had not been proved, could not claim injury that was compensable under the treaty for possibly wrongful local governmental acts.

November 1. Declaring "the judgments of the International Court of Justice . . . represent the world's most authoritative pronouncement on international law," and that some UN members "cannot proceed [there] because of lack of legal expertise or funds," the UN secretary-general announces the creation of a trust fund, to be financed by voluntary contributions, "to provide a practical means of overcoming financial obstacles" to judicial settlement of disputes by the Court.

November 17. UN General Assembly declares 1990–1999 United Nations Decade of International Law, to promote acceptance of international law, and specifically to enhance a "resort to and full respect for the International Court of Justice."

December 15. The UN Economic and Social Council requests an advisory opinion as to the deprivation of rights of a UN expert of Romanian nationality, concealed by his country behind lies about his health. Despite objections by Ceauşescu's Romania, the Court affirms applicability to D. Mazilu of the Convention on Privileges and Immunities of the United Nations.

1990   **February 28.** In a case pending between El Salvador and Honduras over a variety of maritime, island, and border questions, (already referred by agreement to a Chamber of five of the Court's judges), their neighbor Nicaragua makes an application to intervene as a contesting party with regard to its interest in the maritime aspects of the case. The full Court is presented with the application and rules that the application must be referred to the already-constituted Chamber. Three judges dissent.

March 22. Guinea-Bissau, in a case already pending, files to challenge the validity of earlier arbitration award fixing its maritime boundary with Senegal; Court denies application for provisional measure to restrain activities (by Senegalese Navy) in disputed area.

June 22. In Nicaragua case against United States, seeking reparations for law violations as held by Court, the case is called for a hearing after Nicaragua's memorial (brief and calculation of claims) is filed and the United States fails to respond. (Chamorro had been recently elected over Ortega.) Nicaragua's new agent reports his government is studying the "very complex" case and it is inconvenient to make decision what to do. Case is postponed.

September 15. Chamber hearing Honduras–El Salvador case grants (over objection) Nicaragua's request to intervene as party-litigant. Nicaragua is limited to the portion of case dealing with sea regime. The case is said to represent a milestone as the first case in the Court's history where such intervention was granted. Only because parties were already in Court would Nicaragua have jurisdiction.

September 25. Poland consents to optional clause jurisdiction.

October 29. Spain consents to optional clause jurisdiction.

November 20. In regular triennial elections, Judges Jennings and Guillaume are reelected. New judges are:

- Andres Aguilar-Mawdsley of Venezuela, a law school dean, justice minister, and international jurist.
- Raymond Ranjeva of Madagascar, university rector, law dean, diplomat in many capacities, and member, among others, in American Society of International Law.

- Christopher G. Weeramantry of Sri Lanka, justice of the Supreme Court, law professor, and participant in numerous UN affairs.

1991   **February 7.** Sir Robert Jennings is elected president and Shigeru Oda vice president of the Court.

February 22. Portugal brings suit against Australia, asserting her rights as "administrator" (former colonial ruler of a people to whom she had not fully granted independence when island was invaded and occupied by Indonesia) were violated when Australia made a treaty with Indonesia about "Timor Gap" oil exploitation. The principal purpose asserted in Portuguese pleading: to enforce the rights of the people of East Timor to self-determination.

July 29. In a case filed earlier this year, Finland sued Denmark to stop construction of a fixed bridge across the "Great Belt," a channel of water within Danish islands but a natural channel to which all states had peacetime rights of navigation. Finland claims the bridge would obstruct its shipping of oil rigs for offshore drilling. Court denies application for provisional order to stop construction that would impede passage, pending litigation, because Denmark asserts that the part of the bridge that would obstruct won't be built till end of 1994, and Denmark will join the effort to conclude the case before then.

August 14. Taslim O. Elias, Court president 1981–1985 and vice President 1979–1981, dies while there is in preparation a two-volume "Festschrift" (a collection of essays in tribute to his scholarship and character) by many colleagues around the world, including fellow judges, UN officials, and noted Canadian, British, and U.S. scholars of international law.

September 26. Nicaragua's agent at the Court, reporting on U.S. and Nicaragua "agreements aimed at enhancing Nicaragua's economic, commercial, and technical development to the maximum extent possible," requests discontinuance of the case in order to effect termination of proceedings to calculate amount of reparations that are due. U.S. letter, while continuing to deny jurisdiction, does not contradict the assertion that there are "agreements." Case is removed from list.

November 12. Court rules on the merits of Guinea-Bissau's challenge to the arbitration award that had been rendered regarding her maritime boundaries with Senegal. The multiple grounds of challenge are denied.

December 5. Nigerian Prince Bola A. Abijola is elected a member of Court in place of Judge Elias. Abijola was a bencher of Lincoln's Inn; past president of Nigerian Bar Association and of Association of Arbitrators; attorney general; member of PCA.

1992   **March 3.** Libya offers to submit to judicial determination its obligations regarding Lockerbie air crash (PanAm Flight 103) under Montreal Convention for Suppression of Unlawful Acts against the Safety of Civil Aviation, asking among other things that the United States and United Kingdom cease and desist from force or threats against Libya. On same day it asks the Court for provisional measure to enjoin action against Libya to coerce or compel the surrender of accused individuals, pending judicial action.

March 26–28. Court Vice President Oda presides in Libya case hearing on provisional measures, in view of President Jennings's British nationality.

March 31. Three days after the close of the Court hearing on Libya's application, Security Council adopts Resolution No. 748, "determining" that the failure of Libya to respond to a request in a prior resolution is a "threat to international peace and security." Sanctions are to be imposed on Libya if she does not comply, "notwithstanding the existence of any right [under] any international agreement."

April 14. The Court, in twin decisions in cases of Libya against United Kingdom and United States, declines the provisional measure requested. Five judges dissent. Denial is stated to be solely on the ground that Resolution No. 748, adopted after the

Court hearing, prevails under Charter Section 103 (obligations under the Charter prevail over any conflicting agreement). The Court majority declares "the right of the parties to contest issues [of fact and law] must remain unaffected" by denial. (Question of a Court review of the Council's action is avoided.)

May 27. In case of *Nicaragua v. Honduras,* long held in suspense by Nicaragua's consent to indefinite delay in the filing of Honduras's counter memorial, the case is discontinued by consent of the parties.

June 24. Time limits of extended duration are set for merits case of *Libya v. United States and United Kingdom* (December 20, 1993 and June 20, 1995).

June 26. In case of *Nauru v. Australia,* the Court rejects the preliminary objections of Australia to the exercise of jurisdiction or to the admissibility of the case. The objections of waiver, loss of right to sue when the trusteeship was terminated or delayed were all overruled by votes of 12 to 1, with Judge Oda dissenting. The ground of objection based on the absence from suit of United Kingdom and New Zealand won additional dissents from President Jennings, Judge Ago, and Judge Schwebel. The Court held in favor of Australia on a separate claim against the British Phosphate Commissioners' assets.

September 11. In the multiple-issue case of El Salvador–Honduras, with Nicaragua intervening, the Chamber of the Court render its decision. The issues involved and dealt with separately include several specific portions of the land boundary between Honduras and El Salvador; the ownership of a number of different islands in the Gulf of Fonseca; and the legal status of the Gulf of Fonseca, the last as being held jointly by the three parties except for a belt around the coast, three miles wide, assigned to the respective adjoining state. In this instance, the ICJ gave respect to and used as a guide the 1917 decision of the Central American Court of the Justice (see March 9, 1917) that resulted in Nicaragua, then U.S.-controlled, casting veto against continuance of Central American Court.

Finland announces a settlement of the case concerning the Danish construction of a bridge over the "Great Belt" waterway, and the case is discontinued.

October 9. A new case is filed by Guinea-Bissau against Senegal that presents issues left open by the arbitration award that the Court declined to upset, as result of meetings of the parties with the Court president and information about possible settlement. Time for pleadings is postponed indefinitely.

November 2. Iran files a new case against United States, claiming a naval attack/destruction of offshore oil platforms in the Gulf (in October 1987 and April 1988) violated Treaty of Amity.

1993   **January 14.** Court announces with regret the death of longest-serving judge, Manfred Lachs, who played an important role in history of Court as judge and president.

March 20. Bosnia/Herzegovina brings case charging genocide against Yugoslavia (Serbia and Montenegro) and other violations of human rights and aggression. The Genocide Treaty provides for compulsory jurisdiction among parties. It also asks the Security Council to initiate an arms embargo so as not to impair self-defense right.

April 8. In a decision on Bosnia and Herzegovina's application for provisional measures, Yugoslavia is directed "to take all measures within its power to prevent commission of the crime of genocide." The Court limits itself to acting on genocide issues, and also holds, Judge Tarassov dissenting, that "Yugoslavia" should in particular assure that . . . armed units which may be directed or supported by it," do not commit genocide.

May 10. Geza Herczegh of Hungary is elected to the seat left vacant by the death of Manfred Lachs. He was dean of faculty of the University of Pecs; judge of Hungary's Constitutional Court; head of international law faculty at Pecs for twenty-three years; and is a recognized expert on international humanitarian law.

June 14. In the case between Denmark and Norway, delimitation lines for continental shelf and fishing zones in the open sea between Greenland and Jan Mayen Island are fixed. Norway's interpretation of the existing agreements is rejected. The disparity of coastal lengths of big Greenland and little Jan Mayen is taken into consideration, but not so much as to be inequitable to the interests of the much smaller island.
July 5. A new case filed by Hungary and Slovakia (Gabcikovo-Nagymaros Project) concerns the objections of the former to the diversion of waters of the Danube. An intersecting aspect: The dispute arose between Czech-and-Slovak Republic and Hungary but there was no basis for Court jurisdiction, absent a treaty or mutual optional clause acceptance. After Slovakia and Bohemia separate, Slovakia—where the diversion took place—accepts an invitation previously filed with the Court by Hungary and the case is accepted by Court.
July 19. The Court, which has long had the authority to designate chambers for "particular categories of cases; for example labor cases and cases relating to transit and communications," announces the formation of a Chamber for Environmental Matters. The announcement notes that the Court now has eleven cases on its docket of which two, Nauru/Australia and Hungary/Slovakia, have implications for international law on matters that relate to the environment. Note that the Court's reference to the number of cases it has, the first ever in routine communiqués of the Court, points to the fact celebrated in an article by Keith Highet and two letters in the *American Journal of International Law* that the Court for several years has been extremely busy, far more so than ever in its history.
July 28. As a follow-up to an earlier uncomplied-with order indicating provisional remedies, Bosnia applies for wide relief, including the lifting of an arms embargo; Yugoslavia files it own application on August 11; a hearing in both is held August 25–26.
August 26. World Health Organization (WHO) a UN-affiliated body, authorized to ask Court for an advisory opinion as a partial culmination to antinuclear groups' "World Court Project," files for advice: "In view of the health and environmental effects would the use of nuclear weapons by a State in war or other armed conflict be a breach of its obligations under International Law, including the WHO Charter?"
September 13. In a decision and order by the Court in the second round of the Bosnia case, the Court denies further legal order but warns, "The present perilous situation demands, not an indication of provisional measures additional to those indicated by the Court's order of April 8, but immediate and effective implementation of those measures." The broader Bosnian claims for relief were denied as not within the authority conferred on the Court by the Genocide Convention.
September 13. An order is entered noting and approving the settlement of the case of Nauru against Australia by agreement reached out-of-court by the parties.
November 11. The regular triennial election of judges results in the reelection of Judges Oda and Herczegh, and the election of three new judges:

- Shi Jiuyong of China, master of laws in international law at Columbia University, university lecturer in China; author of articles in various periodicals; legal adviser to and member of various international bodies, and delegations for People's Republic; a member of the UN International Law Commission for years.
- Carl August Fleischhauer of Germany, Fulbright scholar at University of Chicago; legal education at Heidelberg; much diplomatic service to Federal Republic and head of international law section of Foreign Office, member of various law-connected Foreign Service delegations since 1983, has been UN under-secretary-general for legal affairs.
- Abdul G. Koroma of Sierra Leone, barrister at Lincoln's Inn; legal adviser and diplomatic representative to United Nations for Sierra Leone, had been ambas-

sador to several European countries; member of a legal committee of UN General Assembly for many years.

December 13. As a sequel to provisional Oslo peace plan for PLO and Israel; Chairman Arafat, as part of visit to Netherlands, pays a courtesy call on the Peace Palace and is received by Vice President Judge Oda and other judges.

1994   **January 27.** In a case concerning oil platforms that were bombed by the United States in the Persian Gulf, the United States files formal objections to jurisdiction, and proceedings are suspended for separate adjudication. Time limits are fixed for briefing.

February 3. In case of *Libyan Arab Jamahiriya v. Chad* for the settlement of a border dispute (which had led to hostilities that were terminated on submission to the Court), the judgment of the Court is announced. The judgment finds, by 16 to 1 (only dissenter is an ad hoc judge) that the correct line of boundary is as established by a treaty between France (as colonial possessor of Chad) and the republic's predecessor, United Kingdom of Libya. The parties quietly comply.

February 7. Officers are elected for the new triennial term: president to be Mohammed Bedjaoui, an Algerian national educated in France; vice president, U.S. jurist and former State Department aide, Stephen M. Schwebel.

February 16. Eduardo Valentia-Ospina is reelected as registrar; Jean-Jacques Arnaldez is elected as deputy registrar.

March 11 Hearings conclude in litigation between Qatar and Bahrain in a contest over oil land borders.

March 14. Chamber of Court for Environmental Matters is redesignated, with Fleischhauer replacing Evenson.

March 21. Yugoslavia, unable to sue for lack of optional clause arrangement, challenges NATO powers to defend in Court, as if they were subject to jurisdiction; Yugoslavia alleges illegal threats of force.

March 30. Republic of Cameroon brings a case against Nigeria. The issue to be settled is the border on Bakassi Peninsula. Each agrees to compulsory jurisdiction.

June 6. Cameroon amends and extends application to bring in the status of all territory from Lake Chad to the sea.

June 22. The Court's president fixes time limits for filing written statements in the advisory opinion case concerning legality of the use of nuclear weapons; all submissions to close June 20, 1995.

July 1. Decision is made on jurisdiction, dependent on interpretation of documents on submission of the dispute between Qatar and Bahrain. Parties held to have agreed to submit the entire controversy. The case deals with sovereignty over oil-rich islands and shoals.

July 8. Former (1988–1991) Court President José Maria Ruda, who had been the ad hoc judge selected by Qatar, dies.

August 11. Public hearing in the case of *Iran v. United States,* scheduled for September 12 (concerning shootdown of passenger plane), is postponed indefinitely without explanation.

September 28. Nikolai Tarassov, a member of Court since 1985, dies in office.

December 15. UN General Assembly, responsive to several years of effort by the so-called World Court Project, adopts a resolution for an additional advisory opinion case as to the legality of the threat or use of nuclear weapons. "Threat" is added.

1995   **January 17.** In case of *Hungary v. Slovakia,* concerning a dam blocking the Danube, the president fixes time for filing briefs after a conference with the parties.

January 18. Case concerning East Timor (*Portugal v. Australia*) is scheduled for a hearing on January 30, 1996.

January 26. UN General Assembly and Security Council elect a successor to Tarassov: V. S. Vereshchetin, chief, since 1981, of International Law Department, Russian Academy, and chair, since May 1994, of the UN International Law Commission; active in domestic and international law societies; former professor of international law and guest professor at the University of Akron; author of numerous publications.

February 2. Court order fixes time limits (final date September 20) for briefs in the advisory case on the Legality of Threat or Use of Nuclear Weapons.

February 15. In the case of Qatar and Bahrain, on border dispute concerning oil-rich lands, the Court votes, 10 to 5, for further decision on jurisdiction and admissibility.

February 24. Judge Roberto Ago dies.

March 28. Spain initiates a case against Canada after incidents in which Canadian vessels attack a Spanish fishing craft on the high seas; the use of force, which gained media attention to the dispute, is a central feature in the filing of the case, which the media ignored.

April 28. The Court, after hearing Qatar and Bahrain, fixes February 29, 1996, as date for filing briefs (memorials).

June 12. Professor Rosalyn Higgins is elected as judge, the first woman. She has long been professor of international law at London School of Economics and previously at University of Kent; author of many articles on international law and a book based on her lectures at the Hague Academy.

June 21. To replace Judge Ago, Luigi Ferraro Bravo is elected by the Assembly and Security Council. He has held professorships in international law or organization in a number of universities, with tenure at the University of Rome; lectured at the Hague Academy; edited several professional journals; and was a delegate to and served on committees of UN General Assembly.

June 27. Former Court President Sir Robert Jennings resigns, to take effect July 10.

June 30. The case concerning East Timor's occupation by Indonesia, brought by Portugal against Australia (each subject to optional clause "compulsory" jurisdiction), is dismissed because Indonesia's actions would be subject of suit, and, not being part of the group agreeing to optional clause, is not a party. The theory of the case was that Australia's "Timor Gap" pact was illegal itself and that Portugal, not yet lacking status as excolonial "administering" power, had the right to participate in challenging treaty.

July 19. In the case of *Bosnia v. Yugoslavia* (Serbia and Montenegro), brought under the Genocide Treaty (which gives universal jurisdiction) seeking injunction and lifting of an arms embargo, the president fixes November 14, 1995, for the filing of Bosnia's comment on Serbian objections.

August 21. To challenge French announcement of further nuclear tests among South Pacific atolls it controls, New Zealand files application to reopen the 1973–1974 case (see chapter 10) that was dismissed after France announced that there would be no more (atmospheric) tests. New Zealand claims threat of adverse effect by the entry into the marine environment of radioactive material.

August 23. Australia, party to an earlier case, seeks to intervene in support of New Zealand's application.

August 24. Independent states of Samoa and Solomon Islands seek to intervene and to oppose nuclear tests.

August 28. State of Marshall Islands and Federated States of Micronesia file in support of New Zealand application.

September 11. A public hearing is held at the Court on New Zealand's petition against France (supported as above), on a request for a temporary emergency injunction.

September 22. New Zealand and allied applications are denied by the Court. Earlier case is limited to atmospheric tests. Three judges dissent.

1996   **January 11.** In case of *Cameroon v. Nigeria,* the latter files preliminary objections to jurisdiction. The Court orders prior hearing on these, separately. Answer is due May 15.

February 5. Extension of time to file memorial on merits to September 1, 1996, in case of *Qatar v. Bahrain.*

February 6. In the case of *Bosnia v. Yugoslavia* a hearing is set for April 29 on the preliminary objections. A hearing is also set for September 16 on preliminary objections in the oil platforms case (*Iran v. United States*).

February 15. Cameroon files a request for provisional measure in case against Nigeria.

February 23. The case of the aerial incident of July 3, 1988, (*Iran v. United States*) is settled after negotiations, following the parties' request to the Court to postpone oral proceedings that were scheduled for September 12, 1994. The United States is to pay indemnity to survivors of passengers of the civilian aircraft that was shot down ($300,000 to employed victims' kin; $150,000 to others). Settlement includes other claims pending at Iran-U.S. Claims Tribunal, set up at The Hague in 1981 after a delayed compliance by Iran with Tehran hostages case.

February 29. Court announces an election to replace Judge Aguilar-Mawdsley, who died October 24, 1995. The new judge is Gonzalo Parra-Aranguren of Venezuela, long a professor and later a judge in Caracas; later elevated to Court of Appeal; also editor and frequently published writer in his field.

March 2. President of Costa Rica is honored during a visit to the Court. President Bedjaoui notes, at time the legality of nuclear weapons is being adjuged, that Costa Rica has no weapons of any kind and no army, "a fact unique in this world." Costa Rican President Figueres Olsen replies, "For the first time in human history, international law is not on the side of force and power."

March 15. In the case of *Cameroon v. Nigeria,* the Court hands down a decision granting provisional remedies as requested (cease hostilities and incursions).

April 19. The fiftieth anniversary of the Court is marked by a special session of Court, with various ambassadors and royal presence.

April 19–May 3. Court hears preliminary objections in case of *Bosnia v. Yugoslavia.*

May 10. Close of written submissions in fisheries case (*Spain v. Canada*). The Court declines further brief by Canada.

May 30. A new case is filed concerning Botswana and Namibia, via the parties' special agreement case filed on border dispute.

July 8. In an application for an advisory opinion by the World Health Organization, petitioner's standing is denied (to request advice as to legality of nuclear weapons). On petition of the UN General Assembly for advice regarding the legality of the use of nuclear weapons, a historic ruling made. Except in one special case (when survival of State is at sake), where no opinion is granted, nuclear weapon use is illegal.

July 11. In genocide case, Yugoslavia's preliminary objections are overruled. (Bosnia is the plaintiff).

September 16–24. Hearings are conducted in the case of *Iran v. United States* on U.S. preliminary objections to being sued in case alleging illegality of destruction of oil platforms in Persian Gulf.

November 7. At a regular triennial election, three judges are reelected: Bedjaoui, Schwebel, and Vereshchetin. Newly elected judges are:

- Peter H. Kooijmans of the Netherlands, professor of international law; foreign minister; chair of boards of Carnegie Foundation and Hague Academy of International Law; served in UN General Assembly and various committees; and author of numerous publications on Law of Nations.
- Francisco Rezek of Brazil, a member of Brazil's Supreme Judicial Tribunal; studied at Sorbonne, Oxford, and Harvard; professor since 1971 of international and

constitutional law; chair of university department, later dean; and author of numerous publications.

December 12. A decision is made in case of oil platforms (*Iran v. United States*). It is held to be justifiable under the Treaty of Amity, Commerce, and so on. U.S. objections to jurisdiction are overruled, 14 to 2. Contention that "amity" treaty does not apply to the use of force is rejected.

1997 **February 17.** In the *Gabcíkovo-Nagymaros* case, concerning the effect of a water development project on the Danube River, the Court accepts an offer of the parties to visit the site for inspection. The visit is accomplished; first such action in Court history.

February 6. Officers are elected for new triennial term. Stephen Schwebel is elected president, Christopher Weeramantry, vice president.

March 19. Mary Robinson, then president of Ireland, visits Court, and stresses the important of role of the ICJ with "special interest in the contributions of the Court to the development of human rights and international humanitarian law." (She later headed the UN Human Rights Commission.)

April 9. Court conducts a visit to the site on the Danube involved in the Gabcíkovo case. Hearings have second round April 10–15 and are concluded.

September 25. Court opens Web site on the Internet: www.ICJ-CIJ.org.

The Court delivers judgment in Gabcíkovo case. Hungary is held not entitled to abandon its part in project, and Hungary/Slovakia are directed to negotiate in good faith and take all necessary measures to ensure completion of project.

October 13–22. Court rules in two cases (Lockerbie) from the aerial incident at Lockerbie and application of 1971 Montreal Convention for Suppression of Unlawful Acts against the Safety of Civil Aviation *Libya v. United Kingdom* and *Libya v. United States* (indication of provisional relief denied in April 1992 (*Lockerbie* I) that continuance of litigation requires a hearing on preliminary objections by the United Kingdom and United States; hearings are conducted and concluded.

1998 **February 27.** Court renders decision in *Lockerbie* II. Preliminary objections as filed in each case (United Kingdom and United States) are overruled. The Court makes it clear (as originally noted in 1992 case, *Lockerbie* I) that the rights of the parties are unaffected by the denial of the provisional measures that Libya then sought. Security Council resolutions that were entered after Court proceedings were begun cannot deprive the Court of jurisdiction to pass on Libya's underlying claims as alleged in opening the case. The votes on specific aspects of ruling range from 13 to 3 to 10 to 6.

February 27. On joint application of parties in *Botswana v. Namibia,* an additional round of pleadings is authorized by order of the Court.

March 11. Hearings are concluded in case of *Land and Maritime Boundaries between Cameroon and Nigeria.*

March 19. In the case concerning oil platforms (*Iran v. United States*), the United States is authorized to file a counterclaim.

April 1. In *Lockerbie* II, the defendants' (United States and United Kingdom) pleadings in response to Libya's allegations had been delayed by two rounds of preliminary proceedings. In view of February 27 ruling that case is to go forward, the Court now fixes the date for answer by defendants as December 30, 1998. This creates an occasion for further settlement talks in view of Libya's previously rejected offer for a trial in a "neutral" country under Scots law.

In *Qatar v. Bahrain* case concerning a maritime border, the Court orders a new round of written pleadings to clarify points in paperwork dispute.

April 3. Paraguay begins a case against United States, based on an alleged violation of the Vienna Convention on the right of an accused or arrested alien to seek advice and assistance from his nation's consular official. In view of "gravity and immediacy" of irreparable harm, Paraguay petitions the Court for a provisional measure to cause the United States to delay the execution of Breard, the national in the case.

April 6. The Court announces a revision of working methods to expedite examination of contentious cases brought to it. "The revision was necessary," the Court states, "owing to the major increase of activity of the Court in recent years and to the budgetary constraints it faces as a result of the financial crisis of the United Nations."

April 9. After hearing both sides in case of Breard (*Paraguay v. United States*), the Court, finding reasonable probability of jurisdiction and of irreparable harm, orders that "United States should take all measures at its disposal to ensure that Breard is not executed pending the final decree in these cases." The decision is unanimous. Judge (and President) Stephen Schwebel says, in a separate opinion, "It is of obvious importance to the maintenance and development of a rule of law among States that the obligations imposed by treaties be complied with and that . . . mutuality of interest in . . . observance of the obligations of the Vienna Convention on Consular Rights is greater today . . . [no state with higher interest than] peripatetic citizens of the United States."

April 12. Breard is executed after U.S. Supreme Court abstains.

May 26. In the case of *Iran v. United States* (destruction of oil platforms), on an application by Iran for an extension of time to plead, the United States consents, with pleadings not to close until May 2000 (indicates possibility of settlement negotiation).

June 9–17. Hearings are held in case of *Spain v. Canada,* precipitated by a Canadian boarding on high seas of Spanish fishing boat. (The raid attracts media attention; the response, a Court filing, draws none.)

June 11. The Court rules on eight preliminary objections in case pending between Nigeria and Cameroon. One holding: filing of a state's consent to jurisdiction under optional clause is to be effective immediately.

June 30. The Court files, with General Assembly comment of some length, on consequences of the increase in volume of cases being brought to the Court. It says in part: "Whereas in the seventies the Court characteristically had one or two cases at a time on its docket . . . throughout the 1990s the figures have been large, standing at 9 in 1990, 12 in 1991, 13 in the years 1992–95, 12 in 1996, 9 in 1997."

August 10. Advisory opinion is requested in a dispute between the United Nations and Malaysia, arising from a filing of multimillion-dollar damage suits against a special rapporteur (designated by the UN Commission on Human Rights) for public statements made. Rules providing immunity claimed to be broken by Malaysia.

September 3. In Danube dam case (*Hungary v. Slovakia*), Slovakia asks for supplemental judgment on claimed breaches by Hungary.

October 27. In his annual report to the UN General Assembly, Court President Schwebel demands an adjustment of the budget to make possible the full effectiveness of Court. The budget problem is the result of the default in payment of dues by the United States.

October 28. Nigeria files an application for an interpretation of an earlier ruling on preliminary objections.

November 2. A new case between Indonesia and Malaysia is filed. Neither sues the other; they agree to submit to the Court a dispute about sovereignty on island in the Celebes Sea.

December 4. In the case of *Spain v. Canada,* regarding the seizure of a Spanish fishing craft, the Court rules that it lacks jurisdiction. An exception in Canada's submission to general jurisdiction that excludes disputes concerning conservation of fisheries is held, over several dissents, to apply to an action at sea well outside protected fishing zones.

December 30. Guinea brings a case against Democratic Republic of the Congo, alleging mistreatment, by imprisonment and taking of properties, of Guinean national, A. S. Diallo.

1999   **February 15.** Hearings are held for ten days in case of Botswana and Namibia, presented by their joint petition for resolution of a dispute concerning the boundary and legal status of an offshore island.

February 16. Eritrea initiates a proceeding against Ethiopia regarding the invasion of the premises formerly used by its diplomatic mission and detention of its staff. This is really a challenge, rather than a legally sufficient action; Ethiopia, the prospective defendant, had not consented to general (optional clause) jurisdiction, and so the filing has the publicity value of a "dare" and the potential for a ruling only if Ethiopia should consent.

March 3. In case of Germany's claim against the United States that rights of two nationals (LeGrand) were violated by the failure to offer contact with a consular officer, the Court in a unanimous vote "indicates," that is, directs, a stay of execution until merits of the case are considered. One execution had in fact already taken place when the Court acted, and in total disregard of the Court's action, the second execution was conducted.

March 25. The Court rejects a request by Nigeria for an interpretation of a judgment for Cameroon.

April 29. In the case of the UN-appointed rapporteur facing multimillion-dollar lawsuits in Malaysia, which he (and the Economic and Social Council) claimed were in violation of a special diplomatic immunity for international civil servants, the Court hands down an advisory opinion ruling that immunity should have been granted.

Federal Republic of Yugoslavia files ten cases against NATO countries, individually, ranging from Belgium to the United States, charging that the bombing in connection with the Kosovo matter violates the obligation of each "not to use force"; complaining of aid to terrorists (KLA) and attacks on targets of historical and cultural value; and charging use of cluster bombs with intended effect on civilians. An immediate application is made for an indication of provisional measures (temporary restraining order).

May 10–11. Hearings are held on each of ten cases Yugoslavia filed against NATO members, to pass on provisional remedy.

June 2. Decisions are made in each of the ten Yugoslavia and NATO cases. Interim measures of protection are rejected in all, with some dissents in each. The Court expresses "profound concern with the use of force" (by bombing Yugoslavia) and adds, "Whether or not a state accepts the jurisdiction of the Court, they remain in any event, responsible for acts attributable to them that violate International Law." Cases against Spain and United States are dismissed because of the absence of a basis of jurisdiction; others are retained to litigate merits, legally unaffected by a denial of temporary relief.

June 23. Democratic Republic of Congo files suit against Burundi, Uganda, and Rwanda, complaining of invasions that constitute intervention in an ongoing civil war.

June 30. State of Equatorial Guinea seeks to intervene and be heard in support of its interest in a pending border dispute case between Cameroon and Nigeria.

July 2. Croatia brings a case against Yugoslavia, claiming violation of the Genocide Convention in recent conflicts.

The cases by Yugoslavia against remaining eight NATO defendants will continue; dates for pleadings are set.

September 22. Pakistan files suit against India; the complaint is based on the downing of a Pakistani naval plane, allegedly over home territory.

October 22. In case between Cameroon and Nigeria (land and maritime boundary), the Court grants Equatorial Guinea the right to intervene, indicating a judicial trend to more leniency in regard to intervention by third states.

October 26. President Stephen M. Schwebel, in an annual report of the Court to the UN General Assembly, declares the failure by member states to pay their dues "has the gravest effect on the life of the organization" and "transgresses the principle of free consent and good faith . . . which are at the basis of international law and relations." The Court, with a growing list of cases, is hit harder than other UN agencies by the U.S. default's effect on the UN budget.

November 3. At a triennial election, Judges Guillaume, Ranjeva, Higgins, and Parra-Aranguren are reelected. Vice President Weeramantry fails to be reelected, saddening some who have followed his career and opinions. He is replaced by Jordanian national A. S. Al-Khasawneh, a Cambridge graduate; member of the Jordanian diplomatic service and Foreign Ministry; and notable more for offices held than for published scholarship.

November 24. In the case of *Pakistan v. India* (aerial incident of August 10, 1999), the Court holds that the question of jurisdiction shall be heard first, separately.

November 26. In A. S. Diallo case (*Guinea v. Congo*), time limits are fixed.

December 6. President of Mongolia visits the Court, Court President Schwebel noting the acceptance of compulsory jurisdiction by the Asian state.

December 8. Nicaragua brings suit against Honduras to bring about a Court delimitation of maritime boundary, the source of a recent conflict.

December 13. A Court decision in Botswana–Namibia case settles ownership of disputed island and holds waters around it to be jointly controlled.

2000   **February 7.** Judge Gilbert Guillaume, a French national, is elected president of the Court on expiration of Schwebel's term; Judge Shi Jiuyong of China is elected vice president.

February 10. The Court elects Chambers of Summary Procedure and for Environmental Matters, and committee chairs are elected.

February 11. Philippe Couvreur, whose principal recent career had been with the Court, is elected registrar. He has lectured and written on international legal matters.

February 16. President Guilaume holds a press conference reporting on the Court's accomplishments and, like his predecessors, calling attention to the impairment of the Court's function due to UN budget difficulties. Court's budget is $10 million with sixty-two employees. The Criminal Tribunal for former Yugoslavia has a budget of $100 million and 900 employees.

February 29. French President Chirac pays respects to Court at visit.

March 3. To replace Judge (and former president) Schwebel, the Assembly and Security Council elect Thomas Buergenthal. He has been a juris doctor since 1960; a professor of international law at several law schools and dean of one; judge and president of the Inter-American Court of Human Rights; a wide-ranging scholar and diplomatic consultant; served on the UN Truth Commission for El Salvador, which reported abuses by death squads.

March 23. In case of Nicaragua and Honduras on Caribbean Sea borders, time is fixed for filing pleadings.

April 3. Four days of hearings open in the case of *Pakistan v. India* concerning the aerial incident of August 10, 1999.

May 12. In the case of *Indonesia v. Malaysia* (concerning sovereignty over two islands), further extensions of time limits are granted.

May 24. Emperor and empress of Japan pay ceremonial visit to the Court and Court president notes Japan's acceptance of compulsory jurisdiction.

May 29–June 29. Sixteen days of hearings are held in dispute between Qatar and Bahrain over oil-rich shoals.

June 7. President Guillaume notes twenty-four cases are now pending at Court, of which twelve will be ready for hearings by year's end.

June 19. In the case of *Democratic Congo v. Uganda,* Congo requests an indication of provisional measures to remove foreign troops from Congo.

June 21. In the case of the aerial incident of August 10, 1999, India's claim that the Court lacks jurisdiction is sustained, enforcing a reservation that no suit between members of the same Commonwealth shall be included.

June 28–29. Hearings are held on Congo's application for provisional measures against Uganda.

July 1. The Court grants provisional measure directing Congo and Uganda to refrain from any armed action and to respect human rights in the conflict zone.

July 7. In Kosovo bombing case (*Yugoslavia v. Belgium, Canada, France, Germany, Italy, Netherlands, Portugal,* and *United Kingdom*), the respondent states file challenge to jurisdiction of the Court.

September 13. In *Lockerbie* II (*Libya v. United Kingdom* and *United States*) concerning Montreal Convention, further extensions of time to answer are granted.

September 14. In the Kosovo bombing case (*Yugoslavia v. NATO members*), time extension is given for Yugoslavia's response to preliminary objections.

October 9. During a visit by the president of Brazil, Court President Guillaume notes that a Brazilian delegate in 1922 initiated the optional plan for limited compulsory jurisdiction.

October 17. Democratic Republic of Congo sues Belgium to challenge the arrest warrant against DRC acting-Minister of Foreign Affairs. Provisional remedy to cancel is sought.

October 26. President Guillaume, in the annual report to the UN Assembly, decries that the limitations of Court budget "decide whether Court is to die slow death."

November 20–23. Hearings are held on DRC application for provisional measures.

December 8. Court denies Belgium's request to dismiss Congo case, but declines provisional measures as sought.

2001   **June 27.** LeGrand case, a suit by Germany against the United States, is settled.

Index